Handbook of Technologic
Content Knowled

This *Handbook* addresses the concept and implementation of *technological pedagogical content knowledge*—the knowledge and skills that teachers need in order to meaningfully integrate technology into instruction in specific content areas. Recognizing, for example, that effective uses of technology in mathematics are quite different from effective uses of technology in social studies, teachers need specific preparation in using technology in each content area they will be teaching. Offering a series of chapters by scholars in different content areas who apply the technological pedagogical content knowledge framework to their individual content areas, the volume is structured around three themes:

- What is technological pedagogical content knowledge?
- Integrating technological pedagogical content knowledge into specific subject areas
- Integrating technological pedagogical content knowledge into teacher education and professional development

The *Handbook of Technological Pedagogical Content Knowledge (TPCK) for Educators* is simultaneously a mandate and a manifesto on the engagement of technology in classrooms based on consensus standards and rubrics for effectiveness. As the title of the concluding chapter declares, "It's about time!"

Handbook of Technological Pedagogical Content Knowledge (TPCK) for Educators

Edited by AACTE Committee on Innovation and Technology

The AACTE Committee on Innovation and Technology

Joel A. Colbert, Ed.D., Chapman University (Chair)

Kim E. Boyd, Ed.D., Oral Roberts University

Kevin A. Clark, Ph.D., George Mason University

Sharon Guan, Ph.D., DePaul University

Judith B. Harris, Ph.D., The College of William and Mary

Mario A. Kelly, Ed.D., Hunter College

Ann D. Thompson, Ph.D., Iowa State University

Published by
Routledge
for the American Association of Colleges
for Teacher Education

Routledge
Taylor & Francis Group

NEW YORK AND LONDON

Serving Learners

First published 2008
by Routledge
270 Madison Avenue
New York, NY 10016

American Association of Colleges
for Teacher Education
1307 New York Ave., N.W., Suite 300
Washington, DC 20005–4701
www.aacte.org

Simultaneously published in the UK
by Routledge
2 Park Square, Milton Park, Abingdon, Oxon OX14 4RN

Routledge is an imprint of the Taylor & Francis Group, an informa business

© 2008 Taylor & Francis

Cover art by Smita Sawai and Punya Mishra
Typeset in Minion by Wearset Ltd, Boldon, Tyne and Wear
Printed and bound in the United States of America on acid-free paper by Edward
Brothers, Inc.

Library of Congress Cataloging in Publication Data
Handbook of technological pedagogical content knowledge (TPCK) for educators /
edited by AACTE Committee on Innovation and Technology.
p. cm.
Includes indexes.
1. Educational technology–Study and teaching–United States–Handbooks, manuals,
etc. 2. Teachers–Training of–United States–Handbooks, manuals, etc. I. American
Association of Colleges for Teacher Education. Committee on Technology and
Innovation.
LB1028.3.H356 2008
371.33071'1–dc22   2007030023

ISBN 10: 0-8058-6355-9 (hbk)   ISBN 13: 978-0-8058-6355-0 (hbk)
ISBN 10: 0-8058-6356-7 (pbk)   ISBN 13: 978-0-8058-6356-7 (pbk)
ISBN 10: 1-4106-1818-8 (ebk)   ISBN 13: 978-1-4106-1818-4 (ebk)

This book is sponsored by the American Association of Colleges for Teacher Education
(AACTE), a national, voluntary association of almost 800 higher education institutions
and related organizations that prepare more than two-thirds of the new teachers
entering schools each year in the United States. AACTE's mission is to promote the
learning of all PK-12 students through high-quality, evidence-based preparation and
continuing education for all school personnel. It operates under the guiding principle of
"Serving Learners," including children in classrooms, the teachers who instruct them,
and the faculty who prepare those teachers. Four strategic goals drive AACTE's work:
(1) build consensus on professional issues; (2) advocate in state and federal policy
arenas; (3) strengthen programs and enhance their capacity; and (4) improve all
educators' ability to serve diverse learners.

AACTE is publishing this document to stimulate discussion, study, and
experimentation among educators. The findings, interpretations, and conclusions
presented herein are entirely those of the author(s) and do not necessarily reflect the
official position or policies of AACTE, nor does sponsorship of the publication imply
endorsement by AACTE. Though AACTE and the author(s) have used their best efforts
in preparing this document, they make no representations or warranties with respect to
the accuracy or completeness of its contents and specifically disclaim any implied
warranties of merchantability or fitness for a particular purpose. Neither AACTE, its
Board of Directors or officers, nor the author(s) of this document shall be liable for any
loss or profit or other commercial damages, including but not limited to special,
incidental, consequential, or other damages.

Contents

Preface

M. CHRISTOPHER BROWN II AND BOBBY CATO, JR.

The twenty-first century has been filled with rapid, continued innovation and advances in the domains of technology, information, and knowledge transfer. Concomitantly, the sociopolitical and educational context of school-aged children is under a period of redefinition and redesign (Sefton-Green, 2006). The means, mode, and manner of instructing the present and forthcoming generations of school-aged children require fundamental shifts in the pedagogical science called teaching. The role of technology and non-tactile information transfer have extended beyond opaque projectors, transparencies, reel-to-reel film, videocassette, typewriters, and recorded albums. Contemporary classrooms are now filled with digital video players, computers, and virtual/online instructional modules. The challenge facing the modern teacher is how to incorporate multimodalities and differentiated educational technologies to facilitate and/or enhance student learning (Mishra & Koehler, 2006). The solution: teachers must acquire and develop *technological pedagogical content knowledge*.

Between autumn 2005 and spring 2007, the Committee on Innovation and Technology of the American Association of Colleges for Teacher Education (AACTE) designed and managed a consensus panel on the role of technology in the classroom with regard to the acquisition and exhibition of teacher knowledge and instructional skill. The chapters that follow are a result of this effort. The Committee and the subject-matter authors were each cognizant of the changing nature of technology and its import for education. Likewise, each realized the dissonance that can occur when classroom students possess technology skills more advanced than those of their teachers. The resultant research posits that the effectiveness of classroom instruction is maximized when teaching and technology are in symbiosis. Moreover, each chapter of this book evinces an understanding of the complicated nexus among pedagogy, technology, and quality of instruction.

Like many teacher educators who are attempting to infuse technology within a teacher development program (e.g., Brush *et al.*, 2001; Dawson & Norris, 2000; Morrow, Barnhart, & Rooyakkers, 2002; Rademacher, Tyler-Wood, Doclar, & Pemberton, 2001; Thomas & Cooper, 2000), the editors of this volume have many questions about whether and how such integration supports students' immediate and long-term professional learning. Their assumption is that information on technology integration should be a clear component of the preclinical training of teachers. The research suggests, however, that this expectation is met with uncertain, inconsistent, and unequal presence in the pre-teaching curriculum at the university level

(Schrum, 1999; Strudler & Wetzel, 1999; Topp, Mortensen, & Grandgenett, 1995). This comparative absence leads to similarly infrequent use when the teacher candidate progresses to the classroom without the technological pedagogical content knowledge necessary for successful technology integration.

Teachers play important roles in determining the time, place, and manner technology is engaged in the classroom—the "if, when, and how" of technology use (National Council of Teachers of Mathematics, 2000, p. 26). Their decisions significantly affect students' learning (Ely, 1996), and include selecting learning objects that enlarge and enrich their repertoire of instructional techniques for presenting content. This handbook describes a broad array of technology-infused learning strategies and explains how teachers can facilitate the use of those learning strategies as a part of curriculum-based instruction. Many of the specific ideas presented herein are not new. What is new is the sense that after years of scholarly work in this area, the realities of educational technology integration and teacher education have matured to a level where a significant conceptual and practical shift is required to effect high-quality teaching across the subject areas via myriad technological modalities.

This handbook offers a series of consensus chapters by scholars in different content areas who apply the technological pedagogical content knowledge framework to their individual content areas. It is simultaneously a mandate and/or manifesto on the integration of technology in classrooms based on established national standards and knowledge of pedagogical effectiveness. As the title of its final chapter declares, "It's About Time." That title brings to mind the invitational import of Arthur C. Clarke's 1982 classic, *2010: Space Odyssey*. In the opening segment of his book, Clarke writes,

> "The time has come," said Dr. Dimitri Moisevitch to his old friend Heywood Floyd, "to talk of many things. Of shoes and spaceships and sealing wax, but mostly of monoliths and malfunctioning computers."
>
> (p. 3)

Likewise, the time has come for schools, colleges, and departments of education to engage their professors, cooperating teachers, and teacher-students in constructive exploration of and dialogue about the role of technological pedagogical content knowledge in facilitating high-quality, effective instruction for all learners.

References

Brush, T., Igoe, A., Brinkerhoff, J., Glazewski, K., Ky, H., & Smith, C. (2001). Lessons from the field: Integrating technology into preservice teacher education. *Journal of Computing in Teacher Education, 17*(4), 16–20.

Clarke, A. C. (1982). *2010: Space odyssey.* New York: Ballantine Books.

Dawson, K., & Norris, A. (2000). Preservice teachers' experiences in a K-12/university technology-based field initiative: Benefits, facilitators, constraints, and implications for teacher educators. *Journal of Computing in Teacher Education, 17*(1), 4–12.

Ely, D. P. (1996, August). Trends in educational technology 1995. *Eric Digest* [Online]. Available: http://ericir.syr.edu/ithome/digests/trendsdig.html.

Mishra, P., & Koehler, M. J. (2006). Technological pedagogical content knowledge: A new framework for teacher knowledge. *Teachers College Record, 108*(6), 1017–1054.

Morrow, L. M., Barnhart, S., & Rooyakkers, D. (2002). Integrating technology with the teaching of an early literacy course. *The Reading Teacher, 56*(3), 218–230.

National Council of Teachers of Mathematics. (2000). *Principles and standards for school mathematics.* Reston, VA: Author.

Rademacher, J., Tyler-Wood, T., Doclar, J., & Pemberton, J. (2001). Developing learner-centered technology assignments with student teachers. *Journal of Computing in Teacher Education, 17*(3), 18–25.

Schrum, L. (1999). Technology professional development for teachers. *Educational Technology Research and Development, 47*(4), 83–90.

Sefton-Green, J. (2006). Youth, technology, and media cultures. *Review of Research in Education, 30*, 279–306.

Strudler, N., & Wetzel, K. (1999). Lessons from exemplary colleges of education: Factors affecting technology integration in preservice programs. *Educational Technology Research and Development, 47*(4), 63–81.

Thomas, J. A., & Cooper, S. B. (2000). Teaching technology: A new opportunity for pioneers in teacher education. *Journal of Computing in Teacher Education, 17*(1), 13–19.

Topp, N. W., Mortensen, R., & Grandgenett, N. (1995). Building a technology-using facility to facilitate technology-using teachers. *Journal of Computing in Teacher Education, 11*(3), 11–14.

Acknowledgments

The members of the AACTE Committee on Innovation and Technology wish to acknowledge Sharon Robinson, President and CEO of the American Association of Colleges for Teacher Education (AACTE); M. Christopher Brown II, former AACTE Vice President for Programs and Administration; Bobby Cato, former AACTE Coordinator of Technology Programs; Jane West, AACTE Vice President for Government and External Relations; and D. Kamili Anderson, AACTE Director of Publications, who shared in the vision for this monograph and provided resources to push the project forward.

It is with sincere appreciation that the Committee acknowledges the following authors who generously gave of their time and their efforts to write chapters for this monograph, and who participated in multiple rounds of constructive criticism and provided feedback on others' chapters: Matthew Koehler, Punya Mishra, Mario Kelly, Denise Schmidt, Marina Gurbo, Joan Hughes, Cassandra Scharber, Marcela Van Olphen, John K. Lee, Neal Grandgenett, Nancy DePlatchett, Joel Colbert, Raven McCrory, Luke Kelly, Maggie Niess, Judi Harris, Glen Bull, Tom Hammond, Ann Thompson, Kim Boyd, Kevin Clark, and Sharon Guan. The production of this material would have been impossible without the scholarly contributions of these individuals.

We also wish to thank Matthew Koehler and Punya Mishra for creating and maintaining the TPCK website and for their ongoing commitment to this publication effort, as demonstrated by their willingness to participate in multiple face-to-face and teleconference meetings throughout the process. Authors and committee members having access to the website was crucial to the successful completion of this project.

We acknowledge the contributions of our reviewers including all of the aforementioned authors; the graduate students in Raven McCrory's CEP 953: "Teachers and Technology" class; and Joel Colbert's student assistant, Rebecca Campbell for their careful reading and thoughtful comments.

Finally, we wish to acknowledge our publisher, Routledge, and Naomi Silverman, the primary editor at Routledge, for this venture.

I
What is technological pedagogical content knowledge (TPCK)?

1

Introducing TPCK

MATTHEW J. KOEHLER[1] AND PUNYA MISHRA

In this chapter we describe *technological pedagogical content knowledge* (TPCK) as a framework for teacher knowledge for technology integration (Mishra & Koehler, 2006). This framework builds on Shulman's construct of pedagogical content knowledge (PCK) to include technology knowledge. We argue that the development of TPCK by teachers is critical to effective teaching with technology. We emphasize teacher knowledge because we view the teacher as an autonomous agent with the power to significantly influence the appropriate (or inappropriate) integration of technology in teaching. In keeping with the goal of this volume (that of situating the idea of TPCK in the realm of teacher education and teacher professional development, and investigating how it differs by content areas) we explore the parameters of the TPCK framework within and between multiple curriculum areas, as well as in varying teaching and learning contexts.

We begin with a brief introduction to the complex, ill-structured nature of teaching. We consider the nature of technologies (both analog and digital), and how the inclusion of technology in pedagogy further complicates teaching. We propose to view teaching with technology as a "wicked problem" (Rittel & Webber, 1973), in which teaching is viewed as a highly complicated form of problem-seeking and problem-solving that derives from flexible and integrated bases of knowledge. We offer our TPCK framework for teacher knowledge in detail, as a complex interaction among three bodies of knowledge: *content, pedagogy,* and *technology.* We describe how these bodies of knowledge interact, in abstract, and in practice, to produce the type of flexible knowledge needed to successfully integrate technology in the classroom. Finally, we argue that the complexity of developing and applying TPCK suggests that a greater emphasis should be placed on the idea of teachers as "curriculum designers."

Teaching as an ill-structured, complex domain

As Spiro and colleagues have argued, ill-structured domains are characterized by a complexity of concepts and cases with a wide variability of features across different cases (Spiro, Coulson, Feltovich, & Anderson, 1988; Spiro & Jehng,

1990). Like expertise in other complex domains including medical diagnosis (Lesgold, Feltovich, Glaser, & Wang, 1981; Pople, 1982), decision-making (Klein, 1999), and writing (Hayes & Flower, 1980; Hillocks, 1986), expertise in teaching is dependent on flexible access to and application of highly organized systems of knowledge (Glaser, 1984; Putnam & Borko, 2000; Shulman, 1986, 1987) that must continually shift and evolve based on the contexts within which they are applied. Teachers practice in a highly complex, dynamic environment (Leinhardt & Greeno, 1986; Spiro, Coulson, Feltovich, & Anderson, 1988; Spiro, Feltovich, Jacobson, & Coulson, 1991) that asks them to integrate knowledge of student thinking and learning, knowledge of the subject matter, and increasingly, knowledge of technology.

In this regard, teaching is akin to other real-world problems that are ill-structured, that lack required information, and do not have a known correct nor best solution (Frederiksen, 1986; Glass, Holyoak, & Santa, 1979; Nickerson, 1994; Reitman, 1964; Roberts, 1994). Other examples of ill-structured domains are biomedicine (Feltovich, Coulson, Spiro, & Dawson-Saunders, 1992), literary analysis (Jones & Spiro, 1992; Spiro & Jehng, 1990), and law (Feltovich, Spiro, Coulson, & Myers-Kelson, 1995; Lawrence, 1988; Williams, 1992). Paradoxically, domains that appear to be well-structured can also be ill-structured, either at advanced levels of study, or when applied to unconstrained, naturally occurring situations (Mishra, Spiro, & Feltovich, 1996; Mishra & Yadav, 2006; Spiro, Feltovich, Jacobson, & Coulson, 1991).

For example, mathematics is typically treated as a very structured field that is concerned with solving problems which have unique, correct answers, developed as the logical consequence of manipulations of a finite set of axioms or postulates. Professional mathematicians, however, hold a very different view of their field, and consider it laden with ambiguity and uncertainty (Davis & Hersh, 1981). Ill-structuredness also appears when abstract mathematical ideas are applied to real-world situations (Resnick, 1988). Similarly, physics appears to be an orderly and regular discipline—except when applied to the real world, as in the case of engineering. Building a bridge, for example, applies principles of physics, but the unique features of each case (including the cost, materials, and setting) prevent the indiscriminate generalization from one case to another (Guzdial, Turns, Rappin, & Carlson, 1995; Petroski, 1985, 1994).

Teaching, consistent with the examples above, is a classic example of an ill-structured discipline with a high level of variability across situations as well as a dense context-dependent inter-connectedness between knowledge and practice. As educators know, the application of knowledge in teaching involves many different conceptual structures and perspectives that play out in novel and unique ways even in instances that may seem superficially similar. The push to integrate technology in teaching further complicates matters by bringing an additional domain of knowledge (technology knowledge) into the mix.

It is important, therefore, that we develop a better understanding of what we mean by the term technology, particularly as it is applied in educational settings. The following sections explore this idea in greater detail.

Understanding technology

We broadly define *technology* as the tools created by human knowledge of how to combine resources to produce desired products, to solve problems, fulfill needs, or satisfy wants (Wikipedia, 2006). This definition implies two uses of the word. The first use describes an individual tool or technique, and the second use encompasses all tools, techniques, and knowledge. If we choose to use the first sense of the term there can be an Internet technology that specifically refers to the tool we call the Internet. Likewise there is a "computer technology," a "word-processing technology," and "microscope technology" (collectively called *technologies*). Using the second sense of the term, there can be educational technology, which describes the sum of the tools, techniques, and collective knowledge applicable to education. This definition includes both analog technologies (e.g., chalkboard, pencil, and microscope) and digital technologies (e.g., the computer, blogging, and Internet). Our view does not distinguish between older technologies (e.g., the chalkboard, the overhead projector, the hand-held calculator, and the pencil) and newer technologies (e.g., the MP3 player and blogs).[2]

One of the most important things to understand about technologies is that *particular technologies have specific affordances and constraints*. Technologies are neither neutral nor unbiased; rather, particular technologies have their own propensities, biases, and inherent attributes that make them more suitable for certain tasks than others (Bromley, 1998; Bruce, 1993). The term *affordance* was originally introduced by Gibson (1977, 1979) to refer to the perceived and actual psychological properties of any object, as a means of explaining how individuals interact with objects in the world. A hammer, for example, easily affords hitting objects (such as nails), due to its handle (affording a grip) and its weighted end. The design of the hammer also constrains what you can do with it—a hammer does not afford turning a screw or designing a website. The use of affordance in the context of educational technology is meant more broadly to include all of the properties of the system that allow certain actions to be performed and encourage specific types of learner behavior (Norman, 1988). Using email to communicate, for example, affords asynchronous communication and easy storage (an archive) of exchanges. Email does not afford synchronous communication in the way that a phone call, a face-to-face conversation, or instant-messaging does. Nor does email afford the conveyance of subtleties of tone, intent, and mood.

In this context, it is important to distinguish between affordances and constraints of a technology that are *inherent* to the technology and those that are *imposed from outside* by the user. We often approach technologies with our own biases and predilections related to appropriate and inappropriate ways of using them. Cognitive scientists use the phrase *"functional fixedness"* to describe the manner in which the ideas we hold about an object's function can inhibit our ability to use the object for a different function (Birch, 1945; German & Barrett, 2005). Functional fixedness often stands in the way of creative uses of technologies. Overcoming this is essential for the intelligent and creative application of technology for learning. For example, a whiteboard has certain constraints and affordances: it is heavy and difficult to move, yet it is easy to write on and erase, and it can function as a public "writing space" to share ideas with others. These constraints and affordances, however, do not necessarily determine how a whiteboard can be used. The manner in which a whiteboard is used in a classroom as opposed to a science lab clearly indicates that the function of a whiteboard is determined very much by the context in which it is used. Similarly, although email is a tool for communication, it can be used to aid creative writing, and PowerPoint, a presentation tool, can be used as a medium for artistic creativity (Byrne, 2003). Thus, creative uses of technology require us to go beyond this "functional fixedness" so that we can innovatively repurpose existing tools toward pedagogical ends. Many excellent examples of such creative repurposing can be found in this book. In particular, see Chapter 13 by Bull, Bell, and Hammond which describes a range of different uses for a spreadsheet program.

Technology and its complex role in teaching

Technology integration (the act of including technology in teaching) is not a new phenomenon. For example, although by today's standards we rarely consider writing to be a technology, early cultures found writing to be "an external, alien technology, as many people today think of the computer" (Ong, 1982, p. 81). Plato, for example, deliberated over the many constraints and affordances of this new technology, reasoning that this new technology may prove to be a crutch that causes the populace to lose the capability to trust their own memory.

There are several reasons why introducing technology complicates the processes of teaching. There are social and institutional contexts that are unsupportive of teachers' efforts to integrate technology. Teachers have often been provided with inadequate training for this task. The diverse contexts of teaching and learning suggest that there is not "one way" that will work for everyone. Even when we restrict our discussion to particular technologies in fixed contexts, the decision to use a technology in one's teaching introduces a myriad of affordances for teaching content and engaging learners, as well as a number of constraints on what functions technologies can serve in the classroom. Understanding the complexities of technology integration requires us to offer a richer description of what we mean by the word "technology."

Issues of technology integration apply to both analog and digital, and new and old technologies. As a matter of practical significance, however, most of the technologies under consideration in the current literature (e.g., computers, software, and the Internet) are newer and digital. Newer digital technologies have some inherent properties that make it difficult for teachers to apply them in straightforward ways. Thus, it is important for us to develop a better understanding of the affordances and constraints inherent in digital technologies, since much of the discussion today is about these technologies.

Most traditional pedagogical technologies are characterized by *specificity* (a pencil is for writing, while a microscope is for viewing small objects); *stability* (pencils, pendulums, microscopes, and chalkboards have not changed a great deal over time); and *transparency of function* (the inner-workings of the pencil or the pendulum are quite simple and directly related to their function) (Simon, 1969). Over time, these technologies achieve a *transparency of perception* (Bruce & Hogan, 1998), they have become commonplace and in most cases are not even considered technologies. Digital technologies—such as computers, and hand-held devices, and software applications—in contrast, are *protean* (usable in many different ways) (Papert, 1980), *unstable* (rapidly changing), and *opaque* (the inner-workings are hidden from users) (Turkle, 1995). We describe each of these factors complicating the inclusion of technology in the sections below.

Digital technologies are protean in nature

The digital computer is unique in its ability to store, deliver, and help manipulate a variety of symbol systems: visual, acoustic, textual, and numerical. As a tool, the computer (or the computer application or system) provides humans with new ability or greater power, allowing people to do things they could not do before, or to do familiar things more easily (Papert, 1980). Computers can dynamically simulate the details of any other medium including those that cannot exist physically, making it a meta-medium with degrees of freedom for representation and expression never before encountered and as yet barely investigated (Kay, 1984).

This protean nature also means that digital technologies are many different things to different people. The digital computer can be a tool for communication (through email or instant messaging), a tool for design and construction (through software for scientific modeling or software for designing websites, themselves very different activities), a tool for inquiry (such as through digital libraries and digital probes), and a tool for artistic expression (through image, movie, and audio design software programs). This protean nature gives digital technologies their greatest strength and is the main reason why computers have applications in nearly every field of human activity. These strengths, however, come at a cost—that of significantly increasing the complexity of having to use these different symbol systems, making them difficult to learn and use. It is no surprise that the introduction of digital technologies into the classroom further complicates the kinds of problems and issues teachers face.

Digital technologies are functionally opaque

That is, the inner workings of most contemporary technologies are hidden from those who use them. The computer becomes a *virtual* domain in which cause and effect relationships are divorced from everyday rules. This quality makes our interactions with computers symbolic and often quite arbitrary (Turkle, 1995). This separation often makes learning to work with computers difficult—akin to learning a new language or culture. The fact that most software tools available today are designed for the world of business and work, not education, further contributes to this opacity (Zhao, 2003). Adapting general-purpose tools created for the world of business (e.g., spreadsheet programs) to the classroom context requires working through this opacity (and our functional fixedness) to reconfigure and repurpose these existing technologies for pedagogical purposes.

Digital technologies are unstable

The instability of digital technologies is manifest in two ways. First, the knowledge required to learn to use digital technologies is never fixed. Technology changes quickly, causing hardware and software applications to become outdated every few years. One has to continually keep up with the changing demands of new technologies, be they Hypercard, Logo, web pages, AJAX, blogs, wikis, podcasts, or the types of social bookmarking software loosely aggregated under the evolving term *Web 2.0*. Moreover, these rapid changes often happen in piecemeal fashion, which leads to users having to work with a variety of versions of software and hardware, some of which may be incompatible with one another. A second consequence of rapid technological change is that the technologies we use are often not fully tested and robust. Most software programs are error-prone and riddled with bugs. Hardware evolution also lends itself to imperfect work environments. For instance, the rapid changes in wireless protocols can leave users frustrated with connections that are too often unreliable. Though the specifics may change, these are issues, in some form or the other, that all users of digital technologies have to contend with. Thus, learning to use the technologies (and integrating into the curriculum) is not a one-shot deal. The instability of digital technologies requires that teachers become life-long learners who are willing to contend with ambiguity, frustration, and change.

These inherent characteristics of digital technology are not the only barriers to technology integration. Another series of barriers are more social, institutional, or contextual in nature. We describe a few of them below.

Teachers often have inadequate (or inappropriate) experience

Teachers often lack experience with using digital technologies for teaching and learning. Many teachers earned degrees at a time when educational technology was at a very different stage of development than it is today. It is, thus, not surprising that many teachers do not consider themselves sufficiently prepared to use technology in the classroom, and oftentimes do not appreciate its value or relevance to the classroom. Acquiring a new knowledge base and skill set can be quite challenging, particularly if it is a time-intensive activity that must fit into a busy schedule. However, these skills are unlikely to be used unless teachers can conceive of technology uses that are consistent with their existing pedagogical beliefs (Ertmer, 2005). Research suggests that an innovation is less likely to be adopted if it deviates too greatly from prevailing values, pedagogical beliefs, and practices of the teachers (Zhao, Pugh, Sheldon, & Byers, 2002). Learning to become flexible, creative educators who can transcend functional fixedness and other barriers is an ongoing and complicated process and must be confronted at both pre- and in-service levels. These topics are addressed by every chapter in this volume, but are the specific focus of Chapters 11 and 12 by Niess and Harris, respectively.

Technology is often considered to be somebody else's problem

Technology integration is made even more complex by the kinds of *social and institutional contexts* in which teachers work. Unfortunately, the problem of technology integration has often become what we have named the "somebody else's problem" (SEP) syndrome (Koehler, Mishra, Hershey, & Peruski, 2004). Technology and pedagogy are often considered domains that are ruled by different groups of people—teachers and instructors, who are in charge of pedagogy; and technologists, who are in charge of the technology. Similar to C. P. Snow's (1959) idea of two cultures of scientists and artists, teachers and techies live in different worlds and often hold curiously distorted images of each other. On one hand, technologists view non-technologists as Luddites, conservative, resistant to change, and oblivious to the transformative power of technology. On the other hand, non-technologists tend to view technologists as being shallowly enthusiastic, ignorant of education and learning theories, and unaware of the realities of classrooms and schools. These two groups read different journals, visit different conferences, and can have fundamentally different visions of the role of technology in the classroom. The chasm between these two groups is not unbridgeable, because it is clear that teachers use technology, either technologies that have become transparent to them (e.g., the chalkboard and the overhead projector) or in personal contexts outside of the classroom (e.g., the Internet, MP3 players, and DVD players). Likewise, technologists in schools know something about teaching and learning. Often they are former teachers or current teachers working full- or part-time. Yet, the phenomenon of two worlds is sociologically and psychologically real, especially as it applies to newer technologies.

It is not easy for teachers to navigate between these two worlds, worlds in which the norms, values, and language can be different. As we argue later, a complete understanding of teaching with technology involves breaking down this false dichotomy between pedagogy and technology. This tension between educators and technologists can complicate the teacher's role greatly, concomitantly discouraging effective technology integration. Chapter 13 by Bull, Bell, and Hammond offers insight into just how these institutional barriers can (and need to) be reduced.

Classroom contexts are varied and diverse

Surrounding all the things that teachers should know about technologies and how to use them in their classrooms are the circumstances, or contexts, in which each teaches. As we argue more fully later, there is no such thing as a "perfect solution" to the problem of integrating technology into a curriculum. Instead, integration efforts should always be custom-designed for particular subject matter ideas in specific classroom contexts.

In several ways, the contexts of teaching reflect several *divides*, each of which further complicates the issue of technology integration in classrooms. One divide, for example, is between the *digital natives* (the first generation of students to live and grow up entirely surrounded by digital technology) and the *digital immigrants* (the teachers who have "migrated" to this technology later in life) (Prensky, 2001). The natives represent a challenge to immigrant teachers, because of differences in comfort levels and knowledge of technology, and a concomitant clash of culture, language, and values. Another divide is the well-known *digital divide* between those who have access to the latest technology, and those who do not (see Digital Divide.org, 2006). This divide takes many forms, and has complex implications for how teachers approach these contexts, as is addressed in Chapter 10 by Kelly.

Teaching with technology as a wicked problem

Technology integration has often been considered a kind of problem-solving, the goal of which is to find the appropriate technological solutions to pedagogical problems. However, matters are not this clear-cut. Integrating technology in the classroom is a complex and ill-structured problem involving the convoluted interaction of multiple factors, with few hard and fast rules that apply across contexts and cases.

One fruitful way of thinking about the complex problem of teaching with technology is to view it as a "wicked problem" (Rittel & Webber, 1973). Rittel and Webber argued that wicked problems, in contrast to "tame" problems (such as those in mathematics, chess, etc.), have incomplete, contradictory, and changing requirements. Solutions to wicked problems are often difficult to realize (and maybe even recognize) because of complex interdependencies among a large number of contextually bound variables. Wicked problems, they argue, cannot be solved in a traditional linear fashion, because the problem definition itself evolves as new solutions are considered and/or implemented. Rittel and Webber stated that while attempting to solve a wicked problem, the solution of one of its aspects may reveal or create another, even more complex problem. Moreover, wicked problems have no stopping rule—and solutions to wicked problems are not right or wrong, simply "better," "worse," "good enough," or "not good enough." Most importantly, every wicked problem is essentially unique and novel. There are so many factors and conditions—all dynamic—that no two wicked problems are alike. Accordingly, solutions to wicked problems will always be custom-designed. For this reason, there is no definitive solution to a technology integration problem. Each issue raised by technology integration presents an ever evolving set of interlocking issues and constraints.

Rittel and Webber show that the biggest mistake that one can make when tackling a wicked problem is to think of it as a "normal" or "tame problem" that can be tackled in conventional ways. Wicked problems always occur in social contexts—in the case of technology integration, that of classrooms. The diversity of teachers, students, and technology coordinators who operate in this social context bring different goals, objectives, and beliefs to the table, and thereby contribute to the wickedness of this problem. Indeed it is the social, psychological complexity of these problems—rarely their technical complexity—that overwhelms standard problem-solving approaches. These solutions become a source for learning, leading to newer knowledge, and unintended consequences, that can lead to more wicked problems, which in turn can lead to newer knowledge and so on in a continuous spiral or development. This process of problem-seeking, problem-solving, and knowledge generation does not typically end when all possible problems are solved but rather when external factors (such as running out of time, money, information, support, or other resources) come into play. As Simon argues, in contexts such as these, the best we can hope for is *satisficing*, i.e. achieving a satisfactory solution, an outcome that, given the circumstances, is good enough.

Describing teaching as a wicked problem, full of complexity and ill-structuredness, does not suggest that this problem lacks structure. Ill-structuredness demands that understanding a typical case in the domain in question requires understanding a variety of complex concepts (and their contextually defined interactions), and that these concepts interact in patterns that are not consistent across cases. Complexity often emerges from a smaller set of tractable and understandable phenomena that interact with one another.

The wicked problems of technology integration require us to develop new ways of confronting this complexity. We argue that at the heart of good teaching with technology are three core components: *content, pedagogy, and technology* and the relationships between them. It is these interactions, between and among these components, playing out differently across diverse contexts, that account for the wide variations seen in educational technology integration. These three knowledge bases (content, pedagogy, and technology) form the core of the TPCK framework. We offer an overview of the framework below, though more detailed descriptions may be found in other published reports (Koehler, Mishra, Hershey, & Peruski, 2004; Koehler & Mishra, 2005a, 2005b; Mishra & Koehler, 2006). It is important to note that this perspective is consistent with other researchers and approaches that have attempted to extend Shulman's idea of pedagogical content knowledge (PCK) to the domain of educational technology.[3]

The TPCK model

The TPCK framework builds on Shulman's (1987, 1986) descriptions of pedagogical content knowledge to describe how teachers' understanding of technologies and pedagogical content knowledge interact with one another to produce effective teaching with technology. (See note #3 for an overview of the evolution of these ideas.) In this model (see Figure 1.1), there are three main components of knowledge: content, pedagogy, and technology. Equally important to the model are the interactions among these bodies of knowledge, represented as pedagogical content knowledge (PCK), technological content knowledge (TCK), technological pedagogical knowledge (TPK), and technological pedagogical content knowledge (TPCK).

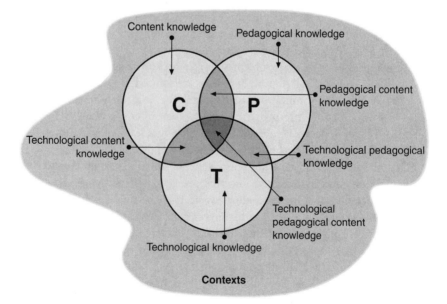

Figure 1.1 The TPCK framework and its knowledge components.

The goal of describing each of these bodies of knowledge is not to engage in philosophical discussions about the nature of knowledge. Although many philosophers have typically defined knowledge as "justified true belief" and have spent decades, if not centuries, attempting to understand each of these words, the definition of knowledge used here is more pragmatic and is influenced by scholars such as Dewey, Schon, and Perkins (Dewey, 1934; Dewey & Bentley; 1949; Perkins, 1986; Schon, 1983, 1987, 1996). Perkins in particular poses a provocative metaphor: that of "knowledge as design" (Perkins, 1986). In fact he goes on to argue that knowledge can be considered a tool that is designed and adapted to a purpose. As he says:

> To think of knowledge as design is to think of it as an implement one constructs and wields rather than a given one discovers and beholds. The kinesthetic imagery implicit in knowledge as design fosters an active view of understanding worthy of emphasis in teaching and learning.
>
> (p. 132)

In this view of knowledge, the truth-value of the knowledge is less important than what you can do with that knowledge—what has also been called usable knowledge (Kelly, 2003; Lagemann, 2002; National Research Council [NRC], 2002). We briefly describe each component of the TPCK model below.

Content knowledge (CK)

Content knowledge is knowledge about the actual subject matter that is to be learned or taught. The content to be covered in middle school science or history is different from the content to be covered in an undergraduate course on art appreciation or a graduate seminar on astrophysics. Knowledge of content is of critical importance for teachers. As Shulman (1986) noted, this would include: knowledge of concepts, theories, ideas, organizational frameworks, knowledge of evidence and proof, as well as established practices and approaches towards developing such knowledge. Knowledge and the nature of inquiry differ greatly between fields and it is important that teachers understand the deeper knowledge fundamentals of the disciplines in which they teach. In the case of science, for example, this would include knowledge of scientific facts and theories, the scientific method, and evidence-based reasoning. In the case of art appreciation, such knowledge would include knowledge of art history, famous paintings, sculptures, artists and their historical contexts, as well as knowledge of aesthetic and psychological theories for evaluating art. The cost of not having a comprehensive base of content knowledge can be quite prohibitive; students can receive incorrect information and develop misconceptions about the content area (National Research Council, 2000; Pfundt & Duit, 2000). Yet content knowledge, in and of itself, is an ill-structured domain, and as the culture wars (Zimmerman, 2002) and the

Great Books controversies (Bloom, 1987; Casement, 1997; Levine, 1996) as well as court battles over the teaching of evolution (Pennock, 2001) demonstrate, issues of content can be areas of significant contention and disagreement. The bulk of the chapters in this book describe how differences among content knowledge domains are reflected in differing strategies to integrate educational technologies in teacher education and classroom practice.

Pedagogical knowledge (PK)

Pedagogical knowledge is deep knowledge about the processes and practices or methods of teaching and learning and encompasses (among other things) overall educational purposes, values, and aims. This is a generic form of knowledge that applies to student learning, classroom management, lesson plan development and implementation, and student evaluation. It includes knowledge about techniques or methods used in the classroom, the nature of the target audience, and strategies for evaluating student understanding. A teacher with deep pedagogical knowledge understands how students construct knowledge and acquire skills, and how they develop habits of mind and positive dispositions towards learning. As such, pedagogical knowledge requires an understanding of cognitive, social, and developmental theories of learning and how they apply to students in the classroom.

Pedagogical content knowledge (PCK)

Pedagogical content knowledge is consistent with, and similar to Shulman's idea of knowledge of pedagogy that is applicable to the teaching of specific content. PCK covers the core business of teaching, learning, curriculum, assessment, and reporting, such as the conditions that promote learning and the links among curriculum, assessment, and pedagogy. An awareness of common misconceptions and ways of looking at them, the importance of forging links and connections between different content ideas, students' prior knowledge, alternative teaching strategies, and the flexibility that comes from exploring alternative ways of looking at the same idea or problem are all essential for effective teaching.

Central to Shulman's conceptualization of PCK is the notion of the transformation of the subject matter for teaching. Specifically, according to Shulman (1986), this transformation occurs as the teacher interprets the subject matter, finds multiple ways to represent it, and adapts and tailors the instructional materials to alternative conceptions and students' prior knowledge. An excellent example of such a transformation can be seen in John Lee's Chapter 6 on the application of TPCK to social studies. As Lee argues, social studies does not exist as a distinct discipline but rather is configured from multiple sources including history, geography, political science, economics, behavioral sciences, cultural studies, and more. According to Lee, the domain of social studies emerges as a consequence of the pedagogical decision to educate students about civic preparation. In other words, without this pedagogical decision, the domain of social studies would not exist.

Technology knowledge (TK)

Technology knowledge is always in a state of flux—more so than the other two "core" knowledge domains in the TPCK framework (pedagogy and content). This makes pinning it down notoriously difficult. Earlier in this chapter, we described the manner in which technology continually changes and how keeping up-to-date with it can become a full-time job, in and of itself. This also means that any definition of technology knowledge is in danger of becoming outdated by the time this text has been written, edited, proofread, and published.[4] That said, we believe that there are certain ways of thinking about and working with technology that can apply to all technology tools.

In that sense, our definition of TK is close to that of fluency of information technology (FITness) as proposed by the Committee of Information Technology Literacy of the National Research Council (NRC, 1999). They argue that FITness goes beyond traditional notions of computer literacy to require that persons understand information technology broadly enough to apply it productively at work and in their everyday lives, to recognize when information technology can assist or impede the achievement of a goal, and to continually adapt to changes in information technology. FITness therefore requires a deeper, more essential understanding and mastery of information technology for information processing, communication, and problem-solving than does the traditional definition of computer literacy. Acquiring TK in this manner enables a person to accomplish a variety of different tasks using information technology and to develop different ways of accomplishing a given task. This conceptualization of TK does not posit an "end state" but rather sees it developmentally, as evolving over a lifetime of generative, open-ended interaction with technology.

Technological content knowledge (TCK)

Technology and knowledge have a deep historical relationship. Progress in fields as diverse as medicine and history, or archeology and physics have coincided with the development of new technologies that afford the representation and manipulation of data in new and fruitful ways. Consider Roentgen's discovery of X-rays or the technique of Carbon-14 dating and the influence of these technologies in the fields of medicine and archeology. Consider also how the advent of the digital computer changed the nature of physics and mathematics, and placed a greater emphasis on the role of simulation in understanding phenomena.[5] Technological changes have also offered new metaphors for understanding the world. Viewing the heart as a pump, or the brain as an information-processing machine, are just some of the ways in which technologies have provided new perspectives for understanding phenomena in the world. These representational and metaphorical connections are not superficial. They often have led to fundamental changes in the nature of the discipline itself.

Understanding the impact of technology on the practices and knowledge of a given discipline is critical if we are to develop appropriate technological tools for educational purposes. The choice of technologies affords and constrains the types of content ideas that can be taught. Likewise, certain content decisions can limit the types of technologies that can be used. Technology constrains the types of possible representations but conversely affords the construction of newer and more varied representations. Furthermore, technological tools can provide a greater degree of flexibility in navigating across these representations.

This book contains many examples of the manner in which representations are changed with the introduction of technology. For instance, consider Grandgenett's Chapter 7 examples of fractals, which require the computational power of the computer to be created and to be taught. Fractals, as we conceive of them now, would not be possible without the computational and visual representational power of the digital computer. McCrory's Chapter 9 on science and DePlatchett's Chapter 8 on art provide excellent examples of how new technologies are changing the very nature of physics and art, respectively.

Thus, we can define TCK as an understanding of the manner in which technology and content influence and constrain one another. Teachers need to master more than the subject matter they teach, they must also have a deep understanding of the manner in which the subject matter (or the kinds of representations that can be constructed) can be changed by the application of technology. Teachers need to understand which specific technologies are best suited for addressing subject-matter learning in their domains and how the content dictates or perhaps even changes the technology—or vice versa.

In some ways, TCK is the most neglected aspect of the various intersections in the TPCK framework. As Thompson (2006) says, this framework "suggests that teachers' experiences with technology need to be specific to different content areas" (p. 46). This monograph attempts to redress this neglect by asking scholars in different disciplinary contexts to describe how technology and content are reciprocally related in their particular domains.

Technological pedagogical knowledge (TPK)

Technological pedagogical knowledge is an understanding of how teaching and learning changes when particular technologies are used. This includes knowing the pedagogical affordances and constraints of a range of technological tools as they relate to disciplinarily and developmentally appropriate pedagogical designs and strategies. This requires getting a deeper understanding of the constraints and affordances of technologies and the disciplinary contexts within which they function.

Consider the whiteboard example provided earlier. As we described, the nature of this technology—which has been in use for a long time—in some ways pre-supposes the kinds of functions it can serve. It is usually placed in the front of the classroom and under the control of the teacher. This, in turn, imposes a particular physical order in the classroom. For example, the use of a whiteboard can determine the placement of tables and chairs and frames the nature of student–teacher interaction. For instance, the teacher has primary ownership of the whiteboard, and students can use it only when called upon by the teacher. However, it would be incorrect to say that there is only one way in which whiteboards can be used. One has only to compare the use of a whiteboard in a brainstorming meeting in a business setting to see a rather different use of this technology. In such a setting, the whiteboard is not under the purview of a single individual, but rather it can be used by anybody in the group, and it becomes the focal point around which discussion and the negotiation/construction of meaning occurs. Thus an important part of TPK is developing creative flexibility with available tools in order to repurpose them for specific pedagogical purposes.

TPK becomes particularly important because most popular software programs are not designed for educational purposes. Software programs such as the Microsoft Office Suite (Word, PowerPoint, Excel, Entourage, and MSN Messenger) are usually designed for a businesses environment. Furthermore, web-based technologies such as blogs or podcasts are designed for purposes of entertainment/communication/social networking. Teachers need to reject functional fixedness, and develop skills to look beyond the immediate technology and "reconfigure it" for their own pedagogical purposes. Thus TPK requires a forward-looking, creative, and open-minded seeking of technology, not for its own sake, but for the sake of advancing student learning and understanding. Harris in Chapter 12 on in-service teacher education, introduces the idea of activity types as one way of assisting novice teachers to develop such an open-minded perspective on repurposing of technology.

Technological pedagogical content knowledge (TPCK)

TPCK is an emergent form of knowledge that goes beyond all three components (content, pedagogy, and technology). Technological pedagogical content knowledge is an understanding that emerges from an *interaction* of content, pedagogy, and technology knowledge. Underlying truly meaningful and deeply skilled teaching with technology, TPCK is different from knowledge of all three concepts individually. We argue that TPCK is the basis of effective teaching with technology and requires an understanding of the representation of concepts using technologies; pedagogical techniques that use technologies in constructive ways to teach content; knowledge of what makes concepts difficult or easy to learn and how technology can help redress some of the problems that students face; knowledge of students' prior knowledge and theories of epistemology; and knowledge of how technologies can be used to build on existing knowledge and to develop new epistemologies or strengthen old ones.

By simultaneously integrating knowledge of technology, pedagogy, and content, TPCK is a form of knowledge that expert teachers bring into play any time they teach. Each "wicked problem" or situation presented to teachers is a unique combination or weaving together of these three factors, and accordingly, there is no single technological solution that applies for every teacher, every course, or every view of teaching. Rather, solutions lie in the ability of a teacher to flexibly navigate the space defined by the three elements of content, pedagogy, and technology and the complex interactions among these elements in specific contexts. Ignoring the complexity inherent in each knowledge component, or the complexity of the relationships among these components, can lead to oversimplified solutions or failure. Thus, teachers need to develop fluency and cognitive flexibility not just in each of these key domains (T, P, and C) but also in the manner in which these domains interrelate, so that they can effect solutions that are sensitive to specific contexts. This is the kind of deep, flexible, pragmatic, and nuanced understanding of teaching with technology that we advocate in this monograph and is further examined by the other chapters in this volume.

The act of seeing technology, pedagogy, and content as three knowledge bases is not straightforward. As we have said before:

> separating the three components (content, pedagogy, and technology) ... is an analytic act and one that is difficult to tease out in practice. In actuality, these components exist in a state of dynamic equilibrium or, as the philosopher Kuhn (1977) said in a different context, in a state of "essential tension" ... Viewing any of these components in isolation from the others represents a real disservice to good teaching. Teaching and learning with technology exist in a dynamic transactional relationship (Bruce, 1997; Dewey & Bentley, 1949; Rosenblatt, 1978) between the three components in our framework; a change in any one of the factors has to be "compensated" by changes in the other two.
>
> (Mishra & Koehler, 2006, p. 1029)

This compensation is most evident whenever a new educational technology suddenly forces teachers to confront basic educational issues and *reconstruct the dynamic equilibrium among all three elements*. This view inverts the conventional perspective that content simply needs to be converted to fit a new technology—that is, the pedagogical goals and technologies are derived from the content area. Things are rarely that simple, particularly when newer technologies are employed. The introduction of the Internet—particularly the rise of online learning—is an example of the arrival of a technology that forced educators to think about core pedagogical issues such as how to represent content on the web, and how to connect students with the subject matter and with one another (Peruski & Mishra, 2004).

In this context, consider the example of cognitive flexibility hypertexts (CFTs) as espoused by Spiro and his colleagues (Spiro, Feltovich, Jacobson, & Coulson, 1991; Spiro & Jehng, 1990). Over the years, many CFT hypertexts have been developed by academics, often for use in research. By their nature, these hypertext environments are constrained to specialty software projects with focused subject matter, with limited availability to other users outside of universities. Thus, most of the work in this area has been restricted to publications, research papers, and journal articles. The advent of community-developed hypertexts and encyclopedias, user-generated metadata (also known as social bookmarking), and their use at popular web sites such as Wikipedia, Furl, Delicious, YouTube, and Flickr has suddenly moved core CFT ideas from the research lab into the real world. Educators are now realizing the constructivist power of folksonomies,[6] and other user-created tagging/categorization schemes, to reconfigure how we understand texts and the relationships among them. In this context, it is the advent of a new technology that "drives" the kinds of decisions we make about content and pedagogy, by highlighting or revealing previously hidden facets of the content, by enabling connections between diverse domains of knowledge, or supporting newer forms of pedagogy. The decision to use hypertext, for example, by necessity restricts the type of pedagogical representations available, and the content that may be represented, thus forcing teachers to select curriculum content that is most appropriate given the affordances of this particular technology.

This influence of technology on pedagogy and content (as the previous examples showed) is not unidirectional. A good example of how the pedagogical constraints of schools can restrict how technology is designed and used relates to the use of educational computer games. A study comparing commercial games with educational games found that commercial games often were more demanding than educational games in terms of cognitive effort as well as in time required for mastery (Heeter *et al.*, 2003). Educational games were easier to install, easier to learn, less complex, shorter, less challenging to play, and required less social interaction than commercial games. Heeter and colleagues asserted that these qualities resulted mainly from the need to fit game-playing into standard school schedule 45–50 minute timeslots. What was clear from the study was that the constraints of working within a school setting led to design solutions that limited playability, particularly related to the length and complexity of game play, and thus limited what students could learn from the game. The authors argue that constraining games to a format that is playable in classroom settings may pose a bigger challenge to designers interested in creating fun, educational games than the need to integrate curriculum-based subject matter. This emphasis on pedagogy through play leads Heeter and colleagues to argue that educational games are schizophrenic, in that they continually try to serve two masters, content learning and fun.

The above examples are intended to illustrate the complex ways in which content, pedagogy, and technology interact with varying levels of success. Teaching with technology is a difficult thing to do well. The TPCK framework suggests that content, pedagogy, and technology have roles to play individually and together. Teaching successfully with technology requires continually creating, maintaining, and re-establishing a dynamic equilibrium between each component. It is worth noting that a range of factors influence how this equilibrium is reached, including subject-matter specific ones (hence the content component of the model), and therefore we recommend the other chapters in this volume for guidance on how subject-matter areas impact teachers' TPCK. However, we do suggest that there are some general implications for teachers who try to achieve this equilibrium, and we explore what this view implies for teaching practice. That is the focus of the next section.

Teacher knowledge in practice, or teachers as curriculum designers

Our description of the unique and case-specific nature of wicked problem solving, and the kinds of knowledge required to function in such contexts, strongly supports the idea that there is no general solution to a teaching problem for every context, every subject matter, every technology, or every classroom. In making his argument for knowledge as design, Perkins suggests that practitioners have to "learn to see through design-colored glasses" and, "be inventive" (p. 36) in how we approach the problems in our fields. Joseph Schwab (1983) offered an apt description of the complexity of the teacher's role and the kinds of flexibility teachers need to possess in order to succeed in classroom environments. This description is also an important reminder that the teacher is the primary, if not exclusive, conduit for any changes that can occur in the classroom. As Schwab says:

> Teachers will not and cannot be merely told what to do … Teachers are not assembly line operators, and will not so behave … There are thousands of ingenious ways in which commands on what and how to teach can, will, and must be modified or circumvented in the actual moments of teaching. Teachers practice an art. Moments of choice of what to do, how to do it, with whom and at what pace, arise hundreds of times a school day, and arise differently every day and with every group of students. No command or instruction can be so formulated as to control that kind of artistic judgment and behavior, with its demand for frequent, instant choices of ways to meet an ever-varying situation.
>
> (p. 245)

What this quote makes clear is that curricula do not exist independently of teachers. Teachers are "an integral part of the curriculum constructed and enacted in classrooms" (Clandinin & Connelly, 1992 p. 363). The teacher, Dewey argued, is not merely the creator of the curriculum, but is a part of it: teachers are *curriculum designers*.[7] The idea of teachers as curriculum designers is based on an awareness of the fact that implementation decisions lie primarily in the hands of particular teachers in particular classrooms. Teachers are active participants in any implementation or instructional reform we seek to achieve, and thus require a certain degree of autonomy and power in making pedagogical decisions. Teachers construct curricula through an organic process of iterative design and refinement, negotiating among existing constraints, to create contingent conditions for learning. This process, of enacting teaching (with or without technology) in ways that are uniquely shaped by their personalities, histories, ideas, beliefs, and knowledge, has been called *bricolage*.[8] Curriculum design as bricolage emphasizes situational creativity and flexibility, through tactically and contingently selecting and unselecting elements from what is available. Teachers constantly negotiate a balance between technology, pedagogy, and content in ways that are appropriate to the specific parameters of an ever-changing educational context.

This view of teaching has significant implications for teacher education and teacher professional development. We list some of them below.

Approaches that merely teach skills (technology or otherwise) do not go far enough

Learning about technology (how to use email, word processing, or the latest version of a computer operating system) is different than learning what to do with it. Clearly, a solid understanding of knowledge in each individual domain would be the basis for developing TPCK. Developing these knowledge bases is necessary but clearly not sufficient. For instance, teaching technology skills alone (the T in our model) does little to help teachers develop knowledge about how to use digital tools to teach more effectively (TP), navigate the relationships between technology and content representations (CT), or how to use technology to help students learn a particular topic (TPC). Likewise, isolating learning about curriculum content (C), or general pedagogical skills (P), will not necessarily help teachers develop an understanding of how to put this knowledge to good use.

The spiral-like development of TPCK

In this chapter we have argued that digital technologies, in particular, require a greater level of thought and work on the part of the teacher seeking to integrate them in their teaching. The TPCK framework, however, should not be seen as being specific to just the application of newer digital technologies. Teacher educators need to be sensitive to the fact that *all* technologies come with pedagogical affordances and constraints, and in that sense the TPCK framework can be applied to any technology, as the range of examples used in this chapter, from whiteboard to wikis, testifies. Thus, teacher-training programs may seek to develop TPCK in a gradual and spiral-like manner, beginning possibly with more standard and familiar technologies (areas in which teachers may already have developed TPCK), and moving on to more advanced or non-familiar technological solutions.

The need for a greater emphasis on the demands of subject matter

This is the main theme of this book, and one that is highlighted in every chapter of this volume. Instead of applying technological tools to every content area uniformly, teachers should come to understand that the various affordances and constraints of technology differ by curricular subject-matter content or pedagogical approach. For example, a teacher interested in integrating technology into history education may consider the use of primary sources available on the Internet, while another may choose to have students develop hypertexts that focus on the inter-linked cause–effect relationships between historical events. A mathematics teacher may focus on the representational capabilities of technology (graphs, symbols, etc.), or on different methods of proof.

Practice (in curriculum design and teaching) is an important route to learning

It is not always the case that conceptual learning precedes the ability to apply that knowledge to practice. Learning in complex and ill-structured domains often happens best through working through problems or cases (Shulman, 1986; Williams, 1992)—that is, working with the wicked problems posed by integrating technology into effective practice. When designers tackle these problems, their solutions are generative, in that each solution leads to newer knowledge, and unintended consequences, which are likely to lead to further wicked problems. The learning of new concepts and their inter-relationships comes from practice; not the rote application of general principles. Teacher educators must find ways to provide preservice teachers multiple opportunities to work through these problems of practice before they enter their first classrooms, whether by internships, case-studies (traditional or video), or problem-based learning scenarios. This is much easier said than done, and the issues/concerns in this domain are discussed in Chapter 11 by Niess.

Context is important to learning and situating teacher knowledge

Because teaching is a complex and ill-structured problem, there are few— perhaps no—general principles that apply in every situation. In short, context matters. Solutions to "wicked problems" require nuanced understanding that goes beyond the general principles of content, technology, and pedagogy. A deep understanding of the interactions among these bodies of knowledge, and how they are bound in particular contexts (including knowledge of particular students, school social networks, parental concerns, etc.), imparts the kind of flexibility teachers need in order to succeed. In viewing teachers as curriculum designers, we acknowledge that they actively adapt to multiple contexts and changing conditions, rather than trying to apply general approaches. Chapters 11 and 12 by Niess and Harris, respectively, investigate the implications of viewing the TPCK framework through the lens of teachers as curriculum designers.

Conclusion

In his book *Life in the Classroom* (1968), Philip Jackson reported the results of one of the first studies that attempted to describe and understand the mental constructs and processes that underlie teacher behavior. In representing the full complexity of the teacher's task, Jackson made conceptual distinctions that fit the teacher's frame of reference—for instance, the preactive and the interactive stages of teaching—and drew attention to the importance of describing the thought processes and planning strategies of teachers (the so-called "hidden side of teaching") in an attempt to develop a more complete understanding of classroom processes. Jackson's pioneering work led to a flurry of research studies that focused attention on teachers' thinking and decision-making processes (Clark & Peterson, 1986), a line of research that hopes to "understand and explain how and why the observable activities of teachers' professional lives take on the forms and functions they do" (p. 255). A major goal of this research was to understand the relationships between two key domains: teacher thought processes; and teachers' actions and their observable effects. In this manner we see the current work—this chapter as well as the others in this book—as extending this tradition of research and scholarship. We need to develop better techniques for discovering and describing how knowledge is implemented and instantiated in practice, and, just as importantly, how the act of doing influences the nature of knowledge itself. The "knowledge as design" notion has at its heart this interactive, bi-directional relationship between thought and action, embedded within ill-structured, complex contexts.

Reitman (1965) described ill-defined or ill-structured problems as those "whose definition included one or more parameters, the values of which are left unspecified" (p. 112). The classic example he gave was the problem of composing a fugue, which in its simplest form has just one requirement: that of having the quality of "fugueness." Of course, this requirement also contains within itself a range of cultural, technical, historical, and psychological values and constraints—its "context," as it were. We particularly like this example as an analogy to instruction, because teaching is similar to creating original music of multiple genres, not only fugues, and represents one of the highest forms of human achievement, which requires the creative dovetailing and melding of both technical and aesthetic skills. The TPCK framework offers insight, we hope, into how the myriad complexities and tensions of teaching and learning can be brought together to mutually develop teachers' and students' knowledge.

Notes

1. Contributions of the two authors to this article were equal. We rotate the order of authorship in our writing. We would like to thank the members of the AACTE Innovation and Technology Committee for initiating this project and for providing feedback on a previous version of this chapter. Thanks are also due to Jim Ratcliffe, Leigh Graves Wolf, and Sue Barratt.

2. There are two reasons to include both older and newer technologies in our definition. First, the distinction between older and newer technologies is fuzzy. Given the rapid rate of technology change, it is difficult to pinpoint exactly at what point a particular technology goes from being "new" to "old." Second, a wide variety of technologies exist side-by-side in today's world, the MP3 Player and the radio, whiteboards and web-based learning management systems (LMS). Any framework that considers technology integration in teaching needs to accept and consider how these different technologies work together in today's classroom. This of course is not to say that all technologies are the same (clearly there are significant differences between analog and digital technologies, as described elsewhere in this chapter) but rather that our framework can (and does) accommodate a range of technologies.

3. The idea of TPCK (though not the term) has been around for a while. A precursor to the TPCK idea was a brief mention of the triad of content, theory (as opposed to pedagogy), and technology in Mishra (1998), though within the context of educational software design. A more specific focus was Pierson (1999, 2001) whose work almost exactly pre-empted the current diagrammatic conceptualization of TPCK. Keating and Evans (2001) and Zhao (2003) describe TPCK as well, while other authors have discussed similar ideas, though often under different labeling schemes. These include *integration literacy* (Gunter & Baumbach, 2004); *information and communication (ICT)-related PCK* (e.g., Angeli & Valanides, 2005); *technological content knowledge* (Slough & Connell, 2006); and *electronic PCK or e-PCK* (e.g., Franklin, 2004; Irving, 2006). Others who have demonstrated a sensitivity to the relationships between content, pedagogy, and technology include Hughes (2004), McCrory (2004), Margerum-Leys and Marx (2002), Niess (2005), and Slough and Connell (2006). *Our* conception of TPCK has developed over time through a series of publications and presentations (e.g., Koehler, Mishra, Hershey, & Peruski, 2004; Koehler & Mishra, 2005a, 2005b; Koehler, Mishra, & Yahya, 2007; Mishra & Koehler, 2003, 2006; Mishra, Koehler, Hershey, & Peruski, 2002), the most definitive one of which is Mishra and Koehler (2006). An updated reference list is maintained at http://www.tpck.org.

4. At the risk of sounding outdated in a few years (months?) we argue that, at this time, knowledge of technology would include a basic understanding of the full range of digital technologies (video, Internet, computers, peripheral devices, etc.) and commonplace educational technologies such as print media and overhead projectors. It also includes the ability to use important and relevant software tools (including word processing, email, and spreadsheets). Increasingly, knowledge of technology has come to include newer technologies made popular through the advancement of the Internet and gaming technologies. For instance knowledge of blogs and wikis, podcasting and tagging/social bookmarking, video games and simulations are increasingly becoming a part of the technologies that teachers need to be familiar with.

5. Though physics and mathematics approach simulation from somewhat opposite directions, physics from the side of grounded experimentation and mathematics from a more abstract axiomatic method, it is interesting to note that they both "meet" in the realm of the virtual.

6. Community-developed hypertexts, such as Wikipedia, have quickly developed a huge, hyper-linked corpus of information by simultaneously circumventing the bottlenecks of the traditional approach (the restricted subject-matter focus and a limited set of experts who could author the text). Folksonomies also expand the development of hypertexts through collaborative, open-ended categorization schemes for web pages, online photographs, and web links. Folksonomies can be best understood by comparing them with taxonomies (such as the Dewey Decimal System or Linneaean system for categorizing living creatures). Taxonomies are often developed by a select few "experts," and have "controlled vocabularies" that other users have to conform to. A folksonomy, on the other hand, is an unsystematic, emergent, bottom-up categorization scheme in which the main users are the authors of the labeling system. As must be obvious, folkonomies are often chaotic and idiosyncratic. Folksonomies are inherently open-ended and can therefore respond quickly to changes and innovations in the way users categorize Internet content (Wikipedia)

7. The word "curriculum" has a complex and tangled definitional history. Traditionally, teachers have come to be seen as separate from curriculum, and various programs (such as programmed instruction, teaching machines, computer-assisted learning, etc.) have, over the years, attempted to limit the teacher's role in curriculum development. However, it has become clear that teacher-proof curricula do not do justice to the teacher agency or the realities of classrooms. Our definition of curriculum is consistent with Clandinin and Connelly's (1992) view that the teacher is an integral part of the curriculum constructed and enacted in classrooms.

8. The word bricolage comes from the French *bricoleur*, which is normally translated as "handyman" or "tinkerer." The pedagogic sense of the word was introduced by Papert (1980) and then again in Turkle and Papert (1992), based on an earlier use by Lévi-Strauss (1962). The idea here is that there are two fundamentally different ways of approaching a problem. The "engineering" way involves making careful plans and writing everything down in full detail ahead of time, while the way of the *bricoleur* is that of doing the best with what is at hand, under existing constraints and within extant contexts. This idea is also close to that of Simon's (1957) idea of satisficing as being the goal of design.

References

Angeli, C., & Valanides, N. (2005). Preservice elementary teachers as information and communication technology designers: an instructional systems design model based on an expanded view of pedagogical content knowledge. *Journal of Computer Assisted Learning, 21*(4), 292–302.

Birch, H. G. (1945). The relation of previous experience to insightful problem-solving. *Journal of Comparative Psychology, 38*, 367–383.

Bloom, A. (1987). *The closing of the American mind: How higher education has failed democracy and impoverished the souls of today's students.* New York: Simon & Schuster.

Bromley, H. (1998). Introduction: Data-driven democracy? Social assessment of educational computing. In H. Bromley & M. Apple (eds), *Education, technology, power* (pp. 1–28). Albany, NY: SUNY Press.

Bruce, B. C. (1993). Innovation and social change. In B. C. Bruce, J. K. Peyton, & T. Batson (eds), *Network-based classrooms* (pp. 9–32). Cambridge, UK: Cambridge University Press.

Bruce, B. C. (1997). Literacy technologies: What stance should we take? *Journal of Literacy Research, 29*(2), 289–309.

Bruce, B. C., & Hogan, M. C. (1998). The disappearance of technology: Toward an ecological model of literacy. In D. Reinking, M. McKenna, L. Labbo, & R. Kieffer (eds), *Handbook of literacy and technology: Transformations in a post-typographic world* (pp. 269–281). Hillsdale, NJ: Erlbaum.

Byrne, D. (2003). *Envisioning emotional epistemological information.* Distributed Art Pub Inc.

Casement, W. (1997). *The great canon controversy: The battle of the books in higher education.* Somerset, NJ: Transaction Publishers.

Clandinin, D. J., & Connelly, F. M. (1992). Teacher as curriculum maker. In P. Jackson (ed.), *Handbook of research on curriculum* (pp. 363–401). New York: Macmillan.

Clark, C. M., & Peterson, P. (1986). Teachers' thought processes. In M. C. Wittrock (ed.), *Handbook of research on teaching (3rd edn)* (pp. 255–296). New York: Macmillan.

Davis, P. J., & Hersh, R. (1981). *The mathematical experience.* Boston: Mariner.

Dewey, J. (1934). *Art as experience.* New York: Perigree.

Dewey, J., & Bentley, A. F. (1949). *Knowing and the known.* Boston: Beacon.

Digital Divide.org (2006). Digital Divide.org. Retrieved July 12, 2006 from http://www.digitaldivide.org.

Ertmer, P. A. (2005). Teacher pedagogical beliefs: The final frontier in our quest for technology integration. *Educational Technology, Research and Development, 53*(4), 25–39.

Feltovich, P. J., Coulson, R. L., Spiro, R. J., & Dawson-Saunders, B. K. (1992). Knowledge application and transfer for complex tasks in ill-structured domains: Implications for instruction and testing in biomedicine. In D. Evans & V. Patel (eds), *Advanced models of cognition for medical training and practice* (pp. 213–244). Berlin: Springer-Verlag.

Feltovich, P., Spiro, R., Coulson, R., & Myers-Kelson, A. (1995). The reductive bias and the crisis of text in the law. *Journal of Contemporary Legal Issues, 6*(1), 187–212.

Franklin, C. (2004). Teacher preparation as a critical factor in elementary teachers: Use of computers. *Society for Information Technology and Teacher Education International Conference, 2004*(1), 4994–4999.

Frederiksen, N. (1986). Toward a broader conception of human intelligence. In R. J. Sternberg & R. K. Wagner (eds), *Practical intelligence: Nature and origins of competence in the everyday world* (pp. 84–116). New York: Cambridge University Press.

German, T. P., & Barrett, H. C. (2005). Functional fixedness in a technologically sparse culture. *Psychological Science, 16*(1), 1–5.

Gibson, J. J. (1977). The theory of affordances. In R. E. Shaw & J. Bransford (eds), *Perceiving, acting, and knowing* (pp. 67–82). Hillsdale, NJ: Lawrence Erlbaum Associates.

Gibson, J. J. (1979). *The ecological approach to visual perception.* Boston: Houghton Mifflin

Glaser, R. (1984). Education and thinking: The role of knowledge. *American Psychology, 39*(2), 93–104.

Glass, A. L., Holyoak, K. J., & Santa, J. L. (1979). *Cognition.* Reading, MA: Addison-Wesley.

Gunter, G., & Baumbach, D. (2004). Curriculum integration. In Kovalchick, A., & Dawson, K. (eds), *Education and technology: An encyclopedia.* Santa Barbara, CA: ABC-CLIO, Inc.

Guzdial, M., Turns, J., Rappin, N., & Carlson, D. (1995). Collaborative support for learning in complex domains. In J. L. Schnase & E. L. Cunnius (eds), *Computer support for collaborative learning (CSCL '95)* (pp. 157–160). Bloomington, IN: Lawrence Erlbaum Associates.

Hayes, J. R., & Flower, L. S. (1980). Identifying the organization of writing processes. In L. Gregg & E. R. Steinberg (eds), *Cognitive processes in writing* (pp. 3–30). Hillsdale, N.J.: Lawrence Erlbaum Associates.

Heeter, C., Chu, C., Maniar, A., Winn, B., Mishra, P., Egidio, R., & Portwood-Stacer, L. (2003). Comparing 14 plus 2 forms of fun (and learning and gender issues) in commercial versus educational space exploration digital games. *Proceedings of the International Digital Games Research Conference.* University of Utrecht: Netherlands.

Hillocks, G. (1986). The writer's knowledge: Theory, research, and implications for practice. In A. Petrosky & D. Bartholomae (eds), *The teaching of writing. Eighty-fifth yearbook of the national society for the study of education, part II* (pp. 71–94). Chicago: University of Chicago Press.

Hughes, J. (2004). Technology learning principles for preservice and in-service teacher education. *Contemporary Issues in Technology and Teacher Education, 4*(3), 345–362.

Irving, K. E. (2006). The impact of technology on the 21st century classroom. In J. Rhoton & P. Shane (eds), *Teaching science in the 21st century* (pp. 3–20). Arlington, VA: National Science Teachers Association Press.

Jackson, P. W. (1968). *Life in the classroom.* New York: Holt, Rinehart & Winston.

Jones, R. A., & Spiro, R. (1992). Imagined conversations: The relevance of hypertext, pragmatism, and cognitive flexibility theory to the interpretation of "classic texts" in intellectual history. In D. Lucarella, J. Nanard, M. Nanard, & P. Paolini (eds), *Proceedings of the ACM Conference on Hypertext* (pp. 141–147). New York: Association for Computing Machinery.

Kay, A. (1984). Computer software. *Scientific American, 251*(3), 53–59.

Keating, T., & Evans, E. (2001). *Three computers in the back of the classroom: Pre-service teachers' conceptions of technology integration.* Paper presented at the 2001 annual meeting of the American Educational Research Association, Seattle, WA.

Kelly, A. E. (2003). Special issue on the role of design in educational research. *Educational Researcher, 32*(1), 5–8.

Klein, G. (1999). *Sources of power: How people make decisions.* Cambridge, MA: MIT Press.

Koehler, M. J., & Mishra, P. (2005a). Teachers learning technology by design. *Journal of Computing in Teacher Education, 21*(3), 94–102.

Koehler, M. J., & Mishra, P. (2005b). What happens when teachers design educational technology? The development of technological pedagogical content knowledge. *Journal of Educational Computing Research, 32*(2), 131–152.

Koehler, M. J., Mishra, P., & Yahya, K. (2007). Tracing the development of teacher knowledge in a design seminar: Integrating content, pedagogy, & technology. *Computers and Education, 49*(3), 740–762.

Koehler, M. J., Mishra, P., Hershey, K., & Peruski, L. (2004). With a little help from your students: A new model for faculty development and online course design. *Journal of Technology and Teacher Education, 12*(1), 25–55.

Kuhn, T. (1977). *The essential tension.* Chicago, IL: University of Chicago Press.

Lagemann, E. C. (2002). *Usable knowledge in education: A memorandum for the Spencer Foundation board of directors* [Memorandum]. Chicago: Spencer Foundation. Retrieved July 15, 2006 from http://www.spencer.org/publications/annual_reports/ar_2002.pdf

Lawrence, J. A. (1988). Expertise on the bench: Modeling magistrates/judicial decision-making. In M. T. H. Chi, R. Glaser, & M. J. Farr (eds), *The nature of expertise* (pp. 229–259). Hillsdale, NJ: Lawrence Erlbaum.

Leinhardt, G., & Greeno, J. G. (1986). The cognitive skill of teaching. *Journal of Educational Psychology, 78*(2), 75–95.

Lesgold, A. M., Feltovich, P. J., Glaser, R., & Wang, Y. (1981). *The acquisition of perceptual diagnostic skill in radiology.* Technical report no. PDS-1. University of Pittsburgh, Learning Research and Development Center, University of Pittsburgh.

Levine, L. W. (1996). *The opening of the American mind: Canons, culture, and history.* Boston: Beacon Press.

Lévi-Strauss, C. (1962). *The savage mind.* Chicago, IL: University of Chicago Press.

Margerum-Leys, J., & Marx, R. (2002). Teacher knowledge of educational technology: A study of student teacher/mentor teacher pairs. *Journal of Educational Computing Research, 26*(4), 427–462.

McCrory, R. (2004). A framework for understanding teaching with the Internet. *American Educational Research Journal, 41*(2), 447–488.

Mishra, P. (1998). Flexible learning in the periodic system with multiple representations: The design of a hypertext for learning complex concepts in chemistry (Doctoral dissertation, University of Illinois at Urbana-Champaign). *Dissertation Abstracts International, 59*(11), 4057. (AAT 9912322.)

Mishra, P., & Koehler, M. J. (2003). Not "what" but "how": Becoming design-wise about educational technology. In Y. Zhao (ed.), *What teachers should know about technology: Perspectives and practices* (pp. 99–122). Greenwich, CT: Information Age Publishing.

Mishra, P., & Koehler, M. J. (2006). Technological pedagogical content knowledge: A framework for integrating technology in teacher knowledge. *Teachers College Record, 108*(6), 1017–1054.

Mishra, P., & Yadav, A. (2006). Using hypermedia for learning complex concepts in chemistry: A qualitative study on the relationship between prior knowledge, beliefs and motivation. *Education and Information Technologies, 11*(1), 33–69.

Mishra, P., Koehler, M. J., Hershey, K., & Peruski, L. (2002). With a little help from your students: A new model for faculty development and online course design. *Proceedings from the Annual Meeting of the Society for Information Technology & Teacher Education*, March 2002, Nashville, TN. Virginia: Association for the Advancement of Computing in Education.

Mishra, P., Spiro, R. J., & Feltovich, P. (1996). Technology, representation and cognition. In H. von Oostendorp (ed.), *Cognitive aspects of electronic text processing* (pp. 287–306). Norwood, NJ: Ablex Publishing Corporation.

National Research Council (1999). *Being fluent with information technology literacy. Computer science and telecommunications board commission on physical sciences, mathematics, and applications.* Washington, DC: National Academy Press.

National Research Council (2000). *How people learn: Brain, mind, experience, and school.* Washington, DC: National Academy Press.

National Research Council (2002). *Scientific research in education.* R. K. Shavelson & L. Towne (eds), Committee on Scientific Principles for Education Research. Washington, DC: National Academy Press.

Nickerson, R. (1994). The teaching of thinking and problem solving. In R. Sternberg (ed.), *Thinking and problem solving* (2nd edn, pp. 215–234). San Diego, CA: Academic Press.

Niess, M. L. (2005). Preparing teachers to teach science and mathematics with technology: Developing a technology pedagogical content knowledge. *Teaching and Teacher Education,* 21(5), 509–523.

Norman, D. A. (1988). *The psychology of everyday things.* New York: Basic Books.

Ong, W. J. (1982). *The technologizing of the word.* London: Methuen.

Papert, S. (1980). *Mindstorms: Children, computers and powerful ideas.* New York: Basic Books.

Pennock, R. (2001). *Intelligent design creationism and its critics: Philosophical, theological and scientific perspectives.* Cambridge, MA: MIT Press.

Perkins, D. N. (1986). *Knowledge as design.* Hillsdale, NJ: Lawrence Erlbaum Associates.

Peruski, L., & Mishra, P. (2004). Webs of activity in online course design and teaching. *ALT-J: Research in Learning Technology,* 12(1), 37–49.

Petroski, H. (1985). *To engineer is human: the role of failure in successful design (1st edn).* New York: St. Martin's Press.

Petroski, H. (1994). *Design paradigms: case histories of error and judgment in engineering.* New York: Cambridge University Press.

Pfundt, H., & Duit, R. (2000). *Bibliography: Student's alternative frameworks and science education (5th edn).* Kiel, Germany: University of Kiel.

Pierson, M. E. (1999). Technology integration practice as a function of pedagogical expertise (Doctoral dissertation, Arizona State University). *Dissertation Abstracts International,* 60(03), 711. (AAT 9924200.)

Pierson, M. E. (2001). Technology integration practice as a function of pedagogical expertise. *Journal of Research on Computing in Education,* 33(4), 413–429.

Pople, H. E. (1982). Heuristic methods for imposing structure on ill-structured problems: The structuring of medical diagnostics. In P. Szolovits (ed.), *Artificial intelligence in medicine* (pp. 119–189). Boulder, CO: Westview Press.

Prensky, M. (2001). Digital natives, digital immigrants. *On the Horizon,* 9(5), 1–6.

Putnam, R. T., & Borko, H. (2000). What do new views of knowledge and thinking have to say about research on teacher learning? *Educational Researcher,* 29(1), 4–15.

Reitman, W. R. (1964). Heuristic decision procedures, open constraints, and the structure of ill-defined problems. In M. W. Shelly & G. L. Bryan (eds), *Human judgments and optimality* (pp. 282–315). New York: John Wiley and Sons.

Reitman, W. R. (1965). *Cognition and thought.* New York: Wiley.

Resnick, L. B. (1988). Treating mathematics as an ill-structured discipline. In R. I. Charles & E. A. Silver (eds), *The teaching and assessing of mathematical problem solving* (pp. 32–60). Hillsdale, NJ: Lawrence Erlbaum Associates.

Rittel. H., & Webber, M. (1973). Dilemmas in a general theory of planning. *Policy Sciences,* 4(2), 155–169.

Roberts, P. (1994). The place of design in technology education. In D. Layton (ed.), *Innovations in science and technology education, vol. V* (pp. 171–179). Paris: UNESCO Publishing.

Rosenblatt, L. M. (1978). *The reader, the text, the poem: The transactional theory of literary work.* Carbondale, IL: Southern Illinois University Press.

Schon, D. (1983). *The reflective practitioner.* London: Temple Smith.

Schon, D. (1987). *Educating the reflective practitioner.* San Francisco: Jossey-Bass.

Schon, D. (1996). *Reflective conversation with materials.* In T. Winograd, J. Bennett, L. DeYoung, & B. Hartfield (eds), *Bringing design to software* (pp. 171–184). New York: Addison-Wesley.

Schwab, J. J. (1983). The Practical 4: Something for curriculum professors to do. *Curriculum Inquiry, 13*(3), 239–265.

Shulman, L. (1986). Those who understand: Knowledge growth in teaching. *Educational Researcher, 15*(2), 4–14.

Shulman, L. S. (1987). Knowledge and teaching: Foundations of the new reform. *Harvard Educational Review, 57*(1), 1–22.

Simon, H. (1969). *Sciences of the artificial.* Cambridge, MA: MIT Press.

Simon, H. A. (1957). *Models of man—social and rational.* New York: John Wiley and Sons.

Slough, S., & Connell, M. (2006). Defining technology and its natural corollary, technological content knowledge (TCK). In C. Crawford, D. Willis, R. Carlsen, I. Gibson, K. McFerrin, J. Price, & R. Weber, (eds), *Proceedings of society for information technology and teacher education international conference 2006* (pp. 1053–1059). Chesapeake, VA: AACE.

Snow, C. P. (1959). *The two cultures and the scientific revolution.* New York: Cambridge University Press.

Spiro, R. J., Coulson, R. L., Feltovich, P. J., & Anderson, D. K. (1988). Cognitive flexibility theory: Advanced knowledge acquisition in ill-structured domains. In V. Patel (ed.), *Tenth Annual Conference of the Cognitive Science Society* (pp. 375–383). Hillsdale, NJ: Lawrence Erlbaum Associates, Inc.

Spiro, R. J., Feltovich, P. J., Jacobson, M. J., & Coulson, R. L. (1991). Cognitive flexibility, constructivism, and hypertext: Random access instruction for advanced knowledge acquisition in ill-structured domains. *Educational Technology, May,* 24–33.

Spiro, R. J., & Jehng, J.-Ch. (1990). Cognitive flexibility and hypertext: Theory and technology for the nonlinear and multidimensional traversal of complex subject matter. In D. Nix & R. Spiro (eds), *Cognition, education, and multimedia: Exploring ideas in high technology* (pp. 163–204). Hillsdale, NJ: Lawrence Erlbaum Associates.

Thompson, A. (2006). Technology pedagogical content knowledge: Framing teacher knowledge about technology. *Journal of Computing in Teacher Education, 22*(6), 46–48.

Turkle, S. (1995). *Life on the screen: Identity in the age of the Internet.* New York: Simon & Schuster.

Turkle, S., & Papert, S. (1992). Epistemological pluralism: Styles and choices within the computer culture. *Signs, 16*(1), 128–157.

Wikipedia (2006). Technology (Wikipedia entry). Retrieved on July 12, 2006 from http://en.wikipedia.org/wiki/Technology.

Williams, S. M. (1992). Putting case-based instruction into context: Examples from legal and medical education. *The Journal of The Learning Sciences, 2*(4), 367–427.

Zhao, Y. (2003). *What teachers should know about technology: Perspectives and practices.* Greenwich, CT: Information Age Publishing.

Zhao, Y., Pugh, K., Sheldon, S., & Byers, J. L. (2002). Conditions for classroom technology innovations. *Teachers College Record, 104*(3), 482–515.

Zimmerman, J. (2002). *Whose America? Culture wars in the public schools.* Cambridge, MA: Harvard University Press.

2

Bridging digital and cultural divides
TPCK for equity of access to technology

MARIO ANTONIO KELLY

That is true culture which helps us to work for the social betterment of all.

Henry Ward Beecher

The focus of this chapter is technological pedagogical content knowledge (TPCK) for addressing issues of equity of access to information and communication technology (ICT), for students from diverse backgrounds. While equity of access to ICT is not a subject area taught by teachers, it is central to the teaching effectiveness of lessons that incorporate technology, and therefore should be an important component of every teacher's pedagogical knowledge base. The issue of equity of access to technology is likely to grow in importance as the role of technology in K-12 teaching and learning increases, while the access of low-income, ethnic, linguistic, and cultural minority families remains limited. Access to technology matters because it is necessary for achieving ICT literacy, and is becoming necessary for achieving in every curriculum subject.

In K-12 classrooms ICT literacy can be the direct learning outcome of technology classes, as well as a byproduct of instruction in English, art, science, and other subjects, when these are taught with technology. The other chapters in this volume present the state of the art of teaching various subjects with technology. The focus of this chapter is teaching any subject with technology in ways that make technology and ICT literacy accessible to all children, including those seemingly placed at a disadvantage by their backgrounds. If teachers are to help children from low-income, ethnic, linguistic, or cultural minority families overcome the potential negative academic and social consequences of limited access to technology, then they must be armed with pedagogical knowledge to not only respond to limited access, but to also provide technology-mediated instruction that is sensitive to cultural differences. Knowing how to do so should be part of the standard repertoire of pedagogical skills provided by teacher education programs.

The goals of this chapter, to be achieved in a non-linear format, are three-fold. First, to describe the current state of equity of access to technology in the

U.S. Second, to present a conceptual framework and knowledge base for pedagogically addressing inequity of access to ICT. Of particular importance in this regard are the potential contributions of teacher TPCK to increasing equity of access. The discussion here will build on Koehler and Mishra's model (in Chapter 1), expanding on the concept of TPCK context. A final goal is to provide and justify teaching strategies for improving equity of access. As a platform for the discussion the next section provides a brief description of twenty-first century literacy.

ICT literacy in the twenty-first century

Our society is arguably experiencing a third industrial revolution, one that Castells (1993, 2000) referred to as "informationalism." Among its major features are an increasing reliance on science and technology, a shift from material production to information processing and management, and networked organizations in which administrative hierarchies are flattened, replaced by team-based work. These are the labor, economic, and social environments in which today's students will have to function (Warschauer, 2003). To be effective in these environments students increasingly have to be able to individually navigate and sort-through vast digital repositories of knowledge and make accurate judgments about the quality, authenticity, relevance, and applicability of what they find. Students also have to be able to work collaboratively with others if they are to be successful in team-based work settings. They must be able to do so in person as well as online over great physical, often global, distances, and frequently with others who are culturally different.

A major challenge for teachers and teacher educators is to foster ICT literacy, and to do so for *all* children. In this regard, children from ethnic minority, low-income, or culturally different families, or whose first language is not English, often exhibit lower achievement than children from mainstream families. This has been true for achievement in reading/writing literacy, and is also true for ICT literacy. Ethnicity, socio-economic status, language, and cultural background are at the core of the "digital divide" that separates students, before they even cross the portals of the school, into groups that have relatively high levels of access to ICT and groups whose access is limited or non-existent. If teachers are to help bridge this digital divide it is important that they understand its nature, pedagogical practices that contribute to its creation and maintenance, and instructional strategies for narrowing it. It is to these that we turn next.

There are multiple digital divides

The discussion of equity of access to ICT, crystallized in the term "digital divide" has largely focused on equal access to technology infrastructure (computers, multimedia equipment, software, the presence or absence of Internet connectivity, and recently, the speed of Internet connections). Following Attewell (2001) this aspect of equity will be referred to in this chapter as the *first digital divide*. However, equity is more complex than the simple presence or absence of equipment. It is multidimensional (Technology Counts, 2001), comprising at least two other aspects of equity: (1) access to achievement-enhancing technology mediated instruction (TMI) in school, and technology mediated activities outside of school; and (2) access to culturally sensitive TMI—teachers knowledgeable about multicultural education, and able to incorporate this knowledge into their pedagogical practice of teaching with technology. The latter two dimensions will be referred to as the *second digital divide* and *third digital divide*, respectively.

In the sections that follow the characteristics of each digital divide will be presented and discussed as the basis for a set of pedagogical practices designed to bridge it. Also incorporated into these discussions will be aspects of the literature on math, science, and "technocentrism" (Damarin, 1998), and the literature on multicultural education. These literatures are based on largely different sets of assumptions and conceptual frameworks and can be construed as oppositional. Yet, they seem to agree on the technological pedagogical practices that are most likely to result in the acquisition of content knowledge and ICT literacy. These pedagogical practices, as Damarin (1998) suggested, are low on the "banking system of education" scale (Freire, 1970), low on student accumulation of pre-selected facts, low on teacher centrism, high on individual constructivism, and high on Vygotskian social constructivism. In other words, in terms of teaching with technology, both theoretical frameworks—"technocentrism" and multicultural education—advocate strategies that involve individuals as well as learning communities seeking answers to challenging, stimulating, often personally relevant questions; supported, guided, scaffolded, or mentored by teachers, more knowledgeable peers, or even peers of equivalent levels of knowledge. Unfortunately, the ideal of this constructivist type of approach seems not to be the reality that poor children typically experience.

The first digital divide: access to technology hardware, software, and the Internet

The first digital divide refers to an actual physical divide between those who have ICT, such as computers, scanners, camcorders and access to the Internet, and those who do not. Recently the term has also been used to distinguish those who have the highest level of technology from those who have the lowest level and those who have broadband or high-speed access to the Internet from those who do not (U.S. Department of Commerce, 2002, 2004). Perhaps far too much of the discussion about the digital divide has revolved around this aspect of equity. Countless theoretical, empirical, and policy articles have documented its existence. In general, the evidence shows that physical access to ICT is greater among middle- and high-income families than among low-income families; greater among White and Asian-American families than among Black and Latino families. For example, the U.S. Department of Commerce (2004) reported that in October 2003, 45 percent of families with annual incomes $75,000 and above had broadband access, while only 7 percent of families with annual incomes below $15,000 had such access. In total, 34 percent of Asian American and Pacific Islanders lived in a broadband household, as did 25 percent of Whites. By comparison, only 14 percent of Blacks and 12 percent of Latinos had broadband access at home. The data also showed that suburban families are more likely to have ICT equipment than urban families, particularly those residing in inner cities, and rural families tend to have the least access, although recently access in some rural areas has increased significantly.

While it is convenient to bifurcate the technology world into the haves and the have-nots, as seen in much of the literature, reality, as Warschauer (2003) pointed out, is a lot more complex. Actual physical access to technology is on a gradient that goes from no access, to access limited in terms of times of access and the quality of equipment or Internet connectivity, to high access. Likewise, inter-group differences on physical access are not as simple as often portrayed. For example, low socio-economic status White and Asian-American households are much more likely to have computers and Internet access at home than similar Hispanic and African-American households of limited income (Gorski, 2005). A recent study by the Corporation for Public Broadcasting (2002) found a home access ethnic divide for older children, but not for preschool-aged children. It found that between 21 percent and 23 percent of Caucasian, African-American and Hispanic children aged two to five used the Internet at home. The authors of the study speculated that the absence of difference may be related to parental age. Parents of younger children are more likely younger and more experienced with the Internet, having experienced it in high school, at college or at their own or a friend's place of employment than parents of older children. Equity of physical access to ICT is also complicated by the distinction between private, as opposed to public access, an issue to be analyzed below in the discussion of the second digital divide. It is sufficient to note here that those who do not own computers and other ICT can often gain access at work and in their communities.

There are many reasons for bridging the first digital divide

CHILDREN NEED PHYSICAL ACCESS TO COMPLETE HOMEWORK ASSIGNMENTS REQUIRING ICT

However, this reason may have been overemphasized in the literature, given that teachers and parents willing to invest the time and energy (important caveats) can offset lack of personal ownership by finding publicly accessible ICT.

PHYSICAL ACCESS HAS BEEN ASSOCIATED WITH HIGHER ICT LITERACY

One way of conceptualizing the highest form of ICT literacy is in terms of what Ching, Basham, and Jang (2005) called *"full spectrum frequency"* users. These are individuals with a high degree of use across a broad range of ICT activities, including: (1) communication technologies (text or voice-based with computers or hand-held devices); (2) construction technologies (Web pages, digital images, spreadsheets, PowerPoint, and other manipulable digital artifacts); and (3) entertainment technologies (e.g., computer video games, digital music). Ching *et al.* found, for a sample of education candidates at a Midwestern college, that the higher the family income (and presumably access to ICT), the more likely the student was to exhibit "full spectrum frequency" of use. (Ethnicity was not found to be a predictor, but the authors acknowledge limitations of the sample that could be responsible for that finding.) They also found that the earlier and the better the access, the higher one's chances for achieving ICT literacy. College students who first started using computers prior to age ten were significantly more likely than those who started after age ten to achieve "full spectrum frequency."

BROADBAND ACCESS TO THE INTERNET AT HOME HAS BEEN ASSOCIATED WITH HIGHER INTERNET ENGAGEMENT, MORE FREQUENT INTERNET USE AND DECREASED TELEVISION WATCHING

It does seem to matter whether students have broadband, as opposed to dial-up Internet access. In one study (U.S. Department of Commerce, 2004) those with broadband access at home were more likely than those with dial-up service to use the Internet daily (66.1 percent to 51.1 percent) and to engage in more types of activities online, including obtaining information. Moreover, at least among teenagers, time spent online and with all types of digital media seems to be increasing at the expense of television watching (Corporation for Public Broadcasting, 2002). In general, children who use the Internet spend 37 percent less time watching television and 16 percent more time with friends and family (Corporation for Public Broadcasting, 2002; North Central Regional Educational Laboratory, 2003). This is a positive outcome given the association of television watching with lower achievement (Shin, 2004), and the high rate of television and entertainment media use by minority children (Roberts, Foehr, Rideout, & Brodie, 1999). However, time spent not watching television is often spent with computer and multimedia forms of entertainment, not pursuing knowledge and achievement, and this is especially true for minority children (Gorski, 2005).

Teachers can help to change this by using homework and other pedagogical practices to engage children in multimedia activities that not only entertain, but provide academic and general knowledge. It is important to bridge the first digital divide, and to do so as early as possible in children's lives to start them on the path to developing high levels of ICT literacy and "full spectrum frequency."

Teachers should play a role in bridging the first digital divide

Bridging this divide, as Gorski and Clark (2001) have suggested, will be most thoroughly and effectively accomplished through systemic social justice change that makes technology accessible to all children. Indeed, much of the discussion about the first digital divide seems to incorporate the tacit assumption that bridging it is primarily the task of local, state, or federal government, and secondarily, of large corporations, philanthropies, and civic organizations. Another tacit assumption seems to be that schools, teachers, and teacher educators are powerless in the face of this obstacle; that their responsibility will begin after others have made the equipment available. This is a delay we can ill afford. To the contrary, the argument here is that inequity of access to all kinds of resources (up-to-date books, well-designed and furnished school buildings, overhead projectors) has always been a challenge to those in low-income brackets, many of whom are minority, and to their teachers. Effective teachers have always improvised bridges across those divides, and the first digital divide is another example of this phenomenon. It is incumbent on teachers to work collaboratively with school administrators, parents, and community organizations to develop strategies for securing access to hardware, software, and the Internet for all children. By extension, it is incumbent on teacher educators to prepare preservice teachers to do so.

To the extent that technology is another area in which individuals from low-income and minority backgrounds may be socially and educationally excluded, the goal, as Warschauer (2003) suggested, must be social and educational inclusion. Accomplishing this goal requires not being daunted by the limitations in the availability of equipment in the ideal locations of home and classroom, but instead developing the resourcefulness to find and use technology where it is available. The assumption here is that effective pedagogy depends on making the best use of available equipment and other resources. It is further assumed that it is part of a teacher's responsibility to incorporate into instruction strategies that help students and parents identify and use public ICT resources. Rather than focus on the real obstacle that not having technology and Internet access are, it is more effective to develop pedagogical practices that attempt to overcome these obstacles. Such a focus is empowering for teachers, students, and parents.

Technological pedagogy for bridging the first digital divide

1. *Work with school administrators to secure after-school access to school ICT.* Where schools have up-to-date technology, especially a computer laboratory, then one strategy is to work with administrators to secure after-school access with technical and academic

support. It may be incumbent on teachers to take the initiative, given that well-intentioned administrators may not spontaneously see the need.

2. *Work with parents and others to identify public ICT facilities in the community.* Develop a list of resources (e.g., after school programs) that are close to the school or students' homes that can provide access for those who lack it at home. Even where a school computer lab exists, it may be insufficient if many children need access. For these situations, as well as for schools without a computer lab, public facilities in the community are often viable supplements or substitutes. Managed and/or supported by a community-based organization, a local civic group, or business, such facilities can be found in communities across the nation. Teachers can work collaboratively with parents and administrators to identify such facilities, make contact with them, and if possible make arrangements for students to use them for homework assignments. Sometimes the facilities have staff with the expertise to tutor, not only regarding technical issues, but also content. The establishment of formal and informal relationships with such programs and staff can not only make technology accessible to students, but can result in equipment time, and even tutors, being set aside for class assignments.

   Teachers are likely to find in some parents a valuable resource in locating public facilities, given that Wilson, Wallin, and Reiser (2003) found that African-Americans were not only less likely to have home computers or Internet access, even when socio-economic status is controlled, but they were also more likely to know of public facilities in their community. Establishing contact and securing time for children should be seen as only the start. Teachers, parents, and staff at public facilities can collaborate to provide an ideal level of support for students. Such facilities often have on staff former teachers or others sufficiently familiar with K-12 education to be an academic resource for students, especially if well informed by teachers about students' needs and homework goals.

3. *Develop strategies to counter problems at public ICT facilities.* There are potential drawbacks to the use of after-school computer programs at schools or other public facilities. These include the possibility that children may have to share computers, the limited hours of access which often require working immediately following school with no break for meals, and that parents are usually not present (Gorski & Clark, 2001). However, there are silver linings to these clouds. With some attention to how children are grouped and the structure of the TMI task, children can derive important learning and social benefits from the sharing of computers. They can acquire

skills that are essential to ICT literacy, as described previously. Since relatively high amounts of television watching (sometimes at the expense of homework) is a characteristic of many children in the group of interest, working immediately after school may not only be an effective alternative to television watching—previously cited data associates increased technology use with decreased television watching—but it is one that many parents have instituted. Regarding the meal issue and parental involvement, arrangements can be made for healthy snacks and many programs can accommodate (and some invite) the participation of parents.

4. *Seek assistance from local colleges and universities.* Gorski and Clark (2001) proposed a strategy similar to the one described above, but built around colleges and universities and their technology resources. They suggested that teachers seek for their students and families physical access to university computer labs, digital access to universities' libraries, and the direct engagement of faculty, especially those whose expertise involves the intersection of multicultural education and technology. Unfortunately this strategy may not be as widely applicable as desired given that some institutions of higher education are finding their technology facilities insufficient to meet the needs of their own students. Moreover, there are insufficient numbers of educators well trained in both multicultural education (and the other content areas) and technology.

5. *Take steps to learn about the ICT access and history of students in the classroom.* Survey the class early in the school year to determine out-of-school access to technology, history of ICT use, and level of skill. Talk not only to students, but also with the person who plays the most significant role in the student's life and education, be that a parent, a legal guardian or an extended family member. A student may have access to ICT and considerable prior experience even though these may be at a friend's or neighbor's home rather than in their own home or a community center. Many students have ICT skills that, while not acquired with a focus on academics, are a sound foundation on which to build. Therefore, the line of questioning must be sufficiently broad, non-threatening, and confidential to elicit this information.

6. *Advocate for the fair and effective distribution of ICT resources.* If teachers lack technology skills, encourage school administrators to provide professional development before the large-scale purchase of equipment that in the absence of training may be poorly used or not used at all. Suggest purchasing one or two carts of laptops that can be shared by many classrooms as opposed to equipping every classroom (Warschauer, 2003).

7. *Plan for equipment failure.* For schools that primarily serve low-income students investigate workability issues—that the equipment will not work is a common problem (Warschauer, Knobel, & Stone, 2004). If the school does not have resources, a plan, and staff in place for dealing with such problems, then identify colleagues with technology skills and set up an informal network. At a minimum ask if it is OK to call on them in emergencies.

The second digital divide: access to achievement-enhancing TMI

The second digital divide refers to disparities in how ICT is used at school as well as outside of school (Attewell, 2001). It has several components:

1. Fewer technologically skilled teachers. In general, schools that primarily serve low-income students have fewer teachers well versed in the integration of technology into instruction and fewer technology support staff than schools that primarily serve middle-class students. This is not surprising in light of the first digital divide.
2. Different technology assignments within the same culturally mixed classroom. Within the same classroom those with the lowest grades are often assigned drill and practice technology activities, while those with higher grades are given more engaging and challenging assignments involving problem-solving components.
3. Fewer technologically skilled parents. Another feature of the second digital divide is that parents of minority and low-income students are generally less accomplished with technology and are less likely to directly provide achievement-enhancing technology activities at home than are the parents of middle- and high-income and White students.

The differences described above should be considered in the larger contexts of K-12 and teacher education, where there is a divide between the pedagogical affordances of current ICT on the one hand, and on the other hand, the daily pedagogical practices in most classrooms. It is arguable that nationally too few teachers (and teacher educators) meet the existing broad standards for the integration of technology into teaching, such as the National Educational Technology Standards (NETS), developed by the International Society for Technology in Education (ISTE), and the Professional Standards of the National Council for Accreditation of Teacher Education (NCATE). The latter standards only require a "commitment" to technology in an institution's conceptual framework. Teachers and teacher education programs may well meet these standards yet lack the ability to use technology in the content-specific, pedagogically appropriate ways described in this volume.

The impact of the second digital divide

In the context of the big picture, the poor uses of ICT in teaching are not unique to low-income and minority students, but poor uses are higher among this group. More importantly, its impact is potentially more deleterious because it is added to, and interacts with, other entrenched factors weighing down the achievement of low-income and minority students. Already relatively low achievement in reading, math, and other content areas may be exacerbated by poor uses of technology in teaching (Warschauer, 2003).

The differences in use of technology matter because it is with this dimension of the digital divide that differences in genuine access to knowledge lies (Natriello, 2001). As Warschauer (2003) demonstrated with examples from around the world, a large infusion of technology resources, when poorly managed and used inappropriately, may be less effective—in terms of promoting ICT literacy, achievement, and social inclusion—than limited resources used well. It follows that with the present state of the second digital divide, even if differences in the physical access to ICT were to be immediately erased, and all schools and families had high-end equipment and the fastest Internet connection, the differences in use would perpetuate the digital divide.

As was true of the first digital divide, the reality of the second digital divide is more complex than the simple binary division of the haves and the have-nots. The second digital divide is really about ineffective TMI strategies, and these can be observed in all kinds of schools. However, what creates and maintains the second digital divide is the disproportionate use of these ineffective strategies with low-income and minority students. This is true in schools that primarily serve such students, compared with schools that primarily serve students who are of higher income and/or White. It is also true of schools that serve demographically mixed students, and is of special concern in such schools. When ineffective strategies are selectively and excessively applied to minority and/or low-income students, due to low expectations and/or as a response to lower achievement in content areas, the outcome is likely to be race or income-based disparity in ITC literacy. Some of the ineffective strategies will be discussed next, followed by a description of effective strategies.

Ineffective TMI strategies

DRILL AND PRACTICE

Wenglinsky (1998) found the racial and income differences in school use of ICT to be significant. White and Asian students were more likely to use computers for simulations and applications, whereas African-American and Latino students were more likely to use computers for drill and practice. The same difference was true for students from low-income families as opposed to those from wealthier families. In terms of learning, achievement, and inclusion in the broader society, the long-term consequences of using computers primarily for drill and practice are most likely negative and substantive for Latino, African-American and/or poor students. Of course there is a place and a need for drill and practice in learning. But the over-reliance on drill and practice is consistent with the industrial model of schooling that consigns students to low-end jobs with limited prospects for professional or personal fulfillment. It is inconsistent with the achievement of the type of twenty-first century ICT literacy described earlier. It is preparing students for an industrial economy, rather than for post-industrialism or informationism (Warschauer, 2003).

DEFENSIVE TEACHING (AND LEARNING)

The term defensive teaching (Fordham & Ogbu, 1986; Ogbu, 1987) was used by Garrison and Bromley (2004) to describe overly restrictive and controlling TMI practices observed in a case study. The term basically means that students are held to very detailed instructions based on the assumption that if they are not, they will misbehave or get into academic trouble. Garrison and Bromley described an observation in a lab where the teacher first controls students by telling them: "If finished, wait patiently, till I finish what I'm doing." Further controlling them with the statement: "Hands in lap." Then waiting a brief interval before saying: "Yes, save." The point is that defensive teaching elevates control beyond what is necessary for safety and learning and may stifle inquisitiveness, exploration, motivation, and even the intended learning.

Defensive teaching has a counterpart in defensive student learning strategies such as *pretending* (faking inability or faking being busy) and *undermining* (preventing work initiation or completion by sabotaging equipment, e.g., unplugging the computer by kicking the power strip or removing the ball from the mouse). Garrison and Bromley found these too. The cause–effect relationship between these variables is not a fruitful discussion to have here. What matters is that they are related and that teachers should try to decrease both.

USING BASIC ACCESS TO ICT AS A REWARD

This strategy can be exhibited in several ways. ICT access may be a "privilege" that has to be earned or maintained by good behavior, or by minimal levels of academic performance in other areas. Garrison and Bromley described the mutually reinforcing role often played by teachers and students in this strategy. Students struggling academically act out to be denied computer "privilege" and the hard work involved in integrating technology use into weak content knowledge. Denial of the "privilege" spares teachers the labor-intensive interaction required to lift the achievement of such students.

The previous statements are not meant to imply that it is more difficult to teach with technology than without. Although the use of technology requires an initial investment of extra time and energy, so does any strategy being used for the first time by a teacher. Nor is technology, by itself, a magical bullet that can substitute for weak content knowledge on the part of teachers or students, or for poor pedagogical knowledge on the part of teachers. It is the integration of technology with sound foundations of content and pedagogical knowledge—TPCK—that is likely to be most effective.

Technological pedagogy for bridging the second digital divide

Part of the solution to the problem of the second digital divide is to build effective technological pedagogical practices into standards-based curricula (Atwater, 2000; Lynch, 2000). Another is to improve the performance outcomes for teachers (and teacher education programs), such as those of ISTE and NCATE. In the absence of such systemic changes there is much that individual teachers can do, building on the second digital divide issues raised above.

1. At the start of an academic term take steps to learn about the prior ICT knowledge and skills of students in the classroom. (See strategy 5 under the first digital divide.)
2. Determine the required technological competencies for each activity and whether all students have them (Chisholm, Carey, & Hernandez, 2002). Do not rely entirely on promotional statements from manufacturers.
3. If there is wide variation in the prior technology or subject knowledge of students, then use this variation as a variable in pairing students or otherwise organizing some TMI activities.
4. Expose students to a variety of ICT, including computers, the Internet, and visualization software. This strategy is important for bridging the first digital divide by providing all children with access to a full range of technology. It is also important for bridging the second digital divide in that effective TMI will incorporate a range of technology in pedagogically appropriate ways for each content area.
5. Avoid educational technological "performativity"—merely running students through a checklist of technology activities or skills for the sake of being able to state that they were exposed, but with little concern about whether they really understand and are able to apply the new knowledge in meaningful, purposeful ways (Lyotard, 1984; Lankshear & Knobel, 2003; Warschauer, Knobel, & Stone, 2004).
6. Use drill and practice when necessary, but not excessively, and not exclusively for any group.
7. Develop activities that encourage students to use ICT to explore

natural phenomena, experience scientific phenomena, extend their thinking, create multiple representations of their understanding, and communicate with teachers and peers (Edelson, 1998; Hug, Krajcik, & Marx, 2005; Linn, 1998; Spitulnik, Stratford, Krajcik, & Soloway, 1998). In addition to increased understanding and higher achievement, another important result is likely to be increased motivation (Blumenfeld *et al.*, 1991).

8. Assign creative, problem-solving activities that require application, analysis, synthesis, and evaluation—e.g., multiple-step projects that require searching the Internet, evaluating what is found and then applying it to the solution of a problem.

9. Avoid using ICT to engage in defensive teaching (Garrison & Bromley, 2004), and especially avoid granting basic access to ICT as a reward.

The third digital divide: access to culture-sensitive technological pedagogy

The third digital divide is a difference in the extent to which the TMI received by students is compatible or at least sensitive to their cultural backgrounds. For many middle-class and White students, instruction, including TMI, is more consistently culturally sensitive than is the case for many minority and low-income students. Cultural sensitivity, like the other kinds of digital divides, is probably more a matter of degree than of presence versus absence. The issue is important to all teaching, whether or not technology is involved. However, it is particularly important that teachers (and teacher educators) deliberately address it in teaching that involves technology because in the absence of such deliberate attempts it is too easy to assume that technology, and by extension teaching with technology, is a-cultural and bias-free. Arguably, technology is not. The choices we make at every level reflect culture and value differences. The kind of hardware and software, their degree of user-friendliness, their language requirements or the degree to which the software reflects the experiences of different children in the room are not culture and bias-free. The ways in which the technology is used, for example whether or not children are grouped for computer work or whether email is used as a principal method of communication with parents, reflect underlying values. In the absence of deliberate attempts to be aware of these issues, to analyze instructional technology choices for bias and to make conscious choices, teachers may unwittingly contribute to the alienation of some groups of students, and to the maintenance of digital divides.

Bridging the third digital divide requires being sensitive to cultural differences, embracing them, and being deliberate about incorporating them into TMI. Sensitivity starts with an understanding of the concept of culture and the ways cultural similarities and differences often play out in the classroom.

This issue will be discussed next, followed by a description of three general approaches for teaching with cultural sensitivity, and finally, by specific strategies for culture-sensitive TMI.

Cultural similarities and differences in the classroom

Culture has been defined in numerous ways. See for example Geertz (1973) and Le Vine (1973). For the present discussion it suffices that most definitions include at least three components: (1) the material products or artifacts that people produce; (2) what people do, the ways they behave (for example, whether or not it is normative in the culture for individuals of different social rank to maintain eye contact); and (3) what people think and believe, their mental processes (including learning styles), and their values and belief systems (Bodley, 1994). In the classroom each of these three components corresponds to an aspect of cultural sensitivity that has to be addressed if students are to be treated equitably (Kinsler, Romero, Kelly, Graves, & Mercado, 1991).

The first component of culture is the most tangible, the most superficial, and the easiest to observe; for example, the foods, clothing, and artwork of different cultures. Perhaps for this reason, this component has received a disproportionate amount of attention in multicultural education and is the area in which teachers seem to exhibit the highest level of cultural sensitivity. Sensitivity to surface culture issues can be seen in the curriculum of schools nationwide, where children learn that foods, clothing, and art, among others, are dimensions along which people and cultures differ, and that such differences are to be respected and embraced.

The second component of culture is less superficial, less tangible, and more difficult to observe than the first. While this component—how people behave, including the normative social interaction patterns of the group—is susceptible to introspective analysis, such analysis requires more deliberate effort than the superficial characteristics. In general, different cultural groups develop different ways of behaving and interacting; for example, allowing small (versus large) personal space around individuals, or persons of unequal social status maintaining (versus avoiding) eye contact. Although this knowledge is provided by many teacher education programs, awareness of these cultural differences is probably not as widespread or as thorough as awareness of superficial differences. Consequently, the sensitivity of teachers is less primed and in the classroom these issues receive less attention than they deserve.

Teachers are even less sensitive and less primed to the third component of culture—mental processes, values, and belief systems—which often differ among cultural groups. For example, in terms of learning styles some groups seem to exhibit a preference for linear reasoning, while others seem to prefer relational reasoning; some lean towards field independence, others towards field dependence (Hale-Benson, 1986). Teaching with sensitivity to this aspect of culture requires at a minimum some awareness of one's own learning and teaching preferences and a willingness to engage other styles.

Another aspect of the third component of culture is the values and belief system cultural groups develop in response to their history and experience. For example, in response to societal racial stereotypes and a long history of segregation in education, employment, and housing, the knowledge base of African-Americans includes a well-established sense of how to identify racism and prejudice, even in its subtler forms. Many African-American parents have come to expect such behavior from at least some teachers and school administrators and in anticipation, psychologically "buttress" their children so that they will be resilient to such experiences (Oden, Kelly, Ma, & Weikart, 1992). Teaching with sensitivity to such values and belief systems has to start with the ability and willingness to find out which systems are actually in place for individual students, and to teach in ways that engage those systems to indirectly impact achievement through interpersonal and intrapersonal variables such as self-esteem and self-efficacy. (See the discussion of teaching–learning context below.) Teaching with cultural sensitivity may require an extra measure of vigilance when technology is involved and the goal is to bridge digital divides.

Culture-sensitive TMI

Twenty-first-century America classrooms are largely culturally mixed. Even though many schools have been re-segregated along income and racial lines (Kozol, 2006) the fact is that most schools are culturally mixed, at least in the sense of having a few students from a different cultural background than the majority in that school. A mix of several cultures is common in many East and West coast schools, and is increasingly true in other parts of the country. Moreover, even in majority minority or low-income schools, the teaching staff is often largely White and middle-class. Cultural diversity among students or between teacher and students is a salient characteristic of the teaching–learning context of many American schools and classrooms. Effective teaching in such contexts requires not just the pedagogical management of cultural issues, but deliberate attempts to incorporate these cultural differences into instruction, in ways that simultaneously tap their affordances while reducing the potential obstacles they create to learning. There are several ways to accomplish this, including aptitude-treatment-interaction pedagogy, "good teaching," and creating and maintaining "equitable classrooms."

ATTRIBUTE-TREATMENT-INTERACTION PEDAGOGY (ATIP)

The school, its curriculum, materials, pedagogy, and ways of processing information and interacting are reflective of the dominant culture in which the school operates (Banks, 2006; Nieto, 2004). When students are from the dominant culture their ways of behaving and learning are generally compatible with those of the school. However, culturally mixed classrooms require managing diversity pedagogically so that all students achieve their academic potential, not only those whose cultural background is dominant and therefore most compatible with the school. Moreover, ideally pedagogy will stretch students beyond their own culture, familiarizing them with other ways. When students in a classroom are from multiple cultures, effective teaching requires a variety of pedagogical accommodations, including attribute-treatment-interactions and enrichment.

The term *attribute-treatment-interaction pedagogy* (ATIP) is a deliberate alteration of the concept of aptitude-treatment-interaction, replacing the term *aptitude* with *attribute* to convey the equality of cultural characteristics. In ATIP students vary on a particular cultural attribute, such as preferred learning style, and it is the teacher's responsibility to figure out which instructional strategies will be the most compatible (interact best with the preferred learning style) to result in the highest achievement (Hale-Benson, 1986). The "treatment" may be different for different students. Of greatest importance is the conscious and deliberate analysis of preferred learning style which can then be used as the basis for an instructional strategy. In its strongest form, ATIP involves making instruction compatible with the cultural preferences of individual students. This is challenging and difficult to achieve. Far more practical is to vary modes of instruction so that the cultural preferences of different students are all covered at different times.

Another important way ATIP must be considered is that pedagogical practices often interact with student cultural attributes in unique ways, resulting in unintended academic, psychological, and social outcomes. Whether or not a teacher is aware, a student will have accumulated a history of experiences and knowledge about how others respond to their cultural background. Intended to or not, pedagogical practices are often interpreted by students, positively and negatively, through the filter of this prior experience. Interpretation matters because it is often the basis for student achievement-related behaviors. Students who interpret an instructional strategy as high or at least neutral teacher expectation are likely to exhibit higher motivation to learn than students who interpret the strategy as low teacher expectations. This is one of the central factors that should guide technological pedagogical practice intended to bridge the third digital divide. Clearly no teacher can know each student's prior history or thought. However, there are practices that decrease the likelihood of negative interpretations (and increase positive ones) for all children. These include creating and maintaining "equitable classrooms," and engaging in "good teaching."

"EQUITABLE CLASSROOMS"

Academic achievement is more likely in an *equitable classroom* (Cohen & Lotan, 2004), which is one in which: (1) teachers and students view all students as capable of acquiring basic skills and high-level concepts; (2) all students have equal access to (and often share) challenging learning materials; (3) all students are challenged by tasks that require higher-order thinking skills; (4) teachers create opportunities that enable English language learners (ELLs) and students reading below grade level to complete activities; and (5) students have equal status in terms of participating in class and openly expressing opinions.

Creating an equitable classroom is not an easy task. It is even more challenging when the classroom is multilingual, multicultural, multiethnic, and multi-income and ICT is the medium of instruction. Classrooms become equitable when: (1) teachers broaden the conception of what it means to be smart to allow multiple ways of demonstrating multiple types of abilities; (2) assess these in multiple ways; and (3) students interact with each other in the context of meaningful group activities that require discussing ideas, deliberating and coming to decisions, and learning to resolve intellectual and social conflicts (Cohen & Lotan, 2004). In addition to creating an equitable classroom the teacher should also engage in "good teaching."

"GOOD TEACHING"

Good teaching (Haberman, 1991) engages students with major concepts and ideas; it has them applying ideals; it encourages them to question common sense; it engages students with important issues in their lives and encourages them to reflect upon these issues; it has them learn to perfect their work by redoing and polishing; and in terms of the third digital divide, it has them using technology in meaningful ways. In contrast, what many poor urban students, who are largely minority and ELLs experience is what Haberman labeled the *"pedagogy of poverty."* They are given information, directions, assignments, homework, tests, and grades; they review assignments, homework, and tests; they are punished for noncompliance. Individually there is nothing wrong with these acts, but they block achievement when they are used collectively and systematically to the exclusion of other pedagogical practices. Bridging the third digital divide will require deliberate efforts to incorporate "good" teaching into TMI.

Technological pedagogy for bridging the third digital divide

1. Analyze TMI before, during, and after lessons. Identify specific culture components and attempt to determine whether and how they may affect teaching and learning.
2. Review software and multimedia programs for bias or insensitivity. For example, are non-Whites depicted in costumes, when these are not relevant to the main discussion (Warschauer, Grant, Del Real, & Rousseau, 2004).
3. Provide a balance of individual assignments and group TMI activities so that the preferences of different cultural groups are alternatively addressed.

4. Make TMI activities consistent with "good teaching." Assign creative, problem-solving activities that require application, analysis, synthesis, and evaluation—e.g., multiple-step projects that require searching the Internet, evaluating what is found and then applying it to the solution of a problem.
5. Use TMI activities to foster an "equitable classroom."
   - Do not lock students into a group for an entire semester or academic year. However, extend groups for sufficient time to enable the development of working relationships and the completion of meaningful projects.
   - Assign different roles or tasks to group members and make sure that all students experience the full range of roles. In particular, make sure minority and low-income students experience leadership roles with technology.
   - Rotate the membership of groups.
6. Use information obtained at the start of the academic year (see first and second digital divide strategies above) to identify and meet the unique needs of students. For example, Chisholm, Carey, and Hernandez (2002) found that computer-based self-efficacy was lower among low-income university students with limited prior computer ownership, information that could be useful in addressing the needs of those students.

Teaching that bridges divides: a case study

A case study of Adelante Elementary School in California (Warschauer, Grant, Del Real, & Rousseau, 2004) can serve to illustrate many of the concepts and strategies discussed in this chapter and as a model of the kind of TMI that can help bridge digital divides. The students in this case happened to be English language learners (ELLs), but the instructional uses of technology made by the teacher could be effective with other groups of students and other content.

While the initial challenge to ELLs is to develop basic interpersonal communication skills, the greater challenge is to develop academic literacy, which is more complex in its vocabulary, syntax, and genre (Cummins, 1988). This is particularly true in the upper elementary grades (Warschauer, Grant, Del Real, & Rousseau looked at fourth grade), where ELLs add the challenge of learning English to the challenge to all students that Chall (1996) described as having to go from the early elementary grades focus on learning to read (emphasis on decoding skills) to the later grades focus on reading to learn (emphasis on comprehension of a variety of texts across content areas).

To facilitate the above process with technology a teacher at Adelante Elementary School, Mr. Molina, infused technology into each of the projects students had to complete as part of thematic literature units. Pre-reading, independent reading, and post-reading activities each used a variety of technology to offer students challenges, choices (and some control), social interaction, and technology skill development, while limiting the monotony of drill and practice.

Pre-reading technology-mediated activities to build student background knowledge for the material to be read included relevant content and images downloaded from the Internet and used to engage the whole class in a discussion. Individual students could also visit websites through a teacher-created Webquest. These activities provided a basis for discussions among students, discussions that provided opportunities for practicing language use in a cooperative group. (Note that these practices were consistent with several strategies described for bridging the digital divides. For example, this was most likely an "equitable classroom" in which there was a level playing field since all students were provided with a means to acquire the relevant background knowledge. Note also that students worked in cooperative groups, which if properly structured, also equalized status.)

Independent reading activities included taking computerized quizzes in the *Accelerated Reader* program (the school library had 16,000 books for which the quizzes were available). The program was used to encourage independent student reading and to evaluate it, *not* to teach reading skills and strategies. The teacher monitored the latter by having students fill out cards describing the strategies they used and discussing these and the books with them. (Note that the computer program was not used for drill and practice. Instead it was used, supplemented by the cards, to empower students to assess themselves and to help the teacher assess each student. The teacher did not abrogate his duties to a computer program. He used the program to enable himself and the students to acquire relevant information about students' knowledge.)

In post-reading activities Mr. Molina used technology extensively to help students deconstruct texts and better understand their structure and genres. They used cognitive mapping software to interpret and outline, often having to reread texts for this purpose. They searched the Internet for visual representations of texts and in doing so enhanced their vocabulary (figuring out the best words for desired images will have that effect) and technology skills. (Note that these practices are consistent with "good teaching" practice of challenging students intellectually and with the second digital divide-bridging strategy of assigning creative, problem-solving activities that require application, analysis, synthesis, and evaluation, as well as that of creating multiple representations of their understanding. Finally, note what is not present in the case study: performativity, defensive teaching, and the use of classroom access to technology as a reward.)

Summary

The first part of this chapter provided a description of the current state of equity of access to technology in the U.S., concluding that in terms of ethnicity, income, and linguistic and cultural background there are at least three digital divides—the first, physical access; the second, access to achievement-enhancing TMI; and the third, access to culturally sensitive TMI. It was also concluded that each of these divides is a matter of degree of access rather than an absolute binary split between the haves and the have-nots. For example, people who lack a home computer often have limited access to computers at local community centers. Teaching strategies for improving equity of access to technology and fostering ITC literacy for all children were discussed. As important as the strategies that were prescribed, were the ones that were proscribed.

The prior discussion thus was about providing equity of access so that all students can achieve ICT literacy. However, issues of technology equity are not restricted to achievement of ICT literacy. Equity issues are also involved in achievement in mathematics, science, and the other subjects in the K-12 curriculum. In all of these subjects, lower achievement and issues of equity existed long before the recent rise of technology as a teaching tool. Whether technology helps to increase achievement for all, or merely exacerbates existing inequities, is largely dependent on how it is used in the schools.

Koehler and Mishra's TPCK model (discussed in Chapter 1) may be particularly useful for framing the equity issues in each subject or content area. While an obvious strength of the model is the framework it offers for conceptualizing how to teach with technology in content-specific ways, the model also offers broad outlines for conceptualizing issues of equity in each content area. At least three types of such issues exist: issues of equity that apply across content areas, whether technology is used to teach the lesson or not; issues of equity unique to individual content areas; and issues of equity that arise in one or more content areas when technology is the medium of instruction. These issues are at the intersection of the TPCK model on the one hand, and multicultural education theory and research on the other hand. This is an intersection that teachers and teacher educators should try to understand well.

The discussion of the digital divides in the first part of the chapter reflected the TPCK–multicultural education intersection. While in that discussion the subject to be learned was ICT literacy, similar issues of equity exist in all content areas. The discussion that follows will make explicit the theoretical assumptions that were used. It is hoped that this description will serve as a foundation for teachers and teacher educators as they wrestle with issues of equity in other content areas. The discussion will include a brief description of Koehler and Mishra's model, expanding on one of its components, the TPCK context.

TPCK

The concept of TPCK refers to a true understanding of the intersection of knowledge about technology, content (content areas or subjects such as mathematics, science, or English), and pedagogy (specific instructional practices that are effective for teaching the subject).

Teachers with high levels of TPCK possess not only general technology skills, but also knowledge about the types and specific uses of technology that are most likely to facilitate teaching and learning in each subject. An elementary school teacher whose level of TPCK is high for example, will not only be skilled with technology applications such as Excel, PowerPoint, digital imaging, and hypertext, but will know which ones to use to teach a particular mathematics lesson and which ones are most suitable for a particular lesson in social studies. See Koehler and Mishra (Chapter 1) for a detailed discussion of the concept of TPCK, and the other chapters in this volume for applications of TPCK across curriculum content areas.

TPCK is a solid foundation for meeting the challenge of teaching all children with technology. Of particular importance in reaching all children is the TPCK context. TPCK is always applied in the context of a specific, idiosyncratic teaching–learning situation, and its effectiveness is highly dependent on the extent to which teachers are able to pedagogically accommodate that context (see Figure 2.1).

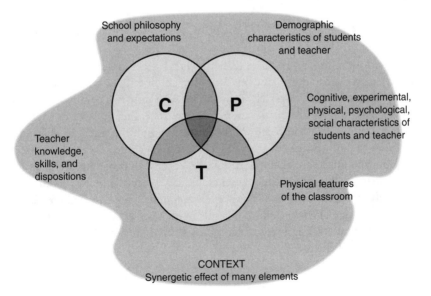

Figure 2.1 TPCK Context.

TPCK context

The TPCK context—hereafter referred to as the context—is essentially the teaching–learning context. It is one of the most complex, important, and least tangible components of the TPCK model and of any teaching–learning situation. The context consists of numerous factors beyond the content to be learned, as well as the interactions of these factors with each other and with the curriculum. Each TMI situation has its own context. This context is much more than a mere setting for the unfolding of teaching and learning with technology, it is an integral part of the process.

THE CONTEXT IS A COMPLEX, MULTI-FACTORIAL PHENOMENON

It includes physical elements, such as the size and learning-conduciveness of the room, the type and arrangement of furniture, and the physical resources available in the classroom, including the quantity and quality of technology. Perhaps most important for the discussion of equity of access to technology, the context also includes the demographic characteristics of the student body, including: the ethnic, socio-economic, cultural, and linguistic backgrounds of individual students; their physical, cognitive, social, psychological, and experiential characteristics; the teacher's characteristics, such as his/her knowledge, skills, and dispositions; and characteristics of the school, such as its philosophy, and its explicit and tacit expectations of parents, teachers, students, and administrators. Most importantly, and most difficult to concretize, the context is the *synergetic effect* of the combination of all these elements in a unique class of students and teacher.

THE CONTEXT INTERACTS WITH OTHER ELEMENTS TO DETERMINE LEARNING OUTCOME

For example, a classroom context that includes a computer and broadband Internet access for every student does not automatically guarantee higher achievement for all. Conversely, a classroom with only two computers for 30 students is not an automatic condemnation to academic failure. In each instance the learning outcome will largely depend on the teacher's ability to envision the affordances of the available technology and place it to its best possible and most equitable use. A skilled teacher with two computers can be more effective than an unskilled teacher with 30. Moreover, in terms of issues of equity, a skilled teacher with only a few computers, but instructional strategies that target and engage all children can be more effective than a teacher with 30 computers, but instructional strategies that only engage children who are already ICT literate.

THE CONTEXT OFFERS POTENTIAL OBSTACLES AS WELL AS POTENTIAL OPPORTUNITIES OR AFFORDANCES

The context is not a static feature of teaching–learning situations; it is not a *fait accompli*. It is dynamic and responsive to the actions of teachers, students, and others. For teachers it should represent affordances, unrealized potential whose actualization is dependent on how well a teacher responds to the context (and is able to encourage students to respond to it) and is able to integrate it into instruction.

The context provides elements—physical, cognitive, linguistic, social, psychological, cultural—which are simultaneously teaching–learning affordances and potential obstacles. Responded to inappropriately during instruction, these elements become obstacles to teaching and learning. Advantageously incorporated into teaching, they enhance instruction and knowledge acquisition. For example, a teacher with a class of children from different cultural backgrounds can choose to focus on the potential obstacles this presents to teaching, or to focus on the opportunity it affords to enhance the presentation of the curriculum with the real-life experiences of students and their families, helping students learn substantive positive lessons about each other's backgrounds.

WHEN THE TEACHING INVOLVES TPCK, THE CONTEXT ELEMENTS THAT PERTAIN TO EQUITY CAN BE OF THREE TYPES

First, the context elements may pertain to general issues of equity that apply across content areas, whether or not technology is used in the lesson. For example, differences among students in their preference or use of learning styles can be handled equitably or non-equitably.

Second, the context elements pertaining to equity may be unique to individual subjects or content areas. For example, Orr (1987) argued that the math achievement of students who primarily speak Ebonics is often lowered by miscommunication between them and teachers who only speak Standard English. While miscommunication can occur in any subject, Orr argued that its negative effects on learning were particularly strong in math; at times resulting in students acquiring the wrong meaning of math concepts or correct student answers being misunderstood by teachers and judged incorrect.

Third, the context elements pertaining to equity may arise in one or more content areas only when technology is the medium of instruction. For example, for some students computer assignments in science or English may only involve drill and practice exercises, while peers in the same class are typically given challenging, engaging computer assignments.

If context issues of equity and diversity are considered to be a knowledge base that teachers should have, then Figure 2.2 represents possible relationships among this knowledge base (represented by E) and the other

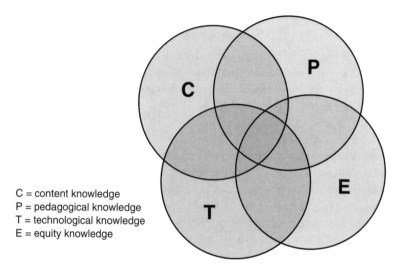

C = content knowledge
P = pedagogical knowledge
T = technological knowledge
E = equity knowledge

Figure 2.2 The relationship between knowledge about equity and TPCK.

components of TPCK. Each of the areas depicted offers affordances and potential obstacles to equity.

MANY CONTEXT ELEMENTS ARE SOCIAL AND PSYCHOLOGICAL
AND AFFECT THE ACHIEVEMENT OF INDIVIDUAL STUDENTS
DIRECTLY AND INDIRECTLY

For example, when linguistic, ethnic, or socio-economic status differences are treated only as obstacles to learning by teachers, the social, psychological, and achievement consequences to some students can be significant. The most direct impact on achievement can come from the differential treatment of students from different backgrounds during instruction. The frequency with which they are called on to display knowledge in class, the level of difficulty of the questions they are asked, and the amount of time they are allowed for answering a question before the teacher moves on to another student are examples of differential treatment. The students who are the most disadvantaged in any class—due, for example, to their limited English proficiency, their low-income status, or their ethnic minority status—are likely to be on the negative end of differential treatment.

Perhaps the deepest and longest lasting achievement effects of context-relevant instructional practices such as those described above are indirect. They affect achievement by chipping away at the psycho-social support mechanisms within individual students; mechanisms such as the student's self-esteem, sense of self-efficacy (Bandura, 1997), and sense of industry (Erikson, 1963), which are a foundation for sustained achievement-enhancing behaviors. When some students are treated, or perceive that they are treated, by teachers in ways that ignore or even implicitly denigrate their backgrounds, the social psychological consequence can be a diminution of their industriousness, their self-esteem, and their sense of self-efficacy. This is likely to be reflected in their classroom behavior. Moreover, because in social psychological matters perception can be a more important determinant of behavior than objective reality, students are likely to respond to what they perceive regardless of what a teacher actually does. It is therefore incumbent on teachers, if they are to implement TPCK well, that they understand how to manage the context in ways that objectively attempt to engage and challenge all students, and that students from different backgrounds will perceive as attempting to engage and challenge them.

THE CONTEXT CONTRIBUTES TO MAKING TEACHING AN ILL-STRUCTURED, "WICKED PROBLEM"

Given the complexity of the context described above, it seems quite appropriate to describe teaching, including teaching with technology, as a "wicked problem" (Koehler and Mishra, Chapter 1). In general, wicked problems have several distinctive features: (1) they are unique and situation-specific, each wicked problem different from other similar problems; (2) they are ill-structured, comprising many elements interacting in idiosyncratic ways; (3) because of their uniqueness, wicked problems, even apparently similar ones, defy solutions that consist of prefabricated strategies, requiring instead tailor-made solutions. In addition, wicked problems of teaching often arise while teachers are actively engaged in instruction, requiring an immediate solution.

Teaching with technology—the "problem" of how to best use technology to help students learn a lesson—is a wicked problem. It is ill-structured; it is subject area and situation specific; it is unique in that even two teaching problems that appear identical are likely to be different in subtle ways. For example, the problem of how to best teach math with technology is in many ways different from the problem of how to best teach social studies with technology. Much of the "wickedness" of the problem of teaching with technology can be attributed to the context. The synergetic mix of the lesson content, the technology and other resources for teaching the lessons, the teacher's characteristics, and the intellectual, social, and psychological characteristics of the students in a math class makes the context of that class different from the context of even other math classes. Indeed, the mere presence or absence of individual students on any given day can make a difference. Therefore, the problem requires a solution custom-made for that context, and TPCK, if it is to be an effective solution, must accommodate to such context elements. In addition, the solution must often be improvised.

SOLUTIONS TO CONTEXT PROBLEMS OFTEN HAVE TO BE
IMPROVISED

Because wicked problems can arise while teachers are actively engaged in the act of teaching, teachers are frequently challenged to *vividly construct solutions at the moment of enactment.* This concept, modified from speech theory, means that the teacher has to actively develop appropriate solutions at almost the very instance that they are required to respond to a problem, and the response has to be specific and appropriate to the synergetic effect of the elements in that context. While the teacher may be able to select from a menu of prefabricated or "canned" strategies, at a minimum these have to be tweaked on the spot to fit the current context. It is not uncommon for teachers to have to construct original solutions from scratch on the spot. This requires engagement at the application, analysis, synthesis, and evaluation levels of Bloom's taxonomy for the cognitive domain (Bloom, Engelhart, Frost, Hill, & Krathwohl, 1956), sometimes in a matter of seconds. Indeed, as Harris (Chapter 12) points out, solving wicked problems of teaching with technology requires that teachers improvise, not unlike the way skilled jazz musicians improvise.

While the context can comprise many elements with their corresponding affordances and potential obstacles, the focus of this chapter has been a set of context elements likely to affect the achievement of ICT literacy in many American classrooms—the diverse backgrounds of students, including their ethnicity, socio-economic status, home language, and culture. These elements also play a role in other subject areas. It is the responsibility of individual teachers to develop an ongoing and incremental understanding of these elements, as well as pedagogical practices to respond appropriately. It is the responsibility of teacher education programs to start teachers on the road to doing so.

Summary

The second part of this chapter described the theoretical framework that was the foundation for the analysis and strategies provided in the first half. This theoretical framework used Koehler and Mishra's TPCK model as a foundation, building on one of the model's elements, the context, as well as multicultural education theory and research, to analyze and explain issues of equity involved in teaching with technology across content areas. The complexity of the context, the synergetic effect of the elements that constitute the context, and the affordances and potential obstacles offered by the context, were discussed. The importance of teachers being able to improvise solutions to context problems at the very instance they must be enacted was also discussed. Finally, the need for teachers to make a life-long commitment to improving knowledge about the context and how to respond to it, and the importance of teacher education programs starting teachers on the path to doing so, were stated.

References

Attewell, P. (2001). The first and second digital divides. *Sociology of Education, 74* (July), 252–259.

Atwater, M. M. (2000). Equity for Black Americans in precollege science. *Science Education, 84,* 154–179.

Bandura, A. (1997). *Self-efficacy: The exercise of control.* New York: W.H. Freeman

Banks, J. A. (2006). *Cultural diversity and education: Foundations, curriculum, and teaching.* New York: Allyn and Bacon.

Bloom, B. S., Engelhart, M. D., Frost, E. J., Hill, W. H., & Krathwohl, D. R. (1956). *Taxonomy of educational objectives.* New York: David McKay.

Blumenfeld, P. C., Soloway, E., Marx, R. W., Krajcik, J. S., Guzdial, M., & Palincsar, A. (1991). Motivating project-based learning: Sustaining the doing, supporting the learning. *Educational Psychologist, 26*(3–4), 369–398.

Bodley, J. H. (1994). *Cultural anthropology: Tribes, states and the global system.* Mountain View, CA: Mayfield.

Castells, M. (1993). The informational economy and the new international division of labor. In M. Carnoy, M. Castells, S. S. Cohen, & F. H. Cardoso (eds), *The new global economy in the information age: Reflections on our changing world.* University Park: Pennsylvania State University Press.

Castells, M. (2000). *The rise of the network society,* 2nd edn. Malden, Mass: Blackwell

Chall, J. S. (1996). *Stages of reading development,* 2nd edn. Fort Worth: Hartcourt Brace College Publishers.

Ching, C. C., Basham, J. D., & Jang, E. (2005). The legacy of the digital divide: Gender, socioeconomic status, and exposure as predictors of full-spectrum technology use among young adults. *Urban Education, 40*(4), 394–411.

Chisholm, I. M., Carey, J., & Hernandez, A. (2002). Information technology skills for a pluralistic society: Is the playing field level? *Journal of Research and Technology in Education, 35*(1), 58–79.

Cohen, E. G., & Lotan, R. A. (2004). Equity in heterogeneous classrooms. In J. A. Banks (ed.), & C. A. McGee Banks (assoc. ed.), *Handbook of research on multicultural education,* 2nd edn. San Francisco: Jossey-Bass.

Corporation for Public Broadcasting. (2002). Connected to the future: A report on children's Internet use. Retrieved 09/21/07 from: http://www.cpb.org/stations/reports/connected/connected_report.pdf.

Cummins, J. (1988). Second language acquisition within bilingual education programs. In L. M. Beebe (ed.), *Issues in second language acquisition.* New York: Harper & Row.

Damarin, S. K. (1998). Technology and multicultural education: The question of convergence. *Theory into Practice, 37*(1), 11–19.

Edelson, D. C. (1998). Realizing authentic science learning through the adaptation of scientific practice. In B. J. Fraser & K. G. Tobin (eds), *International handbook of science education* (pp. 317–332). London: Kluwer Academic Publishers.

Erikson, E. H. (1963). *Childhood and society.* New York: W. W. Norton & Co., Inc.

Fordham, S., & Ogbu, J. U. (1986). Black students' school success: Coping with the "burden of 'actin White.'" *Urban Review, 18*(3), 176–206.

Freire, P. (1970). *Pedagogy of the oppressed.* New York: Continuum.

Garrison, M. J., & Bromley, H. (2004). Social contexts, defensive pedagogies, and the (mis)uses of educational technology. *Educational Policy, 18*(4), 589–613.

Geertz, C. (1973). Thick description: Toward an interpretive theory of culture. In *The interpretation of cultures.* New York: Basic Books, Inc.

Gorski, P. C. (2005). *Multicultural education and the Internet: Intersections and integrations (2nd ed.).* Boston: McGraw Hill.

Gorski, P., & Clark, C. (2001). Multicultural education and the digital divide: Focus on race. *Multicultural Perspectives, 3*(4), 15–25.

Haberman, M. (1991). The pedagogy of poverty versus good teaching. *Phi Delta Kappan, 73,* 290–294.

Hale-Benson, J. (1986). *Black children: Their roots, culture, and learning styles.* Baltimore: Johns Hopkins University Press.

Hug, B., Krajcik, J. S., & Marx, R. W. (2005). Using innovative learning technologies to promote learning and engagement in an urban science classroom. *Urban Education, 40*(4), 446–472.

Kinsler, K., Romero, M., Kelly, M. A., Graves, S. B., & Mercado, C. (1991). *The Quality Urban Elementary School Teachers (QUEST) Program faculty handbook on cultural diversity.* Division of Programs in Education, Hunter College, City University of New York.

Kozol, J. (2006). *The shame of the nation. The restoration of apartheid schooling in America.* New York: Crown Publishers.

Lankshear, C., & Knobel, M. (2003). *New literacies: Changing knowledge and classroom learning.* Buckingham, UK: Open University Press.

Le Vine, R. (1973). *Culture, behavior, and personality.* Chicago: Aldin Publishing Co.

Linn, M. C. (1998). The impact of technology on science instruction: Historical trends and current opportunities. In B. J. Fraser & K. G. Tobin (eds), *International handbook of science education* (pp. 265–294). London: Kluwer Academic Publishers.

Lynch, S. (2000). *Equity and science education reform.* Mahwah, NJ: Lawrence Erlbaum Associates.

Lyotard, J. F. (1984). *The postmodern condition: A report on knowledge.* Minneapolis: University of Minnesota Press.

Natriello, G. (2001). Bridging the second digital divide: What can sociologists of education contribute? *Sociology of Education, 74*(July), 260–265.

Nieto, S. (2004). *Affirming diversity: The sociopolitical context of multicultural education* (4th edn). New York: Allyn & Bacon.

North Central Regional Educational Laboratory. (2003). *enGauge® 21st century skills: Literacy in the digital age.* Retrieved 5/25/06 from: http://www.ncrel.org/engauge/skills/skills.htm.

Oden, S., Kelly, M. A., Ma, Z., & Weikart, D. P. (1992). *Challenging the potential: Programs for talented disadvantaged youth.* Ypsilanti, MI: High/Scope Press.

Ogbu, J. (1987). Variability in minority school performance: A problem in search of an explanation. *Anthropology and Education Quarterly, 18*(4), 312–334.

Orr, E. W. (1987). *Twice as less: Black English and the performance of black students in mathematics and science.* New York: Norton.

Roberts, D. F., Foehr, U. G., Rideout, V. J., & Brodie, M. (1999). *Kids and media @ the new millennium.* Menlo Park, CA: Kaiser-Family Foundation.

Shin, N. (2004). Exploring pathways from television viewing to academic achievement in school age children. *Journal of Genetic Psychology, 165*(4), 367–381.

Spitulnik, M. W., Stratford, S., Krajcik, J. S., & Soloway, E. (1998). Using technology to support student's artifact construction in science. In B. J. Fraser & K. G. Tobin (eds), *International handbook of science education* (pp. 363–381). London: Kluwer Academic Publishers.

Technology Counts 2001: The New Divides. (2001). *Education Week on the Web* 20(35), May 10. Retrieved 10/23/06 from: http://counts.edweek.org/sreports/tc01/tc01article.cfm?slug=35contents.h20.

U.S. Department of Commerce, Economics and Statistics Administration, National Telecommunications and Information Administration. (2002, February). *A nation online: How Americans are expanding their use of the Internet.* Retrieved 9/21/07 from http://www.ntia.doc.gov/ntiahome/dn/anationonline2.pdf.

U.S. Department of Commerce, Economics and Statistics Administration, National Telecommunications and Information Administration. (2004, September). *A nation online: Entering the broadband age.* Retrieved 9/21/07 http://www.ntia.doc.gov/reports/anol/NationOnline-Broadband04.pdf.

Warschauer, M. (2003). *Technology and social inclusion: Rethinking the digital divide.* Cambridge, MA: MIT Press.

Warschauer, M., Grant, D., Del Real, G., & Rousseau, M. (2004). Promoting academic literacy with technology: successful laptop programs in K-12 schools. *System, 32*, 525–537.

Warschauer, M., Knobel, M., & Stone, L. (2004). Technology and equity in schooling: Deconstructing the digital divide. *Educational Policy, 18*(4), 562–588.

Wenglinsky, H. (1998). Does it compute? The relationship between educational technology and student achievement in mathematics. Policy Information Report. Educational Testing Service. Retrieved June 01, 2006 from: http://www.ets.org/Media/Research/pdf/ PICTECHNOLOG.pdf.

Wilson, K. R., Wallin, J. S., & Reiser, C. (2003). Social stratification and the digital divide. *Social Science Computer Review, 21*(2), 133–143.

II
Integrating TPCK into specific subject areas

3
TPCK in K-6 literacy education
It's not that elementary!

DENISE A. SCHMIDT AND MARINA GURBO

One of the most fundamental responsibilities of schools is to teach students to read (Moats, 1999). Researchers estimate that 95 percent of all children can be taught to read (Fletcher & Lyon, 1998), while others claim nearly 20 percent of our elementary students experience problems when learning to read (Moats, 1999). For elementary students to become successful readers, teachers must have a thorough foundational knowledge of both reading and writing processes, and they must also understand how these processes can be effectively taught in classrooms (Moats, 1999; Ruddell, 2006). Although preparing teachers for literacy instruction in elementary classrooms has always been a major component of teacher preparation programs, differences exist in how these programs actually prepare teachers to teach literacy. While experts have attempted to define the knowledge of literacy development and instruction that teachers require for effective classroom practice (International Reading Association, 2004; Moats, 1999; National Reading Panel, 2000; Pearson & Raphael, 2003; Snow, Griffin, & Burns, 2005; Young, 2001), the methods selected for preparing elementary teachers to teach literacy in teacher preparation programs can vary greatly.

While the acquisition of content knowledge (CK) and pedagogical knowledge (PK) are critically important to the preparation of K-6 literacy teachers, the knowledge of how, when, and why to use technology effectively in teaching literacy seems just as relevant for today's teachers. There are numerous descriptions of how technology is used in K-6 classrooms to teach literacy skills and processes (e.g., Anderson & Speck, 2001; Wepner, Valmont, & Thurlow, 2000). Most illustrate highly successful and efficient approaches for using technology to enhance literacy learning for children. Yet, are we preparing current and future literacy educators to critically examine how technology might be used to teach literacy more effectively or how technology might change the way students actually learn to read and write? To answer these questions we must thoughtfully consider and skillfully apply our understanding of technological pedagogical content knowledge (TPCK) and its relationship to literacy learning and teaching.

The purpose of this chapter is to examine the relationships between content knowledge, pedagogical content knowledge, technological content knowledge, and technological pedagogical content knowledge related to teaching literacy in the elementary (K-6) grades. Guided by the work of Shulman (1986) and Mishra and Koehler (e.g., Chapter 1), this chapter suggests how one might begin thinking about the connections and interactions between the knowledge of content, pedagogy, and technology with respect to teaching literacy in elementary classrooms. As Mishra and Koehler (2006) acknowledge, "developing good content requires a thoughtful interweaving of all three key sources of knowledge—technology, pedagogy and content" (p. 1029). Clearly, examining these knowledge bases with respect to literacy is a complex undertaking because the relationships between technology, pedagogy, and content are extremely dynamic. We begin the chapter by providing some general comments on literacy and what it means to be literate today. In the next three sections we highlight the content knowledge, pedagogical content knowledge, and technological content knowledge we see as essential to teaching K-6 literacy. These sections help provide the foundational framework for the section describing technological pedagogical content knowledge. There we provide specific examples of what TPCK might look like in an elementary literacy classroom. Finally, we suggest how preservice and in-service teachers might learn specific knowledge related to TPCK and elementary literacy education.

The changing definition of literacy

What it meant to be literate a decade ago is not what it means to be literate today or will mean for tomorrow's children. Typically, the nature of literacy has evolved and changed due to the historical and cultural contexts with which it has been applied (Kinzer & Leander, 2003; Leu, 2000). Past definitions of literacy originate from the perspective of learning to read from traditional print and tend to focus on the ability to sound out words, or the ability to read and write in a specific language, or the ability to learn the mechanics of reading (Anderson & Speck, 2001; Harris & Hodges, 1995; Kinzer & Leander, 2003; Swenson, Rozema, Young, McGrail, & Whitin, 2005). Contemporary literacy educators are now challenged to broaden the scope of these definitions to include multiple sign systems, verbal and non-verbal, when constructing meaning (Valmont, 2003). Technology's presence in our lives, in schools, and society as a whole, dictates the necessity to accommodate the influence electronic environments and digital media have had on literacy development and instruction. Kinzer and Leander (2003) argue that "as the medium of the message changes, comprehension processes and decoding processes must be learned and taught so that these changes can be reflected in readers' and authors' strategies for comprehension and response" (p. 547). In chapter three of this monograph, Lee stresses that the uneven quality of technologically enhanced resources requires teachers to develop students' critical media skills as a new form of literacy which includes informational literacy, computer literacy, and film and video literacy.

Still, it is difficult to predict the impact new and emerging technologies will have on students and their literacy development in the future. One can only hope classroom teachers will monitor these changes and react positively to them in terms of knowledge and application (Labbo & Reinking, 1999). According to the International Reading Association (2002),

> The Internet and other forms of information and communication technology (ICT) such as word processors, Web editors, presentation software, and e-mail are regularly redefining the nature of literacy. To become fully literate in today's world, students must become proficient in the new literacies of ICT. Therefore, literacy educators have a responsibility to effectively integrate these technologies into the literacy curriculum in order to prepare students for the literacy future they deserve.
>
> (p. 2)

Literacy is a "moving target" that will continually change according to what society expects from a literate person (Kinzer & Leander, 2003, p. 547). Literacy will constantly be redefined as new technologies emerge and as expectations change for what it means to be literate. Students and educators in today's literacy classrooms must use a variety of technological resources and tools as they synthesize information to communicate knowledge. Likewise, literacy educators will be expected to respond to these changes with a solid knowledge base about specific content, pedagogical and technological knowledge related to literacy education.

Defining content knowledge for K-6 literacy

In 2005, Floden and Meniketti conducted a meta-analysis of the research on K-12 prospective teachers' subject matter knowledge in their specific areas. Across the areas these researchers identified there was one consistent finding—a significant number of prospective teachers have only a "mechanical" understanding of the subject they teach. Floden and Meniketti (2005) concluded that "The claim that teachers need to know the subjects they teach has a strong intuitive appeal, but exactly what they need to know to teach at various levels, with what desired outcomes, are still topics for debate" (p. 283). Hence, we would probably all agree in principle that literacy teachers across the board must have a thorough understanding of the content knowledge required to help children learn to read and write.

Mishra and Koehler (2006) define content knowledge (CK) as "knowledge about the actual subject matter that is to be learned or taught" (p. 1026). So what content knowledge defines the knowledge and skills necessary for effective practice related to elementary literacy instruction? Several experts have made rigorous, research-based efforts to recommend a content base for reading education that identifies the knowledge and skills teachers should have in order to teach literacy in K-12 schools (International Reading Association, 2004; Moats, 1999; National Reading Panel, 2000; Pearson & Raphael, 2003; Snow, Griffin, & Burns, 2005; Young, 2001). As Moats (1999) explains, "Professional preparation programs have a responsibility to teach a defined body of knowledge, skills, and abilities that are based on the best research in the field" (p. 14). The content knowledge base we suggest was determined by examining numerous research studies available on literacy development and how children learn to read. Although there was not an actual consensus as to what content knowledge should be required, common themes did emerge from this work that help us frame a content knowledge base for K-6 literacy teachers.

Literacy, as stated earlier, is a complex and multifaceted concept so it is extremely difficult to narrow such a content area down to a prescribed knowledge base. Therefore, we suggest the following content knowledge areas and will discuss each area later in relationship with the TPCK required for teaching elementary literacy. Several areas frequently listed in literature and mentioned as required literacy content knowledge for teachers include knowledge of: language structure, vocabulary, comprehension, fluency, and composition. These areas are directly related to the foundational knowledge cited in Standard 1 from the Standards for Reading Professionals developed by the Professional Standards and Ethics Committee of the International Reading Association (International Reading Association, 2004). New reading teachers who enter the profession are required to demonstrate knowledge in these areas (and more) and then apply this knowledge to effectively plan and implement the appropriate instructional methods for engaging students in the reading and writing processes at the elementary school level.

Understanding pedagogical content knowledge for K-6 literacy

Pedagogical content knowledge (PCK) is the "knowledge of pedagogy that is applicable to the teaching of specific content" (Mishra & Koehler, 2006, p. 1027). To paraphrase with the help from Shulman (1987) as PCK relates to literacy—it is the ability of a teacher to transform content knowledge (i.e. language structure, vocabulary, comprehension, fluency, and composition) in pedagogically powerful ways (i.e. teaching strategies, lesson plan development and implementation, classroom management, student assessment) that adapt to students' abilities and backgrounds in a classroom context (p. 15).

The Standards for Reading Professionals (International Reading Association, 2004) defined five main performance areas that literacy teachers must demonstrate: (1) foundational knowledge, (2) instructional strategies and curriculum materials, (3) assessment, diagnosis, and evaluation, (4) creating a literate environment, and (5) professional development (p. 3).

Within these performance categories, we believe there are several important PCK components to consider while helping us frame the necessary TPCK required for teaching literacy in the elementary grades. The PCK components for literacy we have identified are:

- Teach literacy as a developmental continuum.
- Apply appropriate teaching methods and strategies while considering the diversity of learners and individual differences.
- Create a supportive literacy environment that increases learners' engagement.
- Motivate students to read.
- Select and use a wide range of strategies and tools for assessment.

It is important to emphasize that teachers will not apply this knowledge and these skills in isolation, but will use this information to help address a wide range of instructional challenges they encounter every day in elementary classrooms.

According to Whitehurst and Lonigan (1998), "reading, writing, and oral language develop concurrently and interdependently from an early age from children's exposure to interactions in social context" (p. 849). For the elementary literacy teacher, this means understanding the relationships between how and when literacy develops throughout a developmental continuum. For example, while teaching phonemics and letter-word recognition, a teacher must know how phonemic awareness develops and how it relates to a child's further ability to decode and comprehend. Also because reading and writing are reciprocal processes, a teacher should explicitly connect these processes in the day-to-day literacy instruction of elementary students.

There are many effective, research-based teaching methods and strategies that a teacher can use when teaching children to read. Most elementary teachers who teach literacy are prepared to use pedagogical methods such as guided reading, whole-class literature studies, literature circles, book clubs, reader's theater, and reader's/writer's workshop. In addition, instructional strategies like think aloud, book talks, margin guides, semantic mapping, topic talk, paragraph frames, directed reading thinking activity, word sorts, and discussion webs all contribute to the applications of pedagogical knowledge teachers should have to teach all children to read. In addition, teachers must apply these literacy methods and strategies appropriately by understanding each child's diverse literacy background (i.e. family literacy, multicultural issues, background knowledge). On a practical level, teachers must use various strategies to help each individual child become a successful reader and writer. For example, for children who are learning English as a second language (ELL), the research indicates that a strong background in the first language promotes school achievement in a second language (Cummins, 1979). So while conducting literature circles in a classroom, English language learners might have access to literature books in their first language as well as English. It is about creating classroom environments where children maintain their first language while they are learning to speak and read in English (Wong & Fillmore, 1991).

A teacher's knowledge and ability to create a literacy-rich environment in the classroom enhances the literacy experiences for students who may have limited access to these resources at home (McGill-Franzen & Lanford, 1994). Creating literacy-rich, learning environments is essential in addressing the diverse needs of learners and, at the same time, it emphasizes the importance of developing speaking, reading, and writing on a daily basis. Literacy-rich environments provide access to high-quality literature from a variety of genres, build whole-class community and respect, embrace independent and collaborative work, and value the children's diversity of background knowledge and expertise (e.g. Kelly, Chapter 2).

Since motivating students to read and write is an ultimate objective, teachers should create environments where students are highly motivated to learn. Reading motivation is directly related to students' reading comprehension (Wang & Guthrie, 2004) and also correlates with the amount of time students spend reading (Wigfield & Guthrie, 1997). The time students spend reading seems especially important since students' self-initiated or independent reading increased their proficiency in vocabulary and reading comprehension (Cunningham & Stanovich, 1998; Guthrie, Schafer, & Huang, 2000), as well as increased their knowledge of other subjects, such as history, science, and literature (West, Stanovich, & Cunningham, 1995). There are many instructional strategies teachers can use to increase elementary students' motivation to read. Some of these strategies include providing content goals for reading, supporting students' selection of texts and reading tasks, providing interesting texts, and facilitating social interactions related to reading (Guthrie & Wigfield, 2000; Guthrie et al., 2006).

Literacy learning in the elementary classroom can be strongly influenced by social interaction in the classroom community (Goodman & Wilde, 1992). Teachers should develop classroom environments where individual students interact with the language and each other as they move towards collaborative construction of meaning (Cazden, 1988; Genishi, McCarrier, & Nussbaum, 1988). By implementing such teaching methods as reader's/writer's workshops and literature circles teachers can create a range of opportunities for children to communicate with each other when they read and write (i.e., exploratory talks, self-paced reading, literature logs, guided discussions, response projects). Collaborative and social experiences like these facilitate language acquisition, as teachers and children provide the models and use purposeful and meaningful language in the classroom context (Cambourne, 1984).

Understanding how to select and use assessment tools and strategies in the elementary grades is another important aspect of PCK for literacy teachers.

To assess children's literacy development, teachers must be familiar with what it means to be an excellent reader. This involves various levels of PCK understanding such as constructing meaning of text, responding to the meaning, selecting effective reading strategies, and monitoring reader's comprehension (Pressley *et al.*, 1997) and then applying that knowledge appropriately to assess children. Teachers must also be aware of and use multiple forms of assessments like observations of a child's oral language development, evaluations of a child's written work, interpretations of standardized tests, and assessments of authentic reading and writing activities. With the current emphasis on the assessment requirements for reading achievement brought about by federal and state policy, this knowledge of selecting and using assessment tools and strategies appropriately is vitally important to all teachers.

Although our perception of PCK is not limited to only these areas for literacy educators, we feel these areas will be significantly impacted when integrating technology for teaching literacy. Since technology has the potential to change the nature of literacy and also the way literacy learning occurs, teachers must continually refine their PCK based on what technology can contribute to literacy learning in the elementary classroom. In the next section, we describe how technology has contributed to and changed elementary literacy education and suggest what specific technologies are well suited for teaching K-6 literacy.

Identifying technological content knowledge for K-6 literacy

Technology has actually changed the way we read, create, and interpret texts (Swenson, Rozema, Young, McGrail, & Whitin, 2005). Today, students who access information on the Internet use different decoding and reading strategies as they follow hyperlink after hyperlink about a specific topic. For teachers and teacher educators, this means they must not only understand how to use technology, but they must also determine how technology changes the way literacy is taught. Our task in this chapter is to identify the technological content knowledge (TCK) preservice and in-service teachers should have to provide technology-rich literacy experiences for elementary students. It might be easy to just suggest an exhaustive list that includes all of the hardware, peripherals, software, and interfaces literacy teachers might conceivably use in classrooms. Yet realistically, we know such a list would not be a useful solution in better understanding TCK and its relationship to TPCK in teaching elementary literacy. So to help frame this TCK piece for K-6 literacy, we first examine how teaching literacy has changed as a result of using technology in classrooms.

Literacy, by definition, reacts to the evolution of emerging technologies. Kamil and Lane (1998) cite it is often difficult to evaluate technology's usefulness for literacy and learning because it changes so rapidly. Leu (2000) concurs that both technology and literacy change so quickly that the "importance to our children's future is often clear" before research-based solutions can be reported (p. 762). However, there are documented findings that illustrate how using technology has changed both the content and pedagogical approaches related to literacy instruction.

Many current and newer technologies require us to read and interpret text using different strategies and approaches not typical of print-based reading and writing. Traditionally, when we read text in a book we read from left to right and top to bottom, and then we proceed through the book in a linear fashion (Wepner, Valmont, & Thurlow, 2000). Hypertext and hypermedia have significantly changed how we can read in digital environments and how we create paths to search for information. Hypermedia environments are dynamic and interactive as they support text, graphics, sound, video, and hyperlinks to create a non-linear collection of information. Research indicates that hypermedia and hypertext can increase students' understanding of the material (Anderson-Inman & Horney, 1999; Hillinger & Leu, 1994; Leu & Hillinger, 1994). Leu (2000) reports some learning gains related to comprehension using hypermedia environments because students are more motivated and seem to have a greater sense of control over what they can access and read. Some research even suggests that if designers appropriately combine images and sound, it may enhance students' comprehension and their ability to create text (Daiute & Morse, 1994). In addition, Hughes and Scharber (see Chapter 4) provide a very dynamic example of how learning language while using the writing process changes when incorporating hypertexts into the English language arts classroom.

Composition and the act of writing in classrooms changed when technology tools were introduced that made the process easier, especially in terms of editing and revising. Using word processing programs meant students could focus more on idea generation and organization rather than the mechanical aspects associated with writing (Jones, 1994). Some positive outcomes associated with using word processing for writing are longer written samples, greater variety of word usage, more variety of sentence structure, more accurate mechanics and spelling, more substantial revision, greater responsiveness to teacher and peer feedback, better understanding of the writing process, and more positive attitudes towards writing (Bialo & Sivin, 1990; Office of Technology Assessment, 1988; Rodriguez & Rodriguez, 1986). Typically at the elementary level, technology is not used for the entire writing process (McKenna, Labbo, & Reinking, 2003). This means students are using technology to type in "finished" handwritten stories, thus the technology only facilitates the publishing stage and not the entire writing process.

Students and teachers in elementary classrooms frequently read literature books. Electronic or talking books have even been used in classrooms with some promising results. These books use hypermedia text that links to word pronunciations, definitions, and/or sentences. Most contain audio and animated illustrations as well. Some research suggests that while children listen to an electronic book they develop a sense of story structure, build vocabulary, and increase word knowledge (McKenna, 1998; McKenna, Labbo, & Reinking, 2003). Others saw positive results when using electronic books as an aid to help children improve their comprehension of texts (Hastings, 1997; Lewin, 1997; McKenna, 1998). McKenna and Watkins (1996) note a significant gain in sight–word acquisition while using electronic books with children. After reviewing literature in this area, Leu (2000) reported gains in comprehension when children access digitalized speech while reading, and McKenna (1998) indicated the "point and click" pronunciation support available to children could potentially move them to independent reading levels. In addition, Hasselbring (1999) reported improved comprehension and motivation levels while using electronic books with struggling readers.

Evidence exists that teachers even alter their instructional models to accommodate technology for literacy learning. It seems teachers tend to use more student-centered models of instruction when using technology to teach literacy content (Labbo, Murray, & Phillips, 1995–1996). Leu and Kinzer (2000) note that many of the information and communication environments created by technology permit both teacher-directed and student-directed learning opportunities that strengthen and broaden the learning context. For example, the Internet has created many possibilities (e.g. conversations with authors, contacting experts, collaborating with other classrooms) for student collaboration and social knowledge construction during literacy activities using student-centered teaching approaches. Spitzer (1990) claims, "computers, which were once thought to promote isolation, may in fact prove to be of greatest help in creating cooperative learning environments" (p. 59). Wood (2000) observed that children tended to work together more when technology was involved in the process of writing stories, searching the Web, and creating multimedia presentations.

The aforementioned possibilities for technology in the literacy classroom seem important to mention since they are tools teachers can use to motivate students to read and increase their engagement in reading tasks. One effective instructional strategy we mentioned in the PCK section is students' autonomy in reading. In this sense, technology links students to a wide variety of authentic texts that they can choose to read on their own. The same technology can facilitate more social interaction related to reading (e.g., email, discussion forums, video conferencing, etc.) and, as a result, increase students' motivation and level of engagement with reading text. Building upon this research, we will now suggest specific technological content knowledge (TCK) that appears necessary for teachers who teach K-6 literacy.

Just knowing how to use a computer is not enough anymore for today's K-6 literacy teacher. There are a number of peripherals and related technologies that may positively impact students' literacy learning. Visual literacy is an extremely important concept in today's literacy classroom (Valmont, 2003), so teachers should use digital still cameras and digital video cameras to enhance these types of experiences for young children. Some elementary classrooms have experimented with using handhelds with students. Innovative educational software like GoKnow® (i.e. PicoMap, FreeWrite, Sketchy) provide opportunities for children to write and draw using such devices. It is extremely important for teachers to know about technology that may help students with specific learning difficulties. Assistive technologies like a Reading Pen or an Intellikeys keyboard might be very useful to some elementary students.

Technology can provide teachers with opportunities to communicate and collaborate with others all over the world. A videoconferencing camera offers a unique connection to individual experts and classrooms. New portable tools such as iPods extend the possibilities as elementary teachers begin to explore how audio books, audio recordings, and podcasts might enhance literacy instruction. It will be important for K-6 literacy teachers to stay abreast of emerging technologies so the best learning tools can be used to assist students with reading and writing.

Literacy teachers should be familiar with productivity-type software programs they can use in elementary classrooms. Both teachers and students can use visual learning tools such as Inspiration® and Kidspiration® to create graphic representations for many literacy learning tasks (e.g. brainstorming, story grammar, character map, discussion web). Since writing is a vital curriculum component for elementary classrooms, teachers should be familiar with writing tools designed for younger children like Clicker5 and StoryBook Weaver® Deluxe. Multimedia tools like Kid Pix®, eZedia, and PowerPoint can be used in numerous ways to support literacy instruction and learning. Digital video editing programs such as iMovie and Windows Movie Maker make production tasks for elementary students and teachers relatively easy for larger literacy projects and assignments. It is evident that these programs' architectures will change over time, but the fundamental purpose will remain relatively constant. These are all open-ended, productivity tools that, when tied to learning standards and objectives, can be used to enhance the literacy learning experience for K-6 students. Obviously, there are other software programs available that are more subject-area specific and designed exclusively for teaching elementary reading, writing, and language arts. Teachers must be cognizant of these programs and evaluate them carefully based upon students' individual needs.

There are also numerous online resources and tools that elementary literacy teachers should consider. Online resources like ReadWriteThink (www.readwritethink.org) and A to Z Teacher Stuff® (atozteacherstuff.com) offer teachers access to lesson plans, professional web resources, and classroom materials. In fact, the ReadWriteThink site has a collection of innovative online student tools designed specifically to support K-12 literacy learning activities. Some examples include an acrostic poem builder, a comparison and contrast guide, a flipbook, and a literary elements map. Some online sites offer useful instructional templates for teachers (see www.thinkport.org/default.tp) or inquiry-based activities (see webquest.org) that support research-based literacy practices. Online tools like blogs and wikis offer yet another option for writing and response (with caution) in the classroom. Alternative online assessment tools, like RubiStar (rubistar.4teachers.org), let teachers create rubrics to evaluate project-based learning activities. These online tools and resources are just a small sample of those available to teachers and students for literacy learning.

In 2000, the International Society for Technology in Education (ISTE) developed technology standards and performance indicators for teachers (NETS•T) (International Society for Technology in Education, 2000). Overall, we believe these guidelines provide a helpful framework for teacher educators in any content area to use when selecting the TCK appropriate for preservice and in-service teachers. These guidelines define general profiles for technology-literate teachers as they go through their professional preparation program and up to their first year of teaching. The six standard areas that define the concepts, knowledge, skills, and attitudes teachers should possess for using technology in the classroom are: (1) technology operations and concepts, (2) planning and designing learning environments and experiences, (3) teaching, learning, and the curriculum, (4) assessment and evaluation, (5) productivity and professional practice, and (6) social, ethical, legal, and human issues (ISTE, 2000). A closer examination of the National Educational Standards for Teachers (NETS•T) reminds us that TCK still has to align itself with the pedagogical concerns associated with using technology classrooms. In the next section, we will illustrate how these three knowledge bases (CK, PCK, and TCK) interact with and connect to the technological pedagogical content knowledge necessary for teaching K-6 literacy.

Examining TPCK and K-6 literacy

Using technology effectively for literacy instruction requires one to understand the complex relationships between content, pedagogy, and technology or technological pedagogical content knowledge (TPCK). For K-6 literacy, good teaching with technology will look very different for individual teachers who teach students with diverse instructional needs.

Ultimately, it is the individual teacher who will decide what and how to use technology with students. This decision will be based on the teacher's own perceptions of the value that technology will have on instructional practices, classroom context, and the students' learning. Often this occurs when a teacher discovers the one technology-based activity that connects with their own teaching philosophy and their knowledge of literacy (McKenna, Labbo, & Reinking, 2003). Such an activity usually stimulates the teacher to think about other ways technology might be used in teaching. Zhao (2003) suggests that technology becomes useful for teachers when they use it to solve educational problems. He offers the example that an individual might use a word processor to overcome the perceived problems one encounters while composing and editing text. Zhao (2003) contends "for teachers to use technology, they need to develop knowledge that enables them to translate technological potentials into solutions to pedagogical problems, which are very local and deeply situated in their own contexts" (p. 4). In literacy, this means preparing teachers to thoughtfully consider how to best connect literacy content and technology with research-based practices in their classrooms (e.g. Hughes & Scharber, Chapter 4).

The examples that follow illustrate how the relationships between content, pedagogy, and technology might be formalized into the application of TPCK with respect to teaching K-6 literacy. These examples are modeled with pre-service and in-service teachers enrolled in our own methods and content-specific courses (Merkley, Schmidt, & Allen, 2001; Schmidt, Merkley, Fuhler, & Rinkleff, 2004). We offer these examples as possible classroom scenarios that assume the teachers have the necessary content knowledge, pedagogical content knowledge, and technological content knowledge (as described earlier) to orchestrate the "complex interplay" (Mishra & Koehler, 2006, p. 1025) between these principles to demonstrate what TPCK might look like in elementary literacy classrooms.

Example 1: creating a digital story during literature circles

We use our first example to illustrate the decision-making process an elementary teacher goes through when considering the appropriate content, pedagogical, and technological knowledge needed to design an instructional literacy unit or activity that includes technology. Figure 3.1 represents the decision-making processes that a teacher constructs using the TPCK components while implementing digital storytelling in the classroom. In this example, a fifth-grade teacher decides her students will create a digital storytelling project during literature circles. Digital storytelling, the modern expression of the ancient art of storytelling, involves telling stories and sharing information through multimedia (Armstrong, 2003). Digital storytelling builds upon the content knowledge areas of composition, vocabulary, and fluency.

Students in Ms. Lander's fifth-grade classroom have just self-selected books for their literature circle study on historical fiction. Ms. Landers was careful to select books with different reading levels to match students' individual learning needs. Five groups of between four and six students are in literature circles reading such historical fiction books as *Out of the Dust, Lily's Crossing, Number the Stars,* and *I Have Heard of a Land.* For the next four weeks, students meet each day with their literature circle group to read, discuss, and respond to the text.

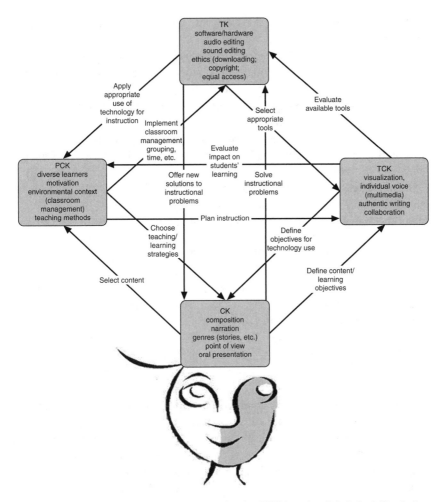

Figure 3.1 Teacher's decision-making process related to TPCK for using digital storytelling in the classroom.

Typically, each day begins with the teacher conducting a mini lesson and reviewing learning tasks and responsibilities for the day. Today, Ms. Landers introduces an extension project involving digital storytelling that students will work on during their student-led group time. Ms. Landers gives a short electronic presentation (e.g. PowerPoint, Keynote) on digital storytelling and informs the students that each group will be creating a digital story about a historical event that impacted a person or group of people. Then, Ms. Landers shows the students a digital story example that tells the story about Native American boarding schools in America. After answering a few student questions, Ms. Landers hands out the grading rubric (created on RubiStar) she will use to assess each group project. She reminds students they can use either the computer stations located in the classroom or checkout laptops from the media center to complete the project. Then, students break into their literature circles and begin the reading and response activities assigned for the day. This includes beginning their digital storytelling projects by selecting a topic. Over the next few weeks, students work collaboratively to conduct research about their topic, design a storyboard, and produce a digital story (using iMovie, Windows Movie Maker, etc.).

This short scenario provides some insight on how a digital storytelling project begins with students within the context of using literature circles in an elementary classroom. Figure 3.1 helps us understand the decisions Ms. Landers makes throughout this four-week literacy unit. Ms. Landers will constantly be revisiting and readjusting her TPCK decisions based on classroom observation and practice throughout the entire unit.

Example 2: developing fluency using predictable text

Fluent readers read text with speed, accuracy, and proper expression (National Reading Panel, 2000). Most agree that fluent reading is the result of repeated practice. According to Padak, Rasinski and Mraz (2002), "A beginning reader needs opportunities to read in context and to hear examples of fluent reading" (p. 2). Situated in a first-grade classroom, this next example provides multiple opportunities for young children to hear and practice fluent reading by using a predictable story that uses repetitive language and phrases.

Ms. Johnson settles into a chair in the reading corner with twenty-four, first graders sitting anxiously on a rug in front of her. Today, Ms. Johnson will read aloud the story *It Looked Like Spilt Milk* by Charles G. Shaw. She takes her time reading each page fluently with proper expression. Students laugh at the illustrations that resemble clouds in the shape of various objects. At times, Ms. Johnson reads a page aloud and then lets the students read the page aloud together. After completing the story, Ms. Johnson announces that the entire class will create their own book about spilt milk using Kid Pix®. These first-grade students have used Kid Pix® for other projects, so they are somewhat familiar with the program as they enter the computer lab. In preparation for the lesson, Ms. Johnson created a template for the children to use for the activity (see Figure 3.2) and loaded it on the computers. After a few directions from Ms. Johnson, students quickly start sharing and brainstorming their ideas with others and then soon begin creating their "page" for the class book using the template. Ms. Johnson also reminds students to record what they write using the program's built-in, audio recording feature.

The next day, Ms. Johnson presents the "spilt milk" slideshow to the entire class (see Figure 3.2). Of course the students want to watch it again, so Ms. Johnson mutes the sound and this time through each student reads their page aloud when it appears. Ms. Johnson also prints a few copies of the book so

Figure 3.2 Teacher template and student example using predictable story to build fluency.

students can read it during sustained silent reading time or read it with another student during paired reading. The book can also be taken home to share and read with parents.

Guided repeated oral reading practices, like those described in this example, have a positive impact on word recognition, fluency, and comprehension (National Reading Panel, 2000). Technology provided multiple opportunities for these young children to experience listening to and reading the same text in several ways. This example also illustrates that when using technology it doesn't always have to take a significant amount of time to produce projects that motivate and teach students to read fluently.

Example 3: composing during the writing process with technology

One CK literacy area that has received a significant amount of attention in terms of using technology is composition. The use of word-processing software in schools creates opportunities for developing students' writing that replicates how real writers write. Recent technology innovations illustrate how the act of teaching composition can change considerably using appropriate TPCK approaches. As Swenson *et al.* (2005) so aptly state, teachers of writing are now faced with using multimodal and multimedia technologies so they "must be prepared to facilitate a more textured and complex approach to the composing process" (p. 224). These technology tools help scaffold students' writing development as they support authentic, collaborative writing activities in classrooms.

Although there are various methods that teachers use to teach writing, writer's workshop is one approach that is commonly practiced in elementary classrooms. Writer's workshop provides students with time to write each day and focuses on the authentic processes involved in learning how to write (i.e., prewriting, drafting, revising, editing, publishing) (Atwell, 1984; Calkins, 1986; Graves, 1983). The process approach to teaching writing is recursive and flexible in nature and builds upon some pedagogical content components like time, choice, structure, response, and community similar to those mentioned earlier in this chapter (Atwell, 1987; Hansen, 1987). In this hypothetical TPCK example, adding technology as a tool with which to compose text during writer's workshop capitalizes on the collaborative nature of writing and the importance of peer response and feedback in classrooms.

Mr. Cole implements writer's workshop using technology in his fourth-grade classroom. During their scheduled writing time each day, his fourth-grade students have one-on-one access to wireless laptops in the classroom. Each student begins a new story by choosing a topic of interest based upon his/her own background experiences and knowledge. At the prewriting stage students begin to brainstorm and generate their story ideas using Inspiration®. Using this software students create concept maps to visually represent their thoughts and ideas before beginning to write their story (see Figure 3.3).

Next, the students use the concept map to guide their thinking while composing the first draft of their stories using SubEthaEdit. SubEthaEdit is a text editor that allows collaborative editing so compositions can be shared online with others for the purpose of providing feedback and response. Once the first draft is complete, students participate in a recursive process that involves several exchanges back and forth between peers and/or teachers while revising, editing, and re-drafting the stories. Using SubEthaEdit, a student sends his/her draft to a peer in the classroom (or anyone in the world) who reads the piece and makes suggestions revising the document (see Figure 3.4). Another unique feature of SubEthaEdit is that it is available in multiple languages like Chinese, Russian, Korean, Japanese, German, and French so communicating and collaborating with a diverse audience is possible. After students have re-drafted their writing using the suggestions offered during the revising stage, the collaborative editing process is later replicated by using SubEthaEdit during the editing stage focusing on correcting mechanics and spelling.

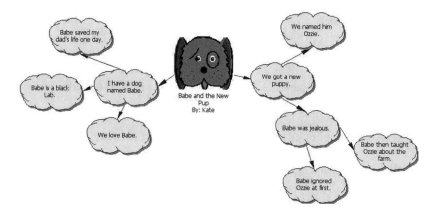

Figure 3.3 Student's concept map created using Inspiration® during the prewriting stage of the writing process.

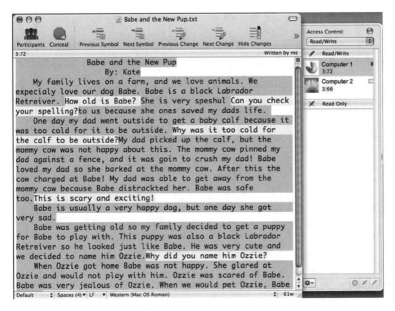

Figure 3.4 Student receives online revisions from peer using SubEthaEdit.

Finally, after revising and editing their stories the students publish their compositions. Although publishing in writer's workshop can have multiple purposes and be done in a variety of ways, technology can still play a significant role in completing the writing process cycle. After completing edits and revisions, the students might print out their stories and then during author's chair time (Hansen, 1987) the students share their stories with the entire class. At times, Mr. Cole provides the opportunity for his students to publish their work online as a means to motivate them to write. Karchmer (2000) noted that when students felt that their work could have "far-reaching effects," it encouraged them "to put more effort into it" (p. 83). Mr. Cole encourages his students to post their stories on a classroom website he developed or he might manage a class website on KidPub (www.kidpub.org), a website designed specifically for children who are interested in publishing their work on the Internet. This TPCK example illustrates how multiple technologies can be used with a research-based pedagogical approach to change how writing is taught in the elementary classroom.

Collectively, these three examples model TPCK and its "practical" application for teaching literacy in elementary classrooms. These classroom scenarios also illustrate the "complex interplay" that occurs between the knowledge components in TPCK. Teachers must be prepared to plan for and then facilitate learning environments where elementary students are engaged with learning literacy using proven pedagogical and technological approaches.

Now, teacher educators must critically examine how preservice and in-service teachers are being prepared for using TPCK in classrooms.

Learning these knowledge components

One thing is clear—it has been extremely difficult over the years to find the "perfect model" or the "best approach" for helping teachers (at all levels) acquire TPCK. Efforts to integrate technology into teacher preparation programs and methods courses are well documented and rather extensive (Brush *et al.*, 2003; Schmidt, Merkley, Fuhler, & Rinkleff, 2004; Strudler, Archambault, Bendixen, Anderson, & Weiss, 2003; Thompson, Schmidt, & Davis, 2003; Vannatta & O'Bannon, 2002). Many of these efforts have significantly impacted teacher preparation programs with respect to connecting content, pedagogy, and technology. A general conclusion might be that there is no single solution or correct model for integrating technology into a teacher preparation program. As Pellegrino and Altman (1997) conclude, "There is not a simple descriptive schema for what it takes to create the kinds of learning environments, courses, and integrated teacher preparation programs necessary to ensure that the next generation of teachers have the capabilities needed to function well in the 21st-century schools" (pp. 92–93). With this in mind, we now offer a few suggestions to assist teacher educators as they prepare teachers who will thoughtfully consider TPCK and its implications for literacy classrooms.

With the complex relationships involved in learning about TPCK it seems obvious that the skills and knowledge teachers require will not be realized anymore by just taking the one "technology course" offered by many institutions. In such a course students typically learn how to use technologies, but the pedagogical knowledge and content knowledge required for subject area application are often ignored. Currently, there seems to be agreement that the content taught in most technology courses should be strengthened and extended throughout the teacher preparation program by other faculty who model technology for instructional and administrative tasks (Becker & Ravitz, 1998; Brush, 1998; Strudler & Wetzel, 1999). In practice, this is extremely difficult to accomplish unless the appropriate support structures for teacher education faculty are in place. For the past 15 years, faculty at Iowa State University have had the opportunity to participate in a technology mentoring program (www.ci.hs.iastate.edu/mentor/about.htm) in which a teacher education faculty member works one-on-one each week with a graduate student enrolled in an advanced technology in teacher education course (Thompson, Schmidt, & Hadjiyianni, 1995). The one-on-one support that the faculty member receives as a result of this mentoring experience has significantly increased the technology use and modeling in content-specific courses at our institution. We acknowledge that this may not be a viable solution for everyone, but when it comes to learning about and using technology, one-on-one support meets the needs of most individuals and should be considered.

As teacher education faculty use technology, they will naturally begin making connections to the content and pedagogical approaches taught in their courses. When that happens, teacher education faculty can develop specific learning activities that model TPCK approaches for their students—like the examples described in this chapter's TPCK section. Modeling the use of technology proved to be a highly effective strategy for helping preservice teachers understand how technology might be used in classrooms (Faison, 1996; Kovalchik, 1997; Nicaise & Barnes, 1996). Participating in modeling activities where technology is used to teach elementary literacy skills and concepts can only help future teachers understand what it takes to translate TPCK into classroom practices. Ertmer (2003) concludes,

> Models can provide important information about how to complete a complex task, as well as increase the confidence of those who observe them. Given the complexity involved in creating and implementing technology-rich lessons, it is likely that teachers (at all levels) will benefit from observing varying degrees of expert performance as they move toward more advanced levels of technology use themselves.
>
> (p. 126)

These suggested models of use associated with TPCK must follow preservice teachers into K-12 classrooms. Although modeling the use of technology within specific content area courses increases preservice teachers' confidence about their own abilities to teach these subjects with technology (Dawson & Norris, 2000; Strudler, Archambault, Bendixen, Anderson, & Weiss, 2003), we still need to collaborate with our K-12 school partners to make sure these TPCK modeling experiences are extended into practicum and student teaching experiences. In fact, observing in-service teachers making technology-based instructional decisions in diverse, multicultural learning environments may help preservice teachers develop sensitivity to digital equity and may enable them to use this knowledge to bridge what Kelly defines as the third digital divide (e.g., Kelly, Chapter 2).

Preservice teachers spend a considerable amount of time in K-12 classrooms during practicum and student teaching experiences so working with in-service teachers becomes an extremely important consideration. Providing preservice teachers with opportunities to observe models of technology use in elementary classrooms, combined with opportunities for "hands-on" experience teaching in those environments may enhance their TPCK skills (see Niess, Chapter 11). Several teacher education institutions have established strong, ongoing relationships with K-12 school districts that offer innovative solutions for preparing both preservice and in-service teachers to use technology (Dawson, Pringle, & Adams, 2003; Strudler, Archambault,

Bendixen, Anderson, & Weiss, 2003; Strudler & Grove, 2002; Thompson, Schmidt, & Davis, 2003).

Communication with instructors and practicing teachers may also contribute to preservice teachers' understanding of TPCK. Nicaise and Barnes (1996) found that using communication technologies such as email with classroom teachers gave preservice teachers a mechanism to share their thoughts with or pose questions to practicing teachers. In our elementary literacy methods course at Iowa State, an in-service teacher (i.e., Voice from the Trenches) communicates with the preservice teachers each week using a blog (voice378.blogspot.com). This experience provides them with a valuable model of critical reflection and practice as it relates to literacy education (e.g., Niess, Chapter 11). In fact, teacher candidates who had the opportunity both to observe and to communicate with practicing teachers who used technology became more critical users of technology themselves (Nicaise & Barnes, 1996; Wilkerson, 2003).

In sum, we suggest providing one-on-one support for teacher educators as they learn and integrate technology into their own courses, modeling effective TPCK applications in K-6 literacy courses, providing "hands-on" experiences for preservice teachers to practice TPCK applications in methods courses, practicums, and student teaching, and creating multiple opportunities for preservice teachers to communicate and reflect on their TPCK experiences in K-6 literacy. These types of experiences will foster preservice teachers' understanding of TPCK applications in elementary literacy and build their capacity to transfer TPCK practices into their own classrooms.

Conclusion

Understanding TPCK and how it relates to K-6 literacy education requires a critical and thoughtful examination of all components and their interactions with each other. As Figure 3.1 illustrates, TPCK involves a complex interplay of instructional decisions made by the teacher that include content, pedagogy, and technology—*it's not that elementary*. A teacher's decision-making process is extremely complex and multifaceted as she must consider many classroom and instructional variables related to designing learning activities that incorporate TPCK thought and application. The classroom examples provided in this chapter illustrate how these components (i.e. technology, content, and pedagogy), taken collectively, comprise a synergistic approach for designing TPCK applications for K-6 literacy instruction. Preparation and professional development experiences for teachers must include opportunities for them to observe, participate, and reflect upon what they will teach, how they will teach it, and how technology might be used to enhance and expand K-6 literacy learning in their classrooms.

Clearly, preservice and in-service teachers need exposure to TPCK models that demonstrate making effective technology-related decisions for content area instruction and that also show an understanding of the relationship between technology, pedagogy, and content. With respect to K-6 literacy, our goal as teacher educators is to prepare teachers who can teach a child to read and write. We must provide learning opportunities for preservice and in-service teachers that model and apply the ideas of TPCK and its relationship to the content and pedagogy being taught in our methodology courses. Hopefully the examples shared in this chapter will inspire others to discover the possibilities for TPCK in K-6 literacy education.

References

A to Z Teacher Stuff, L.L.C. (1997–2006). *A to Z Teacher Stuff*. http://atozteacherstuff.com.

ALTEC, the University of Kansas. (2000–2006). *RubiStar*. http://rubistar.4teachers.org/index.php.

Anderson, R. S., & Speck, B. W. (2001). *Using technology in K-8 literacy classrooms*. Upper Saddle River, NJ: Prentice-Hall, Inc.

Anderson-Inman, L., & Horney, M. A. (1999). Electronic books: Reading and studying with supportive resources. *Reading Online* [Online]. Retrieved May 22, 2006, from http://www.readingonline.org/electronic/ebook/index.html.

Armstrong, S. (2003). The power of storytelling in education. In S. Armstrong (ed.), *Snapshots! Educational insights from the Thornburg Center* (pp. 11–20). The Thornburg Center: Lake Barrington, Illinois.

Atwell, N. (1984). *Coming to know: Writing to learn in the intermediate grades*. Portsmouth, NH: Heinemann.

Atwell, N. (1987). *In the middle: Writing, reading and learning with adolescents*. Portsmouth, NH: Heinemann.

Becker, H., & Ravitz, J. (1998). The influence of computer and Internet use on teachers' pedagogical practices and perceptions. *Journal of Research on Computing in Education, 31*(4), 356–384.

Bialo, E., & Sivin, J. (1990). Report on the effectiveness of microcomputers in schools. Washington, DC: Software Publishers Association.

Brush, T. A. (1998). Teaching preservice teachers to use technology in the classroom. *Journal of Technology and Teacher Education, 6*(4), 243–258.

Brush, T., Glazewski, K., Rutowski, K., Berg, K., Stromfors, C., Hernandez Van-Nest, M., *et al.* (2003). Integrating technology into a pre-service teacher training program: The PT3@ASU project. *Educational Technology Research and Development, 51*(1), 57–72.

Calkins, L. M. (1986). *The art of teaching writing*. Portsmouth, NH: Heinemann.

Cambourne, B. (1984). Language, learning, and literacy (reproduced from *Towards a Reading-Writing Classroom* by permission of Primary English Teaching Association, Sydney, Australia). Crystal Lake, IL: Rigby.

Cazden, C. (1988). *Classroom discourse*. Portsmouth, NH: Heinemann.

Center for Technology in Learning and Teaching, Iowa State University. *Faculty technology mentoring*. Retrieved May 31, 2006, from http://www.ci.hs.iastate.edu/mentor/about.htm.

Cummins, J. (1979). Linguistic interdependence and the educational development of bilingual children. *Review of Educational Research, 49*, 222–251.

Cunningham, A. E., & Stanovich, K. E. (1998, Spring/Summer). What reading does for the mind. *American Educator, 22*, 8–15.

Daiute, C., & Morse, F. (1994). Access to knowledge and expression: Multimedia writing tools for students with diverse needs and strengths. *Journal of Special Education Technology, 12*, 221–256.

Dawson, K., & Norris, A. (2000). Pre-service teachers' experiences in a K-12/university technology-based field initiative: Benefits, facilitators, constraints, and implications for teacher educators. *Journal of Computing in Teacher Education, 17*(1), 4–12.

Dawson, K., Pringle, R., & Adams, T. (2003). Providing links between technology integration, methods courses and traditional field experiences: Implementing a model of curriculum-based and technology-enhanced microteaching. *Journal of Computing in Teacher Education, 20*(1), 41–47.

Dodge, B. WebQuest Portal. Retrieved May 31, 2006, from http://webquest.org.

Ertmer, P. A. (2003). Transforming teacher education: Vision and strategies. *Educational Technology Research and Development, 51*(1), 124–128.

Faison, C. (1996). Modeling instructional technology use in teacher preparation: Why we can't wait. *Educational Technology, 36*(5), 57–59.

Fletcher, J. M., & Lyon, G. R. (1998). Reading: A research-based approach. In W. Evers (ed.), *What's gone wrong in America's classrooms?* (pp. 49–90). Stanford, CA: Hoover Institution Press.

Floden, R. E., & Meniketti, M. (2005). Research on the effects of coursework in the arts and sciences and in the foundations of education. In M. Cochran-Smith & K. M. Zeichner (eds), *Studying teacher education: The report of the AERA Panel on Research and Teacher Education* (pp. 261–308). Hillsdale, NJ: Erlbaum.

Genishi, C., McCarrier, A., & Nussbaum, N. R. (1988). Research currents: Dialogue as a context for teaching and learning. *Language Arts, 65*, 182–191.

Giff, P. R. (1997). *Lily's crossing.* New York: Delacorte.

Goodman, Y. M., & Wilde, S. (eds) (1992). *Literacy events in a community of young writers.* New York: Teachers College Press.

Graves, D. H. (1983). *Writing: Teachers and children at work.* Portsmouth, NH: Heinemann.

Guthrie, J. T., & Wigfield, A. (2000). Engagement and motivation in reading. In M. L. Kamil, P. B. Mosenthal, P. D. Pearson, & R. Barr (eds), *Handbook of reading research* (3rd edn). New York: Longman.

Guthrie, J. T., Schafer, W. D., & Huang, C. (2000). Benefits of opportunity to read and balanced reading instruction for reading achievement and engagement: A policy analysis of state NAEP in Maryland. *Journal of Educational Research, 94*(3), 145–162.

Guthrie, J. T., Wigfield, A., Humenick, N. M., Perencevich, K. C., Taboada, A., & Barbosa, P. (2006). Influences of stimulating tasks on reading motivation and comprehension. *The Journal of Educational Research, 99*(4), 232–245.

Hansen, J. (1987). *When writers read.* Portsmouth, NH: Heinemann.

Harris, T. L., & Hodges, R. E. (1995). *The literacy dictionary: The vocabulary of reading and writing.* Newark, DE: International Reading Association.

Hasselbring, T. (1999, May). *The computer doesn't embarrass me.* Paper presented at the meeting of the International Reading Association, San Diego, CA.

Hastings, E. (1997). Effects of CD-ROM talking storybooks on word recognition and motivation in young students with reading disabilities: An exploratory study. Unpublished manuscript, Syracuse University.

Hesse, K. (1997). *Out of dust.* New York: Scholastic Press.

Hillinger, M. L., & Leu, D. L. (1994). Guiding instruction in hypermedia. *Proceedings of the Human Factors and Ergonomics Society's 38th annual meeting*, 266–270.

International Reading Association. (2002). *Integrating literacy and technology in the curriculum.* Newark, DE: International Reading Association.

International Reading Association. (2004). *Standards for reading professionals—revised 2003.* Newark, DE: International Reading Association.

International Society for Technology in Education. (2000). *National educational technology standards for teachers.* Eugene, OR: International Society for Technology in Education.

IRA/NCTE. (2002–2006). *ReadWriteThink.* http://www.readwritethink.org.

Jones, I. (1994). The effect of a word processor on the written composition of second-grade pupils. *Computers in the Schools, 11*(2), 43–54.

Kamil, M. L., & Lane, D. M. (1998). Researching the relationship between technology and literacy: An agenda for the 21st century. In D. Reinking, M. C. Mckenna, L. D. Labbo, & R. D. Kieffer (eds), *Handbook of literacy and technology: Transformation in a post-typographic world* (pp. 323–341). Mahwah, NJ: Lawrence Erlbaum Associates.

Karchmer, R. A. (2000). Understanding teachers' perspectives of Internet use in the classroom: Implications for teacher education and staff development programs. *Reading and Writing Quarterly, 16*(1), 81–85.

KidPub Children's Publishing. Retrieved May 31, 2006, from http://www.kidpub.com/kidpub.

Kinzer, C. K., & Leander, K. (2003). Technology and the language arts: Implications of an expanded definition of literacy. In J. Flood, D. Lapp, J. R. Sauire, & J. M. Jensen (eds), *Handbook of research on teaching the English language arts* (2nd edn., pp. 546–565). Mahwah, NJ: Lawrence Erlbaum Associates.

Kovalchik, A. (1997). Technology portfolios as an instructional strategy: designing a reflexive approach to pre-service technology training. *TechTrends, 42*(9), 31–36.

Labbo, L. D., & Reinking, D. (1999). Negotiating the multiple realities of technology in literacy research and instruction. *Reading Research Quarterly, 34*(4), 478–492.

Labbo, L. D., Murray, B. A., & Phillips, M. (1995–1996). Writing to read: From inheritance to innovation and invitation. *The Reading Teacher, 49,* 314–321.

Leu, D. J., Jr. (2000). Deictic consequences for literacy education in an information age. In M. L. Kamil, P. Mosenthal, P. D. Pearson, & R. Barr (eds), *Handbook of reading research* (Volume III, pp. 743–770). Mahwah, NJ: Erlbaum.

Leu, D. J., & Hillinger, M. (1994). *Reading comprehension in hypermedia: Supporting changes to children's conceptions of a scientific principle.* San Diego, CA: National Reading Conference.

Leu, D. J., Jr., & Kinzer, C. K. (2000). The convergence of literacy instruction with networked technologies for information and communication. *Reading Research Quarterly, 35,* 108–127.

Lewin, C. (1997). Evaluating talking books: Ascertaining the effectiveness of multiple feedback modes and tutoring techniques. In C. K. Kinzer, K. A. Hinchman, & D. J. Leu (eds), *Inquiries in literacy theory and practice* (pp. 360–371). Chicago: National Reading Conference.

Lowry, L. (1989). *Number the stars.* Boston: Houghton Mifflin Co.

Maryland Public Television, & Johns Hopkins University Center for Technology in Education. (2006). *Thinkport.* http://www.thinkport.org/default.tp.

McGill-Franzen, A., & Lanford, C. (1994). Exposing the edge of the preschool curriculum: Teachers' talk about text and children's literacy understanding. *Language Arts, 71,* 264–273.

McKenna, M. C. (1998). Electronic texts and the transformation of beginning reading. In D. Reinking, M. C. McKenna, L. D. Labbo, & R. D. Kieffer (eds), *Handbook of literacy and technology: Transformations in a post-typographic world* (pp. 45–59). Mahwah, NJ: Erlbaum.

McKenna, M. C., & Watkins, J. H. (1996, December). *The effects of computer-mediated trade books on sight word acquisition and the development of phonics ability.* Paper presented at the meeting of the National Reading Conference, Charleston, SC.

McKenna, M. C., Labbo, L. D., & Reinking, D. (2003). Effective use of technology in literacy instruction. In L. M. Morrow, L. B. Gambrell, & M. Pressley (eds), *Best practices in literacy instruction* (2nd ed., pp. 307–331). New York: The Guilford Press.

Merkley, D., Schmidt, D., & Allen, G. (2001). Addressing the technology standards in a secondary reading methodology class. *Journal of Adolescent & Adult Literacy, 45*(3), 220–231.

Mishra, P., & Koehler, M. J. (2006). Technological pedagogical content knowledge: A framework for teacher knowledge. *Teachers College Record, 108*(6), 1017–1054.

Moats, L. C. (1999). *Teaching reading is rocket science: What expert teachers of reading should know and be able to do.* Washington, DC: American Federation of Teachers. (ERIC Document Reproduction Service No. ED445323.)

National Reading Panel. (2000). *Teaching children to read: An evidence-based assessment of the scientific research literature on reading and its implications for reading instruction.* Jessup, MD: National Institute for Literacy. Retrieved May 20, 2006 from http://www.nichd.nih.gov/publications/nrp/smallbook.pdf.

Nicaise, M., & Barnes, D. (1996). The union of technology, constructivism, and teacher education. *Journal of Teacher Education, 47*(3), 205–212.

Office of Technology Assessment. (1988). *Power on! New tools for teaching and learning.* Washington, DC: U. S. Government Printing Office.

Padak, N., Rasinski, T., & Mraz, M. (2002). *Scientifically-based reading research: A primer for adult and family literacy educators. Research to practice.* Kent State University, OH: Ohio Literacy Resource Center. (ERIC Document Reproduction Service No. ED469865.)

Pearson, D. P., & Raphael, T. E. (2003). Toward a more complex view of balance in the literacy curriculum. In L. M. Morrow, L. B. Gambrell, & M. Pressley (eds), *Best practices in literacy instruction* (2nd edn, pp. 23–39). New York: The Guilford Press.

Pellegrino, J. W., & Altman, J. E. (1997). Information technology and teacher preparation: Some critical issues and illustrative solutions. *Peabody Journal of Education, 72*(1), 89–121.

Pressley, M., Wharton-McDonald, R., Rankin, J., El-Dinary, P., Brown, R., Afflerbach, P., *et al.* (1997). Elementary reading instruction. In G. D. Phye (ed.), *Handbook of academic learning: Construction of knowledge* (pp. 151–198). New York: Academic Press.

Rodriguez, D., & Rodriguez, J. J. (1986). *Teaching writing with a word processor, grades 7–13.* Urbana, IL: ERIC Clearinghouse on Reading and Communication Skills and National Council of Teachers of English.

Ruddell, R. B. (2006). *Teaching children to read and write: Becoming an effective literacy teacher* (4th edn). New York: Pearson Education, Inc.

Schmidt, D. A., Merkley, D. J., Fuhler, C. J., & Rinkleff, S. (2004). Technology for engaged learning in a literacy methods course, *Reading Online, 7*(4). Retrieved May 25, 2006, from http://www.readingonline.org/articles/art_index.asp?HREF=/articles/schmidt.

Schmidt, J. A voice from the trenches. Retrieved May 31, 2006, from http://voice378.blogspot.com.

Shaw, C. G. (1947). *It looked like spilt milk.* New York: Harper.

Shulman, L. S. (1986). Those who understand: Knowledge growth in teaching. *Educational Researcher, 15*(2), 4–14.

Shulman, L. S. (1987). Knowledge and teaching: Foundation of the new reform. *Harvard Educational Review, 57*(1), 1–22.

Snow, C. E., Griffin, P., & Burns, M. S. (eds). (2005). *Knowledge to support the teaching of reading: Preparing teachers for a changing world.* San Francisco, CA: Jossey-Bass.

Spitzer, M. (1990). Local and global networking: Implications for the future. In D. H. Holdstein & C. L. Selfe (eds), *Computers and writing: Theory, research, practice* (pp. 58–70). New York: Modern Language Association.

Strudler, N., & Grove, K. (2002). Integrating technology into teacher candidates' field experiences: A two-pronged approach. *Journal of Computing in Teacher Education, 19*(2), 33–39.

Strudler, N., & Wetzel, K. (1999). *Lessons from exemplary teacher education programs.* Paper presented at the ninth annual conference of the Society for Information Technology and Teacher Education, Washington, DC.

Strudler, N., Archambault, L., Bendixen, L., Anderson, D., & Weiss, R. (2003). Project THREAD: Technology helping restructure educational access and delivery. *Educational Technology Research and Development, 51*(1), 41–56.

Swenson, J., Rozema, R., Young, C. A., McGrail, E., & Whitin, P. (2005). Beliefs about technology and the preparation of English teachers: Beginning the conversation. *Contemporary Issues in Technology and Teacher Education, 5*(3/4), 210–236.

Thomas, J. C. (1998). *I have heard of a land.* New York: HarperCollins Publishers.

Thompson, A., Schmidt, D. A., & Davis, N. E. (2003). Technology collaboratives for simultaneous renewal in teacher education. *Journal of Educational Technology Research and Development, 51*(1), 73–89.

Thompson, A. D., Schmidt, D. A., & Hadjiyianni, E. (1995). A three year program to infuse technology throughout a teacher education program. *Journal of Technology and Teacher Education, 3*(1), 13–24.

Valmont, W. J. (2003). *Technology for literacy teaching and learning.* Boston: Houghton Mifflin.

Vannatta, R. A., & O'Bannon, B. (2002). Beginning to put the pieces together: A technology infusion model for teacher education. *Journal of Computing in Teacher Education, 18*(4), 112–123.

Wang, J. H. Y., & Guthrie, J. T. (2004). Modeling the effects of intrinsic motivation, extrinsic motivation, amount of reading and past reading achievement on text comprehension between U.S. and Chinese students. *Reading Research Quarterly, 39*, 162–186.

Wepner, S. B., Valmont, W. J., & Thurlow, R. (eds) (2000). *Linking literacy and technology: A guide for K-8 classrooms.* Newark, DE: International Reading Association.

West, R. F., Stanovich, K. E., & Cunningham, A. E. (1995). Compensatory processes in reading.

In R. Dixon & L. Backman (eds), *Compensating for psychological deficits and declines: Managing losses and promoting gains* (pp. 275–296). Hillsdale, NJ: Erlbaum.

Whitehurst, G. J., & Lonigan, C. J. (1998). Child development and emergent literacy. *Child Development, 68*, 848–872.

Wigfield, A., & Guthrie, J. T. (1997). Relations of children's motivation for reading to the amount and breadth of their reading. *Journal of Educational Psychology, 89*, 420–432.

Wilkerson, T. L. (2003). A triad model for preparing preservice teachers for the integration of technology in teaching and learning. *Action in Teacher Education, 24*(4), 27–32.

Wong Fillmore, L. (1991). When learning a second language means losing the first. *Early Childhood Research Quarterly, 6*, 323–346.

Wood, J. M. (2000) Literacy: Charlotte's web meets the World Wide Web. In D. T. Gordon (ed.), *The digital classroom: How technology is changing the way we teach and learn* (pp. 117–126). Cambridge, MA: Harvard Education Letter.

Young, E. E. (2001). *Improving reading in America: Are teachers prepared? NCREL policy issues.* Oak Brook, IL: North Central Regional Educational Laboratory. (ERIC Document Reproduction Service No. ED464041.)

Zhao, Y. (ed.) (2003). *What should teachers know about technology?* Greenwich, CT: Information Age Publishing, Inc.

4

Leveraging the development of English TPCK within the deictic nature of literacy

JOAN E. HUGHES AND CASSANDRA M. SCHARBER

In this chapter, we will illustrate preservice and practicing English teachers' technological pedagogical content knowledge (TPCK), note the impact TPCK has on teachers' English language arts instruction (and subsequently their students' learning experiences), and discuss two strategies to employ in teacher education contexts that we suspect must be in place to foster more knowledge development. We also recommend that teachers and teacher educators attend both to the developing technology knowledge and the emerging practices that such knowledge enables.

The first author's past research (Hughes, 2000) generated the TPCK concept specific to the English discipline, at that time referred to as: E(nglish)-TPCK. The E-TPCK concept emerged from case study research of practicing English teachers with a range of teaching experience, technology learning experiences, and technological access in their schools (see also: Hughes, 2005), serving as contrasts in accordance with theoretical replication within multiple cases (Yin, 1994).

The fundamental premise and value of the E-TPCK concept (see Figure 4.1) is that differences in teachers' technology learning and classroom technology use can be explained in terms of the kinds of existing teacher knowledge or teacher knowledge under development. This E-TPCK theory and its components (see Figure 4.1) corresponds with the technology knowledge framework framing all the chapters in this monograph, as introduced in Chapter 1 by Koehler and Mishra.

The E-TPCK concept built upon Shulman's (1987) conceptual categories of pedagogical knowledge, subject matter knowledge, and pedagogical content knowledge. General pedagogical knowledge, such as cooperative learning, human cognitive development, and classroom management techniques, or more specific strategies such as promoting classroom discourse during which students' thinking becomes explicit, earns respect, and is challenged by all involved in the discussion, is knowledge teachers use across all subject areas for general instructional planning and decision-making. Subject matter knowledge is the depth and breadth of knowledge in a content area such as, in our case, English Education (see Chapter 3 by Schmidt and Gurbo for more information on early literacy). Teachers know facts and concepts of the discipline, frameworks for explaining such disciplinary facts and concepts, and the path(s) new content takes to become part of the discipline. The breadth of English discipline is truly substantial. Teachers of English in middle and high school know and teach topics and concepts such as: theater, film and media studies, remedial reading, American/British/world literature, contemporary literature, creative writing, journalism, critical approaches to analyzing literature, grammar, speech and debate, language acquisition and development, mythology, and Shakespeare. They understand how to sequence their curriculum, choose texts to represent genres or periods, and use frameworks or representations to help learners understand the content. They also recognize the evolving and developing nature of English language arts and may add concepts, authors, and topics into their curriculum as the field recognizes new content (e.g., contemporary American writers). Pedagogical content knowledge is specific for each content area; teachers within a discipline make pedagogical decisions about instruction and learning based on what they believe to be the purpose(s) for teaching the content, what knowledge they believe students should be developing (noting what has been taught in previous and subsequent grade levels), what discipline-based teaching materials are available, and what representations or activities have been successfully used in their past teaching. For example, teachers build reading, listening, viewing, and writing communities where learners grapple with each others' idea through deep consideration and interpretation; teachers lead learners in the writing process and conferencing; teachers invite and guide learners into transactions with literature, ultimately improving their individual comprehension and interpretation of texts.

At the time of Hughes' earlier study (2000) when technology was becoming more conspicuous within educational settings, the TPCK concept emerged as a way to explain and emphasize how these technological tools, concepts, activities, and perspectives connected with the recognized literature on teachers' knowledge (i.e., Shulman, 1987). E-TPCK, and its related TPK, TK, and TCK, served as conceptual categories that described knowledge English teachers develop and use to craft learning opportunities for their students that pointedly use technologies to help students engage in learning and engaging with English content. Then and now, we argue that E-TPCK and TPCK in general are *temporary* concepts that draw attention to the interconnections between technological tools, concepts, activities, and perspectives and the well-developed teacher knowledge, content knowledge, pedagogical knowledge, and pedagogical content knowledge. TPCK has and will continue to help teachers and teacher educators focus explicitly on these overlaps when they might otherwise not do so. Eventually, as technology and technology integration becomes more culturalized in schools, the teacher education preparation and professional development, the concepts we

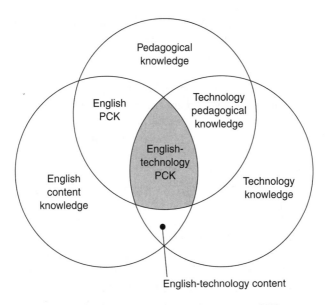

Figure 4.1 English-technology pedagogical content knowledge (Hughes, 2000).

describe here, essentially, will be incorporated as aspects of CK, PK, and PCK. However, our field needs the *explicitness* of the TPCK concept at this point in time.

English educators and English education teacher educators are already intimate with the content knowledge, general pedagogical knowledge, and pedagogical content knowledge that we are aiming to develop within new and veteran English teachers. Our chapter, therefore, focuses on explaining cases and examples of English teachers' TPCK and how the possession of such knowledge impacts English classroom practices. Toward that end, we offer a model of technology integration in English education teacher preparation. We interpret examples from research and commentary of English preservice teachers' preparation through the TPCK lens as well as discuss the role the learning context plays in developing these new teachers' technology knowledge. We then discuss two teacher cases, Laura, a three-year novice teacher teaching 9th grade English, and Nell, a 26-year veteran teacher who teaches 7th and 8th grade English, specifically in regards to the existence and development of technology-related knowledge and its impact on their practice in English classrooms. These teachers never experienced or observed technology-supported English practice in their professional teacher preparation. The cases of Nell and Laura illustrate that, in the absence of an "apprenticeship of observation" (Lortie, 1975), each developed her own approach to learning TK (the skills in technology knowledge), which, in turn, impacted the development of TPK and E-TPCK. Why and how a teacher learns technology determines if and how TPK and E-TPCK is developed. Overall, we discuss approaches to preservice and in-service education that can increase the likelihood of the development of TPCK among preservice and practicing/in-service teachers.

Our chapter provides illustrations of both preservice and in-service English teachers' TPCK in practice. We do not attempt to catalogue TPCK because we conceptualize TPCK as adaptive to conditions and context. We do show how teachers use their varying levels of TPCK to make curricular decisions regarding technology in the classroom. We illustrate the complexity of E-TPCK, and it is this very complexity that does not lend itself to creating a "list" of elements of E-TPCK. The ever-changing and emerging technologies, the evolving content area of English literacy, the variations within schools and among students, and the capabilities of teachers all impact how and what TPCK teachers develop and use to make curricular decisions. Our chapter's goal is to help teacher educators recognize TPCK's complexity, be able to identify the depth of TPCK within English teachers with whom they work/teach, and create learning experiences that will further develop these teachers' TPCK so that it positively impacts English learners in schools. It is with that focus that we begin at the beginning—with preservice teachers who are just learning to become a teacher. We focus in on an innovative preservice English education program that we believe creates learning opportunities that work towards developing E-TPCK within enrolled preservice teachers so that they are poised to make thoughtful technology integration decisions as novice teachers.

Developing E-TPCK within an innovative preservice teacher education program at the University of Minnesota

Ed-U-Tech: content-specific technology integration

Preparing teachers to use technology within the context of their content areas rather than in a separate, general technology skills course is an emerging trend in the field of education (Dexter, Doering, & Riedel, 2006; Sprague, 2004). As instructors with first-hand experiences in working with teachers on technology integration, we view the model of content-area specific technology integration currently in use within the teaching licensure programs of the College of Education and Human Development at the University of Minnesota (Dexter, Doering, & Riedel, 2006) as an exemplary way of fostering E-TPCK in preservice English teachers. Initially supported by a 1999 Implementation grant from the U.S. Department of Education's Preparing Tomorrow's Teachers to Use Technology (PT3) initiative (http://www.pt3.org/), this model began as the grant initiative called Ed-U-Tech (Dexter, Doering, & Riedel, 2006). Seven years after the introduction and implementation of the model and three years post-funding, the content-specific technology model introduced by Ed-U-Tech at the University of Minnesota has become "part of 'the way we do things here'—a part of the culture of the teacher education institution" (Dexter *et al.*, 2006, p. 341).

At its core, Ed-U-Tech and its legacy is a college-wide commitment to developing content-area specific technology integration skills in preservice teachers. The preservice teacher education program was redesigned to include content-based educational foundations courses that are taken concurrently with content-based methods courses. For example, English preservice teachers form a cohort that simultaneously enrolls in the English educational technology course and an English-methods course. Doering, Hughes, and Huffman (2003), three faculty members who taught/teach under the Ed-U-Tech model explain, "we wanted the preservice teacher experience to provide a content-area community for students as well as a network of content-related peers to share their technology integration ideas" (p. 7). Thus, the content-specific design of the program at the University of Minnesota creates spaces and opportunities for preservice teachers to observe and experience the blurring between, and the intersection and integration of English-specific technological, pedagogical, and content knowledge.

Through taking licensure courses as content-based cohorts, UMN preservice English teachers are able to explore, refine, model, and develop E-TPCK. As illustrations of E-TPCK being fostered in preservice English teachers at UMN, we highlight one project that has been completed by preservice English teachers during their participation in the UMN teaching licensure program. This project was possible due to the restructuring of the English education program during Ed-U-Tech and the dedication of the English/Literacy faculty to the concept of content-specific technology integration.

Co-inquiry multi-genre writing project

An English composition methods course instructor, Dr. Richard Beach, and the English-focused technology foundations course instructor, Dr. Aaron Doering, collaborated on a multi-genre writing project involving both preservice English teachers and middle-school students (Doering & Beach, 2002) in which the

> project was an assignment with parts that counted in both courses, with the technology course introducing the necessary software and its application to this assignment and the methods course reinforcing how its use could further the language arts development in K-12 students and add value to instruction.
>
> (Dexter, Doering, & Riedel, 2006)

In addition to taking the two courses, the preservice teachers were also participating in a practicum experience in a middle school that made possible the collaboration between K-12 students and preservice teachers. The multi-genre project, which included the development of a biographical sketch, a newspaper report, and a narrative about a famous person (content knowledge), was co-constructed by the preservice teachers and the middle-school students over the course of one semester. Each preservice teacher was assigned to work with between two and four middle-school students. The teams met face-to-face weekly (as part of the practicum) and communicated as needed via email and discussion boards (technological pedagogical knowledge). In addition, the preservice teachers engaged in web-based communication with each other about their experiences (technology knowledge/ pedagogical knowledge)—the middle school students were not part of these latter discussions. Inspiration™, StorySpace™, HyperStudio™, ClarisWorks, a web-based asynchronous communication tool, and the Internet (technology knowledge/technology content knowledge) were used during the project.

We discern from Doering and Beach's (2002) discussion and analysis about the multi-media project that the English preservice teachers were developing E-TPCK. In the conclusion to their article, Doering and Beach (2002) observe, "technology serves to *mediate both* preservice teachers' acquisitions of teaching strategies and the development of literacy practices" (pp. 142–143; emphasis ours). This mediation, when viewed through a lens of TPCK, highlights the effectiveness of the project in developing E-TPCK in the preservice teachers. While we can identify when technologies or topics were first introduced to the preservice teachers, in the subsequent enactment of the project over time it is difficult to separate out and identify parts of the project that individually developed technology knowledge, pedagogical knowledge, and content knowledge because they were developed simultaneously and interdependently, which is exactly what Pope and Golub (2000) have described: "English language arts education and technology are no longer separable." During the UMN preservice teachers' experiences with this co-inquiry project, they (a) were positioned as both teacher and student, facilitating their pedagogical knowledge (*PK*), (b) were provided with online and face-to-face spaces and tools to interact and communicate in both roles, helping to develop their technology knowledge and pedagogical knowledge (*TK and PK*), and (c) co-developed a project that promoted the development of literacy practices in the middle school students and for themselves to use/teach as future English instructors (i.e. adoption of multiple voices, intertexuality, hypermedia, technology-mediated research and sharing of information, multi-genre writing) (Doering & Beach, 2002), enabling the development of content knowledge, technological knowledge, pedagogical knowledge, technological content knowledge, and technological pedagogical content knowledge (*CK, TK, PK, TCK, TPCK*).

The innovative preservice English education program in place at the University of Minnesota creates learning opportunities that aid development of preservice teachers' E-TPCK so they are poised to make technology integration decisions as novice teachers. Next, we highlight aspects of the UMN program that could be transferred to other preservice education programs in order to promote the development of TPCK.

Dexter, Doering, and Riedel (2006) state, "Ed-U-Tech's goals focused on faculty development, curriculum development, establishing opportunities for preservice teachers to plan for and practice using technology as a support to instruction and receive feedback about those efforts ... and preparing teachers to use technology" (p. 328). These goals provide a solid starting point for infrastructure and support as other institutions and programs seek to promote the development of TPCK in its preservice and novice teachers. These goals translate into several, concrete operations at the University of Minnesota. First, both students and faculty have access to content-specific hardware and software that is continually purchased and upgraded to facilitate the learning and teaching experiences. In addition to computer labs, the Department of Curriculum and Instruction maintains its own library where faculty and students can check out technology including laptop computers, LCD projectors, digital cameras, video cameras, and audio recorders. Faculty and students are also supported in their use of technology; both the computer labs and the C&I library are staffed with technology support personnel who are knowledgeable in many general and educational applications. In addition, faculty and staff are knowledgeable about technology and are continually provided opportunities to be trained and supported to encourage modeling and use of technology in their teaching practices. These technical affordances provide "just-in-time" access and support to technologies and technology professional development. Because the integration of technology and content is "the way we do things" in preservice teacher education at the University of Minnesota, there is curricular collaboration (design, assignments, goals) between methods and technology foundations instructors. Preservice teachers are expected to incorporate the technology tools learned in the technology foundations course into their lesson plan development and classroom activities in the methods courses while being supported by both the Learning Technologies and English Education faculty. Finally, the commitment of the English faculty and staff to technology integration and meaningful learning and the structure of providing content cohorts (i.e., English, in this case) who engage iteratively in English methods, technology foundations, and practicum experiences, culminate in providing preservice English teachers authentic teaching and learning experiences, such as the co-inquiry project highlighted in this chapter. Ed-U-Tech's initial goals still provide the foundation and motivation for collaborative, meaningful preservice teacher experiences at the University of Minnesota that explore technology, content, and pedagogy in concert, as integrated and intertwined knowledge bases, which fosters the development of TPCK as preservice teachers.

Yet, in the wider field of teacher education, preservice teachers either report a low number of instances of integrating technology into their teaching practicums or the inability to create new technology-integrated lessons in the field. For example, Bowman (2000), in response to Pope and Golub (2000), described her observations of English language arts preservice teachers that were unable to use technologies in their teaching practicum for planning, teaching, or assessment. Fifty-five percent of the students reported either lacking a vision for appropriate "fit" of technology with English language arts or were unable to "discern how to use technology with the assignments" taught. Bowman concluded that modeling was gravely important, as "preservice teachers need guidance and support to make important connections between course material and technology applications." Yet, other research (Doering, Hughes, & Huffman, 2003; Wright & Wilson, 2005–2006) reports preservice teachers relying so heavily on the examples or models that are demonstrated during their preservice education that the preservice teachers do not or are not able to independently create new technology-integrated lessons. We agree with Bowman (2000) that integration "cannot be accomplished through isolated technology experiences or without ongoing discussion, modeling, and evaluation." Yet, despite our best efforts to reform our technology-integrated English language arts preparation courses, such as the approach described above at the University of Minnesota, we have observed that the difficulty in preservice teachers enacting TPCK in developing new lessons is due to a lack of meta-cognitive awareness of their nascent knowledge and its impact on lesson preparation and student learning.

Pope and Golub (2000) emphasized that preservice teachers need "to be critical consumers of technology, to be thoughtful users who question, reflect, and refract on the best times and ways to integrate technology." They recommend establishing a process of questioning and probing, evolving preservice teachers into becoming teacher researchers. While we applaud positioning new teachers to become teacher researchers, we believe being a critical consumer, or more so, a teacher researcher, requires preservice teachers to be explicitly aware of their developing knowledge, especially in the English language arts. Unlike other disciplines, Leu, Mallette, Karchmer, and Kara-Soteriou (2005) describe how changes in technology create new literacies: "Today, continuous, rapid change regularly redefines the nature of literacy as changing technologies regularly generate new literacies" (p. 2). We believe existing learning principles (Hughes, 2004; Pope & Golub, 2000) and rhetoric surrounding developing teachers to design technology-supported lessons does not emphasize enough the need for teachers' explicit meta-cognitive awareness of their own learning and knowledge development.

We know that teachers' knowledge is developed out of teachers' past experiences, skills, and dispositions as it contends with new experiences and information in social situations (Borko & Putnam, 1996a, 1996b; Bransford, Brown, & Cocking, 2000; Bransford & Schwartz, 1999). We might expect preservice teachers, who tend to be younger, to experience technology-supported instruction in high school, yet research has shown such experiences to be inconsistent (Banister & Ross, 2005–2006). Therefore, as new teachers build their knowledge across the components of the knowledge framework (see Figure 4.1), teacher educators must also guide them in explicitly tracking their knowledge development, including TK, TCK, TPK, and E-TPCK, to enable them to set learning goals and/or classroom-based research goals for themselves and, in turn, make thoughtful decisions for technology integration.

Assisting preservice teachers in developing knowledge across this framework as well as helping them become meta-cognitively aware of such knowledge over their preservice preparation program implies that English language arts preparation programs must comprehensively and continually integrate technology throughout coursework and across the duration of the program. It is generally agreed that stand-alone technology courses are insufficient and inferior to an integrated programmatic approach (Dexter, Doering, & Riedel, 2006; Sprague, 2004). The preservice example we provided in this chapter demonstrates an integrated, cooperative relationship between Learning Technology faculty and English Education faculty that create technology-infused learning opportunities in both the Technology and English education courses. Yet, we still see room for improvement. Most important, the mechanisms and strategies employed for the preservice teachers to explicitly acknowledge their knowledge base, including TK, TCK, TPK, and E-TPCK, begun in the Technology and English methods courses, need to extend into the student teaching, in final education program courses, and be portable enough to enable the teachers to continue tracking their knowledge into their teaching career. A simple strategy to help preservice teachers become meta-cognitively aware of their developing knowledge is to have them use concept mapping software (e.g., Inspiration, MindGenius, c-map) to recognize their knowledge and capture its changing forms over time. Such a knowledge map(s) could be incorporated into portfolio systems in place in teacher education institutions.

Preparation programs also need to have a consistent evaluation and evolve in a deictic manner (Dutt-Doner, Allen, & Corcoran, 2005; Swenson, Rozema, Young, McGrail, & Whitin, 2005), especially to understand if the preparation is providing the necessary skills, knowledge, and dispositions for novice teachers to succeed. Our next section provides two cases of practicing English teachers' development and use of technology knowledge. These teachers were not prepared within the UMN program but represent the numerous practicing teachers whose past technological preparation ranges from some, to little, to no technological preparation prior to becoming a teacher.

Cases of practicing English teachers' technology knowledge base

Laura

Laura, a new teacher having taught for only three years, grew up using technologies both in her own education and for her personal use. She taught in a new school with a high-tech "teacher desk" that had a networked computer, VCR, multi-use cameras, satellite access, and two large class monitors (affordances). The school had invested in computer technologies instead of print materials for their library under the philosophy of offering the most up-to-date information.

Laura learned to navigate the Internet during college with assistance from her husband. After his introduction, Laura managed to play with it occasionally (technology knowledge) and browsed for interesting web sites. As a teacher, Laura participated in a National Writing Project and began thinking about the web's applicability in education (technology content knowledge/technology pedagogical knowledge). There, she learned to compose her own web page (technology knowledge) and examined many more. She saw demonstrations of web authoring, and with assistance from project leaders, she had time to develop her own web site. In her teaching context, the library was extremely limited, as the school did not choose to spend money on book and periodical acquisitions (constraint). Consequently, she saw web browsing as a possible solution to these limitations.

With Laura's immediate access to the web at her teaching station (affordance), she began using the web in her daily teaching, as demanded by student questions. For example, while reading Edgar Allan Poe's "The Cask of Amontillado," she found students had difficulty understanding the story. She thought having a better image of the story's setting might help them. In the moment, she searched for "catacombs" on the web and found the Vatican offered an electronic field trip through catacombs and shared that with her students (technological pedagogical knowledge). In another instance, Laura used the web as a learning resource for herself. She had difficulty explaining the Cold War to her students—as background for a story they read. After school, she found resources on the web to educate herself, so she could explain the concepts to the students adequately (content knowledge). Laura found that using the web to access information, sometimes instantaneously, offered her students the supplementary information required to understand concepts and stories they read about in class but that were not available in the school library (technological pedagogical knowledge).

LAURA'S TPK

This example, representative of Laura's technology use in the classroom for presentation, information, and administrative purposes, depicts technologies in use to support her *teaching* but not in direct support of her students' *learn-*

ing English content or processes. Laura developed and used TPK in her instructional decision-making, but she did not appear to possess E-TPCK as her presentational and informational uses, while pedagogically-driven, did not extend to deep curricular matters. She used an affordance of the web, immediate access to a wide range of information, to tackle her students' questions or misunderstandings. Yet, any teacher across any subject matter could use this pedagogical affordance of the web.

Nell

With a move to middle-school English 13 years after beginning her teaching career, Nell actively sought professional growth. Nell reflected on her practice and chose to change it often. She wanted to learn more about teaching English and had already learned about and implemented a writing workshop approach in her classroom and had become a prolific user of listserv communication where she "tested out her ideas" with colleagues. She had completed a Masters degree in Education and was pursuing a Ph.D. in English Education because she had not learned as much about educational theory as she had hoped in her Masters program.

Nell took a doctoral-level rhetoric course where she learned about hypertext theory (content knowledge) and web authoring to construct hypertext narratives (technology content knowledge). Though Nell had difficulty mastering the challenging technology, she managed to learn web authoring because she had time and assistance during the software learning process and was very interested in the topic. During the course, Nell undertook ambitious hypertext projects that frustrated her due to their complexity and her inexperience with the technology. She sought help from her professor, but ultimately relied upon technology consultants at the writing lab. Her vested theoretical interest in the project motivated her even during the most frustrating moments. She resonated with hypertext theory (content knowledge), as she felt "it closely mirrored the way I think my mind works." She thought that "hypertext is going to change us because … it's gonna move us away from that sort of false linearity that book technology has imposed upon us." She also felt it focused attention on the roles of readers, writers, and content since "it kind of makes the writer think more about content and so … you're not focusing so much on structure, you're focusing on content." Hypertext offered new theories of writing to contemplate.

During and after completion of the course, Nell developed a great interest and "was so intrigued by" hypertext theory. She wanted to expose her students to this non-traditional approach to writing and reading, and in the future, she imagined investigating children's writing processes when authoring hypertexts (pedagogical content knowledge). Before actually teaching about hypertext with technology, Nell assessed her own facility with the technology—to determine if she could actually use the technology with her students in the ways she imagined (technology content knowledge). She had authored hypertexts using the web, but her school did not have web access (constraint). She decided to explore other alternatives.

She considered HyperCard (technology knowledge) software owned by the school that creates hypertexts by compiling media (text, graphics, etc.) on individual cards or screens and allowing links to be created between information on different cards. A colleague who had used HyperCard in the past had forgotten how to use it and handed Nell the manual, but the manual did not make sense to Nell. With no coach, she attempted to learn the software on her own but could not penetrate the manual.

Nonetheless, Nell was committed to exposing her students to hypertext. She decided to teach hypertext using a non-computer approach—paper and string (pedagogical content knowledge). She described,

> I had my students write a piece of hypertext fiction and put it on paper and then had string connecting it. And they highlighted the word and then made decisions. Ok, now this word relates to this page of the story that somebody else wrote over here ... that got the idea across.

While Nell felt that this approach successfully communicated the theory, she still sought software that might support hypertext writing. In many articles, chapters, and books about hypertext theory, Nell discovered StorySpace, another computer software program that allowed links between information (technology knowledge). Nell purchased the program and started learning it on her own.

Nell went to work,

> And so [I] kind of played with it [StorySpace] and played with it ... and even after a couple of months of dinking around with it, and I'd play around with it for a while and get frustrated and do something else, I finally had to call them [helpline] and say, "Okay, how do you make a link?" And it's really easy.

Once comfortable with StorySpace software, Nell wanted to use it to support her teaching of hypertext concepts to her students (technological pedagogical content knowledge). Nell earned a grant that supplied her school with 50 computer licenses for StorySpace software. StorySpace was loaded on new PCs (affordance), and she started teaching about hypertext using this software.

Nell's students participated in an interdisciplinary Slavery Project with a group of students from Ghana (pedagogical content knowledge). The two groups of students shared in writing an African's story from his/her life in Africa, capture and deportation to America, and sale as a slave to an owner. The Ghana students collaboratively wrote four versions of the first half of the story depicting the African's life up until he/she boards a slave ship. Nell's students chose one of the four versions and completed the story to the point when the African is sold as a slave at auction. Nell's students imported the first half of the story into the StorySpace software and constructed it as a hypertext narrative (technological pedagogical content knowledge). As they crafted the second half of the narrative, they constantly developed a web of links within and between the two halves of the story.

In this case, the curriculum content goals were completely different from traditional 8th grade English language arts. After learning about and writing hypertext herself, Nell expanded her English goals to include the teaching of hypertext writing (content knowledge). When she took on this goal, she truly stepped out onto the cutting edge of the field at this time. Hypertext was not an explicit goal even in one of the most forward-looking documents available to Nell—her state's English Language Arts content standards. Technology enabled Nell to "transform" her goals for student learning. Instead of writing what Nell called "straight" stories (i.e., linear), students wrote complex intertextual collaborative pieces. Years earlier, Nell first attempted to teach hypertext using string and paper (pedagogical content knowledge). Later, using computer software, her students better understood and grasped the concepts than with other non-computer-based approaches. Though Nell believed the most effective way to communicate notions of text, writing, and reading to her students required the technology (technological pedagogical content knowledge), she was able to use a non-computer based approach. Instructionally, Nell felt StorySpace allowed simpler and clearer illustrations of the concepts (technological pedagogical content knowledge). With the string and paper approach, textual passages were connected intertextually, denoted with string connectors. Representing more lengthy writing, as one can imagine, was a mess of string. StorySpace provided several ways to view text and the intertextual links.

NELL'S TPCK

In this example, we see Nell developing and expanding her English content knowledge in a university course in rhetoric. Intrigued by readings of Bakhtin and Derrida and the concept of hypertext (content knowledge), she develops her intention to teach her own 8th grade students about this form of writing (pedagogical content knowledge). In that university course, she learns how web authoring can be the form hypertext takes as well as its ability to easily illustrate the interconnected linking inherent in hypertext. With a specific curricular intent in mind (teaching her students to write hypertexts and understand the differences between linear and nonlinear texts) and experience with one technological option, which is not available at her own school (constraint), she engages in a quest to find the right pedagogical approach to teaching hypertext for her students—from web authoring, to HyperCard, to string and paper, to StorySpace. Her pedagogical decision-making was grounded in her curricular goal, but also was affected by her school's technological capabilities, her comfort zone with particular technologies, and her evaluation of the most efficacious way for her students to learn the content. Ultimately, Nell developed and used her TPCK to design a lesson in which her students used the technology to engage in writing nonlinear, hypertext narratives, co-authored with African students.

Cross-case issues

We present these two cases as illustrations of practicing teachers' developing technological knowledge but offer insights that emerged from our larger study (see also: Hughes, 2005). We found that informal learning sufficiently facilitated teachers' awareness, familiarity, and understanding of technology, acknowledging that some teachers also seek formal learning opportunities like university education or district in-services. We discovered, not surprisingly, that content-focused technology learning experiences yielded content-based technology integration in the classroom. The content connections could be provided by someone introducing a new technology, like a colleague or a university instructor, but also could be supplied by the teacher and induce him/her to learn a new technology. These content-rich technology learning experiences led practicing teachers, with content and pedagogical knowledge, to develop TPCK and make instructional decisions that put the technologies into the hands of the students for learning content concepts. Laura's case, above, illustrates the degree to which novice practicing teachers, with emergent content and pedagogical knowledge, can be constrained when their school supplies general pedagogical technologies, such as grading and attendance programs, Internet, productivity software, and even "high-tech" teacher desks but do not provide content-focused professional development with regard to these technologies. If novice teachers are to develop TPCK, we need to design more content-rich technology learning opportunities that simultaneously strengthen their English content and pedagogical knowledge and TPCK.

The example of Nell illustrates a veteran teacher developing and applying E-TPCK in her 8th grade English teaching. The literature that chronicles veteran teachers' achievements with technology integration tends to highlight early adopters who possess deep content knowledge and a thirst for understanding technology's intersections with content, instruction, and student learning and/or veteran teachers with copious external support, such as university collaborations. The challenge is that this pool of veteran teachers who have a thirst for and/or support for technology integration is small across the nation's teacher population. Literacy researchers (Bromley, 2006; Hobbs, 2006; McKenna, Labbo, & Reinking, 2003) recount English teachers' resistance to integrate technology. McKenna, Labbo, & Reinking (2003) summarize,

It is hard for some teachers to consider, let alone accept, that emerging forms of electronic reading and writing may be as informative, pedagogically useful, and aesthetically pleasing as more familiar printed forms. To consider that electronic forms of text may be in some instances even be superior is undoubtedly more difficult.

(p. 325)

We need to develop situations in which critical masses of teachers "tip" over the point toward knowledgeable technology integration. We contend that the "tipping point" factor to establish in formal education programs and in-service opportunities is creating cognitive conflict within practicing teachers by immersing them in new literacy and new media literature, critical literacy perspectives to recognize the deictic nature (Leu, 2000, 2006) of evolving technologies and new literacies. In this way, practicing teachers are exposed to new technologies *primarily through* new content perspectives that place technology inextricably within evolving English content. The teachers are cognitively engaged at the English content knowledge (CK) level, which they cannot deny an interest if they profess to be an English teacher, and will be required to also grapple with changes in the field of literacy as inextricably woven with advancements in technology, as Leu, Kinzer, Coiro, & Cammack (2004) describe:

> Today, technological change happens so rapidly that the changes to literacy are limited not by technology but rather by our ability to adapt and acquire the new literacies that emerge. Deixis is a defining quality of the new literacies of the Internet and other ICTs. This will continue into the future but at a much faster pace as new technologies repeatedly appear, requiring new skills and new strategies for their effective use. As literacy increasingly becomes deictic, the changing constructions of literacy within new technologies will require all of us to keep up with these changes and to prepare students for a vastly different conception of what it means to become literate.

Theory and research has shown cognitive dissonance or conflict to be a strategy to raise questions and reflection in learners' minds that positions learners to possibly break down their strongly held beliefs (Hughes, 2003; King, 2002; McGrail, 2005; Piaget, 1964/1972).

With the advent of technological innovations and their increasing roles in the world, the redefinition and reconceptualization of literacy have been constant conversations in the fields of literacy and literacy education. To signal varying meanings and the changing nature of the term *literacy*, the words *new, critical, multi,* and *media* have been appended (Cope & Kalantzis, 2000; Lankshear & Knobel, 2003; Kist, 2005). Leu, Kinzer, Coiro, & Cammack (2004) acknowledge that the term, "new literacies," holds multiple definitions with no comprehensive theory, so they have outlined principles of a new literacies perspective, including: (a) the Internet and other ICTs are central technologies for literacy within a global community in an information age; (b) the Internet and other ICTs require new literacies to fully access their potential; (c) new literacies are deictic; (d) the relationship between literacy and technology is transactional; (e) new literacies are multiple in nature; (f) critical literacies are central to the new literacies; (g) speed counts in important ways within the new literacies; (h) learning often is socially constructed within the new literacies. With these recent reconceptualizations of literacy, practicing teachers have ample room to learn about new perspectives on English language arts. In doing so, the teachers will also begin to recognize how technological changes in our society affect these reconceptualizations of literacy (McGrail, & Rozema, 2005), creating pathways toward formation of TCK and E-TPCK.

In much the same way, we can expose practicing teachers to the perspective of critical literacy, in which readers and writers "disrupt dominant social practices through resistant reading and writing of texts" (Rogers, 2002, p. 773) that reveal power structures in social and cultural contexts and multiple discourses (Fairclough, 1989, 1995; Selfe, 1999). In K-12 classrooms, teachers of critical literacy help students see these power structures and create contexts in which all students can be heard (Delpit, 1995; Freire, 1970; Luke, 2000; Luke & Freebody, 1997, 1999; McLaren, 1989; Morrell, 2002). While we should create situations in which practicing teachers learn about critical literacy perspectives (content knowledge) and its importance for literacy development among children, we can correspondingly raise teachers' critical eye toward technology to develop "critical technological literacy, ... a reflective awareness of these social and cultural phenomenon ... literate citizens should be able to carefully analyze, to pay attention to, the technology–literacy link at fundamental levels of both conception and practice" (Selfe, 1999, p. 148). Teachers, in turn, must help students "to learn how to think critically about technology and the social issues surrounding its use" (Selfe, 1999, p. 152).

The significant difference between the two cases of Nell and Laura was the exposure to, availability of, and preparation to use content-focused technology. Nell was steeped in English content knowledge (e.g., rhetoric, hypertext), English technologies (e.g., Storyspace), and general technologies (e.g., Hypercard, web). Laura was immersed in general technologies (e.g., Internet, grading programs, productivity software) and though participating in a National Writing Project, she did not reveal instances of grappling with the interconnections between technologies and English content as Nell had. The NWP context could be a content-rich learning opportunity to facilitate English teachers' engagement with new media and critical literacy concepts, as already described. We must engage both novice and veteran teachers simultaneously in new technologies and new literacies to create moments of cognitive conflict during which they will evaluate and deliberately think about their professional knowledge, creating an opening for development of E-TPCK.

Discussion and conclusion

We believe developing TPCK ultimately leads to better technology integration decision-making by teachers. Elsewhere (Hughes, 2004), it has been argued that becoming a "technology integrationist" necessitates teachers being able to understand, consider, and choose to use technologies when they uniquely enhance the curriculum, instruction, and/or students' learning in a subject matter area. Thus, technology integrationists have developed TPCK, enabling them to engage in this critical analysis and planning for technology integration in their classrooms. Yet, based on the emergent technology use in schools today (Cuban, 2001; McNabb, 2005), we can infer that not enough preservice, novice, and veteran teachers are developing TPCK to reveal an impact discernible by researchers in technology-integration decision-making and/or exemplary technology uses with children in our nation's schools. Our chapter aimed to illustrate preservice, novice, and veteran teachers' development of technology-related knowledge, including TPCK. In this discussion, we identify distinctive strategies that we feel may generate a tipping point (Gladwell, 2002), effecting more widespread development of TPCK among English teachers. While we believe past design and practice principles (Hughes, 2004; Pope & Golub, 2000) do assist teacher educators, the two strategies that we believe may lead to a tipping point in which more teachers develop TPCK and use it for decision-making include: (a) helping preservice and novice teachers become more meta-cognitively aware of their knowledge base, including TK, TPK, TCK, and TPCK, over time, and (b) creating cognitive conflict within practicing teachers by immersing them in new literacy and critical literacy literature and recognizing the deictic nature (Leu, in press) of evolving technologies and new literacies.

Our examples of preservice, novice, and veteran teachers developing and applying their technological knowledge indicate that teachers are developing TPK and E-TPCK that enable them to make decisions regarding technology integration in their English language arts classrooms. Yet, this knowledge development is not widespread or streamlined. We continue to observe preservice and novice teachers struggling with technology-integration decisions (often, quickly giving up on using technology at all) and veteran teachers who lack the intrinsic interest in technology to forge a learning pathway toward developing TPCK. Acknowledging the already well-developed design principles for teacher educators (Hughes, 2004) and English educators (Pope & Golub, 2000) interested in designing courses and teacher education programs that dispose teachers toward developing TPCK, we conclude that two additional strategies, the explicit meta-cognitive awareness of developing aspects of TPCK and creating openings for the development of TPCK through moments of cognitive conflict with English content knowledge, may help develop a critical mass of teachers developing TPCK. First, within preservice programs, we need to guide preservice and novice teachers in becoming more meta-cognitively aware of their knowledge base, including TK, TPK, TCK, and TPCK. The forms in which they capture this awareness (e.g., written reflections, concept maps, video analyses, portfolios) need to be portable into their beginning teacher careers to encourage life-long learning, goal-setting, and teacher research. Second, in learning contexts for practicing teachers, we suggest focusing on content knowledge, specifically new perspectives within literacy such as new literacies and critical literacy, in order to create cognitive conflict within teachers' minds. Because these new perspectives on literacy are intertwined with the evolving technology in society, the veteran teachers, in turn, must tackle issues of technology in the English discipline and, ultimately, begin to develop TCK, TPK, and E-TPCK.

References

Banister, S., & Ross, C. (2005–2006). From high school to college: How prepared are teacher candidates for technology integration? *Journal of Computing in Teacher Education, 22*(2), 75–80.

Borko, H., & Putnam, R. T. (1996a). Expanding a teacher's knowledge base: A cognitive psychological perspective on professional development. In T. R. Guskey & M. Huberman (eds), *Professional development in education* (pp. 35–65). New York: Teachers College.

Borko, H., & Putnam, R. T. (1996b). Learning to teach. In D. C. Berliner & R. C. Calfee (eds), *Handbook of educational psychology* (pp. 673–708). New York: Macmillan.

Bowman, C. A. (2000). Infusing technology-based instructional frameworks in the methods courses: A response to Pope and Golub. *Contemporary Issues in Technology and Teacher Education.* Retrieved January 28, 2002, from http://www.citejournal.org/vol1/iss1/currentissues/english/article2.htm.

Bransford, J. D., & Schwartz, D. L. (1999). Rethinking transfer: A simple proposal with multiple implications. In A. Iran-Nejad & P. D. Pearson (eds), *Review of research in education* (pp. 61–100). Washington, DC: American Educational Research Association.

Bransford, J. D., Brown, A. L., & Cocking, R. R. (eds). (2000). *How people learn: Brain, mind, experience, and school.* Washington, DC: National Academy Press.

Bromley, K. (2006). Technology and writing. In M. C. McKenna, L. D. Labbo, R. D. Kieffer, & D. Reinking (eds), *International handbook of literacy and technology, volume II* (pp. 349–353). Mahway, NJ: Lawrence Erlbaum Associates.

Cope, B., & Kalantzis, M., for the New London Group. (eds). (2000). *Multiliteracies: Literacy learning and the design of social futures.* London: Routledge.

Cuban, L. (2001). *Oversold and underused: Computers in the classroom.* Cambridge, MA: Harvard University Press.

Delpit, L. D. (1995). *Other people's children: Cultural conflict in the classroom.* New York: New Press.

Dexter, S., Doering, A. H., & Riedel, E. S. (2006). Content-area specific technology integration: A model for educating teachers. *Journal of Technology and Teacher Education, 14*(2), 325–345.

Doering, A., & Beach, R. (2002). Preservice English teachers acquiring literacy practices through technology tools in a practicum experience. *Language, Learning and Technology, 6*(3), 127–146.

Doering, A., Hughes, J. E., & Huffman, D. (2003). Preservice teachers: Are we thinking with technology? *Journal of Research on Technology in Education, 35*(3), 342–361.

Dutt-Doner, K., Allen, S. M., & Corcoran, D. (2005). Transforming student learning by preparing the next generation of teachers for type II technology integration. *Computers in the Schools, 22*(3/4), 63–75.

Fairclough, N. (1989). *Language and power.* London: Longman.

Fairclough, N. (1995). *Critical discourse analysis.* Boston: Addison Wesley.

Freire, P. (1970). *Pedagogy of the oppressed.* New York: Herder and Herder.

Gladwell, M. (2002). *The tipping point: How little things can make a big difference.* Boston: Back Bay Books.

Hobbs, R. (2006). Multiple visions of multimedia literacy: Emerging areas of synthesis. In M. C. McKenna, L. D. Labbo, R. D. Kieffer, & D. Reinking (eds), *International handbook of literacy and technology, volume II* (pp. 15–28). Mahway, NJ: Lawrence Erlbaum Associates.

Hughes, J. E. (2000). Teaching English with technology: Exploring teacher learning and practice. Unpublished doctoral dissertation, Michigan State University, East Lansing, MI.

Hughes, J. E. (2003). Toward a model of teachers' technology-learning. *Action in Teacher Education, 24*(4), 10–17.

Hughes, J. E. (2004). Technology learning principles for preservice and in-service teacher education [Electronic version]. *Contemporary Issues on Technology in Education,* 4 from http://www.citejournal.org/vol4/iss3/general/article2.cfm.

Hughes, J. E. (2005). The role of teacher knowledge and learning experiences in forming technology-integrated pedagogy. *Journal of Technology and Teacher Education, 13*(2), 277–302.

King, K. P. (2002). Educational technology professional development as transformative learning opportunities. *Computers & Education, 39*(3), 283–297.

Kist, W. (2005). *New literacies in action: Teaching and learning in multiple media.* New York: Teachers College Press.

Lankshear, C., & Knobel, M. (2003). *New literacies: Changing knowledge and classroom learning.* Buckingham, England: Open University Press.

Leu, D J., Jr. (2000). Literacy and technology: Deictic consequences for literacy education in an information age. In M. L. Kamil, P. Mosenthal, P. D. Pearson, & R. Barr (eds), *Handbook of reading research, volume III.* Mahway, NJ: Lawrence Erlbaum.

Leu, D J., Jr. (2006). New literacies, reading research, and the challenges of change: A deictic perspective (NRC Presidential Address). In J. Hoffman, D. Schallert, C. M. Fairbanks, J. Worthy, & B. Maloch (eds), *The 55th yearbook of the National Reading Conference* (pp. 1–20). Milwaukee, WI: National Reading Conference. Video available: http://www.newliteracies.uconn.edu/nrc/don_leu_2005html.

Leu, D. J., Jr., Kinzer, C. K., Coiro, J. L., & Cammack, D. W. (2004). Toward a theory of new literacies emerging from the Internet and other information and communication technologies. In R. B. Ruddell & N. J. Unrau (eds), *Theoretical models and processes of reading* (5th edn, pp. 1570–1613). Newark, DE: International Reading Association.

Leu, D. J., Mallette, M. H., Karchmer, R. A., & Kara-Soteriou, J. (2005). Contextualizing the new literacies of information and communication technologies in theory, research, and practice. In R. A. Karchmer, M. H. Mallette, J. Kara-Soteriou, & D. J. Leu (eds), *Innovative approaches to literacy education: Using the Internet to support new literacies* (pp. 1–10). Newark, DE: International Reading Association.

Lortie, D. (1975). *Schoolteacher.* Chicago: University of Chicago Press.

Luke, A. (2000). Critical literacy in Australia: A matter of context and standpoint. *Journal of Adolescent and Adult Literacy, 43*(5), 448–461.

Luke, A., & Freebody, P. (1997). The social practices of reading. In S. Muspratt, A. Luke, & P. Freebody (eds), *Constructing critical literacies: Teaching and learning textual practice.* Sydney: Allen & Unwin.

Luke, A., & Freebody, P. (1999). Further notes on the four resources model. *Reading online.* Retrieved May, 29, 2006 from http://www.readingonline.org/research/lukefreebody.html.

McGrail, E. (2005). Teachers, technology, and change: English teachers' perspectives. *Journal of Technology and Teacher Education, 13*(1), 5–24.

McGrail, E., & Rozema, R. (2005). Envisioning effective technology integration: A scenario for English education doctoral programs. *Contemporary Issues in Technology and Teacher*

Education. Retrieved February 13, 2006, from http://www.citejournal.org/vol5/iss3/languagearts/article2.cfm.

McKenna, M. C., Labbo, L. D., & Reinking, D. (2003). Effective use of technology in literacy instruction. In L. M. Morrow, L. B. Gambrell, & M. Pressley (eds), *Best practices in literacy instruction* (2nd edn, pp. 307–331). New York: Guilford Press.

McLaren, P. (1989). *Life in schools: An introduction to critical pedagogy in the foundations of education.* New York: Longman.

McNabb, M. L. (2005). Raising the bar on technology research in English language arts. *Journal of Research on Technology in Education, 38*(1), 113–119.

Morrell, E. (2002). Media literacy: Toward a critical pedagogy of popular culture: Literacy development among urban youth. *Journal of Adolescent and Adult Literacy, 46*(1), 72–77.

Piaget, J. (1964/1972). Development and learning. In R. E. Ripple & V. N. Rockcastle (eds), *Piaget rediscovered.* Cornell University: A report of the Conference on Cognitive Studies and Curriculum Development.

Pope, C., & Golub, J. (2000). Preparing tomorrow's English language arts teachers today: Principles and practices for infusing technology. *Contemporary Issues in Technology and Teacher Education.* Retrieved January 28, 2002, from http://www.citejournal.org/vol1/iss1/currentissues/english/article1.htm.

Rogers, R. (2002). "That's what you're here for, you're supposed to know": Teaching and learning critical literacy. *Journal of Adolescent and Adult Literacy, 45*(8), 772–787.

Selfe, C. L. (1999). *Technology and literacy in the twenty-first century: The importance of paying attention.* Carbondale: Southern Illinois University Press.

Shulman, L. S. (1987). Knowledge and teaching: Foundations of the new reform. *Harvard Educational Review, 57*(1), 1–22.

Sprague, D. (2004). Technology and teacher education: Are we talking to ourselves. *Contemporary Issues in Technology and Teacher Education, 3*(4), 353–361. Retrieved May 22, 2006 from http://www.citejournal.org/vol3/iss4/editorial/article1.cfm.

Swenson, J., Rozema, R., Young, C. A., McGrail, E., & Whitin, P. (2005). Beliefs about technology and the preparation of English teachers: Beginning the conversation. *Contemporary Issues in Technology and Teacher Education.* Retrieved February 13, 2006, from http://www.citejournal.org/vol5/iss3/languagearts/article1.cfm.

Wright, V. H., & Wilson, E. K. (2005–2006). From preservice to inservice teaching: A study of technology integration. *Journal of Computing in Teacher Education, 22*(2), 49–56.

Yin, R. K. (1994). *Case study research: Design and methods* (2nd edn). Thousand Oaks, CA: Sage.

5
TPCK
An integrated framework for educating world language teachers

MARCELA VAN OLPHEN

Introduction

Over the last three decades, critical changes have occurred in the field of education. These changes, chiefly driven by rising educational theories, have had an effect on the ways that the learning and teaching of second and foreign languages (L2) are conceptualized and practiced. As educational and intellectual environments move toward more critical and socio-constructivist approaches to teacher education, we ought to consider the scope of the knowledge base of language teachers vis-à-vis current and emerging needs in the world languages education (WLE) field.

Today's teachers are confronted with a broader range of needs than teachers were a few decades ago. These changes affect the body of knowledge that teachers need to have in order to thrive in their profession as well as to promote successful learning experiences among their students. To this end, current research on teacher cognition has been consistently linked to research on pupil cognition. Pupil cognition has also been considered a critical component of research on teacher education (Alton-Lee & Nuthall, 1992; Freeman & Johnson, 2005b; Morine-Dershimer, 2001). Morine-Dershimer (2001) asserts that the strengthening of this linkage stems from experienced teachers who became researchers and whose insightful experiences have added to the development of and discussions in the field.

The knowledge base of world languages teacher education[1] (WLTE) has been under discussion for several decades (Bernhardt & Hammadou, 1987; Schulz, 2000; Tedick & Walker, 1994). Researchers have embarked on a quest for agreement regarding what should constitute the knowledge base of WLTE (Adger, Snow, & Christian, 2002; Freeman & Johnson, 1998, 2005a; Tarone & Allwright, 2005) as well as who is in charge of teacher development (Schulz, 2000). There have been lengthy and fruitful discussions about this important topic. Yet, as Tedick (2005, p. 2) noted when addressing Tarone and Allwright's (2005) response to Freeman and Johnson's (1998) article, in some cases, researchers have "agreed to disagree" about what constitutes the knowledge base for WLTE. Professional and learned associations such as the

107

American Council of Teachers of Foreign Languages (ACTFL) and the Teachers of English to Speakers of Other Languages (TESOL) have undertaken the task of writing standards for students as well as standards for professional preparation. Both ACTFL and TESOL have joined efforts and worked collaboratively with the National Council for Accreditation of Teacher Education (NCATE) to develop program standards for the preparation of world languages teachers.

The ACTFL/NCATE *Program Standards for the Preparation of Foreign Language Teachers* document is structured around six content standards: (1) language linguistics, comparisons; (2) cultures, literatures, cross-disciplinary concepts; (3) language acquisition theories and instructional practices; (4) integration of standards into curriculum and instruction; (5) assessment of languages and cultures; and (6) professionalism. Each standard is further divided into supporting standards, accompanied by explanations and rubrics as well. The TESOL/NCATE *Standards for Accreditation of Initial Programs in P-12 ESL Teacher Education* document is structured around five domains: (1) language, (2) culture, (3) instruction, (4) assessment, and (5) professionalism, at the core. These domains are divided into standards (13 total), which are also broken down into performance indicators (Tables 5.1 and 5.2). These program standards provide a framework from which teacher education programs may draw while outlining what should constitute the knowledge base for world languages teacher candidates.

As teachers and teacher educators prepare to educate new generations, new needs and dimensions arise, as the dynamic nature of the evolving socio-cultural contexts of education is considered. Specifically, the study of world languages teachers' cognition as it relates to their knowledge of educational technology has not received a great deal of attention (Lam, 2000; Rodriguez-van Olphen, 2002). Furthermore, although an opportunity for teacher candidates to experience technology is mentioned as one of the requirements for programs of world languages teacher preparation (ACTFL, 2002, p. 2), neither the ACTFL/NCATE nor the TESOL/NCATE professional preparation standards includes a specific standard that relates to a teacher's understanding of educational technology, computer-assisted language learning (CALL), or the integration of technology into the curriculum. Instead, it is briefly mentioned but not developed as a stand-alone standard.

Table 5.1 ACTFL/NCATE Content Standards for the Preparation of Foreign Language Teachers

Standard 1	Language, Linguistics, Comparisons
Standard 2	Cultures, Literatures, Cross-Disciplinary Concepts
Standard 3	Language Acquisition Theories and Instructional Practices
Standard 4	Integration of Standards into Curriculum and Instruction
Standard 5	Assessment of Languages and Cultures
Standard 6	Professionalism

Table 5.2 TESOL/NCATE Standards for the Accreditation of Initial Programs in P-12 ESL Teacher Education

Domains	Standards
Domain 1: Language	1.a. Describing Language
	1.b. Language Acquisition and Development
Domain 2: Culture	2.a. Nature and Role of Culture
	2.b. Cultural Groups and Identity
Domain 3: Planning, Implementing, and Managing Instruction	3.a. Planning for Standards-Based ESL Content Instruction
	3.b. Managing and Implementing Standards-Based ESL Content Instruction
	3.c. Using Resources Effectively in the ESL and Content Instruction
Domain 4: Assessment	4.a. Issues of Assessment for ESL
	4.b. Language Proficiency and Assessment
	4.c. Classroom-Based Assessment for ESL
Domain 5: Professionalism	5.a. ESL Research and History
	5.b. Partnerships and Advocacy
	5.c. Professional Development and Collaboration

This chapter attempts to advance the current understanding of the kinds of knowledge world languages teachers need to have to integrate technology in thoughtful and pedagogically sound ways into the curriculum. To accomplish this goal, I examine Koehler and Mishra's (2005) concept of technological pedagogical content knowledge (TPCK) as a framework for a sound integration of technology into the curriculum as it relates to WLTE. The following sections look at (a) two of Shulman's (1987) categories of the knowledge base for teachers—content knowledge (CK) and pedagogical content knowledge (PCK)—as they relate to world languages teachers' knowledge and as predecessors of TPCK; (b) technological content knowledge (TCK) as it relates to CALL; and (c) Koehler and Mishra's (2005) concept of TPCK as it pertains to current research about teachers' cognition and the integration of technology into the teaching and learning of foreign and second languages. Although CK, PCK, TCK, and TPCK have been described in different sections for organizational purposes, they "exist in a state of dynamic equilibrium" (Koehler & Mishra, 2005, p. 14) and often involve overlapping or related attributes.

Content knowledge in foreign language teacher education

Shulman (1987) explains his definition of CK within teachers' scholarship in their content discipline. That is, CK is referred to as the "knowledge, understanding, skill, and disposition that are to be learned by school children" (p. 9). Drawing from Shulman's definition of CK, world languages educators have to develop the knowledge, understanding, skills, and disposition of their target language. Moreover, students seeking to learn another language need to develop a working knowledge, understanding, and disposition, as well as a set of skills, for their target language while learning to communicate across cultures. Thus, the CK of language educators consists of, but should not be limited to, proficiency in and knowledge about the target language and its culture(s).

Richards (1998) proposes six domains of expertise, knowledge, and skill for second language teacher education as a blueprint for designing programs and advancing professional development. The components of two of those domains, (a) subject matter knowledge and (b) communication skills and language proficiency, are closely related to CK. For Richards, subject matter knowledge involves a teacher's understanding of (a) the nature of language and language use, (b) the nature of second language learning, and (c) approaches to language teaching, curriculum development, testing and evaluation, and materials development (p. 15). The remaining four domains are discussed in the next section of this chapter, as they are more closely related to PCK.

Lafayette (1993), in his overview of the specialist education that world languages teachers need to achieve, states that CK in WLTE includes (a) language analysis, (b) language proficiency, and (c) an understanding of civilization and culture. These components are not simple pieces of the world languages teachers' CK. Instead, each is made up of a complex web of interconnected elements that I will not address further here (for more information, see Schulz, 2000). When these components are taken into consideration, CK for teachers broadly encompasses the study of language-specific linguistics (morphology, phonetics, phonology, pragmatics, second language acquisition, semantics, socio-linguistics, and syntax) and the development of both cross-cultural awareness and near-native language proficiency. Ideally, CK for language teachers includes all the necessary elements that help language learners to communicate both verbally and non-verbally across linguistic and cultural borders. Understanding how second languages are acquired has a direct effect on how languages should be taught. The next section, which offers a brief and non-exhaustive account of current approaches to second language acquisition (SLA), aims to provide some insights into the basics of SLA.

Current approaches to SLA

Current research in SLA[2] has shed light on the teaching and learning of languages. Understanding the theoretical underpinnings of current approaches to language learning and teaching is a crucial component of effective language teaching and, by extension, to meaningful integration of technology.

Chomsky (1959), reviewing Skinner's work, criticized existing approaches to language learning and proposed that languages are not learned solely by memorization. Instead, human minds possess a language acquisition device (LAD) that enables children to learn the grammar rules of their language. Hymes (1961) foregrounds the importance of language use in social settings as it pertains to language performance. Chomsky (1965) made the distinction between competence and performance. According to Chomsky (1965), competence refers to the knowledge of how a linguistic system works, how the grammar rules and syntax work, whereas performance refers to the person's ability to produce language. In other words, competence addresses what one knows about the language, and performance, what one can do with the language. Drawing from these two concepts, linguists elaborated on the role of social interactions (Halliday, 1975), and Chomsky's definition evolved into a broader notion, communicative competence (Berns, 1990; Campbell & Wales, 1970; Canale & Swain, 1979; Hymes, 1972; Savignon, 1972). Canale and Swain (1979) state that communicative competence consists of four components: (a) grammatical competence, (b) sociolinguistic competence, (c) discourse competence, and (d) strategic competence.

Krashen (1981, 1982) proposed the monitor model as a theory of SLA. According to this model, adults acquire language structures in a predictable order provided that they are exposed to comprehensible input and within a low anxiety environment while an internal monitor acquires and makes sense of correct language functions. The Monitor Model is organized around five hypotheses. These hypotheses are (a) the acquisition-learning hypothesis, (b) the natural order hypothesis, (c) the input hypothesis, (d) the monitor hypothesis, and (e) the affective filter hypothesis. Despite the wide criticism this model has received and the controversies raised, it has provided the theoretical basis for the Natural Approach and has had a strong influence on classroom practices.

Long (1980, 1983), when proposing his Interaction Hypothesis, contends that native speakers make modifications to interact with non-native speakers. These modifications have two dimensions: (a) the adjustments made in order to prevent glitches when communicating, and (b) the adjustments made to repair communication when glitches happen. Also, he states that input can be made comprehensible by (a) simplifying the input (i.e., using cognates and familiar vocabulary), (b) using linguistic and extralinguistic features such as gestures and background knowledge, and (c) modifying the structural interactions of conversations with non-native speakers.

Swain (1985, 1995) takes one step further than Krashen and Long and proposes the Output Hypothesis. She argues that input alone is not enough to acquire native-like language competence. Swain, while conducting a study of productive skills of French immersion students in Canada, observed that comprehensible input alone did not help students to move to higher levels of language proficiency. These observations served as a springboard to claim that language production or output that is accurate is necessary to reach higher levels of language proficiency.

Cummings' theories of bilingualism and cognition emphasize that being bilingual poses a cognitive advantage and that the first language provides the foundation for the acquisition of the second language. Cummings' (1979, 1980, 1981) concepts of basic interpersonal communication skills (BICS), cognitive academic language proficiency (CALP), separate underlying proficiency (SUP), and common underlying proficiency (CUP) are major contributions to the understanding of bilingual education as well as to dispelling the myths about a first language hindering the acquisition of second languages.

Finally, but not least important, it is necessary to point out the role of Sociocultural Theory. Vygotsky (1978) highlighted the importance of social interactions as they pertain to language development. Within this theoretical framework, language development is socially constructed and is as much a cognitive process as a social process, as opposed to the theory of Piaget, who stressed the importance of individual cognitive development as a relatively solitary act (stages). According to Vygotsky (1978) learning occurs within a "zone of proximal development" defined as "the distance between the actual developmental level as determined by independent problem solving and the level of potential development as determined through problem solving under adult guidance or in collaboration with more capable peers" (p. 86). Therefore, a language teacher working within this framework will provide a classroom learning environment that fosters communicative pair or group work and that provides ample opportunities for students of varied proficiency levels to interact within a safe and rich environment.

Pedagogical content knowledge (PCK)

According to Shulman (1987) PCK, a special fusion between content and pedagogical knowledge, "represents the blending of content and pedagogy into an understanding of how particular topics, problems, or issues are organized, represented, and adapted to the diverse interests and abilities of learners, and represented for instruction" (p. 8). To this end, Shulman introduces the concept of pedagogical reasoning as the ability of teachers to progress from their role as learners as they make sense of, reorganize, and elucidate the subject matter in original ways so that it can be learned by students. Hence, building upon what constitutes the CK for language teachers, which is the form of knowledge that calls for all the necessary elements to help language learners to communicate both verbally and non-verbally across linguistic and cultural borders, PCK for WLTE refers to what teachers know about teaching the target language to empower students to communicate across linguistic and cultural borders.

Teacher educator researchers have long discussed the PCK for language teachers as a relevant category of the knowledge base within WLTE and have tried to promote PCK-relevant research that advances current understandings in the field. For instance, Lafayette (1993) recommends that research be performed to specify the PCK of foreign and second language teachers. Further, he questions the similarities and differences among fields (social studies, math, science, etc.) and languages (French, German, Latin, Spanish, etc.) and how they interact when trying to outline PCK for foreign language teachers. Wing (1993) contends that it is imperative for teachers to understand the content from the student's perspective as well as to scrutinize precedent and up-to-date teaching and learning practices if they are to advance in their preparation as foreign language teachers. To this end, Wing discusses Jarvis' (1983) observations and warns the teacher education community about relegating PCK to methods courses instead of incorporating it throughout the teachers' professional education. Thus, language teacher education programs should sustain the pedagogical reasoning development of teachers as an ongoing matter.

Richards' (1998) four remaining domains draw from Shulman's (1987) concepts of PCK and pedagogical reasoning. In this regard, Richards' proposed domains are (a) theories of teaching, (b) teaching skills, (c) pedagogical reasoning, and (d) contextual knowledge. The aim of these domains is to provide second language teacher education with an agenda that promotes and strengthens the teachers' engagement in the exploration of knowledge, beliefs, attitudes, and thinking as they inform their teaching endeavors.

To the same effect, Freeman and Johnson (1998) raise awareness of the need for more articulated approaches to bridge content and pedagogical knowledge. They contend that the activity of teaching itself, the teacher who performs it, the contexts in which teaching occurs, and the pedagogy involved must be the core of the knowledge base. Then PCK becomes a crucial component of WLTE within this emerging reconceptualization.

Technological content knowledge (TCK)

TCK pertains to what teachers know about how technology and subject matter knowledge are interconnected (Koehler & Mishra, 2005). Specifically, TCK for foreign language teachers is defined as the body of knowledge that teachers have about their target language and its culture and how technology is used to represent this knowledge. In order to promote curriculum integration and technology-capable students and teachers, the International Society of Technology in Education has published the *National Educational Technology Standards for Students: Connecting curriculum and technology* (NETS), a comprehensive document for connecting curriculum and technology. Among the aims of this project are refining and developing sets of standards for students and for the professional preparation of teachers. Other important components of this document are the sections that specifically provide examples of connecting curriculum and technology by demonstrating the effective infusion of technology into content areas. In addition to national efforts such as this, researchers have widely studied the impact that new technologies have when foreign languages are learned, giving birth to a new field of study that is referred to as computer-assisted language learning (CALL). CALL research looks at how technology shapes foreign language educators and assists them in representing content knowledge. Understanding the contributions that CALL can make to the field of foreign language education is essential for the development of TCK among teacher candidates. In fact, one of the key elements for integrating new technology is that teachers understand how the technology can enhance the learning process (van Olphen, 2003).

Impact of computer-assisted language learning (CALL)

During the last decade, a wealth of research has documented the impact of technology on language learning. The pervasive presence of technology in L2 teaching and learning and WLTE triggers the need for developing pedagogy that benefits from it (Chapelle, 2005). Evidence of these efforts exists in the body of research published in specialized scholarly journals such as *CALICO, Language Learning and Technology*, and *System*, not to mention research studies that have been published in general second language education and applied linguistics journals such as *Foreign Language Annals, Modern Language Journal, TESOL Quarterly*, and *Studies in Second Language Acquisition.* Specifically, researchers have looked at CALL and its impact on both the teaching and learning processes (Bax, 2003; Bush & Terry, 1997b; Chapelle, 1998; Egbert, Paulus, & Nakamichi, 2002; Garrett, 1991; Salaberry, 2000; Warschauer, 2002). It is fundamental for teachers to understand how CALL shapes their teaching practices. The contributions of CALL to the field of foreign language education are crucial to the understanding of TCK. This section describes the growing body of research as it pertains to CALL and its impact on second and foreign language learning.

The following account, although brief, offers examples and an overview of how new technologies can shape the ways teachers represent their subject matter knowledge. Engaging language students in contextualized and meaningful conversations in the target language is always a challenge for the language teacher, not to mention providing students with a challenging environment that sustains the development of this skill. By means of synchronous (real-time) communication, researchers have found a way to allow students to "virtually" speak to one another. Findings from studies that document students' progress when exposed to synchronous networked discussions (such as those in Internet chatrooms) are consistent across the board. The students' writing, reading, and conversational skills seem to benefit from the use of these real-time networks (Beauvois, 1997). Asynchronous environments (such as email) can also be useful for extending conversational classroom practice (Gonglewski, 1999).

Finding authentic and up-to-date materials for practicing listening comprehension used to be an ordeal. Now the World Wide Web offers an ample spectrum of authentic materials for teachers and students. These materials are most commonly found in the format of audio files, online dictionaries with sound, digitized short stories, etc. Gonglewski (1999) states that these materials facilitate the implementation of standards and promote students' success in reaching benchmarks.

Like opportunities for listening comprehension, vocabulary acquisition and retention are issues that teachers find troublesome. Each new chapter of a foreign language text features a myriad of words and expressions that students need to master. Ideally, students should not learn vocabulary by rote memorization. Instead, they should have opportunities to infer the meanings of these new words and expressions. Fortunately, the implementation of hypertext and hypermedia applications has proven to be of great benefit for the acquisition and retention of new vocabulary. Grace (1998) looked at vocabulary retention when presented in contexts that promote inference instead of word-to-word translation while addressing the specific design of software for CALL.

Reading is another important skill that both teachers and students work diligently to improve. Reading in the second language is not the same as achieving literacy in the first language (L1) (Martinez-Lage, 1997). In an attempt to elucidate how to help students develop their second language reading skills, researchers have looked at the effects of multimedia packages, hypermedia technologies, CALL software, and other media. For instance, Hong (1997) evaluated the effectiveness of multimedia computer-assisted reading in business Chinese. The findings suggest that learners performed more efficiently with the support of multimedia technology. Martinez-Lage (1997) examined the application of interactive hypermedia technology to the teaching of reading modern languages.

A common example of technology integration in the language classroom is the facilitation of the students' writing process. Researchers have found the use of Microsoft Word (and its editing tools) to be beneficial for both student-teacher and peer-review activities. Another example is the use of concordancing and other packages in teaching both English as a second language and modern languages (Chavez, 1997; Howells, 1998). Telecommunication networks have also been proven to enhance the students' writing process, particularly when students had to write email messages and respond to those they received (Allen & Thompson, 1995). In general, researchers have found that asynchronous networks help to advance students' writing skills while providing a low-anxiety atmosphere (Beauvois, 1997).

New technologies have expanded the horizon for second and foreign language classrooms. The Internet, chatrooms, email, video-conferencing, and digital communications have shaped the ways in which teachers introduce culture to their students. When students are learning a second language, a tight connection to an understanding of that culture is important. One of the best assets that teachers can have for teaching culture is access to authentic materials and environments that, in most cases, are physically far away. New technologies grant both the students and teachers opportunities to build cultural bridges. Kern (1998), who studied a group of students using email, states that networked environments cultivate the development of cultural literacy. Another example is Kubota's (1999) successful implementation of four projects using the World Wide Web and word processing to address cultural topics and to raise cultural awareness in an intermediate Japanese college classroom. Sehlaoui (2001) examined the use of computer technology to develop critical cross-cultural awareness. Pearson (2004) proposes a web portfolio to strengthen cultural awareness while teaching Spanish reading. Drawing from research studies, Pearson contends that this type of Internet-based project to raise cultural awareness helps students increase linguistic proficiency. All these findings suggest that a major strength of CALL is its potential for opening doors to connect people and to build communities while promoting cross-cultural communicative competence.

As newer technologies such as podcasting, blogging, text-messaging, and digital video emerge, research studies will follow that provide information about how these potential tools affect language learning as well as how they shape teaching practices. CALL has much to offer the field of foreign language education. It is imperative that this body of knowledge becomes part of the knowledge base of teacher candidates. If teachers are not fully aware of these findings and if their beliefs make them hesitant to incorporate this technology into their teaching practice, they will be unable to integrate technology in a pedagogically sound way. It is vital that we use the emerging research about how CALL affects the teaching and learning of languages to inform teachers' PCK. The combination of PCK and the impact of CALL leads one to consider the conceptual framework designed by Mishra and Koehler (2006) for educational technology as a robust structure for advancing the current understanding of teacher cognition, as the fields of second language teacher education and educational technology intersect.

Technological pedagogical content knowledge (TPCK)

Mishra and Koehler (2006) contend that "thoughtful, pedagogical uses of technology require the development of a complex, situated form of knowledge we call *Technological Pedagogical Content Knowledge*" (p. 1017). Koehler and Mishra (2005) coined the term TPCK as they attempted to provide a framework that incorporates the indispensable trait of an educator's knowledge as he/she integrates technology into his/her teaching practice at the same time as attending to the complexities of this particular kind of knowledge. TPCK is an emergent form of knowledge as a response to the growing need for a scaffold that supports the sound integration of technology. TPCK is not an extension or appendix of content, pedagogy, and technology but rather a complex form of knowledge that blends all three components (CK, PCK, and TCK) and the dynamic relationships that exist among them. Furthermore, Mishra and Koehler (2006) assert that "there is no single technological solution that applies for every teacher, every course, or every view of teaching" (p. 1029). Thus, teachers' knowledge and their ability to integrate technology into their pedagogy are intricate and multidimensional phenomena.

These phenomena are not made any less complex when analyzed within the context of second language teacher education. Following Mishra and Koehler's (2006) explanation of how TPCK lies at the core of teaching with technology, it is possible to assert that the foundation of good language teaching with technology requires (a) an understanding of how linguistic and cultural concepts can be represented using technology; (b) educational approaches to language teaching that draw from socio-constructivist philosophies to develop students' language and cultural competence; (c) an awareness of what facilitates or hinders the acquisition of language and the development of language competence and how technology, specifically CALL or computer-mediated communication (CMC), can revamp common problems that students ordinarily face; (d) an awareness of students' previous knowledge, and particularly a knowledge of second language acquisition (SLA) and cognitive development theories; and (e) an understanding of how current and emerging technologies can be used to advance present knowledge and to develop new epistemologies and sustain previous ones.

Grosse (1993) analyzed 157 foreign language methods course syllabi to gain a better understanding of the knowledge base for WLTE. Her analysis revealed integration of technology as one of the five areas that need further development in the world languages methods courses. These findings emphasize the need for teacher educator and teacher education programs to prepare world languages teachers to opt for, adapt, implement, and even design meaningful technology-based activities that are aligned with current approaches to language learning and teaching. That is, meaningful technology-based materials and CALL should be rooted in the theoretical underpinnings of the social construction of knowledge.

Teaching and learning languages through CALL is an ever-evolving process that is intertwined with CK, PCK, and TCK. Within Mishra and Koehler's (2006) framework, a change in one of the components generates a change in the others. These changes happen as compensatory mechanisms to maintain the dynamic equilibrium. For example, consider a Spanish writing class where the students have to write and edit an essay about cross-cultural differences between holidays in the U.S. and in Spain. Writing the essay in Spanish (stylistics, syntax, cultural differences—i.e., content) drives the types of representations to be used (analysis of Spanish writing samples, semantic maps, visual representations of how to structure writing in Spanish, editing exercises—i.e., pedagogy), plus the necessary technologies to influence them. In this case, the Internet, web-based resources, Microsoft Word and its "track changes" tool, wikis, or even blogs would fit the purpose for interactively creating, developing, and writing the essay. Had the teacher not had all these technologies at hand, she/he would have to implement other ways of representing content. Obviously, this change when representing knowledge would also generate an adaptation or modification at the pedagogical level. As Mishra and Koehler (2006) note, newer technologies upset the status quo and demand that teachers reconfigure their current understanding of technology as well as of the three components. Such is the case for the example above in the event that a teacher decides to use only Word and the "track changes" tool in contrast to seeking to integrate newer technologies like wikis and/or blogs.

Raven McCrory's (see Chapter 9) example of a virtual dissection illustrates an important point. Specifically, she states that technology should be used to carry out activities that would otherwise be impossible to accomplish. In the same vein, world languages students often cannot afford studying abroad and being exposed to the magnificent art in museums such as the Louvre, the Prado, or even national art galleries. In this case, a virtual tour of a museum or culturally relevant places can afford students a better understanding of their target language. As Neal Grandgenett (see Chapter 7) points out, it is a matter of thinking imaginatively about "how" technology may support teaching and learning more than focusing too much on "what" technologies may be used. In addition to Mishra and Koheler's (2006) theoretical framework, there have been other attempts to propose curricular models for the meaningful integration of technology (Angeli & Valanides, 2005; Otero *et al.*, 2005; Wildner, 1999). Angeli and Valanides (2005), in their study about preservice elementary teachers as information and communication designers, propose an instructional design system (IDS) model to develop information and communication technology (ICT)-related PCK. They contend that this model was effective in developing some aspects of ICT-related PCK. Otero *et al.* (2005) also provide a critical framework drawing from the concept of situated practice and communities of discourse in their college of education. In their study, they present and discuss how understandings of meaningful technology use were negotiated among graduate students and faculty through their interactions. Wildner (1999) uses national technology standards and institutional features as a framework to propose a model of technology integration into foreign language preservice teacher education. This model provides graduates with a pedagogical and technological foundation that enhances their teaching practices and, in turn, their future students' learning. These curricular models all have their strengths and weaknesses, but they provide guidance to administrators and faculty who have to update teacher preparation programs.

Mishra and Koheler's (2006) concept of TPCK provides a robust framework for professionals seeking to understand the complexities of meaningful integrative approaches for technologies as they pertain to the knowledge base of second language teacher education.

TPCK, the knowledge base of world language teacher education, and technology integration into the second language classroom: current trends and practices

Traditionally, research involving technology use in the field of world languages has focused on the learner and the learning process—particularly on how to enhance the students' learning and the teachers' practices (Beauvois, 1998; Biesenbach-Lucas, 2005; Borras & Lafayette, 1994; Bush, 1997; Bush & Terry, 1997a; Chambers, 2005; Cui & Bull, 2005; Davis & Lyman-Hager, 1997; Horst, Cobb, & Nicolae, 2005; Joiner, Bush, & Terry, 1997; Ware & Kramsch, 2005; Weinberg, Peters, & Sarma, 2005). Conversely, little attention has been paid to the processes that teacher candidates experience as they learn to integrate new technologies. The study of world languages teachers' cognition as they learn to integrate technology into their practices is an emerging area of research. Evidence of this is the scarcity of empirical research on how foreign language teachers learn to integrate technology into their curricula (Lam, 2000; Rodriguez-van Olphen, 2002). In fact, in September, 2000, Y. Zhao and S. Tella underscored this shortcoming when they called for papers for a Special Issue of *Language Learning and Technology* with a theme of Technology and (Language) Teacher Education that was to be published a year later. The editors highly recommended that potential contributors submit original research that focuses on teachers' integration of technologies into their pedagogical practices and necessary conditions that should be met to successfully integrate technology, among others.

Kassen and Higgins (1997), when addressing technology integration in the WLTE, identify three central issues in the preparation of WL teachers: (a) comfort level, (b) technology integration, and (c) critical skills to use technology. Moreover, they state that "Integration entails not only the use of the computers in the classroom but also its use to support curriculum goals" (p. 266). From their perspective, the integration of technology should be cultivated within a program's goals. Likewise, Rubio and Sedersten (2001), when presenting an account of how they integrated technology throughout their program, discuss the importance of helping students develop pedagogical knowledge. Ely (1994) points out that when making decisions regarding how to prepare second language teachers, the challenge is how to help them develop their pedagogical belief system. This belief system should serve as a springboard for teachers to develop their personal and professional guidelines, which will inform their decision-making process. As Freeman (1996) notes, teacher decision-making has provided researchers with "a cognitive map of teachers' mental world and intentions while teaching" (p. 361). Teachers' thinking is divided into two broad categories: (a) preactive decisions and (b) interactive decisions. Language teachers who are integrating technologies make decisions prior to teaching (preactive) in light of their subject matter and their knowledge about how to make the content more readily available to students. For instance, during this decision-making process, TCK is involved as teachers use chat tools to present content. Thus, the use of chat tools modifies the way teachers present content to the students. While teaching, teachers make decisions (interactive) that shape their teaching practices.

The dynamic amalgamation of CK, TCK, and PCK inform and shape each other. To this end, Shaffer and Richardson (2004), who studied student teachers' views of the use of information and communication technologies (ICT), report how the students came to realize that they had to change their teaching practices as a result of the use of ICT. Specifically, participating students linked the use of ICT with a transformation in the nature of classroom exchanges and the restructuring of teaching and learning.

Reasons that hinder or promote the integration of technology by teachers

The survey "Technology Counts '99: Building the Digital Curriculum" showed that just 29 percent of the teachers participating stated that they had more than five hours of technology training in curriculum integration during the past year. Furthermore, this report states that a shortage of training is the chief barrier that deprives teachers from integrating technology into their subject matter. This is consistent with previous and more current findings (Akins, 1992; Lam, 2000). Preservice teachers' methods courses are generally taught separately from those education courses that provide training in technology; this arrangement does not facilitate the meaningful and contextualized integration of technology. In some cases, uncertainty becomes an obstacle for teachers who seek to integrate new technologies. The sources of these uncertainties vary along the continuum offered by social, temporal, and spatial factors. Shaffer and Richardson (2004) found that although preservice teachers who participated in their study showed a strong desire to infuse technology into their teaching, they were uncertain as to what extent and how frequently this should happen. Lam (2000) found that teachers were reluctant to use technology for teaching because of a lack of (a) knowledge about teaching second language with computers, (b) confidence that was due to an absence of the necessary skills, (c) sustained access to computers, and (d) understanding of students' needs. Obviously, some of these teachers felt very insecure about using technology because of social and academic factors.

Ertmer and Hruskocy (1999), in a study where teachers were provided with professional and instructional support through in-service workshops, found an increase in the teachers' instructional and professional use of computers. Some of Lam's (2000) participants decided to use technology because it motivates students and offers a different mode of introducing materials. Ma, Anderson, and Streith's (2005) findings suggest that preservice teachers' perceptions of the usefulness of technology had a significant impact on their intentions to use it. This is consistent with Sime and Priestley's (2005) findings. The participants reflected on technology integrated in teaching and used in meaningful situations vis-à-vis technology used as an end in itself. Basically, if teachers see and understand how technology can affect the content to be represented, they are more likely to integrate it into their teaching. Similarly, the teachers' level of reflectivity can be considered another factor that promotes the meaningful integration of technology. Zhao, Pugh, and Sheldon (2002) found that when teachers are more reflective, they are more likely to integrate technology consciously and in accordance with their pedagogical beliefs. It seems that when there are no broken links among CK, PCK, and TCK, the integration of technology naturally slides into TPCK. Another way of presenting this idea is that when the integration of technology is conceived within the TPCK framework, each component falls into place. That is, all three components are assumed to be interconnected and to be dynamically balanced.

But what can be done?

Bailey *et al.* (1996), when examining Lortie's (1975) idea of "apprenticeship of observation" and how the 13,000 hours that students have spent throughout their K-12 school years shapes and informs the ways in which teachers teach, make a strong case for modeling the types of behavior that teacher educators would like to encourage for preservice teachers. An example of the initiatives that teacher educators have undertaken to provide both fellow teacher educators as well as language teachers with learning opportunities is the National Foreign Language Resource Center (NFLRC) at Iowa State University. This center's mission is to sustain opportunities for educators' professional development as well as to advance student learning of foreign languages across the nation. Specifically, the NFLRC provides professional development institutes that model sound integration of technology for both K-12 language teachers and faculty involved in teacher preparation courses.

Another example of projects for professional development that promote good models for pre- and in-service teachers is The Technology Collaboratives (TechCo) for Simultaneous Renewal in Teacher Education project. According to Thompson, Schmidt, and Davis (2003), TechCo is a collaborative project that draws from Goodland's (1994) theory of simultaneous renewal. This project envisions technology as a tool that facilitates renewal in both K-12 and teacher education programs. To accomplish this project's goals, the College of Education at Iowa State University (ISU) and four K-6 schools work in concert to integrate technology into both teacher education and K-6 curriculum. In addition, New Visions in Action, also hosted at the NFLRC (Iowa State University), has identified exemplary programs that prepare preservice teachers to integrate technology-based activities and assessments for the elementary and/or secondary classrooms.[3] To this end,

Chuang and Rosenbusch (2005) stress the importance of faculty teaching education courses that model the meaningful uses of technology and learning environments.

An additional example of what universities can do to support teacher education faculty and teachers is The Florida Center for Instructional Technology (FCIT), located in the College of Education, University of South Florida (Tampa). The center is funded by the Florida Department of Education, Office of Instructional Technology, and USF, and exists in part to keep the College of Education abreast of pedagogical developments with relation to technology. FCIT staff members and graduate assistants offer training and support to USF faculty and preservice teachers via a "one-stop-shop" regardless of instructional need, topic, or content. In addition, the center maintains and coordinates a wide variety of teaching and learning resources (online and on site), and promotes workshops, training sessions, and classroom techniques that model best teaching practices to assist Florida's schools and districts with technology integration. As the primary support center for teachers and teacher educators at USF, the FCIT offers learning opportunities in a supportive and diverse environment, not only at the university, but also throughout K-20 education in the state of Florida (for further information visit http://fcit.usf.edu/) (J. Takacs, personal communication, October 21, 2006).

The use of web-based courseware tools such as WebCT and BlackBoard in methods courses and practica has proved beneficial for world languages teacher candidates (WLTC). Kamhi-Stein (2000), who studied the use of WebCT by TESOL candidates in a practicum, states that the use of computer-mediated communication in a practicum can help teacher candidates learn more about integrating technologies and develop a reflective approach to technology integration. In the same vein, van Olphen (2007a) reported that WLTC found that the use of WebCT in a methods course was beneficial; it also promoted reflective practice when used as a medium to develop teacher candidates' digital portfolios (van Olphen, 2007b). Participants in van Olphen's (2007a) study also reported that the use of web-based courseware tools helped them increase their confidence in the use of technology while increasing their awareness of how technology could be integrated into the world languages classroom. Similarly, Asan (2003) focused on preservice teachers who used a self-paced multimedia tutorial that had two modes of information delivery—traditional and interactive multimedia; the interactive multimedia group, but not the traditional group, responded positively to integrating technology. Thus, teacher education programs can provide preservice teachers and in-service teachers with models and opportunities to achieve professional experience in learning how to integrate technology in pedagogically sound ways.

Conclusion

The adoption of the TPCK framework provides educators of second language teachers with a venue to enhance classrooms with technology while making them more culturally and linguistically valuable. Furthermore, TPCK offers a conceptual blueprint for language teacher education programs and language teacher educators who envision the seamless and pedagogically meaningful integration of technology in their programs. Specific examples have illustrated the interconnected nature of how language and culture, the teachers' understanding of how to translate this subject matter to their students, and the teachers' understanding of how different technologies shape and inform content and representations within second and foreign languages. Research findings indicate that when teachers have an understanding of TPCK, they have the foundation to enhance second language learning with a purpose (Rodriguez-van Olphen, 2002). Conversely, if teachers do not have a solid knowledge base, technology becomes one more object—or simply an ornament—in the lesson plan. In sum, the concept of TPCK, when used as a framework, is intended to further our understanding of foreign language teachers' cognition to achieve a sound infusion of technology into their content areas, which in turn advances students' second language competence.

Notes

1. I have used the term "world languages teacher education" to refer to English as a second language (ESL), foreign languages (FL), and English as a foreign language (EFL) teacher education to reflect some of the commonalities, shared body of knowledge, and interrelatedness among ESL, EFL, and FL teacher education. However, generalizations of research findings from one context into another one should be carefully analyzed. For instance, findings about L2 learning in the EFL context should be carefully examined before being generalized to the ESL context and vice versa. For further information on this topic see Bernhardt and Tedick (1991), Bigelow and Tedick (2005), Guntermann (1993), Hammadou (1993), and Tedick, Walker, Lange, Paige, and Jorstad (1993).
2. See Johnson (2004), Ellis (1985, 1997), for further information about SLA.
3. Although this project is no longer funded, the following site provides valuable information, http://www.nflrc.iastate.edu/nva/homepage.html.

References

Adger, C., Snow, C., & Christian, D. (2002). *What teachers need to know about language.* McHenry, IL: Delta Systems and The Center for Applied Linguistics.

Akins, K. (1992). Revolution or rhetoric: Factors affecting teachers' decisions about computers in classrooms. Unpublished (Masters' thesis, University, 1992). *Masters' Abstracts International, 32,* 795

Allen, G., & Thompson, A. (1995). Analysis of the effect of networking on computer-assisted collaborative writing in a fifth grade classroom. *Journal of Educational Computing Research, 12*(1), 65–75.

Alton-Lee, A. G., & Nuthall, G. A. (1992). A generative methodology for classroom research. *Educational Philosophy and Theory: Special Issue on Educational Research Methodology, 24*(2), 29–55.

American Council on the Teaching of Foreign Languages (ACTFL). (2002). ACTFL/NCATE program standards for the preparation of foreign language teachers. Yonkers, NY: Author.

Angeli, C., & Valanides, N. (2005). Preservice elementary teachers as information and communication technology designers: An instructional systems design model based on an expanded view of pedagogical content knowledge. *Journal of Computer Assisted Learning, 21*(4), 292–302.

Asan, A. (2003). School experience course with multimedia in teacher education. *Journal of Computer Assisted Learning, 19*(1), 21–34.

Bailey, K. M., Berghold, B., Braunstein, B., Jagodzinski Fleishchman, N., Holbrook, M. P., Tuman, J. *et al.* (1996). The language learner's autobiography: Examining the "apprenticeship of observation." In D. Freeman & J. C. Richards (eds), *Teacher learning in language teaching* (pp. 11–29). New York: Cambridge University Press.

Bax, S. (2003). CALL—past, present and future. *System, 31*, 13–28.

Beauvois, M. H. (1997). Computer-mediated communication: Technology for improving speaking and writing. In M. D. Bush & R. M. Terry (eds), *Technology-enhanced language learning* (Vol. 1997, pp. 165–213). Lincolnwood, IL: National Textbook Co.

Beauvois, M. H. (1998). Write to speak: The effects of electronic communication on the oral achievement of fourth semester French students. In J. A. Muyskens (ed.), *New ways of learning and teaching: Focus on technology and foreign language education* (pp. 93–115). Boston, MA: Heinle & Heinle.

Bernhardt, E., & Hammadou, J. (1987). A decade of research in foreign language teacher education. *Modern Language Journal, 71*(3), 289–299.

Bernhardt, E., & Tedick, D. J. (1991). On paradoxes and paradigms in language education research. In E. S. Silber (ed.), *Critical issues in foreign language instruction* (pp. 43–63). New York: Garland.

Berns, M. S. (1990). *Contexts of competence: Social and cultural considerations in communicative language teaching.* New York: Plenum Press.

Biesenbach-Lucas, S. (2005). Communication topics and strategies in e-mail consultation: Comparison between American and international university students. *Language Learning & Technology, 9*(2), 24–46.

Bigelow, M., & Tedick, D. J. (2005). Combining foreign and second language teacher education: Rewards and challenges. In D. J. Tedick (ed.), *Second language teacher education: International perspectives* (pp. 273–280). Mahwah, NJ: Lawrence Earlbaum Associates.

Borras, I., & Lafayette, R. C. (1994). Effects of multimedia courseware subtitling on the speaking performance of college students of French. *Modern Language Journal, 78*(1), 61–75.

Bush, M. D. (1997). Implementing technology for language learning. In M. D. Bush & R. M. Terry (eds), *Technology-enhanced language learning* (Vol. 1997, pp. 287–349). Lincolnwood, IL: National Textbook Co.

Bush, M. D., & Terry, R. M. (1997a). *Technology-enhanced language learning.* Lincolnwood, IL: National Textbook Co.

Bush, M. D., & Terry, R. M. (eds). (1997b). *Implementing technology for language learning* (Vol. 1997). Lincolnwood, IL: National Textbook Co.

Campbell, R., & Wales, R. (1970). The study of language acquisition. In J. Lyons (ed.), *New horizons in linguistics* (pp. 242–260). Harmondsworth, England: Penguin Books.

Canale, M., & Swain, M. (1979). *Communicative approaches to second language teaching and testing.* Toronto, Canada: The Minister of Education.

Chambers, A. (2005). Integrating corpus consultation in language studies. *Language Learning & Technology, 9*(2), 111–125.

Chapelle, C. (1998). Analysis of interaction sequences in computer-assisted language learning. *TESOL Quarterly, 32*(4), 753–757.

Chapelle, C. (2005). Computer-assisted language learning. In E. Hinkel (ed.), *Handbook of research in second language teaching and learning* (pp. 743–755). Mahwah, NJ: Lawrence Erlbaum Associates.

Chavez, C. L. (1997). Students take flight with Daedalus: Learning Spanish in a networked classroom. *Foreign Language Annals, 30*(1), 27–37.

Chomsky, N. (1959). Review of B. F. Skinner "Verbal Behavior." *Language, 35*, 26–58.

Chomsky, N. (1965). *Aspects of theory of syntax.* Cambridge, MA: MIT Press.

Chuang, H. H., & Rosenbusch, M. H. (2005). Use of digital video technology in an elementary school foreign language methods course. *British Journal of Educational Technology, 36*(5), 869–880.

Cui, Y., & Bull, S. (2005). Context and learner modelling for the mobile foreign language learner. *System, 33*(2), 353–367.

Cummings, J. (1979). Cognitive/academic language proficiency, linguistic interdependence, the optimum age question and some other matters. *Working Papers in Bilingualism, 19,* 121–129.

Cummings, J. (1980). The cross-lingual dimensions of language proficiency: Implications for bilingual education and the optimal age issue. *TESOL Quarterly, 14*(2), 175–187.

Cummings, J. (1981). The role of primary language development in promoting educational success for language minority students In C. Leyba (ed.), *Schooling and language minority students: A theoretical framework* (pp. 3–49). Sacramento: California State Department of Education.

Davis, J. N., & Lyman-Hager, M. A. (1997). Computers and L2 reading: Student performance, student attitudes. *Foreign Language Annals, 30*(1), 58–72.

Egbert, J., Paulus, T. M., & Nakamichi, Y. (2002). The impact of CALL instruction on classroom computer use: A foundation for rethinking technology in teacher education. *Language Learning and Technology, 6*(3), 108.

Ellis, R. (1985). *Understanding second language acquisition.* Oxford: Oxford University Press.

Ellis, R. (1997). *Second language acquisition.* Oxford: Oxford University Press.

Ely, C. M. (1994). Preparing second language teachers for strategy instruction: An integrated approach. *Foreign Language Annals, 27,* 335–342.

Ertmer, P., & Hruskocy, C. (1999). Impacts of a university-elementary school partnership designed to support technology integration. *Educational Technology Research and Development, 47,* 81–96.

Freeman, D. (1996). The "unstudied problem": Research on teacher learning in language teaching. In D. Freeman & J. C. Richards (eds), *Teacher learning in language teaching* (pp. 351–378). Cambridge, UK: Cambridge University Press.

Freeman, D., & Johnson, K. E. (1998). Reconceptualizing the knowledge-base of language teacher education. *TESOL Quarterly, 32*(3), 397–417.

Freeman, D., & Johnson, K. E. (2005a). Response to Tarone and Allwright. In D. J. Tedick (ed.), *Second language teacher education: International perspectives* (pp. 25–32). Mahwah, NJ: Lawrence Earlbaum Associates.

Freeman, D., & Johnson, K. E. (2005b). Toward linking teacher knowledge and student learning. In D. J. Tedick (ed.), *Second language teacher education: International perspectives* (pp. 73–95). Mahwah, NJ: Lawrence Earlbaum Associates.

Garrett, N. (1991). Language pedagogy and effective technology use. *Applied Language Learning, 2*(2), 1–14.

Gonglewski, M. R. (1999). Linking the Internet to national standards for foreign language learning. *Foreign Language Annals, 32,* 348–362.

Goodland, J. (1994). *Educational renewal.* San Francisco, CA: Jossey-Bass Publishers.

Grace, C. A. (1998). Retention of word meanings inferred from context and sentence-level translations: Implications for the design of beginning-level CALL software. *Modern Language Journal, 82*(4), 533–544.

Grosse, C. U. (1993). The foreign language methods course. *Modern Language Journal, 77*(3), 303–312.

Guntermann, C. G. (1993). Developing language teachers for a changing world: Prospects for progress. In C. G. Guntermann (ed.), *Developing language teachers for a changing world* (pp. 1–6). Lincolnwood, IL: National Textbook Co.

Halliday, M. (1975). *Learning how to mean: Explorations in the development of language.* London: Edward Arnold.

Hammadou, J. (1993). Inquiry in language teacher education. In C. G. Guntermann (ed.), *Developing language teachers for a changing world* (pp. 76–104). Lincolnwood, IL: National Textbook Co.

Hong, W. (1997). Multimedia computer-assisted reading in business Chinese. *Foreign Language Annals, 30*(3), 335–344.

Horst, M., Cobb, T., & Nicolae, I. (2005). Expanding academic vocabulary with an interactive on-line database. *Language Learning & Technology, 9*(2), 90–110.

Howells, G. (1998). Problems and possibilities of information technology in the initial teacher training of teachers of English and modern languages. *Revista de Lenguas para Fines Específicos, 5–6,* 257–269.

Hymes, D. (1961). The ethnography of speaking. In T. Gladwin & W. Sturtevant (eds), *Anthropology and human behavior* (pp. 13–53). Washington, DC: Anthropological Society of Washington.

Hymes, D. (1972). On communicative competence. In J. P. Pride & J. Holmes (eds), *Sociolinguistics* (pp. 269–293). Harmondsworth, England: Penguin Books.

International Society for Technology in Education (ISTE). (2000). *National educational technology standards for students: Connecting curriculum and technology.* Eugene, OR: Author.

Jarvis, G. A. (1983). Pedagogical content knowledge for the second language teacher. In J. E. Alatis, H. H. Stern, & P. Strevens (eds), *Applied linguistics and preparation of second language teachers: Toward a rationale* (pp. 234–241). Georgetown University Round Table on Language and Linguistics. Washington, DC: Georgetown University Press.

Johnson, M. (2004). *A philosophy of second language acquisition.* New Haven: Yale University Press.

Joiner, E. G., Bush, M. D., & Terry, R. M. (1997). Teaching listening: How technology can help. In M. D. Bush & R. M. Terry (eds), *Technology-enhanced language learning* (pp. 77–120). Lincolnwood, IL: National Textbook Co.

Kamhi-Stein, L. D. (2000). Integrating computer-mediated communication tools into practicum. In K. E. Johnson (ed.), *Teacher education* (pp. 119–136). Alexandria, VA: Teachers of English to Speakers of Other Languages, Inc.

Kassen, M. A., & Higgins, C. J. (1997). Meeting the technology challenge: Introducing teachers to language-learning technology. In M. D. Bush & R. M. Terry (eds), *Technology-enhanced language learning* (pp. 263–285). Lincolnwood, IL: National Textbook Co.

Kern, R. G. (1998). Technology, social interaction, and FL literacy. In J. A. Muyskens (ed.), *New ways of learning and teaching: Focus on technology and foreign language education* (pp. 57–92). Boston, MA: Heinle & Heinle.

Koehler, M. J., & Mishra, P. (2005). What happens when teachers design educational technology? The development of technological pedagogical content knowledge. *Journal of Educational Computing Research, 32*(2), 131–152.

Krashen, S. (1981). Bilingual education and second language acquisition theory. In *Schooling and language minority students: A theoretical framework* (pp. 51–79). Los Angeles: Evaluation, Dissemination and Assessment Center, California State University, Los Angeles.

Krashen, S. (1982). *Principles and practice in second language acquisition.* Oxford, England: Pergamon Press.

Kubota, R. (1999). Word processing and WWW projects in a college Japanese language class. *Foreign Language Annals, 32*(2), 205–218.

Lafayette, R. C. (1993). Subject matter content: What every foreign language teacher needs to know. In C. G. Guntermann (ed.), *Developing language teachers for a changing world* (pp. 124–154). Lincolnwood, IL: National Textbook Co.

Lam, Y. (2000). Technophilia vs. technophobia: A preliminary look at why second-language teachers do or do not use technology in their classrooms. *Canadian Modern Language Review, 56*(3), 389–420.

Long, M. (1980). Input, interaction and second language acquisition. Doctoral dissertation, University of California, Los Angeles.

Long, M. (1983). Linguistic and conversational adjustments to non-native speakers. *Studies in Second Language Acquisition, 12,* 251–285.

Lortie, D. (1975). *Schoolteacher: A sociological study.* Chicago: University of Chicago Press.

Ma, W. W. K., Anderson, R., & Streith, K. O. (2005). Examining user acceptance of computer technology: An empirical study of student teachers. *Journal of Computer Assisted Learning, 21*(6), 387–395.

Martinez-Lage, A. (1997). Hypermedia technology for teaching reading. In M. D. Bush & R. M.

Terry (eds), *Technology-enhanced language learning* (pp. 121–163). Lincolnwood, IL: National Textbook Co.

Mishra, P., & Koehler, M. J. (2006). Technological pedagogical content knowledge: A new framework for teacher knowledge. *Teachers College Record, 108*(6), 1017–1054.

Morine-Dershimer, G. (2001). "Family connections" as a factor in the development of research on teaching. In V. Richardson (ed.), *Handbook of research on teaching* (pp. 47–68). Washington, DC: American Educational Research Association.

Otero, V., Peressini, D., Meymaris, K. A., Ford, P., Garvin, T., Harlow, D., *et al.* (2005). Integrating technology into teacher education: A critical framework for implementing reform. *Journal of Teacher Education, 56*(1), 8–23.

Pearson, L. (2004). The web portfolio: A project to teach Spanish reading and Hispanic cultures. *Hispania, 87*(4), 759–769.

Richards, J. C. (1998). *Beyond training: Perspectives on language teacher education.* New York: Cambridge University Press.

Rodriguez-van Olphen, M. M. C. (2002). *Integrating technology into the foreign language teacher education curriculum: A phenomenological study.* Unpublished dissertation/thesis, Purdue University, West Lafayette, Indiana.

Rubio, R., & Sedersten, D. S. (2001, March). How we integrated technology throughout our education program. Paper presented at the *12th Annual Meeting of the Society for Information Technology and Teacher Education,* Orlando, FL.

Salaberry, M. R. (2000). Pedagogical design of computer mediated communication tasks: Learning objectives and technological capabilities. *Modern Language Journal, 84*(1), 28–37.

Savignon, S. (1972). *Communicative competence: An experiment in foreign language teaching.* Philadelphia, PA: Center for Curriculum Development.

Schulz, R. A. (2000). Foreign language teacher development: MLJ perspectives—1916–1999. *Modern Language Journal, 84*(4), 495–522.

Sehlaoui, A. S. (2001). Developing cross-cultural communicative competence via computer-assisted language learning: The case of pre-service ESL/EFL teachers. *Association for Learning Technology Journal, 9*(3), 53–64.

Shaffer, S., & Richardson, J. (2004). Supporting technology integration within a teacher education system. *Journal of Educational Computing Research, 31*(4), 423–435.

Shulman, L. S. (1987). Knowledge and teaching: Foundations of the new reform. *Harvard Educational Review, 57*(1), 1–22.

Sime, D., & Priestley, M. (2005). Student teachers' first reflections on information and communications technology and classroom learning: Implications for initial teacher education. *Journal of Computer Assisted Learning, 21*(2), 130–142.

Swain, M. (1985). Communicative competence: Some roles of comprehensible input and comprehensible output in its development. In S. Gass & C. Madden (eds), *Input in second language acquisition* (pp. 235–253). Rowley, MA: Newbury House.

Swain, M. (1995). Three functions of output in second language learning. In G. Cook & B. Seidlhofer (eds), *Studies in honour of H. G. Widdowson* (pp. 125–144). Oxford: Oxford University Press.

Tarone, E., & Allwright, D. (2005). Second language teacher learning and student second language learning: Shaping the knowledge base. In D. J. Tedick (ed.), *Second language teacher education: International perspectives* (pp. 5–23). Mahwah, NJ: Lawrence Earlbaum Associates.

Teachers of English to Speakers of Other Languages (TESOL). (2002). *TESOL/NCATE standards for the accreditation of initial programs in P-12 ESL teacher education.* Alexandria, VA: Author

Tedick, D. J. (ed.). (2005). *Second language teacher education: International perspectives.* Mahwah, NJ: Lawrence Earlbaum Associates.

Tedick, D. J., & Walker, C. L. (1994). Second language teacher education: The problems that plague us. *Modern Language Journal, 78*(3), 300–312.

Tedick, D. J., Walker, C. L., Lange, D. L., Paige, R. M., & Jorstad, H. L. (1993). Second language education in tomorrow's schools. In C. G. Guntermann (ed.), *Developing language teachers for a changing world* (pp. 43–75). Lincolnwood, IL: National Textbook Co.

Thompson, A. D., Schmidt, D. A., & Davis, N. E. (2003). Technology collaboratives for simultaneous renewal in teacher education. *Educational Technology Research and Development, 51*(1), 73–89.

van Olphen, M. (2003). Integrating new technologies into the foreign language classroom. In K. H. Cárdenas & M. Klein (eds), *Traditional values and contemporary perspectives in language teaching* (pp. 71–79). Valdosta, GA: Lee Bradley & Valdosta State University.

van Olphen, M. (2007a). Perspectives of foreign language pre-service teachers on the use of a web-based instructional environment in a methods course. *CALICO Journal, 25*(1), 91–109.

van Olphen, M. (2007b). Digital portfolios: Balancing the academic and professional needs of foreign language teacher candidates. In M. A. Kassen, R. Lavine, K. Murphy-Judy, & M. Peters (eds), *CALICO volume on teacher education and technology* (pp. 265–294). San Marcos, TX: CALICO.

Vygotsky, L. (1978). *Mind in society.* Cambridge, MA: Harvard University Press.

Ware, P. D., & Kramsch, C. (2005). Toward an intercultural stance: Teaching German and English through telecollaboration. *The Modern Language Journal, 89*(2), 190–205.

Warschauer, M. (2002). A developmental perspective on technology in language education. *TESOL Quarterly, 36*(3), 453–475.

Weinberg, A., Peters, M., & Sarma, N. (2005). Learners' preferences for the use of technology in learning languages. *Canadian Journal of Applied Linguistics/Revue Canadienne de Linguistique Appliquée, 8*(2), 211–231.

Wildner, S. (1999). Technology integration into preservice foreign language teacher education programs. *CALICO Journal, 17*(2), 223–250.

Wing, B. H. (1993). The pedagogical imperative in foreign language teacher education. In C. G. Guntermann (ed.), *Developing language teachers for a changing world* (pp. 159–186). Lincolnwood, IL: National Textbook Co.

Zhao, Y., Pugh, K., & Sheldon, S. (2002). Conditions for classroom technology innovations. *Teachers College Record, 104*(3), 482–515.

6

Toward democracy
Social studies and TPCK

JOHN K. LEE

Theoretical considerations in practice are sometimes tenuous and almost always subject to re-evaluation. Such is the case with the theory of technological pedagogical content knowledge (TPCK) as applied to social studies. Conceived of as the intersection of three domains of knowledge, the general idea of TPCK continues to evolve and envelop new conceptualizations and advancements in technology, pedagogy, and academic content. The most common way of thinking about TPCK is to separately conceive of technology, pedagogy, and content and then consider their interplay. Researchers and scholars have conceptualized a Venn diagram illustrating the intersection of these three forms of knowledge as the province of TPCK (Mishra & Koehler, 2006). This conceptualization requires clearly established domains for technology, pedagogy, and academic content. Shulman's (1986) work establishes a viable conceptual framework within which to consider pedagogy as including knowledge of learners, contexts, curriculum, and ends as well as general pedagogical practices. Similarly, in Chapter 1 of this book, Mishra and Koehler clearly conceptualize technologies in education as traditional (specific, stable, and transparent) and digital (protean, unstable, and opaque).

Despite the clarity of these conceptualizations of pedagogy and technology, TPCK in social studies is complicated by the nature of social studies, which itself lacks clearly established academic or disciplinary structure. Schwab's (1964) work suggests that academic disciplines have syntactic and substantive structures which enable scholars working within an academic discipline to contribute new knowledge and verify these new forms of knowledge as legitimate. Social studies lacks substantive and syntactic structures for producing knowledge and thus subject matter in social studies is culled from various disciplines including history, geography, political science, economics, behavioral sciences, and cultural studies among others. Thornton (2001) suggests this social studies subject matter takes form as disciplinary content is selected, adapted, and essentially transformed for teaching purposes. Such a conceptualization of social studies subject matter is inherently pedagogical, so in this chapter I reflect on ten pedagogical actions that frame teaching and learning social studies with technology. These reflections lead to a more complete consideration of the role of technology in social studies given the theory of technological pedagogical content knowledge. Specifically, I present technology use in the context of preparation for democratic life.

Pedagogical actions framing teaching and learning social studies with technology

When developing pedagogical knowledge, teachers recreate for communicative purposes various parts of the organizational characteristics of established forms of subject matter knowledge (Shulman, 1986). Shulman called these actions transformative, suggesting that these transformations might include preparation, representation, adaptation, and tailoring of subject matter. When social studies teachers consider technology as a dynamic component in this transformative process, I would suggest that at least two things happen.

1. Teachers engage social studies subject matter given some built-in technological affordance related to the preparation, representation, adaptation, and/or tailoring of social studies subject matter. This subject matter might be thought of as inherently technological.
2. Teachers engage social studies subject matter given some *added* technological affordance related to the preparation, representation, adaptation, and/or tailoring of studies subject matter. This subject matter might be thought of as being improved by technology.

Both of these occurrences result in pedagogical action. In this chapter, I consider six inherently technological pedagogical actions in social studies and four areas of social studies subject matter as they are enhanced by technology.

Inherently technological affordances affecting the preparation, representation, adaptation, and/or tailoring of social studies-related resources might result in numerous pedagogical actions, including:

1. locating and adapting digital resources for use in the classroom,
2. facilitating students' work in non-linear environments, requiring students to make critical decisions about how to select their own resources and navigate through a wide variety of interfaces,
3. working to develop critical media literacy skills among students,
4. providing students with opportunities to utilize the presentational capabilities of the Web to motivate and encourage students,
5. using the Internet to extend collaboration and communication among students, and
6. extending and promoting active and authentic forms of human interaction in technology enabled social networks.

In addition to actions social studies teachers take given inherent technological affordances, teachers might also enhance, transform, or otherwise reorganize social studies subject matter given technological pedagogical contexts. Such enhancements or transformations might include social studies teachers,

1. making use of historical source materials available through online sources,
2. promoting understandings of spatial, human, and physical systems as aided by technology,
3. expanding social experiences using technology, and
4. encouraging economic literacy through the use of technology.

Each of these ten pedagogical actions is discussed below followed by the presentation of a conceptual framework for considering how technology influences social studies content and pedagogy. This framework emerges given the unique nature of content knowledge in social studies. As previously noted, social studies might be considered as the study of subject matter for democratic life. Such an approach helps resolve problems resulting from the lack of disciplinary structure in social studies by refocusing social studies as a more practical educational matter. I suggest in the last section of this chapter that the ten technological pedagogical actions inform a conceptual understanding of social studies as a school subject aimed at supporting democratic experiences.

Social studies teachers locating and adapting digital resources for use in the classroom

Given the plentitude of instructional resources available online, being able to locate and then quickly adapt resources for use in the social studies classroom is a major pedagogical undertaking. Teachers must be very detailed and deliberate as they make use of these materials. Unlike education-related print resources available for teacher use, online materials are often unsorted, uncatalogued, and/or poorly arranged. Navigating through these resources requires knowledge of the content related to the source. As teachers navigate through available resources, the application of critical strategies related to the selection and consideration of resources will enable them to make more meaningful use of resources.

Research has illustrated a three-part strategy for teachers in locating and using social studies digital pedagogical resources (Lee & Molebash, 2006). The first strategy requires teachers to develop a context for the identification of resources. These contexts are built from curricular and secondary source-derived content knowledge. Within these contexts, subject matter knowledge begins to emerge as teachers make subsequent decisions about what resources to use. For example, a teacher may select a particular letter from a collection of historical letters available online because the given letter has some content value (perhaps it was written by a significant character in history) and because the letter has some pedagogical value (perhaps the letter is readable or includes some topic to which students can relate). In this example, the selection process is aided by the teachers' knowledge of content and their knowledge of pedagogy.

The second strategy involves the delimitation of a specific resource given the characteristics of the resource. Delimitation means the resource must be vetted, in a sense, after it is located to determine its value given specific learner-sensitive characteristics such as length, complexity, relevance, and accessibility. Teachers make these decisions based on their knowledge of the learners in their class and their knowledge of the constraints and restraints which frame their teaching. This strategy requires that teachers go beyond the initial considerations which guided their selection to consider children's specific needs such as their reading level. The third strategy involves a pedagogical manipulation of the resource. In this process, the teacher is beginning to think actively about how the resource must be adapted and tailored for specific student use. At this point, a teacher decides and plans for appropriate use in their classroom given knowledge of learners, knowledge of curriculum, the needs of the school community, and the goals or purposes of the course and subject.

Social studies teachers facilitating their students' work in non-linear environments

Non-linear environments abound on the Web. In fact, most web sites have non-linear or hypertext structures and these structures often confound traditional linear print. Neilson (1995), Landow (1992), and Bolter (1991) have all expounded on the uniqueness of hypertext as an associative assemblage of information. Landow conceptualizes hypertext as "multilinear or multisequential" (p. 4) nodes of information with unique meanings. Landow further argues that hypertext blurs the boundaries between reader and writer by empowering the reader with the authority to, in a sense, write the text as they follow links and read, potentially altering the cognitive load for hypertext readers while allowing users freedom to navigate various nodes according to their needs.

Perhaps the most important consequence of technologically enabled non-linearity has to do with how students switch from linear to non-linear environments. Teachers need to help their students develop critical skills that will enable them to make decisions relating to navigating non-linear resources (particularly web-based). Students need similar skills for using linearly structured resources such as the book, but non-linear web-based resources require students to be more active in their decision-making about how to select resources and navigate through interfaces. Instead of the more linear table of contents or an index, social studies resources online often have menus or browsable and searchable collections. Social studies teachers need to facilitate students as they use both forms of resources.

The discipline of history offers a good context to consider how unique non-linear technological attributes can affect learning and teaching in social studies. Darnton (2000) suggests that historical hyper-environments might have layers of information including historical and analytical narratives as well as documentary, historiographic, pedagogical, and collaborative resources and information. Teachers might use heuristics such as Darnton's to conceptualize online historical resources or resources in other content areas and then plan to use them with their students. These resources can be contrasted with linear resources such as the book, but ultimately students need skills to use both types of resources.

Social studies teachers working to develop critical media literacy skills among their students

Although technology offers a number of affordances for both teaching and learning, challenges exist as well. The uneven quality of technologically enhanced resources requires teachers and students to use critical media skills. These skills require new forms of media literacy, which have been conceptualized as skills that include informational literacy, computer literacy, film and video literacy, and cultural literacy (Scheibe, 2004). Whether teachers and students are using web-based resources, television, film, or other technological outlets, the skills needed to negotiate these spaces are important. For example, consider how we use web-based information. Although popular search engines such as Google have significantly improved in recent years and academic search capabilities in libraries have also greatly improved, student users are still being challenged as they attempt to wade through the breadth of what they find. Without proper focus, students with less training and sophistication can get frustrated, if not totally lost. Fitch (1997) has expressed concern that allowing social studies students to use web resources uncritically may encourage them to "take the easy way out," resulting in limited research skill development. There is also the related and increasingly ominous potential for plagiarism. Access to so much material easily invites the theft of intellectual property. Such concerns clearly illuminate the importance of carefully preparing students to engage in the sophisticated and systematic literacy work that is part and parcel of what it means to teach and learn social studies.

Social studies primary purpose of preparing young people for citizenship positions the field as an ideal context for the development of critical media literacy skills. In fact, Hobbs (2005) suggests that media literacy might be "so far embedded in social studies education as to be hidden from view" (p. 77). Citizenship in a democracy implies critical thought, and critical thought requires information (Parker, 1991). Technology can make more information available to students than ever before. The Internet, in particular, is dramatically increasing the amount of information available to students. The teacher's role in these new learning environments is one of a facilitator. When students are learning in an environment that integrates technology and subject matter, teaching is no longer didactic and learning is no longer passive. Students are helping create their own knowledge and the teacher is assisting the student in the critical analysis that is a part of the knowledge creation process.

Social studies teachers providing students with opportunities to utilize the presentational capabilities of the Web to motivate and encourage students

Teachers know all too well the importance of sharing and making public their students' work. Whether it is the walls outside the classroom, the media center, or the Web, providing students a public forum for their work enhances motivation and encourages authenticity. Technology, in particular the distributive capability of the Web, can facilitate the presentation and sharing of student work. Student web publishing has taken form through archival class projects such as the *Cherokee Digital History Project* (Clarke & Lee, 2004) and the *Bland County History Archive*[1] as well as oral interview projects such as *Always Lend a Helping Hand: Sevier County, Utah, Remembers the Great Depression*[2] and *What Did You Do in the War Grandma?*[3] both of which are high school history class projects focused on interviewing people about their historical recollections. These four projects require a committed teacher with time and technological resources.

More dynamic publication opportunities are available on school web sites and newer interactive web publishing tools such as weblogs and wikis. These new technologies collectively known as Web 2.0 allow teachers to more seamlessly enable students as they creatively present their work (Bull, 2006). Making use of technologies such as digital storytelling, podcasting, news aggregators, file sharing, and online writing can motivate students to develop subject matter knowledge through the presentation of their work. Fred Newmann (Newmann & Associates, 1996) calls such sharing *authentic intellectual work* arguing that among other things students' public work generates value beyond school and generates personal, aesthetic, or social significance. Web-based resources can facilitate such authentic experiences for students and social studies with its "human" subject matter is well-suited for utilizing these technologies.

Social studies teachers using the Internet to extend collaboration and communication among students

The Internet can also encourage communication and student collaboration (Boldt, Gustafson, & Johnson, 1995). Synchronous communications such as instant messaging, telephony, audio and video conferencing, chat, and asynchronous communications such as discussion boards, news groups, and email all enable teachers to expand the forms of interaction their students can have inside and outside the classroom. Discussion groups are being used successfully in thousands of social studies classes. The instructional use of email can make social studies more meaningful and realistic. Tele-collaboration between students from different schools can advance inquiry and distributive problem solving among students (Berenfeld, 1996).

Lakkala, Lallimo, and Hakkarainen (2005) argue that technology-supported collaborative collective inquiry is possible, but teachers must work hard to overcome existing pedagogical tendencies toward individualistic learning. The pedagogy of collaboration cannot simply be grafted on top of school settings which value and support individualistic learning environments. Instead, teachers must develop pedagogical strategies and scaffolds to support less practiced forms of collaboration as assisted by technology enhanced communication.

Social studies is well suited for collaborative and communicative learning. The field includes subject matter from a wide range of social constructs where collaboration and communication exist as normative structures. For example, when studying about geography, students in social studies learn about concepts such as cross-cultural communication. Social studies related communicative technology resources such as the International Education and Resource Network (iEARN), KidLink, and ThinkQuest are all designed to facilitate students as they learn about cross-cultural communication, through technology assisted communication and collaboration. Abbott (2005) argues that innovative and inquiry-oriented teachers can use such resources to help their students become more confident and self-directed learners. A variety of collaborative learning environments (CLEs), including web-based, computer-supported, and virtual environments, provide teachers with opportunities to extend pedagogical approaches to teaching that are focused on student-centered problem-based collaborative learning (Ligorio & Veermans, 2005). These environments are conducive to work in social studies given the relevance of problem-based learning in the field (Gregory, 1998).

Social studies teachers extending and promoting active and authentic
forms of human interaction in technology-enabled social networks
Social studies educators must deal with the impact of technology on the development of human communities (Gooler, 1995) and on human interaction (McKay, 1996). The communities involved in this human interaction include both the students and teachers in schools and extended communities across the globe; all of whom have similar educative interests. Human interaction in these social studies classroom contexts has been impacted by technology in three critical ways. (1) Electronic forms of communications such as email, chat, and audio/video conferencing have facilitated previously unexpected and impossible forms of dialog. (2) Computer technologies have facilitated the planning and implementation of cooperative-based instruction. (3) The wide and diffuse array of information available through technology has allowed students to actively construct new

knowledge that can vie with other versions of the same knowledge in public spaces such as the Web.

These three areas of impact are facilitated through personal computer use, but when these computers first made their appearance in schools, there was concern over the impact of this new technology on the system of social interactions present in the classroom. The development of the social and citizenship communication skills needed to use information was seen in these early days as an important consideration (Diem, 1983). At the same time, fear of the social consequences of technology (and in particular the personal computer) drove some to call for the deceleration of the information revolution. One fear was that human interaction would dissipate in a school as computers took the place of teachers and students interacted only with the computer screen (Langeveld, 1983). Despite these concerns, teachers are using computers to facilitate a wide range of existing and wholly new interaction (Kearsley & Shneiderman, 1998).

The notion that social studies experiences help to prepare students for participation in democratic society implies that schools can reproduce some of the structures that exist in society. In doing so, schools can create authentic interactive experiences for students and technology offers new and creative ways to capture the reality of this life (Bull, 2006; Tally, 1996). Using the Internet, students can interact with other students and subject matter experts. Students can use real-world software applications to produce reports, manipulate data, and create knowledge. These interactions and software applications are not reproductions of the real world; they are the real world. Students are using the actual programs and environments they will use as adult citizens. The contributions they make through conversations or technology-enabled shared work are very real and have the potential to impact other people. Technology can also facilitate active learning through student-developed design learning environments (Resnick, 1994). Technology-enabled constructivist approaches to teaching and learning social studies can generate authenticity within the classroom, allowing students to pursue ideas of personal interest while building on prior knowledge in autonomous, creative, and intellectual environments (Doolittle & Hicks, 2003). These forms of learning are propelled by student activity (Puntambekar & Kolodner, 2005).

Social studies teachers making use of historical source materials available through online sources

Teaching and learning history are being affected by developments in technology, as have so many facets of our lives. Technological change in history is facilitating a form of historical practice known as "digital history" (Ayers, 1999). Digital history has emerged as a result of new technologies which enable the storage of extensive historical records in electronic form as well as remote access to these resources via the World Wide Web (Rosenzweig,

1999). These changes present new pedagogical challenges for teachers. The uniqueness and likely most important pedagogical characteristic of digital history emerges from the availability and growth of digital historical resources, both primary and secondary. The development of digital archives has enabled new forms of teaching and learning in history which involve new strategies related to the unique characteristics of digital environments (Lee, 2002b). The historical work done in digital environments involves the study of the past using a variety of electronically reproduced primary source texts, images, and artifacts as well as the constructed historical narratives, accounts, or presentations that result from digital historical inquiry (Lee, 2002a).

Social studies and history teacher educators are beginning to teach about the methods for using technological or specifically digital resources (Bolick, Berson, Coutts, & Heinecke, 2003). These methods include the important tasks of locating appropriate resources and situating these resources in relevant curriculum. Once located and situated in curriculum, digital historical resources can be utilized for their pedagogical qualities. Metaphors, symbols, images, visual aids, and textual scaffolds can be developed to frame digital historical resources and invite active engagement and constructive interpretation (Lee, 2002b). Well-designed digital historical resources should enable authenticity and student interest, facilitate student interaction with a wide range of practical and authentic historical subject matter, encourage creative and public applications of students' emerging historical knowledge, and aid students as they design learning opportunities and construct tangible artifacts that represent personal and shared historical understandings (Calandra & Lee, 2005).

Social studies teachers promoting understandings of spatial, human, and physical systems as aided by technology

Social studies educators have a considerable collection of new tools and resources available for teaching geography. These tools enable mapping, visualizing, and the conceptualization of spatial arrangements (Sanders, Kajs, & Crawford, 2002). For example, increasingly ubiquitous web applications which make use of aerial photography are reorganizing the way that humans visualize place. Earlier imaginary and artistic "bird's-eye-views" that marked human efforts to accurately represent human life on the surface of earth have rapidly been replaced by a high-resolution matrix of millions of aerial photographs. Social studies teachers in the twenty-first century teach children who, for the most part, do not have to imagine what their neighborhood or city looks like from above; they can see an array of photographs depicting these places. Such spatial representations can change the way we teach about place while positioning students to more affectively incorporate knowledge about their surroundings in more dynamic and intuitive ways.

Geography instruction has also been impacted by technological applications such as geographic information systems (GIS) and graphical positioning systems (GPS) (Alibrandi, 2003). The use of technological geographic systems allows teachers to provide students with real-time data and authentic contexts for learning. These authentic contexts may not be represented in curriculum which is developed often years before being implemented. Efforts to implement a GIS-infused geography curriculum require personal commitment on the part of the teacher and interdisciplinary approaches (Kerski, 2003) as well as careful integration into existing curriculum (Patterson, Reeve, & Page, 2003).

Geography-related technologies can also enhance student inquiry into citizenship-related problems. Given citizenship-related needs for information, social studies teachers can use current technologies in order to prepare today's student to be tomorrow's citizen. Teachers need to understand concepts and issues within geography education related to new ways of representing space and understanding geography-oriented problems citizen face. Teachers can also use technology-informed transformative geography to help students study issues related to the well-being of the planet (Kirman, 2003). Such geographic learning experiences enable children to think about the social, geographic, and ecological benefits and costs of certain human activities. Technologies which monitor human activity relying on large amounts of data such as pollution emission tracking technologies can be used by teachers and students to analyze and evaluate the value of specific human actions in real-time geographic contexts.

Social studies teachers expanding social experiences using technology

In 1994, the National Council for the Social Studies defined social studies as "the integrated study of the social sciences and humanities to promote civic competence." The citizenship rationale of social studies reflects a variety of content areas and requires constant adaptation to changes in society. Technological change represents one such change currently influencing society. With regard to civics, technology has deeply influenced the way citizens access information, participate, and act in democracies. Teachers need to prepare students in a technological age where democratic citizens have access to not only information, but to the political process and authentic discourse and dialog about political issues (Crowe, 2006). New modes of communication and interaction require that students be prepared in etiquette, responsibility, rights, safety, and security (Ribble, Bailey, & Ross, 2004).

Some have argued that technology has the potential to threaten democracy by extenuating inequalities in our society (Smith-Gratto, 1989). The digital divide has separated haves from have-nots and potentially limited access to the political process for those have-nots. Teachers and schools must insure that students are prepared to use public and private resources in an effort to bridge socio-economic differences in access to democracy-related technology.

Social studies teachers must stay abreast of recent developments in technology and make use of current technologies in order to prepare students as critical citizens.

Civic competence infers an understanding of the democratic process and an ability to practice citizenship-related skills. Technology-related critical literacy skills for detecting bias and ideology are increasingly important (Lee, 2006). Low barriers to publication on the Web and widespread use and acceptance of alternative media outlets require that social studies teachers be prepared to filter political information and prepare their students to be critical in their use. Beyond accessing and using information, social studies teachers should make their students aware of the resources that can facilitate their participation in democratic life. Students can lobby their congressperson, participate in activist movements, and vote online. To encourage online voting, social studies teachers can use online student polling, mock elections, and voter registration as well as online resources that facilitate students' critical thinking related to making civic decisions.

Social studies teachers encouraging economic literacy through the use of technology

As the world economy has changed and become more interdependent, technologies have evolved alongside in an iterative and dynamic manner. Given the demands of this evolving global economy, social studies teachers need to help their students develop advanced communication, critical thinking, problem solving, and inter-personal skills (McBeath, 1994). Furthermore, social studies teachers can make use of technology to access information when teaching in the data-rich field of economics (Robinson, 1999). The skills students develop when working with economic data translate into the human capital that individuals carry with them as they move through life. Possession of these skills allows individuals to confidently pursue knowledge-related jobs and opportunities.

Effective citizenship in knowledge-dependent economies requires a range of technology skills for manipulating knowledge (Martorella, 1998). Economic knowledge is increasingly being assembled or arranged in technologically facilitated environments. For example, access to financial markets now requires interacting with electronic Internet-driven interfaces. A corresponding decentralization or diffusion of information has accompanied each of these new knowledge arrangements. As workplace technological skills continue to evolve, schools must prepare students to be successful in these environments (Wilson & Marsh, 1995). Learning environments that incorporate such workplace skills might incorporate simulated economic activities such as stock or commodities trading, cross-school research projects, and the computer-supported intentional learner environment (Scardamalia & Bereiter, 1989). These examples of school-based projects all are based on assumptions about knowledge, economics, and learning. Advanced economies require the creation of new knowledge and students will need to serve as the co-creators of this new knowledge with social studies teachers facilitating students as they use economic data and communicate among themselves and with teachers and experts.

A conceptual framework for technology and pedagogy in the social studies

When computer technologies were just beginning to impact education, Hepburn (1983) called for the establishment of a conceptual framework within which to consider how content, materials, and strategies in social studies are designed for the "information revolution." In the context of TPCK, this call continues to resonate. Given the unique purpose of social studies and the lack of disciplinary structure within the field, one potential framework for considering TPCK in social studies could relate to democracy. In this sense, we would need to reach beyond civics and the political meaning of democracy for a democratic ideal John Dewey called a way of life. Dewey (1927) argued that democratic life is associative and constructive, involving continual change. Life in a democracy according to Dewey requires citizens to deliberate and reflect in a communal arena where barriers to participation are minimal and individuals act in practical and meaningful ways to improve their own life and contribute to the progress of humanity.

Social studies has long been situated to prepare young people for the role of citizen in a democracy. Technology improves and enlivens this process. Social studies educators can use technology to promote the goals of education in a democratic society by creating authentic experiences that encourage critical and active student learning. Technology can play an effective role in lowering barriers to participation in democratic arenas. Social studies students are able to use technologies to have communicative experiences that were once impossible. Using communicative and collaborative technologies, students are able to interact with and share more information than they ever have before. Technology has the capability of bridging educational achievement gaps and external social gaps by changing the nature of students' interaction with people and the information they are learning.

The notion that social studies will help to prepare students for participation in our democratic civic culture implies that schools can reproduce some of the structures that exist in society without reproducing the inequities that are also present in society. Schools have continually struggled to create authentic and fair democratic classrooms and economically viable experiences for students. Technology offers a way to authentically represent American society in students' lived school experiences. Using the communicative and collaborative technologies, students can interact with other students and experts in a given field. Students can use real-world applications to produce reports, manipulate data, and create knowledge. Students can develop workplace skills they will need to be productive adult citizens. In all of these endeavors, social studies students are using disciplinary content knowledge that is culled from the real world and pedagogically repackaged to enable democratic experiences.

All social studies students live and will work in a democratic society and economy which assumes they can access information and have the ability to manipulate that information. These include personal, social, political, and economic activities which require skills, understanding, and knowledge that can be actively developed with technology. By using technologies that allow teachers to make social studies more authentic, critical, and active social studies can become more democratic and meaningful for students. But, democracy means more than economic and social freedom. Democracy is also a disposition which encourages an expansive and plural cultural experience and values opportunity for all. The disproportionate availability of technology resources for some in advanced and developing societies potentially discourages democratic pluralism. Those in control and possession of technological resources have a decided advantage in technology-enhanced learning environments. Mario Kelly in Chapter 2 of this book has identified numerous technological pedagogies which bridge three overlapping digital divides based on access to infrastructure, access to achievement-oriented technologies, and access to culturally compatible resources. Through careful assessment of resource availability and consideration of the needs and abilities of learners in the classroom, teachers can begin to utilize technological resources in more democratic and pluralist ways.

One final consideration relates to the direct needs of young people given their social lives. In the final chapter of this book, the ACCTE Committee on Innovation and Technology writes about the changing lives of children with respect to technology. These changes involve new forms of social organization and communication facilitated by social networking technologies and interactive devices. Many children bring experiences from outside the class, which are technologically rich, into classrooms which are poorly configured with regard to social and collaborative technologies. Such conditions create what some call a digital disconnect (Levin, Arafeh, Lenhart, & Rainie, 2002). Unlike educational solutions to digital divides which address technological disparities in society, the digital disconnect suggests that schools are not doing enough to enable learning and experience in the technological contexts which are "normal" for young people. Social studies for democracy focused on the practical social experiences of young people should consider how young people live their social lives. Without over-emphasizing the social conditions of young people's lives, social studies educators can create meaningful experiences for their students by utilizing the technological habits and experiences which frame their lives.

Conclusion

Social studies teachers can take deliberate and purposeful pedagogical actions to enable meaningful and authentic uses of technology with their students. The affordances of technology in social studies enable a wide variety of enhancements in school social studies. These affordances relate to the use of technology for locating and adapting digital resources, facilitating students' work in non-linear environments, enabling students to make critical decisions about how to select and navigate through resources, developing critical media literacy skills, utilizing presentational capabilities of the Web to motivate and encourage students, using the Internet to extend collaboration and communication among students, and extending and promoting active and authentic forms of human interaction. Although social studies lacks its own disciplinary structure, the related disciplines of history, geography, political science, and economics are enhanced by technology as these disciplines are represented in social studies. These enhancements relate to historical source materials available through online sources, specific understandings of spatial, human, and physical systems, expansive democratic civic experiences, and economic literacy.

Lacking its own academic structure social studies is well suited for practical experiential learning focused on democratic life. Such experiences can benefit from the affordances of technology. Young people living in technologically enhanced social environments can be encouraged to develop skills and dispositions, which promote healthy democratic life. For those who live in environments with less technology, social studies teachers can and must address their needs through pedagogical action. When used thoughtfully for democratic aims, technology can meaningfully enhance social studies related pedagogical content knowledge.

Notes

1. http://www.bland.k12.va.us/bland/rocky/gap.html.
2. http://newdeal.feri.org/sevier/index.htm.
3. http://www.stg.brown.edu/projects/WWII_Women/tocCS.html.

References

Abbott, L. (2005). The nature of authentic professional development during curriculum-based telecomputing. *Journal of Research on Technology in Education, 37*(4), 379–398.

Alibrandi, M. (2003). *GIS in the classroom: Using geographic information systems in social studies and environmental science.* Portsmouth, NH: Heinemann Publishers.

Ayers, E. L. (1999). The pasts and futures of digital history. Retrieved May 19, 2006 from http://jefferson.village.virginia.edu/vcdh/PastsFutures.html.

Berenfeld, B. (1996). Linking students to the infosphere. *Technology Horizon in Education (T.H.E. Journal), 23*(9), 76–83.

Boldt, D., Gustafson, L., & Johnson, J. (1995). The Internet: A curriculum warehouse for social studies teachers. *The Social Studies, 86*(3), 105–112.

Bolick, C., Berson, M., Coutts, C., & Heinecke, W. (2003). Technology applications in social studies teacher education: A survey of social studies methods faculty. *Contemporary Issues in Technology and Teacher Education, 1*(1). Retrieved March 13, 2006 from http://www.citejournal.org/vol1/iss1/currentissues/socialstudies/article1.htm.

Bolter, J. D. (1991). *Writing space.* Watertown: MA: Eastgate Systems.

Bull, G. (2006). Colaboration in a web 2.0 environment. *Learning and Leading with Technology, 33*(7), 23–24.

Calandra, B., & Lee, J. K. (2005). The digital history and pedagogy project: Creating an interpretative/pedagogical historical website. *The Internet and Higher Education, 8*(4), 323–333.

Clarke, W. G., & Lee, J. K. (2004). The promise of digital history. *The Clearing House, 78*(2), 84–87.

Crowe, A. R. (2006). Technology, citizenship, and the social studies classroom: Education for democracy in a technological age. *International Journal of Social Education, 21*(1), 111–121.

Darnton, R. (2000). An early information society: News and the media in eighteenth-century Paris." *American Historical Review, 105*(1), 1–35.

Dewey, J. (1927). *The public and its problems.* Athens, OH: Shallow Press.

Diem, R. (1983). Social implications of technology innovations: A study of ethics and attitudes. (ERIC Document Reproduction Service No. ED 255 403.)

Doolittle, P., & Hicks, D. (2003). Constructivism as a theoretical foundation for the use of technology in social studies. *Theory and Research in Social Education, 31*(1), 71–103.

Fitch, N. (1997). History after the web: Teaching with hypermedia. *The History Teacher, 30*(4), 427–441.

Gooler, D. D. (1995). Perspectives: Technology as content in social studies curricula for young learners. *Social Studies and the Young Learner, 7*(3), 27–30.

Gregory, V. M. (1998). *Problem-based learning in social studies: Cues to culture and change.* Thousand Oaks, CA: Crown Press.

Hepburn, M. (1983). The new information technology: critical questions for social science educators. (ERIC Document Reproduction Service No. ED 231 735.)

Hobbs, R. (2005). Media literacy in the K-12 content areas. *Yearbook for the National Society for the Study of Education, 104*(1), 74–99.

Kearsley, G., & Shneiderman, B. (1998). Engagement theory: A framework for technology-based teaching and learning. *Educational Technology, 38*(5), 20–23.

Kerski, J. (2003). The implementation and effectiveness of geographic information systems technology in secondary education. *Journal of Geography, 102*(3), 128–137.

Kirman, J. M. (2003). Transformative geography: Ethics and action in elementary and secondary geography education. *Journal of Geography, 102*(3), 93–98.

Lakkala, M., Lallimo, J., & Hakkarainen, K. (2005). Teachers' pedagogical designs for technology-supported collective inquiry: A national case study. *Computers & Education, 45*(3), 337–56.

Landow, G. (1992). *Hypertext.* Baltimore: Johns Hopkins University Press.

Langeveld, W. (1983). Alternative teaching aids: or why we can do without new technology in political education. (ERIC Document Reproduction Service No. ED 231 737.)

Lee, J. K. (2002a). Digital history in the history/social studies classroom. *The History Teacher, 35*(4), 503–518.

Lee, J. K. (2002b). Principles for interpretative digital history web design. *Journal for the Association of History and Computing, 5*(3). Retrieved May 16, 2005 from http://mcel.pacificu.edu/JAHC/JAHCV3/K-12/lee.html.

Lee, J. K. (2006). Pre-service social studies teachers using digital civic resources. *International Journal of Social Education, 20*(1), 95–110.

Lee, J. K., & Molebash, P. (2006). Teachers and digital historical resources: Seeing the forest and the trees. Paper presented at the annual conference of the *Society for Information Technology and Teacher Education,* Orlando.

Levin, D., Arafeh, S., Lenhart, A., & Rainie, L. (2002). *The digital disconnect: The widening gap between Internet-savvy students and their schools.* New York: Pew Internet & American Life Project.

Ligorio, M. B., & Veermans, M. (2005). Perspectives and patterns in developing and implementing international web-based collaborative learning environments. *Computers & Education, 45*(3), 271–275.

Martorella, P. (1998). Technology and the social studies or which way to the sleeping giant? *Theory and Research in Social Education, 25*(4), 511–514.

McBeath, R. J. (1994). The impact of paradigm shifts on education. *Educational Media International, 31*(3), 165–170.

McKay, R. (1996). Keep the "social" in social studies. *Canadian Social Studies, 31*(3), 11–16.

Mishra, P., & Koehler, M. J. (2006). Technological pedagogical content knowledge: A new framework for teacher knowledge. *Teachers College Record, 108*(6), 1017–1054.

National Council for the Social Studies. (1994). *Expectations for excellence: Curriculum standards for social studies.* Washington, DC: National Council for the Social Studies.

Neilson, J. (1995). *Multimedia and hypertext: The Internet and beyond.* Boston: Academic Press.

Newmann, F. M., & Associates. (1996). *Authentic achievement: Restructuring schools for intellectual quality.* San Francisco: Jossey-Bass.

Parker, W. C. (1991). Achieving thinking and decision-making objectives in social studies. In J. Shaver (ed.), *Handbook of research on social studies teaching and learning* (pp. 345–356). New York: Macmillan.

Patterson, M. W., Reeve, K., & Page, D. (2003). Integrating geographic information systems into the secondary curricula. *Journal of Geography, 102*(6), 275–281.

Puntambekar, S., & Kolodner, J. L. (2005). Toward implementing distributed scaffolding: Helping students learn science from design. *Journal of Research in Science Teaching, 42*(2), 185–217.

Resnick (1994). *Turtles, termites, and traffic jams: Explorations in massively parallel microworlds.* Cambridge, MA: MIT Press.

Ribble, M. S., Bailey, G. D., & Ross, T. W. (2004). Digital citizenship: Addressing appropriate technology behavior. *Learning and Leading with Technology, 32*(1), 6–9, 11.

Robinson, W. (1999). Technology, the economics profession, and pre-college economic education. *Journal of Education, 181*(3), 77–91

Rosenzweig, R. (1999). Crashing the system?: Hypertext and scholarship on American culture. *American Quarterly, 51*(2), 237–246.

Sanders, R. L., Kajs, L. T., & Crawford, C. M. (2002). Electronic mapping in education: The use of geographic information systems. *Journal of Research on Technology in Education, 34*(2), 121–130.

Scardamalia, M., & Bereiter, C. (1989). Conceptions of teaching and approaches to core problems. In M. C. Reynolds (ed.), *Knowledge base for the beginning teacher* (pp. 37–46). Oxford: The American Association of Colleges for Teacher Education.

Scheibe, C. (2004). A deeper sense of literacy: Curriculum-driven approaches to media literacy in the K-12 classroom. *American Behavioral Scientist, 48*, 60–68.

Schwab, J. (1964). Structure of the disciplines: Meanings and significances. In G. W. Ford and L. Pugno (eds), *The structure of knowledge and the curriculum* (pp. 6–30). Chicago: Rand McNally and Company.

Shulman, L. S. (1986). Those who understand: Knowledge growth in teaching. *Educational Researcher, 15*(2), 4–14.

Smith-Gratto, K. (1989). Computer literacy and citizenship in a democracy. *Louisiana Social Studies Journal, 16*(1), 30–33.

Tally, W. (1996). Up against authentic history: Helping teachers make the most of primary source materials on-line. *Electronic Learning, 16*(2), 40–41.

Thornton, S. (2001). From content to subject matter. *Social Studies, 92*(6), 237–242.

Wilson, E. K., & Marsh, G. E. (1995). Social studies and the Internet revolution. *Social Education, 59*(4), 198–202.

7

Perhaps a matter of imagination
TPCK in mathematics education

Imagination is more important than knowledge. For knowledge is limited to all we now know and understand, while imagination embraces the entire world, and all there ever will be to know and understand.

Albert Einstein

Introduction

Albert Einstein was fond of discussing the need to mix imagination and knowledge in understanding the world of mathematics. His opinions on the topic often surfaced during his public conversations and various presentations, especially those after his 1921 Nobel Prize in Physics. When you examine his many different quotes and thoughts related to mathematics, education, and life, you get a sense of the dynamic and engaging educational environment that we are still striving for today in our nation's schools. His frequent comments on independent thinking, questioning, and connecting mathematics to the real world all seem relevant today when considering what teaching and learning should look like in today's mathematics classroom (for a good source on Einstein see the Priwer and Phillips book *Everything Einstein*, 2003).

But the world has changed considerably since Albert Einstein died in 1955, and especially the technology of our world and the tools that we now have available to us as educators in the mathematics classroom. A mere 50 years has seen us move from slide rulers to graphing calculators and from thick books of computational tables to the impressive computing power of laptop computers. Throw into the mix the educational potential of the Internet and even an impressive thinker like Albert Einstein might be challenged to imagine just how it all comes together for an effective learning environment in a mathematics classroom. Yet, for the preservice and in-service mathematics teachers of today, there is an expectation that upon graduation from our teacher education programs they will be able to design creative and effective learning activities that take full advantage of educational technology. We as the leaders of those teacher education programs are perhaps challenged most of all, as we try to systematically help these preservice and in-service teachers imagine how such technologies might be used in developing lessons that engage, excite, and enhance the learning of an increasingly diverse set of students.

The effective use of technology in the mathematics classroom has long been a topic for consideration by mathematics educators. One simply needs to read some of the many discussions on when calculators should be used with students in the learning of mathematics to get a sense of this historical and sometimes conflicting dialog related to the use of technology in the learning of mathematics (Ball & Stacey, 2005; Heid & Edwards, 2001). Some questions have surfaced time and again in these discussions. Questions such as should students who don't know the fundamentals of basic arithmetic operations be allowed to use a calculator? How about if those same students are doing a real-life application activity that requires a great deal of repetitive arithmetic, should calculators be allowed then? The answer to many of these technology-related questions would probably be given by most mathematics educators today as "it depends." It essentially depends upon how the content, pedagogy, and technology might best intersect within the learning of a specific mathematical topic. It also depends on the individual learners themselves, with the diverse needs and background experiences that they each bring to the mathematics classroom.

When considering the overall use of technology in mathematics education, like other fields, it would seem that we have suffered from too much of a focus on "what" technologies to use and too little imaginative thinking on "how" these technologies might be used to support teaching and learning (Heid, 2005; Sinclair & Crespo, 2006; Horwitz & Tinker, 2005). Most of all, we have not had a framework or programmatic theme upon which to build that imaginative thinking and technology use (Hofer, 2005). The current emphasis on technological pedagogical content knowledge (TPCK) as represented in this monograph and foundational articles (such as Mishra & Koehler, 2003, 2006) is quite timely for those of us with a particular interest in preparing teachers of mathematics. How and when technology should be used within our field has never been an easy question for us, or one that is taken lightly.

For mathematics educators, defining the most effective uses of technology in the teaching of mathematics can certainly be described as a "wicked problem," as represented by Koehler and Mishra in the first chapter of this monograph. A number of challenging instructional questions are associated within this wicked problem, such as: When should teachers incorporate calculators when teaching arithmetic? How should teachers incorporate the powerful new symbolic processing programs within basic algebra instruction? Should teachers allow student use of the many new online homework assistance web sites for mathematics? Such instructional questions illustrate how the problem of effective technology integration into the teaching of mathematics fits the parameters of a wicked problem that is indeed ill-structured, complex, and exists within a dynamic context of interdependent variables (Rittel & Webber, 1973). Instructional questions within this context continue to lead to contextually and politically charged discussions among mathematics educators (Ball & Stacey, 2005).

Part of our current challenge in understanding how and when we use technology effectively has been that the mathematics content itself is a rapidly moving "target." Look at most new books on mathematics that reside on the shelves in one of your local mega-bookstores and it is relatively easy to see that technology has had a considerable impact on the content of the mathematics discipline itself. Consider the concept of "fractals." Fractals are essentially a representation of objects that have "fractional" geometric dimensions. Moving beyond the traditional geometry of points, lines, and planes, fractal geometry instead uses computer-like "algorithms" that replicate relatively intricate geometric patterns (Lesmoir-Gordon, 2001; Peterson, 1988; Turner, Blackledge, & Andrews, 1998). A representative and relatively famous fractal is the Sierpinski Triangle, which was named after the Polish mathematician Waclaw Sierpinski, who investigated some of its interesting properties. The triangle illustrates a common fractal property of "self-similarity," where the larger triangle divides into smaller similar triangles, that then divide into even smaller triangles, and the pattern continues. A computer-generated Sierpinski Triangle is shown in Figure 7.1.

Fractal algorithms like Sierpinski's Triangle help us to define some real world phenomena in ways that we never could before using fractional dimensions. For example, clouds, coastlines, plant growth, lightning, and even blood vessels are now routinely defined with fractals and systematically

Figure 7.1 A computer-generated Sierpinski Triangle, which is a public domain image from Wikimedia Commons.

investigated with computer technology, due to the iterative nature of these phenomena (Falconer, 2003). Striving for accuracy in defining or measuring various geographic features like coastlines or rivers is a particularly good example of how fractal mathematics and computer technology can be useful today. When someone (such as a map maker) attempts to measure a coastline, the often jagged line of where water meets shore can actually be measured from many perspectives, ranging from the height of a satellite to the very close viewpoint of a person kneeling on the shore. Using fractal algorithms that make allowances for such considerably different scales, computers can now provide a much more accurate and consistent measurement of coastlines. Another good example of where fractals and computer technology can be useful is for predicting the flooding of rivers with certain geographic patterns. In some rivers, a branching pattern is formed as various tributary streams flow into the larger river. This "branching pattern" can significantly impact water flow and is at times associated with a potential for devastating flooding. Fractal algorithms and computers have greatly increased our understanding and possible prediction of flooding in such river systems. A public domain NASA image from the SeaWiFS satellite of a river system in Norway illustrates this fractal branching pattern of some rivers (Figure 7.2).

Fractals have become a mathematical topic that probably should now be included in every high school curriculum, if for no other reason than that they have considerable real-life applications and connections. Yet the mathematics of fractals can be confusing. For students to understand fractional geometric dimensions they need to understand "fractional exponents," a topic that relies heavily on understanding both fractions and exponents. How and when a teacher might facilitate the learning of fractals, using computer technology to its full advantage, is probably a good example of our need to help mathematics teachers develop strong backgrounds in TPCK.

Figure 7.2 A public domain NASA image from the SeaWiFS satellite of a river system in Norway (visible within snow fields and taken on June 6, 2000).

Fractals are just one illustration of the many important topics in mathematics that have evolved and changed due to technology. Topics such as statistics, graphing, coordinate geometry, matrices, probability, combinatorics, and many other mathematics-related topics are in an ongoing state of change and evolution (Heid, 2005). For example, technology has enabled a wide array of advanced and multivariate statistical methods to recently evolve for analyzing complex data sets (Mertler & Vannatta, 2005). Mathematics is not the only discipline evolving and as one might imagine, other disciplines are being impacted by technology as well. Schmidt and Gurbo's discussion of K-6 literacy education in Chapter 3 is a good illustration, where hypermedia technology is changing how we fundamentally read and search for information.

Recent national studies in mathematics education (and in related fields such as science) have left little doubt that pedagogy and content must be interwoven by teachers to achieve dynamic and effective educational environments within this evolving context for mathematics (Kim, 2003; Martin, Mullis, Gonzalez, & Chrostowski, 2004; National Science Board, 2003). As technology's role in this instructional mix continues to expand and evolve, it would seem increasingly important that teachers be adept at deciding where technology fits in such mathematics instruction. If technology is left out, teachers may well be missing an important opportunity for aiding their students' understanding; or perhaps worse for some topics, teachers may even misrepresent mathematical concepts that are tied closely to computers (such as fractals). On the other side, if teachers use technology inappropriately or too freely (such as having students rely too heavily on calculators in the learning of basic arithmetic), they run the risk of deepening student misconceptions and expanding bad habits. Thus, addressing TPCK carefully within teacher preparation may well be the difference between students having an effective or ineffective mathematics teacher.

What really is the study of mathematics?

For us to consider the TPCK needed by teachers in the effective instruction of mathematics, one might first review a bit about the discipline of mathematics itself. What really is the study of mathematics? What are we trying to learn when we study it in our classrooms? Such questions are actually more difficult than they may seem to be at first. Ask many elementary level students and their teachers to define mathematics and it will often be defined as a study of arithmetic and simple geometry. Middle level and high school level students and teachers might also mention variables, and perhaps various mathematical topics such as algebra, geometry, trigonometry, and calculus. However, you can definitely expect a long pause before any of these individuals answer your question, because it is not a simple question to answer.

In many ways, defining mathematics by its topics (such as involving arithmetic, geometry, algebra, etc.) is much like defining music as a mere sequence of sounds. The "human" or creative element is missing from such a definition, and that human element helps give mathematics, like music, its own interest and beauty. A superficial definition of mathematics can miss its spirit and depth, ignoring the joy, excitement, and even utility that may be found in its study. For those who take the time to look more deeply, mathematics often represents a rich and dynamic excursion into trying to know and control our world through its patterns. It is a discipline that helped mankind build pyramids, navigate oceans, and send rockets into space. It is a discipline in which the imagination and logic of the human mind strive to structure the reality of our existence.

An excellent contemporary discussion and definition of mathematics is the discussion presented by Steen, who suggests:

> Mathematics involves observing, representing and investigating patterns and relationships in social and physical phenomena and between mathematical objects themselves: Mathematics is often defined as the science of space and number ... [but] a more apt definition is that mathematics is the science of patterns. The mathematician seeks patterns in number, in space, in science, in computers, and in imagination. Mathematical theories explain the relations among patterns ... Applications of mathematics use these patterns to "explain" and predict natural phenomena ...
>
> (1988, p. 616)

To see and teach the discipline of mathematics in this exciting way, especially in the complex world of today, a teacher must have the knowledge and overlapping skills represented by TPCK. For teachers of mathematics, it would seem that adequate knowledge in each of the three areas of technology, pedagogy, and content is relatively critical to a teacher's effectiveness in today's mathematics classroom. When considering the content of mathematics, the teacher must know enough of the content of mathematics to be able to appreciate and represent the depth of this important discipline. Second, the teacher must comprehend enough of the pedagogy of teaching mathematics to help students systematically build toward an understanding of mathematics similar to the teacher's own understanding. And finally, since much of the mathematics of today is intricately interwoven with technology, the teacher must be able to understand and use the technology of mathematics in its instruction. But as stated by Mishra and Koehler, TPCK is much more than the individual three components and "represents a thoughtful interweaving of all three key sources of knowledge—technology, pedagogy, and content" (2006, p. 14).

Mathematics teaching and TPCK

Consider the rapid growth of technology in our society, the variety of peda-gogical strategies available to teachers, and the evolving nature of mathemat-ics itself. Anyone reflecting upon how to develop TPCK in mathematics teachers quickly discards the strategy of trying to have teachers gain an experience in all of the potential combinations where technology, pedagogy, and content come together in the mathematics classroom. Such a listing would no doubt be more of an exercise in understanding the mathematical concept of infinity than it would be a strategy conducive to strong teacher preparation. Instead, since it would appear that we cannot possibly provide teachers with all of the potential TPCK that they might use within a mathe-matics classroom, we must instead help them to imagine "possibilities" and develop an open mind for using a variety of approaches and strategies with their students.

We must also help teachers to make sure that the mathematics learned in the classroom is truly mathematics, and not some limited or "watered-down" version of mathematics in the pursuit of a more engaging classroom. Current recommendations, such as those presented within the American Educational Research Association's panel report, *Studying teacher education*, emphasize the importance of a strong sequence of college mathematics coursework for teachers at all levels engaged in the teaching of mathematics (AERA, 2005). This document references correlations between the college coursework of prospective teachers and the general mathematics achieve-ment of their students. Strong content preparation is clearly important for mathematics teachers.

Yet content in mathematics is a much broader realm than many people, including most novice teachers, might realize. This realm is also expanding rapidly. Consider what has been called "discrete mathematics." This field of mathematics involves the study of objects or ideas that can be divided into discrete (separate or discontinuous) parts (Rosen, 1999). Where continu-ous mathematics is typically dealing with measurement, discontinuous mathematics is more focused on counting. For a simple definition, some authors have also described discrete mathematics as "the mathematics most relevant to computing" (Gardiner, 1991). There are actually some problems in discrete mathematics that seem simple at first glance, but really need significant computing power to solve. Problems that have been called "knapsack problems" are good examples. Consider the classroom problem presented by Caldwell and Masat (1991), which has various real-life connections.

> You are taking a two-week hike and will be backpacking everything you need. You have made a list of eight possible items to take of a total of 77 pounds, and your list has each item's weight and its value to you rated

from 1 to 5, with 5 being the highest. If you carry only 30 pounds, what should you take along to get the highest number of value points?

(p. 228)

This problem seems simple at first and you might make some initial headway using a spreadsheet and ordering the items by weight, or by value points, or even by a ratio of weight per value point for each item. However, you eventually find that for the lesser items, you also need to try various combinations. To try all possible combinations you will be trying 2^8 or 256 combinations, and even with access to a spreadsheet with sorting capabilities, all of a sudden writing a computer program to try all possible combinations doesn't sound so bad (and is actually probably a better strategy). Such real-life "knapsack" problems are common in today's world, such as when NASA tries to decide what experiments (each with relative value and weight) might be included on a space mission. Teaching such new computer-based mathematics relies directly on teachers with strong TPCK backgrounds.

Carefully chosen examples, such as the discrete mathematics backpack problem, can go a long way toward providing teachers with strategies for approaching the instruction of various mathematics topics. As Shulman mentions, building pedagogical content knowledge (PCK) is basically related to providing "the most powerful analogies, illustrations, examples, explanations, and demonstrations" to make the subject accessible and comprehensible (1986). Such foundational experiences can have a significant relationship to later teacher attitudes and classroom strategies (Shulman, 1987; Frykholm & Glasson, 2005). As disciplines get more complex and abstract for teachers, such carefully chosen examples will become even more important (Gates, 2004). Providing examples that connect to technology will also be important for addressing the changing nature of mathematics due to technology. Beyond new areas such as discrete mathematics, even more foundational mathematical areas such as algebra are being impacted by their relationship to technology (Heid & Edwards, 2001; Hegedus & Kaput, 2004). For example, some authors suggest that a renewed focus on algebraic thinking is due to the significant role that algebra now plays in technology-related careers and the usefulness of understanding algebra to help comprehend the symbolic nature of how computers process information, while better ensuring an equitable education for all students (Checkley, 2006; B. Moses, 2000; R. P. Moses, 1994).

In the mathematics classrooms of today's schools, teachers may often find themselves helping their students to "imagine" the relationships and patterns in numbers, space, science, computers, and even in thinking itself. The National Council of Teachers of Mathematics (NCTM) has embraced this dynamic approach to mathematics instruction in its *Principles and standards for school mathematics* published by NCTM in 2000. The instructional principles represented in this document provide a "vision" for equity in student expectations, a coherent curriculum, dynamic teaching, constructivist learning, and formative assessment. In its vision of mathematics instruction, the document describes two strands of standards, that of content and that of process. Content standards address the important aspects of mathematical content that should be learned and include numbers and operations, algebra, geometry, measurement, and data analysis/probability. Process standards cover the ways and strategies in which mathematics might be used and include problem solving, reasoning/proof, communication, connections, and representation. For further refinement of the mathematics content to be taught at the elementary and middle school levels, the NCTM recently published the 2006 document *Curriculum focal points for prekindergarten through grade 8 mathematics: A quest for coherence*, which strives to limit the number of mathematics topics taught at each of the PreK through 8th grade levels so that teachers can cover this content more efficiently and in more depth. Thus, when considering the pedagogy and content aspects of TPCK needed for encouraging effective mathematics instruction, it is important to remember that the NCTM standards and curriculum focal points represent a strong foundation upon which to build.

The NCTM has clearly started to address the interaction of technology more directly within the general context of TPCK. In 2003, the NCTM published a position paper on technology that gives significant insight into how technology should be used in the mathematics classroom and the potential role of TPCK. This position statement makes it clear that technology is an essential part of a current mathematics curriculum and states that "using the tools of technology to work within interesting problem contexts can facilitate a student's achievement of a variety of higher-order learning outcomes, such as reflection, reasoning, problem posing, problem solving and decision making" (p. 1). The position paper also makes a series of five recommendations that support this premise and recommends that all levels and all courses should include strong and thoughtful uses of technology. One of the most interesting recommendations in this document is the fourth recommendation, which states: "Programs of preservice teacher preparation and in-service professional development should strive to instill dispositions of openness to experimentation, with ever-evolving technological tools and their pervasive impact on mathematics education" (p. 2). Such a recommendation reflects a subtle but significant change for mathematics education and recognizes that it is, to some degree, the role of the individual mathematics teacher to "imagine" how new technologies might be used in the mathematics classroom and to involve students in experimentation with these important tools in the context of their learning.

Some of the most recent and carefully undertaken research in mathematics education today appears to be consistent with a systematic march toward

TPCK as a unifying theme in which we can conceptualize good mathematics teaching with technology. A good example is the NCTM 2005 Yearbook. It is entitled *Technology-supported mathematics learning environments* and includes 23 excellent articles that carefully suggest technology-supported activities for the mathematics classroom, while also carefully mapping these strategies to both content and pedagogy. Many of the titles themselves suggest such connections. For example, an article by Vincent, entitled "Interactive geometry software and mechanical linkages: Scaffolding students' deductive reasoning" does an excellent job of linking specific technologies to particular geometry concepts, using a strong research-based pedagogy (pp. 93–112). Other articles also reflect a more collaborative approach in defining such TPCK-based activities, such as an excellent article by eight university researchers and public school teachers (Reece *et al.*, 2005) which is entitled "Engaging students in authentic mathematics activities through calculators and small robots" (pp. 319–328). Similarly, many of the more established professional journals in mathematics education are also showing a new context for TPCK, such as the May 2006 issue of *Teaching Children Mathematics*, which had a lead article by Sinclair and Crespo that was entitled "Learning mathematics in dynamic computer environments."

How we approach the instruction of mathematics in our schools and our corresponding preparation of mathematics teachers is evolving due to technology. The future of technology use in the mathematics classroom is typically seen as an exciting one by mathematics educators. Consider the recent work of Heid (2005), who interviewed 22 leading educators in technology and mathematics education and identified areas that seemed to be the most promising in technology use for the mathematics classroom. These technology applications included various innovations, such as: dynamic computation tools, or software that facilitates interactive computation; microworlds, which allow focused experimentation of various mathematical relationships; intelligent tutors, which facilitate flexible instruction of mathematical content; computer algebra systems, which facilitate symbolic manipulation of algebraic symbols; handheld devices, which permit convenient technology access; web-based instruction, which allows systematic, cost-effective instruction; and interactive learning communities, that can facilitate educational collaboration in classrooms across many different states and even nations.

Beyond instruction, technology can also play an important administrative role for mathematics teachers and their schools. *Education Week* recently showcased the role of computer technology in helping teachers with administrative tasks in their classroom, such as recording and tracking criterion referenced tests, class assignments, and attendance, as well as connecting that information to suggestions for lessons (Hoff, 2006; Zehr, 2006). Districts are steadily becoming more "data wise" and helping their teachers to store, access, and interpret information within an electronic format to aid them in making pedagogical decisions in the classroom (Borja, 2006). Some authors are even declaring Internet access within most classrooms today as generally "ubiquitous," while also suggesting that more needs to be done with teacher professional development to help teachers better understand how to use such pervasive computer access to improve instructional decisions at the classroom level (Swanson, 2006).

As technology is becoming ever more pervasive in our society it is also being more formally recognized as a critical tool for facilitating both the effective doing and learning of mathematics. The Association of Mathematics Teacher Educators (AMTE) succinctly reinforced this critical importance of technology in the teaching and learning of mathematics in their recent position paper, when they stated that "AMTE recognizes that technology has become an essential tool for doing mathematics in today's world, and thus that it is essential for the teaching and learning of mathematics" (2006, p. 1). The AMTE position paper is a strong endorsement of the idea that one cannot truly be an effective teacher of mathematics in today's classroom unless one has "the knowledge and experiences needed to incorporate technology." The two-page AMTE position paper also reinforces a mathematics teacher's need to be both flexible and creative in their application of technology.

Qualities of a mathematics teacher with TPCK

A teacher who has a strong background in TPCK offers her students a considerable advantage in the learning of mathematics. Consider the advantages that such a teacher might have in introducing algebra into a middle school classroom on the first day of an algebra class. I had the chance to witness this advantage first hand while watching a middle school teacher with 20 years of classroom experience and strong TPCK skills. She first approached the introduction of algebra by showing how it generalizes arithmetic by giving examples of specific triangles and finding their areas. This was first illustrated by having students use an electronic geoboard (an applet where virtual rubber bands are stretched on virtual pegs) available at the National Library of Virtual Manipulatives site (http://nlvm.usu.edu/en/nav/vlibrary.html). The teacher then decided to use a spreadsheet on her display device to further illustrate the area formula for a triangle by showing various examples and reinforcing the mathematical relationship between the triangle's base, height, and area, as well as identifying how algebra within the spreadsheet helped students to more efficiently compute the areas of any triangle. The teacher then further illustrated algebra in real life by having students visit various web sites and investigate several careers where algebra played a significant role. Much of the teacher's lesson was relatively spontaneous and relied on her ability to "imagine" the next step in the instructional process. It was easy to see by the attentive looks of the students and their nodding heads that they better understood the "power and utility" of algebra and that they were now ready to start their year of algebra study.

Could this introduction of algebra have been done without the computer, or facilitated by a teacher with little TPCK? Perhaps, but considering that several aspects of this lesson were initiated in response to student questions (such as the possible career connections to algebra) it would seem doubtful that a teacher without strong TPCK could have assembled such an effective lesson so quickly. A teacher without TPCK would not have decided to use a virtual geoboard for their initial illustration and even with regular geoboards available (obviously a worthy tool in its own right), the focus of the lesson was not on the triangles, but rather on the generalizing of arithmetic represented by algebra. The visible connection between the individual triangles and the area formula for triangles was a further advantage offered by a computer spreadsheet in this context, and the teacher knew that this was an excellent opportunity to take advantage of that tool. Using a spreadsheet also show-cased the power of algebra within a real-life computational environment represented by the spreadsheet itself. The web sites associated with the algebra-related careers (perhaps her most spontaneous part of the lesson) established a further real-life context for students and helped to directly answer the age-old classroom question, "why do we need to know this?" before it ever surfaced. A mathematics teacher without the aid of technology, or even one with technology access but little TPCK would be hard pressed to do so much in so little time with this introductory lesson. Algebra by its very nature is abstract and many an algebra student has spent their first few weeks, and some their first full year of algebra instruction, without really being able to define algebra (Noddings, 2000; Steen, 1992). These particular students now had an excellent working definition for algebra, as well as several examples of its use in real life, before they commenced study of this critically important body of mathematical content.

This talented teacher's ability to imagine potential applications of computer technology and then "weigh" the relative benefit of these various instructional options within the context of a specific mathematical topic may be what TPCK for mathematics teachers is all about in today's classroom. Ever since the first *A nation at risk* report was published (National Commission on Excellence in Education, 1983) reform in mathematics education has been steadily striving to make the learning of mathematics more relevant, more engaging, and in many ways, more imaginative. Imagining technology connections, determining the benefit of related instructional strategies, and putting it all together for an effective mathematics lesson is really a growing responsibility for the mathematics teacher of today. As suggested by the NCTM position statement on technology: "Technologies are essential tools within a balanced mathematics program. Teachers must be prepared to serve as knowledgeable decision makers in determining when and how their students can use these tools most effectively" (NCTM, 2003).

Imagination is more than a component of good mathematics instruction; it is really at the core of mathematics itself. Like the initial quote from Albert Einstein at the beginning of the chapter, few mathematicians and their colleagues in mathematics education would argue against the importance of using one's imagination in the study of mathematics. In fact, in some mathematical topics, such as with complex (or imaginary) numbers, the human imagination plays a critical role in understanding the content. Some works associated with mathematics are even known for their use of imagination, such as the paintings of M. C. Escher and his engaging use of tessellations. Interestingly, Escher was rarely successful at traditional mathematics learning and once said in an interview, "I never got a pass mark in math ... just imagine—mathematicians now use my prints to illustrate their books."

Reaching all students in the mathematics classroom, such as talented artists like Escher, or students with different learning styles, genders, races, and backgrounds, may well become steadily more linked to effective technology use. The computers' flexibility with instructional scaffolding, alternative representations, screen displays, audio languages, assessment, and teacher feedback makes reaching a wider range of students increasingly more possible as computers become more pervasive and ubiquitous (Horwitz & Tinker, 2005). Such innovation and classroom flexibility has also been identified by the National Council of Teachers of Mathematics as a key to narrowing mathematics achievement gaps (NCTM, 2005). Yet, the ability of a teacher to take advantage of such technology-based instructional flexibility in reaching all students may well depend significantly upon that teacher's knowledge of which technologies and pedagogies to employ for which content.

It would make sense then, that if a teacher education program wants to build strong TPCK within its mathematics education students (both undergraduate and graduate), such a program might need to consider how to encourage these future and current teachers to approach mathematics instruction more imaginatively and creatively and to strive for lessons that engage, excite, and educate the students within their own classrooms. But first, how would we recognize mathematics teachers who have successfully achieved such skills? In other words, what qualities might be observable in mathematics educators who are strong in their TPCK? What qualities were observable in the teacher mentioned earlier, who represented algebra so well using technology? Based on the previous discussion, it makes sense that mathematics teachers with strong backgrounds in TPCK would most likely demonstrate the following characteristics.

1. Mathematics teachers with strong backgrounds in TPCK would probably have a relative openness to experimentation with the

ever-evolving technological tools available to them in the mathematics classroom. In other words, they will "try" new technology-based lessons with their students on a regular and sometimes spontaneous basis, confident that if done thoughtfully and interactively, their students can learn something of value each time they attempt something new.

2. Such mathematics teachers would also probably strive to be consistently "on-task" for the mathematical topic or content being taught. Teachers with strong pedagogical content knowledge, regardless of technology, would stay relatively focused on the content being discussed or explained during their lessons. In other words, teachers with strong TPCK are effective at focusing on the mathematics concepts, while still taking advantage of the instructional opportunities offered by technology.

3. Mathematics teachers with strong TPCK backgrounds would also approach their mathematics instruction with clear and systematic pedagogical strategies in mind. In other words, these teachers would strive to know "where" their students are conceptually, "what" they need to do to achieve the next step in an instructional process, and "how" they generally want their students to proceed through careful sequences of classroom interactions and tasks.

4. Mathematics teachers with strong TPCK would try to make periodic connections for their students as to "why" a particular technology is useful for instructing a particular mathematics topic. In other words, these teachers would consistently offer explanations to their students on what they are doing with the technology, why a specific tool is appropriate for a particular mathematical situation, and perhaps even how a selected technology fundamentally works. Such explanations of some classroom technologies (such as computer-based lab equipment, graphing calculators, or wireless Internet access) can also have an added benefit of contributing to a student's understanding of the sciences related to the technology, as suggested by McCrory in the science chapter of this monograph (Chapter 9).

5. Strong TPCK teachers would also characteristically embrace the administrative capabilities of technology to help guide their mathematics instruction using student assessment data such as criterion-referenced tests. Such assessment data can help a teacher identify gaps in student understanding which might form the rationale for switching instructional strategies or taking a different pedagogical approach with some or all of the students. This "data-driven" decision-making process can help a teacher select lessons that more directly address where students are in their current understanding of a topic. It also models for students how the computer might aid in the management of information.

6. Perhaps most of all, mathematics teachers with strong TPCK would also do their best to be caring teachers who are comfortable and optimistic for change. Consistent with a definition of mathematics as the dynamic discipline that it is in today's world, a teacher with a rich TPCK background would expect change, not only in the technologies available to them in the classroom, but quite likely in the content of the mathematics that they should be teaching. They must be caring instructional leaders that are welcoming to all students as they enter this changing and evolving world of mathematics.

Mathematics teacher education programs and TPCK

How do we develop dynamic and caring teachers with TPCK like the one described above? Are they "super teachers" who are born to excel in a technology-enabled classroom, or are they simply teachers who have been prepared to excel with the necessary background experiences? Most teacher educators would no doubt suggest that an effective teacher education program can indeed have a significant impact on later teacher and student achievement, or why have such a program in the first place? It would make sense that if we are to develop TPCK within the preservice and in-service mathematics teachers of a teacher preparation program, then like most programmatic objectives, we must consciously address this goal across our program operations (Education Commission of the States, 2003). What then might such a program look like? What might be its observable features? Consistent with Einstein's endorsement of imagination, let's take a few last moments to "imagine" how such a teacher preparation program in mathematics education might approach building TPCK within their preservice and in-service teachers.

Since software, hardware, and computer applications are changing so rapidly, it is probably quite impossible for a teacher preparation program to directly teach its students all the individual applications and possibilities that might arise in their use of technology within the context of content and pedagogy. Instead, such programs can essentially only hope to foster a "disposition" for the use of such technologies in a flexible, experimental, and thoughtful way. This might seem to be particularly true as we move into educational environments that become ever more pervasive in computing technologies (Kaput, 2000).

In many ways, to be successful, an effective teacher preparation program must be relatively dynamic, reflective, and transformative (Thompson & Zeuli, 1999). Some foundational glimpses of what is important in such teacher preparation environments for mathematics appear to be steadily evolving from research and are becoming more directly related to how students at all levels learn effectively. In the National Research Council's 2005 report *How students learn*, a total of 179 out of the 600 pages are dedicated to the learning of mathematics. Within this extensive discussion, Fuson,

Kalchman, and Bransford (2005, pp. 217–256), reinforce that there are three important principles for teachers to follow in helping provide a foundation for the learning of mathematics. These principles include: (1) teachers must engage student prior understandings; (2) teachers must help students build a deep foundation of factual knowledge, give students a conceptual framework, and help them to organize knowledge; and (3) teachers need to help students take a meta-cognitive approach in taking control of their own learning. For mathematics education, perhaps more than in many other disciplines, the newest studies are reinforcing that such learning principles must also be strongly grounded in content preparation, as well as practiced in multiple contexts and field experiences (AERA, 2005; U.S. Department of Education, 2005). Such guiding principles related to how students need to learn, when grounded in strong content preparation and technology use, would seem to provide an excellent framework upon which to help mathematics education programs organize instruction and instill strong TPCK in their graduates.

In today's environment of teacher preparation, programs that successfully address the TPCK of their preservice and in-service teachers would also need to ensure that such teachers are prepared for the many culturally diverse settings in which they might teach. Various studies have shown that there is a definite obstacle to minority students' mathematics achievement, possibly even more so in urban settings, when there is a mismatch between teachers' personal knowledge of students' cultures and the actual cultural environments of their schools (Seilar, Tobin, & Sokolic, 2001). For example, urban teachers sometimes find that they are better able to build the mathematical understanding of their students when they use urban illustrations for challenging mathematical topics, such as explaining network optimization by use of a traffic flow example. When teachers are not aware of such potential cultural contexts, they miss out on a very powerful way of connecting with their students (Kaser, Bourexis, Loucks-Horsley, & Raizen, 1999; Ladson-Billings, 1995).

As teacher preparation programs strive to more systematically embrace TPCK as a foundational goal for preparing mathematics teachers and for reaching all students regardless of their culture, then TPCK may well become a useful "organizational construct" for helping prioritize technology-related experiences. When a program's leaders or instructors consider a particular technology-related activity for potential inclusion in a mathematics education program, then experiences that are more directly compatible with TPCK may be worthy of a higher priority. For example, a spreadsheet activity that explores and addresses student misconceptions of algebraic functions would seem to be a relatively important experience, while using Photoshop to modify images for illustrating the cover of a math journal might seem less important (although perhaps worthy for another context).

Assuming that TPCK indeed represents a key construct for a strong mathematics education program in today's teacher preparation environment, it would make sense that successful programs might exhibit the following characteristics as they strive to develop a strong TPCK foundation in their students.

1. A successful program would most likely need to encourage an "imaginative openness" for classroom experimentation in using technologies for learning mathematical content. This encouragement would no doubt be most observable in how the professors or instructors themselves experiment with technology and various learning strategies in pursuit of their own learning goals within the program's coursework. Such experimentation is consistent with the "disposition" recommendation as mentioned in the NCTM position statement on technology.

2. A successful program would probably not overly separate technology, content, and pedagogy across the coursework of teachers. In other words, the required courses within the mathematics department would include strong technology use and an effective pedagogy of presentation; while correspondingly, the methods and core education courses would also strive to periodically connect to a strong mathematical context.

3. It would seem that a teacher preparation program must carefully select the TPCK-related examples or problems that would be included in a methods class or other program coursework. Instructional opportunities represented in this way may well form one of the more important strategies for building TPCK within teachers when considering that modeling can be so powerful in teacher professional development (Education Commission of the States, 2003).

4. As suggested by Mishra and Koehler (2006), TPCK itself may well represent an important framework for restructuring the professional development experiences for teachers. This framework seems particularly important within the context of mathematics, as the discipline itself continues to evolve and expand related to technology.

5. TPCK experiences in which a teacher might be involved within a program should be as culturally relevant as possible. It is important for a teacher to recognize that all strategies do not work for all students and having teachers consider the cultural relevance of an instructional activity may well be a key to helping them to determine how to reach all students (Darling-Hammond, 1997).

6. Although TPCK appears to be a strong foundational framework for restructuring teacher preparation and professional development, it is important for teachers within successful teacher preparation programs to still recognize that not all effective uses of technology are

tied directly to content and pedagogy. The effective use of technology is a relatively broad spectrum. In other words, teachers need to be aware that technology can also be an effective element of classroom management, parent communication, and many other aspects of being a good "teacher."

7. As computers become more ubiquitous and pervasive, technology must still never overshadow the focus on students as individuals, an educational priority that helps to make teachers such a powerful catalyst for positive growth in young people. Teachers of mathematics, like all teachers, must exhibit a "demonstrated caring" that encourages students to take intellectual chances. As suggested by Davis, Maher, and Noddings (1990), "children who feel cared for are more likely to engage freely in the kind of intellectual activity [constructivist dialogue] that we have described here" (p. 191). When a trusted and caring teacher is leading the class discussions, patiently giving alternate explanations for difficult concepts, or simply helping students to periodically "mess around with mathematical ideas," then these students will indeed be more willing to push their personal limits in understanding mathematics.

A few final thoughts

As institutions who prepare mathematics teachers continue to refine their programs to be more effective in the integration of technology and to more directly address the TPCK of their students, it will be important for these programs to be fully aware of what professional associations like NCTM and AMTE are recommending in this context. Professional associations and coalitions of professional associations, such as the National Technology Leadership Coalition described in the organizational structures chapter of this monograph (Chapter 13, Bull, Bell, and Hammond), are beginning to play a key leadership role in helping to advance an understanding of TPCK as these organizations facilitate collaborative dialogs among professionals. Such collaborative discussions will go a long way toward helping institutions to refine their programs related to technology integration, as we strive to be as effective as possible in preparing teachers for the technological and dynamic world of today.

To help prepare caring, engaging, and imaginative mathematics teachers for today's world, it would make sense that those of us in teacher preparation have that goal clearly in mind as we design our programs. Such a goal in our programs is not an easy task and in a final connection to our most imaginative mathematical thinker, it is worthy to consider that Albert Einstein also once said that "every theory should be as simple as possible, but no simpler." In this attempt to look at TPCK in the mathematics classroom and in the preparation of mathematics teachers, I may well have oversimplified the complexity of this important intersection between technology, pedagogy, and content. However, striving for such "simplicity in statement," is itself a time-honored approach in the discipline of mathematics, as mathematicians are always striving to state things as simply as possible when we try to understand complex relationships. Simplicity has been a goal of all mathematicians as they define a difficult problem, use symbolic representations, or refine a proof. As an organizing construct for preparing mathematics teachers to use technology effectively in the teaching and learning of their discipline, TPCK would appear to be a worthy construct. It offers additional program focus in helping conceptualize how content, pedagogy, and technology might come together effectively in a teacher preparation program within the context of a mathematics discipline that is itself rapidly evolving due to technology. Mix in a bit of imagination from both the program and the individual, and the teachers graduating from such programs may well have a significant advantage in helping their students to enter the very useful and imaginative realm that has always been mathematics.

References

American Educational Research Association. (2005). *Studying teacher education: The report of the AERA panel on research and teacher education.* Edited by M. Cochran-Smith and K. M. Zeichner. Mahwah, NJ: Lawrence Erlbaum Associates.

Association of Mathematics Teacher Educators. (2006). *Preparing teachers to use technology to enhance the learning of mathematics.* An AMTE position statement, published January, 2006. Accessible at http://www.amte.net.

Ball, L., & Stacey, K. (2005). Teaching strategies for developing judicious technology use. In W. J. Masalski, & P. C. Elliott (eds), *Technology-supported mathematics learning environments,* the Sixty-Seventh Yearbook of the National Council of Teachers of Mathematics. Reston, VA: National Council of Teachers of Mathematics.

Borja, R. R. (2006). Voices of experience. In the focus issue entitled, The information edge: Using data to accelerate achievement, of *Education Week, 25*(35), 35.

Caldwell, J. H., & Masat, F. E. (1991). A knapsack problem, critical-path analysis, and expression trees. In M. J. Kenney & C. R. Hirsch (eds), *Discrete mathematics across the curriculum, K-12,* the 1991 Yearbook of the National Council of Teachers of Mathematics. Reston, VA: National Council of Teachers of Mathematics.

Checkley, K. (2006). "Radical" math becomes the standard: Emphasis on algebraic thinking, problem solving, communication. *Education Update,* newsletter within the *Association for Supervision and Curriculum Development, 48*(4), 1–2, 8.

Darling-Hammond, L. (1997). *The right to learn: A blueprint for creating schools that work.* San Francisco, CA: Jossey-Bass.

Davis, R. B., Maher, C. A., & Noddings, N. (1990). Suggestions for the improvement of mathematics education. In *Constructivist views on the teaching and learning of mathematics,* Monograph Number 4. Reston, VA: National Council of Teachers of Mathematics.

Education Commission of the States. (2003). *Eight questions on teacher preparation: What does the research say?* Denver, CO: ECS. Available from www.ecs.org/treport.

Falconer, K. (2003). *Fractal geometry: Mathematical foundations and applications.* Chichester, West Sussex, England: John Wiley and Sons.

Frykholm, J., & Glasson, G. (2005). Connecting science and mathematics instruction: Pedagogical context knowledge for teachers. *School Science and Mathematics, 105*(3), 127–141.

Fuson, K. C., Kalchman, M., & Bransford, J. D. (2005). Mathematical understanding: An Introduction. In M. S. Donovan, & J. D. Bransford (eds), *How students learn: History, mathematics, and science in the classroom.* Committee on How People Learn, A targeted report for teachers from the National Research Council, Washington, DC: The National Academies Press.

Gardiner, A. D. (1991). A cautionary note. In M. J. Kenney & C. R. Hirsch (eds), *Discrete mathematics across the curriculum, K-12*, the 1991 Yearbook of the National Council of Teachers of Mathematics. Reston, VA: National Council of Teachers of Mathematics.

Gates, P. (2004). *Proceedings of the Annual Meeting of the International Group for the Psychology of Mathematics Education*, held in Bergen, Norway, July 14–18.

Hegedus, S. J., & Kaput, J. J. (2004). An introduction to the profound potential of connected algebra activities: Issues of representation, engagement and pedagogy. *Proceedings of the 28th conference of the International Group for the Psychology of Mathematics Education*, 3(1), 129–136.

Heid, M. K. (2005). Technology in mathematics education: Tapping into visions of the future. In W. J. Masalski & P. C. Elliott (eds), *Technology-supported mathematics learning environments*, the Sixty-Seventh Yearbook of the National Council of Teachers of Mathematics. Reston, VA: National Council of Teachers of Mathematics.

Heid, M. K., & Edwards, M. T. (2001). Computer algebra systems: Revolution or retrofit for today's classrooms? *Theory into Practice, 40* (Spring), 128–136.

Hofer, M. (2005). Technology and teacher preparation in exemplary institutions: 1994 to 2003. *Journal of Computing in Teacher Education, 22*(1), 5–14.

Hoff, D. J. (2006). Delving into data: States and districts are beginning to build digital data systems that can drive decisions in the classroom and the boardroom. In the focus issue entitled, The information edge: Using data to accelerate achievement, *Education Week*, 25(35), 12–14, 20–22.

Horwitz, P., & Tinker, R. (2005). Universal design with technology. *The Concord Consortium*, 9(1), 1, 4–5.

Kaput, J. J. (2000). Implications of the shift from isolated, expensive technology to connected, inexpensive, diverse and ubiquitous technologies. *Proceedings of the International Conference on Technology in Mathematics Education*, Auckland, NZ.

Kaser, J., Bourexis, P. S., Loucks-Horsley, S., & Raizen, S. A. (1999). *Enhancing program quality in science and mathematics*. Thousand Oaks, CA: Corwin Press.

Kim, J. (2003). *Overcoming challenges in urban education: CPMSA achievement highlights and case stories of five sites*. Boston, MA: Systemic Research, Inc.

Ladson-Billings, G. (1995). Toward a theory of culturally relevant pedagogy. *American Educational Research Journal, 32*, 465–491.

Lesmoir-Gordon, N. (2001). *Introducing fractal geometry*. Duxford, Cambridge, England: Icon Publishers.

Martin, M. O., Mullis, I. V. S., Gonzalez, E. J., & Chrostowski, S. J. (2004). *Findings from IEA's trends in international mathematics and science study at the fourth and eighth grades*. Chestnut Hill, MA: TIMSS & PIRLS International Study Center, Boston College.

Mertler, C. A., & Vannatta, R. A. (2005). *Advanced and multivariate statistical methods*, 3rd edn. Glendale, CA: Pyrczak Publishing.

Mishra, P., & Koehler, M. J. (2003). Not "what" but "how": Becoming design-wise about educational technology. In Y. Zhao (ed.), *What should teachers know about technology? Perspectives and practices* (pp. 99–121). Greenwich, CT: Information Age Publishing.

Mishra, P., & Koehler, M. J. (2006). Technological pedagogical content knowledge: A new framework for teacher knowledge. *Teachers College Record, 108*(6), 1017–1054.

Moses, B. (2000). Exploring our world through algebraic thinking. *Mathematics Education Dialogues*, April. Reston, VA: National Council of Teachers of Mathematics.

Moses, R. P. (1994). Remarks on the struggle for citizenship and math/science literacy. *Journal of Mathematical Behavior*, 13, 107–111.

National Commission on Excellence in Education. (1983). *A nation at risk: The imperative for educational reform*. A report to the nation and the Secretary of Education, United States Department of Education.

National Council of Teachers of Mathematics. (2000). *Principles and standards for school mathematics*. Reston, VA: NCTM. Accessible at http://www.nctm.org.

National Council of Teachers of Mathematics. (2003). The use of technology in the learning and teaching of mathematics. *NCTM position statement*, published October. Accessible at http://standards.nctm.org.

National Council of Teachers of Mathematics. (2005). Closing the achievement gap. *NCTM position statement*, published April. Accessible at http://standards.nctm.org.

National Council of Teachers of Mathematics. (2006). *Curriculum focal points for prekindergarten through grade 8 mathematics: A quest for coherence.* Reston, VA: NCTM. Accessible at http://www.nctm.org.

National Research Council. (2005). *How students learn: History, mathematics, and science in the classroom.* Committee on How People Learn, A targeted report for teachers, M. S. Donovan & J. D. Bransford, (eds) Washington, DC: The National Academies Press.

National Science Board. (2003). *The science and engineering workforce realizing America's potential.* Washington, DC: National Science Foundation.

Noddings, N. (2000). Algebra for all? Why? *Mathematics Education Dialogues*, April. Reston, VA: National Council of Teachers of Mathematics.

Peterson, I. (1988). *The mathematical tourist: Snapshots of modern mathematics.* New York: Freeman and Company Publishers.

Priwer, S., & Phillips, C. (2003). *The everything Einstein book.* Avon, MA: Adams Media Corporation.

Reece, G. C., Dick, J., Dildine, J. P., Smith, K., Storaasli, M., Travers, K. J., *et al.* (2005). Engaging students in authentic mathematics activities through calculators and small robots. In W. J. Masalski, & P. C. Elliott (eds), *Technology-supported mathematics learning environments*, the Sixty-Seventh Yearbook of the National Council of Teachers of Mathematics. Reston, VA: National Council of Teachers of Mathematics.

Rittel, H., & Webber, M. (1973). Dilemmas in a general theory of planning. *Policy Sciences, 4*(2), 155–169.

Rosen, K. H. (1999). *Discrete mathematics and its applications.* San Francisco, CA: McGraw Hill.

Seilar, G., Tobin, K., & Sokolic, J. (2001). Design, technology, and science: Sites for learning, resistance, and social reproduction in urban schools. *Journal of Research in Science Teaching, 48*(7), 746–767.

Shulman, L. S. (1986). Those who understand: Knowledge growth in teaching. *Educational Researcher, 15*(2), 4–14.

Shulman, L. S. (1987). Knowledge and teaching: Foundations of the new reform. *Harvard Educational Review, 57*(1), 1–22.

Sinclair, N., & Crespo, S. (2006). Learning mathematics in dynamic computer environments. *Teaching Children Mathematics, 12*(9), 437–444.

Steen, L. A. (1988). The science of patterns. *Science, 240*, 29.

Steen, L. A. (1992). Does everybody need to study algebra? *Mathematics Teacher, 85*(4), 258–260.

Swanson, R. R. (2006). Tracking U.S. Trends. In the focus issue entitled, The information edge: Using data to accelerate achievement, *Education Week, 35*, 50–55.

Thompson, C., & Zeuli, J. (1999). The frame and the tapestry: Standards-based reform and professional development. In L. Darling-Hammond and G. Sykes (eds), *Teaching as a learning profession: Handbook of policy and practice* (pp. 341–375). San Francisco: Jossey-Bass.

Turner, M. J., Blackledge, J. M., & Andrews, P. R. (1998). *Fractal geometry in digital imagery.* San Diego, CA: Academic Press.

United States Department of Education. (2005). *The secretary's fourth annual report on teacher quality, from the office of Postsecondary Education.* Jessup, MD: Educational Publications Center, U.S. Department of Education.

Vincent, J. (2005). Interactive geometry software and mechanical linkages: Scaffolding students' deductive reasoning. In W. J. Masalski & P. C. Elliott (eds), *Technology-supported mathematics learning environments*, the Sixty-Seventh Yearbook of the National Council of Teachers of Mathematics. Reston, VA: National Council of Teachers of Mathematics.

Zehr, M. A. (2006). Monthly checkups: A new principal works with teachers to get the most out of district benchmark assessments. In the focus issue entitled, The information edge: Using data to accelerate achievement, *Education Week, 25*(35), 35.

8

Placing the magic in the classroom
TPCK in arts education

NANCY DePLATCHETT

Introduction

The Internet, email, cell phones, and innovative software applications have drastically altered the way we live and work in this twenty-first century. As you read this essay, new technologies are being developed that will likely alter the way we live and work in the years to come. Author David Thornburg stated in his book, *The new basics: Education and the future of work in the telematic age* (2002), that the core skills necessary for the present-day worker are digital-age literacy, inventive thinking, effective communication, and high productivity. The Partnership for 21st Century Skills, in their report, *Learning for the 21st century* (2000), cited the following learning skills as necessary to meeting the demands of the twenty-first century:

- information and media literacy skills
- communication skills
- critical thinking and systems thinking
- problem identification, formulation, and solution
- creativity and intellectual curiosity
- interpersonal and collaborative skills
- self-direction
- accountability and adaptability
- social responsibility

Most educators agree that training in technology use is essential for preparing the next generation of workers for successful careers. But in order to hone the learning skills imperative for today's ever-changing workplaces, educators should not overlook the value of visual and performing arts in education.

Every single one of the skills listed above can be enhanced through arts education. When students create original artworks, most—if not all—of their choices are self-directed. They make decisions based on their own judgments of "rightness of fit." They use creativity and critical thinking to find the best vehicles to communicate their ideas and to solve complex visual, aural, verbal, or spatial problems. In art making, learning is a process of self-discovery.

During this process, goals change as unexpected opportunities arise; thus, students develop flexibility and adaptability. Moreover, the process is often more personally satisfying than traditional, "read-and-regurgitate" learning approaches. Students are more invested in their work and are more apt to exercise personal responsibility to ensure success. In group projects like plays, concerts, and class murals, accountability becomes even more important as each individual is responsible for contributing to a collective goal and must work with a team to ensure that the goal is being reached.

The national standards for all subject areas, including the arts, have content standards that cross disciplines and enable teachers to include this type of instruction in their classroom. Several examples of these standards that are easily integrated into lessons both in the arts and other content areas follow. First, in the National Standards in the Arts, Content Standard 5 in Dance is demonstrating and understanding dance in various cultures and historical periods and Content Standard 8 in Music is understanding relationships between music, the other arts, and disciplines outside the arts. Second, in the National Science Standards, students understand the nature of scientific inquiry, and explore the fact that learning can come from careful observations and simple experiments. As a last example, in the National Standards for History, students understand and know how to analyze chronological relationships and patterns.

These are just a few examples of content standards that can be used for integration of subject areas and there are many more that overlap. The National Standards do not limit you to a single subject. They allow you to interpret and expand your teaching. Furthermore, the arts enhance information and media literacy skills as students use programs like Photoshop, iMovie, and iTunes, as they design virtual galleries and flyers to promote their exhibits and as they work the sound and lighting boards for dance and theater performances.

There are many readily available online resources for teachers to access to incorporate technology into instructional planning. For example, *edutopia* magazine, www.edutopia.org, is published in print and on line by The George Lucas Educational Foundation (GLEF). The GLEF publishes stories of innovative teaching and learning through a variety of media—a magazine, an e-newsletter, CD-ROMs, DVDs, books, and their web site. Here, you will find detailed articles, in-depth case studies, research summaries, instructional modules, short documentary segments, expert interviews, and links to hundreds of relevant resources. You will also be able to participate as a member of an online community of people actively working to reinvent schools for the twenty-first century. It is a free resource for educators and was founded in 1991 as a nonprofit operating foundation to celebrate and encourage innovation in schools. Since that time, they have been documenting, disseminating, and advocating for exemplary programs in K-12 public schools to help these practices spread nationwide.

In the June 2006 edition of *edutopia* magazine, teachers responded to the question, "What did you learn this year?" Two teachers responded with favorable remarks about their experiences integrating technology in their classrooms:

> Eager to try some new approaches with my eighth graders, I dove into the world of iPhoto, iMovie, PowerPoint, and online discussion forums—all in one semester. It has been exhilarating watching my students spread their wings to try these various media-laden activities, many of which they use more competently than I do. I have learned many computer tricks, but the most useful information I can pass to colleagues is this: Know your software and hardware requirements and capabilities before launching into a project that may be doomed by incompatibility or school-network crashes. Work closely with your tech people before you begin, and you'll see triumph, not disappointment, on your students' faces.
>
> (Margaret Herberger, Eighth Grade and College English Language
> Acquisition Teacher, Buffalo, New York)

> Of all the things I learned this year, the most important is how to give students the tools to find their voices. We have blogged with soldiers in Iraq, used a wiki to write collaboratively across classes, made movies to promote childhood safety in our community, and experimented with podcasting the news at our school. Through all these twenty-first-century tools, their voices are being heard loud and clear!
>
> (April Chamberlain, Technology Team Leader, Paine Intermediate
> School, Trussville, Alabama)

Both of these responses highlight the benefits of using technology to enable students to express themselves and create. The first quote is particularly pertinent in that it reveals the potential dangers of utilizing technology without sufficient preparation. In short, the benefits of using technology to tap into students' creativity are endless; but to ensure the successful integration of technology, it is essential to train pre-service teachers in all of their methods courses and to offer continuing education classes to in-service teachers.

TPCK in arts education

Koehler and Mishra point out (see Chapter 1) that there are many reasons to integrate technology into all subject areas, but it does complicate the process of teaching. While the opportunities to integrate technology into arts education are delineated later in this chapter, it is noteworthy to describe the link between teacher knowledge of the subject matter, in this case, the arts, and the integration of the arts in teacher preparation, i.e., using technology to teach children about the visual and performing arts, particularly how technology integration is taught in arts methods classes. Koehler and Mishra stated, "…the decision to use a technology in one's teaching introduces a myriad of affordances for teaching content and engaging learners, as well as a number of constraints on what functions technologies can serve in the classroom" (see Chapter 1). Because the arts encompass both visual and performing domains, the problem is even more complex.

The nexus of subject matter, pedagogy, and technology in the arts presents yet another example of a "wicked problem" (Rittel & Webber, 1973). At the multiple subject, pre-service level, when students take a variety of methods classes, the arts methods class rarely, if ever, receives the same emphasis as the core subjects, e.g., reading-literacy, mathematics, science, and social studies. In many instances, art and music are combined into one methods class, and even then, at a reduced number of units. As a result, the attention devoted to art and music methods in the preparation of elementary teachers is minimal. Considering that the amount of content and pedagogy is no less than in other subjects, how are the visual and performing arts methods instructors supposed to address all of the standards *and* integrate technology into the curriculum? As a result, the art and music methods classes rarely have enough time to adequately address content and pedagogy, leaving the technology component out completely or addressing TPCK inadequately, at best.

It should also be noted that TPCK differs among the arts, adding another level of complexity to this already wicked problem. For example, using digital movies to study dance movements demands a certain level of sophistication as a user of technology as well as being an expert in dance movement as opposed to using a virtual tour of an art museum for an art history lesson. Where do the pre-service teachers learn the continuum of possible uses for integrating technology into their instruction when the variety of uses of technology differs widely and the classes they take to learn to integrate their technology skills into instruction often meet for fewer hours than other core classes?

When we add the diverse needs of learners to the mix, another level of complexity is introduced. Koehler and Mishra pointed out that, "Wicked problems always occur in social contexts … The diversity of teachers, students, and technology coordinators who operate in this social context bring different goals, objectives, and beliefs, to the table, and thereby contribute to the wickedness of this problem" (see Chapter 1). If instruction needs to be differentiated to meet the needs of each child, which it certainly should, then the arts may be the perfect place for TPCK to be addressed, since the arts are an expression of individual preferences and emotions. Therefore, the arts curriculum is an excellent vehicle for teaching children to use technology to express themselves in a wide variety of creative ways.

In the following sections, we explore the many ways technology can be effectively integrated with dance, visual arts, media arts, drama, and music—

not just in the arts classroom, but also across all subjects. Before we begin this exploration, however, it may be useful to synthesize the research-based principles that justify the need for arts education as a non-negotiable element of all students' education. Specifically, we discover that one of the most powerful rationales for emphasizing the arts is their clear and sustained relationship between how human beings learn and how we can best facilitate that process.

All arts education, for example, is highly consistent with contemporary research on cognitive learning theory, from the groundbreaking work of Vygotsky (1978) and Feuerstein, Hoffman, and Miller (1980) to contemporary theorists such as Brown, Cocking, and Bransford, the editors of the groundbreaking publication, *How people learn* (2000). These researchers contend that human beings learn most effectively when they: (1) construct meaning by attaching new knowledge to existing schema, a term first identified by Vygotsky; (2) engage in opportunities for self-exploration, self-expression, and non-linear investigations; and (3) acquire and adapt the protocols and procedures within disciplines and program areas, moving toward growing proficiency in transfer and independent use and application, following Vygotsky's construct of "zone of proximal development."

All learning experiences within the area of arts education align with these precepts, including an active emphasis upon placing the student at the heart of the learning process, with the teacher functioning as a modeler of process and an ultimate facilitator and coach, rather than the clichéd "sage on the stage." Similarly, all arts education is predicated upon a commitment to students' authentic, real-world application of what they are learning and to self-generated products and performances that are a logical and appropriate extension of initial modeling and shaping experiences. As cognitive theorists emphasize, great arts educators also help students to see the "big picture" of what they are learning, i.e., its connection to their internal or inner landscape as well as its relationship to the world beyond the classroom. Finally, arts education integrates assessment and instruction, emphasizing the power of cognitive-theory-based experiential learning, inquiry, and exploration. These processes inevitably supersede lecture and "transmission" of information, a problem seen in many traditional "academic" settings and classrooms.

The power of arts education is also evident in its fundamental alignment with brain-based teaching and learning theory, as articulated by such researchers as Jensen (2000) and Sylwester (2003). All experiences in the visual and performing arts attend to such fundamental brain-based needs as the compulsion to answer "Why?" How, for example, does this learning experience enhance my survival, my well-being, and my self-actualization? These questions are an inevitable and inherent part of all effective arts education. Similarly, the arts allow learners to maximize their use of both brain hemispheres and transitioning from analytical and evaluative processes typically associated with the left hemisphere of the brain to the more open-ended, visual, and imaginative experiences associated with the right hemisphere.

Additionally, arts education is highly consistent with the work of such groundbreaking theorists as Gardner (2006), Goleman (2006), and Csikszent-mihalyi (2002). Students of the arts, for example, inevitably receive a wide range of opportunities to express the multiple forms of intelligence as identified by Gardner. These include the typically less emphasized forms apparent in many academic classroom settings: i.e., visual, spatial, musical, bodily or kinesthetic, interpersonal, intrapersonal, and, a recently added one to Gardner's lexicon, the existential. The latter involves the learner in exploring the universal cosmic issues that are at the heart of the humanities: Who are we? How do we relate as individuals to the universe? How can we wrestle with and answer the great metaphysical questions? Arts students also receive extensive opportunities to engage in what Goleman has labeled "emotional intelligence," moving beyond strict emphasis in their learning process upon the cognitive/intellectual/academic and exploring issues related to relationships, personal efficacy, and evolving social consciousness.

Finally, arts education is supremely positioned to enhance students' experience with what Csikszentmihalyi has called "flow," a condition in which we experience a sense of timelessness, engagement, and stress-free challenge. All effective arts classrooms and related learning experiences encourage students to expand their proficiency in such flow-related processes as creative self-expression, exploration and tolerance of ambiguity and open-ended inquiry, and the process of pushing one's knowledge and ability.

As we explore the relationship between arts education and technology in this essay, it may be useful to consider these research-based learning principles, especially as we develop and reinforce political bases to sustain arts education as a fundamental building block of students' school-based education and their ultimate life-long learning process.

Visual arts and technology in the classroom

I am still learning.

Michelangelo

Even geniuses like Michelangelo admitted that learning is a continual process. In visual arts instruction, life-long learning is particularly relevant. Since new methods and materials for creating and learning about art are constantly being developed, continuing education is essential for all visual arts teachers. For the classroom teacher who is interested in incorporating visual art into the curriculum, the task of keeping up with arts-relevant, technology-based learning tools is even greater. Fortunately, technology itself has made this task less challenging. With just a few clicks of the mouse, teachers can turn to the

Internet to find everything from step-by-step Photoshop instructions to in-depth sites on individual artists, complete with virtual galleries, video interviews, and web-based learning activities for students. Arts institutions, local and state arts agencies, museums, and theaters, all offer courses and summer camps to help educators use these resources and integrate these ideas in the classroom.

With arts programs declining in the wake of a nationwide focus on standardized testing, responsibility is falling more and more to the classroom teacher to expose students to the benefits of arts instruction. It is well researched and documented that visual art provides its practitioners with the ability to find creative solutions to problems and to work cooperatively with others. When a visual art component is incorporated into any subject area—from science to history—teachers can increase student interest in that subject and foster excitement for learning. When students are given the opportunity to demonstrate their understanding of a subject through creative work, the resulting artwork gives teachers a hands-on method of assessment. Visual arts learning is an enriching experience for any student at any grade level. Adding technology to the equation only enhances the learning experience.

The Internet is key to art instruction in our ever-changing society. Whether an art teacher is interested in teaching an unfamiliar visual art process or a classroom teacher wants to incorporate visual arts in a social studies or language arts lesson plan, a wealth of information is available on the Internet. Teachers can find specific information on how to effectively teach the use of specific mediums, making for more authentic teaching techniques.

The following two educational web sites provide a wealth of arts education resources activities for children; e.g., lesson plans for teachers, information and materials for parents, and much more for all arts and crafts lovers:

- www.crayola.com
- www.sanford-artedventures.com

Children ages 4–12 can learn the building blocks of art and creativity through this interactive web site from Albright-Knox. They can learn about portraits, still lifes, landscapes, color, and materials. They can also create their own works in the interactive studio section.

- www.albrightknox.org/artgames/index.html

This site is a resource for artists and art students, focusing on the fundamentals of perspective, shading, color, and painting.

- www.studiochalkboard.evansville.edu

ARTSEDGE—the National Arts and Education Network—supports the placement of the arts at the center of the curriculum and advocates creative use of technology to enhance the K-12 educational experience. ARTSEDGE empowers educators to teach in, through, and about the arts by providing the tools to develop interdisciplinary curricula that fully integrate the arts with other academic subjects. ARTSEDGE offers free, standards-based teaching materials for use in and out of the classroom, as well as professional development resources, student materials, and guidelines for arts-based instruction and assessment.

- www.artsedge.kennedy-center.org

Classroom teachers are prone to falling back on prescriptive arts lessons that just skim the surface of arts instruction, but now they can turn to the Internet for access to countless in-depth lesson plans, many of which are complete with ready-to-print handouts for teachers' convenience. For example, in a unit on Egypt, classroom teachers might only point out that hieroglyphs were a means of communicating through pictures. A lesson like EDSITEment's "Egyptian Symbols and Figures: Hieroglyphs" (http://edsitement.neh.gov/view_lesson_plan.asp?id=348), provides teachers with comprehensive and credible information on hieroglyphs so teachers can offer students a deeper understanding of Egyptian culture. The National Endowment for the Humanities, in partnership with the National Trust for the Humanities, created EDSITEment. This educational partnership brings online humanities resources from some of the world's great museums, libraries, cultural institutions, and universities directly to the classroom.

Many lessons available on the Internet are combined with online educational games that make learning fun for students. Illuminations, an educational site produced by The National Council of Teachers of Mathematics, contains a lesson called "Powerful Patterns." In this lesson, students are directed to use an applet called "Shape Tool" which allows them to choose from a variety of shapes, sizes, and colors to create two-dimensional patterns on the computer. The URL for Illuminations is illuminations.nctm.org. In both the Illuminations and EDSITEment lessons, classroom teachers are encouraged—and shown how—to integrate visual arts in their lessons.

Both classroom teachers and visual arts teachers can also find a wealth of lesson plans and activities on the following site:

- www.nga.gov/education/classroom

You can access lessons and resources by curriculum, topic, or artist; borrow free-loan teaching materials; find games and activities for kids of all ages; and access the *Super-Learner Interactives* link.

The Metropolitan Museum of Art in New York City has been recognized in *Child Magazine* March 2006 as the second-most family friendly museum in the U.S. Click on "Explore & Learn" at www.metmuseum.org/explore/index.asp and experience a multitude of activities that students can participate in and learn from.

KinderArt®, www.kinderart.com/, is the largest collection of free art lessons on the Internet. A truly interactive experience, KinderArt® provides an opportunity for parents, educators, artists, students, and children to have fun while exchanging ideas, finding information, conducting research, and learning new things.

The Freer Gallery of Art and the Arthur M. Sackler Gallery of Art are part of the Smithsonian Institution. They house a collection of Art from the Near and Far East. The link, www.asia.si.edu/education/onlineGuides.htm, to the Education Department has a wealth of information, guides, artwork, and activities for educators.

The Internet is also essential to viewing a variety of artworks from around the world and throughout history. Although there is nothing like viewing a Van Gogh or Picasso in person, not every teacher can provide museum experiences for their students due to restrictive field trip policies, financial constraints, or geographical limitations. Fortunately, students can be taken on virtual field trips to any museum in the world—any museum with a web site, that is—via the Internet. Students will understand the influences that one artistic genre has on another—specifically, the similarities between the New York School poets and Abstract Expressionist visual artists. After examining work by Jackson Pollock, students can analyze and imitate poetry by Frank O'Hara. The University of Virginia has compiled a list of key museum web sites for educators at www.curry.edschool.virginia.edu/it/projects/Museums/Teacher_Guide/Hotlist.

Access to museum resources via the Web is particularly useful when teaching about cultures that the teacher and/or students do not identify themselves with. Because there is a risk of bias and inaccuracy in reference and teaching materials not developed by culturally sensitive experts, it is best to go straight to the source for such materials. The National Museum of the American Indian, www.nmai.si.edu, produces online exhibits that give voice to the side of history that is not often explored in textbooks. For example, while many teachers use George Catlin's images of Indian tribes, teachers may not explain that Catlin also contributed to the exploitation and sensationalism of Indians through his Wild West shows. The Smithsonian Institution's *Campfire Stories with George Catlin* at http://www.catlinclassroom.si.edu/cl.html presents many of George Catlin's artworks along with historical documents and commentary from experts. With the use of LCD projectors, teachers can present enlarged views of artworks accompanied by informative text, and the entire class can be involved in discovery, discussions, and activities—all at the same time.

The Internet is most commonly used in the arts classroom for research purposes. If students' only reference is their school library, their access to information about a particular subject would be extremely limited, and often out-of-date. With information updated every second on the Internet, students can learn about the latest news in the art field and the legacy of legendary artists. And, there is no better place than the Internet to read the most up-to-date information about artists creating works today. Both the Museum of Modern Art's Red Studio, http://redstudio.moma.org/, specifically geared towards teens, and PBS's Art:21, www.pbs.org/art21/, contain videos of interviews with contemporary artists. The challenge for teachers assigning research projects may be to limit students' research. It may be beneficial for teachers to provide students with specific web sites that they know are safe and reliable. In beginning your search for these sites you might want to try the Thinkfinity search engine, www.marcopolosearch.org/MPSearch. This gateway to high-quality educational Internet content is a partnership among the leading national and international educational organizations. Their search engine only includes sites and resources that have been carefully screened by panels of educational professionals and reviewers.

Not only can teachers connect students to artists and their artworks via the Internet, but they also can connect students to their peers in other parts of the world. Through the use of digital cameras, web cams, and instant messaging or iChat, students can share and discuss their works of art with peers on the other side of the globe in real time. These students share ideas and concepts while simultaneously learning about other countries, cultures, and methods of art making.

In high school, most students are required to take one art class as an elective. At this level, the art teacher works with a wide variety of students with multiple levels of talents and skills—often in one class. Technology can be a very valuable tool to help beginning students progress faster with basic concepts while keeping more advanced students engaged and challenged. For example, beginning students can review the building blocks of design on interactive sites like The Minneapolis Institute of Art's "Artist's Toolkit," www.artsconnected.org/toolkit/. Artists use visual elements and principles like line, color, and shape as tools to build works of art. Students can watch an animated demonstration, find examples of the concept in works of art from museums, and create their own compositions. More advanced students use web-based learning tools like the Museum of Modern Art's "Remix: An Interactive Collage" and "youDESIGN" at redstudio.moma.org/activities to put the elements and principles of design into practice via collage and architecture techniques, respectively. Despite the wealth of technological innovations available to teachers, art educators will still rely on traditional, hands-on teaching methods in order to teach students how to paint, draw, sculpt, and take photographs and rightly so. With just a point-and-shoot camera and a background in composition techniques, students can create beautiful works of art. For example, students at Mark Twain Middle School in Los Angeles, California, partnered with the Getty Museum and 826LA, a local writing organization, to produce an exhibit of student-created photographs. The results of the project can be viewed in a virtual gallery at http://artsedge.kennedy-center.org/content/3903/. Such a virtual gallery—a source of pride to students at Mark Twain—can be replicated on school web sites to promote any student exhibit with the help of an aspiring web designer or a savvy student.

In conclusion, while traditional hands-on teaching methods should be maintained in the visual arts classroom, there are many ways to enhance students' learning experiences through technology. Students are able to access more visual examples, more in-depth reference materials, and special web-based learning tools to help them explore their artistic ideas. The use of technology has only enhanced the reliable content knowledge that students are learning on a daily basis—and teachers are learning along with their students!

Music and technology in the classroom

Where words fail, music speaks.

Hans Christian Andersen

Technology and music are perfect partners in the classroom. Technology adds additional layers of learning and excitement to music education while music makes technology education even more creative and fun. Moreover, technology can make both vocal and instrumental music more easily understandable and accessible. Students who cannot afford their own instruments can use school computers and mixers to create new sounds. MIDI technology allows students to compose and record songs with relative ease. Technology can also help English language learners (ELL) through web-based interactive activities that emphasize visual and aural cues over verbal cues.

Educators are enriching students' study of music through technology in a variety of ways. At Berwyn Heights Elementary School in Berwyn Heights, Maryland, K-6 students are composing soundtracks for clay animation movies. Students improvise a melody, create chord progressions, then use a software program called Band-in-a-Box (www.band-in-a-box.com) to hear their chord progressions come to life in a five-instrument accompaniment comprising bass, drums, piano, guitar, and strings. Another Berwyn Heights class uses Band-in-a-Box software to reinforce math concepts. Students explored rhythm and counting sequences by keeping time to the beats in a familiar song. They wrote new lyrics to the song then played the instrumental version of the song so the class could sing along—karaoke-style.

At McCormick Elementary School in Langley Park, Maryland, music is used to bridge the divide between native English speakers and non-native English speakers. In a school with a very high population of ELLs, music is seen as a universal language that can level the playing field. One general music class utilized the Mobile Apple Computer Lab so each student could create their own unique songs. Students began by writing poetry in which they incorporated experiences and ideas unique to their cultures and individual viewpoints. Using a software program called Garage Band (www.apple.com/ilife/garageband), students put together previously created loops of music to accompany their poems, then recorded their voices to complete their songs. In this cross-disciplinary lesson, students explored music, technology, and language arts and ended up with a recording which made them proud.

Technology use is reaching new heights in high school music classes. According to Barbara Liedahl, Instructional Technology Coordinator in Prince George's County Public Schools, Maryland, many new high schools are being built with music technology labs. These labs will feature electronic keyboards, computers, and software that will enable the school to offer such courses as Music Theory, Music Composition, and an integrated course on Music Appreciation/Careers.

Many music teachers, however, can only fantasize about high-tech music labs. The reality is that even a simple stereo system can be hard to come by in schools with limited funding. For such situations, the Internet provides much-needed, free teaching resources. Teachers can find valuable background information and valuable resources for music educators and students of all areas and educational levels at www.isd77.k12.mn.us/music/k-12music/and www.si.edu/RESOURCE/FAQ/nmah/music.htm. They also can access step-by-step lesson plans and innovative activities on sites such as Music Notes, Inc., www.musicnotes.net/ti.html, which offers methods for introducing music literacy into the classroom, and ARTSEDGE, http://artsedge.kennedy-center.org/teach/les.cfm, which provides you with complete lesson plans on music integrated with other subjects. Through streaming video, teachers can watch live music performances on the other side of the country or globe, such as performances on the Kennedy Center's Millennium Stage, www.kennedy-center.org/programs/millennium/. A venue located at the John F. Kennedy Center for the Performing Arts in Washington, DC, the Millennium Stage showcases free performances every day of the year. And every day of the year, streaming videos of each performance are available on the Internet free of charge. In addition, through sites like CNET's music.download.com/, teachers can download a plethora of free music in the public domain. And just in case they have any qualms about downloading music from the Internet, educators can find out information about copyright rules in education settings through web sites of organizations like MENC, the National Association for Music Education, www.menc.org.

Teachers can also expose students to the range of multimedia resources available on the Internet by exploring musical performances and artists across countless styles, genres, and countries of origin. ARTSEDGE's resource on Mexican corridos, www.artsedge.kennedycenter.org/content/3772/ offers audio clips of *corridos* with Spanish and English versions of the lyrics. PBS's Great Performances Multimedia Archive, www.pbs.org/wnet/gperf/multimedia/multimedia.html, features a wealth of videos, background information, jukeboxes, photo galleries, and interviews on everything from the musical *Oklahoma!* to John Lennon. DSOKids, www.dsokids.com, provides online interactive activities in which students can learn about symphonic instruments and different periods in classical music history. They can also play educational games that teach students about classical composers.

As is the case with all the arts, technology opens many new doors in the music classroom—so many doors that teachers may find it difficult to keep up. By the time teachers are comfortable with—and have access to—iPods, for example, a new resource will have been developed that will require more training and will incur more costs. MENC has somewhat eased the burden on teachers struggling to keep abreast of educational innovations by publishing informative publications on classroom uses of technological tools. One publication, *Strategies for teaching: Technology* (Reese, 2002), offers copious standards-based lesson strategies for the classroom teacher and music teacher that incorporate a variety of technological tools and equipment.

There are countless ways that technology can be used to enhance learning in the classroom with innumerable benefits for students and teachers. But one of the most poignant results of technology use in the music classroom is an increased, more accurate understanding of other cultures. The Internet provides access to music and information that teachers used to have to comb through specialty catalogues to find. Students are becoming more aware of the many different instruments common in other countries, as well as the sounds that arise from playing them. More and more contemporary music composers, in fact, combine Western instruments and Eastern instruments in their compositions. With the many videos, audio clips, photographs, and teaching tools available on the Internet, students can come to understand that, regardless of instrumentation or style, music is practiced and enjoyed in similar ways around the world.

Through technology, we are able to connect to one another speaking the universal language of music.

Dance and technology in the classroom

Dance is so important in the world. It needs no language. Our bodies speak a language of its own.

Ibrahim Farrah

As dancer and choreographer Ibrahim Farrah states in the quote above, dance is a language in itself. You could attend a dance performance in any region of the world and appreciate the experience, regardless of whether you can understand the event's program notes or not. But it's not just the audience who benefits from a dance performance. Dancers revel in the thrill of communicating in the universal language of body movements; meanwhile, they are building self-confidence, non-verbal reasoning, expressive skills, creative thinking, and originality through the practice of this graceful art form. Students of dance also learn about the history and culture of various countries and regions through the study of dances from around the world. The knowledge and life skills obtained from dance education are relevant to any student's learning experiences, regardless of age or skill.

Unfortunately, dance is rarely taught in most K-12 schools and many students do not get to experience the joy, creativity, and exhilaration of a dance class. Dance instruction—if it exists in a school at all—is left up to the classroom teacher or the physical education teacher. If a dance component is included in a class activity, it is often taught with little or no attention paid to the dance's history or cultural significance. For example, many schools celebrate Cinco de Mayo with a perfunctory representation of the Mexican Hat Dance, but the students participating in the dance are not given the background information or the dance vocabulary to fully comprehend the importance of the dance in Mexican culture. Thankfully, technology can ease the burden on teachers who want to enrich their students' learning of a dance but do not have the time or resources to research and prepare culturally authentic lesson plans.

Through distance learning programs and instructional videos that can be easily ordered (if not available for free) online, teachers can provide resources for their students that were written and approved by experts. In Debbie Allen's musical, *Brothers of the Knight*, available online at www.kennedy-center.org/multimedia/storytimeonline/brothers.html, the boys sneak out every night to dance, and Rev. Knight dances as he gives a sermon. But what makes one want to dance? Why dance? The dance-learning experience becomes more than just a fun diversion; it becomes an exploration of a culture and a study of an art form's craft.

Fortunately, the Internet provides access to videos of many dance performances and styles from various cultures and time periods. For students and teachers who cannot attend a live dance performance due to time conflicts in school schedules or financial or geographic constraints, the next best thing is to study the works of great dancers and choreographers through performances captured on video. From streaming videos of current dance groups to archived video footage of folk dances or bygone eras, such resources enable students to see culturally accurate and authentic dance performances. Web sites like *Dance: The Spirit of Cambodia*, www.asiasource.org/cambodia/, provide a wealth of free educational resources. A project of the Royal University of Fine Arts in Phonm Penh, *Dance: The Spirit of Cambodia* teaches readers about classical and folk dance, and music from Cambodia, through articles, video clips, and photo galleries.

To access videos of ballet, tap, modern, folk, and jazz dances, teachers simply search for their dance style, genre, artist, or company of choice on the online archives of the Kennedy Center's Millennium Stage at www.kennedy-center.org/programs/millennium/archive.html#search. Throughout the year the Kennedy Center features dance companies from around the world. These performances are placed online for all to view. With the help of a computer and LCD projector, teachers can screen such performances in their class-rooms and can pause, rewind, and forward to specific sections as necessary to fulfill curricular goals.

Resources such as the Millennium Stage's archives also enable educators to stay current with the latest dance movements and styles. By occasionally accessing local performing arts organizations' web sites or the season calendar of esteemed institutions such as the 92nd Street Y, http://www.92y.org/Default.asp, in New York City, educators will keep abreast of the most modern in modern dance. One relatively new dance company called Project Bandaloop fuses dance and rock climbing. Project Bandaloop dancers rappel from vertical surfaces while creating graceful dance movements. If physical education teachers and dance teachers incorporated elements of Project Bandaloop's techniques in their classes, they would surely generate excitement for both strength training activities and dance practice. For more information on this company, see the Kennedy Center's education guide at www.kennedy-center.org/education/cuesheets/single_cuesheet.cfm?asset_id=55032.

Since dance instruction is scarce outside of the physical education class, particularly at the elementary level, students learn little dance vocabulary, let alone the fundamental elements of dance. Resources such as American Ballet Theater's multimedia Ballet Dictionary, www.abt.org/education/library.asp, explain key moves that a classroom teacher may not be able to adequately define without an illustrative video of a dancer demonstrating that move. Moreover, students can learn how to perfect a certain step by viewing the same step performed by a professional dancer. With video cameras more readily available in schools, teachers can videotape students, then have them watch themselves practice. This allows students to view their performance and observe first-hand what they need to change and improve upon. Of course, in order to conduct a positive and meaningful critique without dam-aging students' self-confidence, teachers must establish clear guidelines. The teacher who is uncomfortable with leading critiques can find a wealth of informative resources on the Internet, such as http://www.artsci.wustl.edu/~marchant/critguidelines.htm. This site gives you a wealth of questions and guidelines for teaching about a dance critique and help in preparing one. If you need an excellent dance rubric to work from, one can be accessed at www.hcesc.com/pdfs/HCTA2004CritDance.pdf.

If teachers not trained in dance lack the confidence to bring dance into the classroom, they can turn to the Internet to find state art agencies that have lists of artists who are willing to come to their classroom and either teach or help the teacher learn to teach their students. As the documentary *Mad Hot Ballroom* (Agrelo, 2005) attests, students can learn ballroom dance successfully with the help of professional instructors and the important participation of their teachers as well. In bringing artists into the classroom, the teacher should always become a part of the learning, not disappear from the classroom or fade out of site in the corner. Students are more willing to learn when they see their teacher is not afraid of learning and making mistakes as well. The documentary showcases students in New York City public schools taught by dancers affiliated with American Ballroom Theater's Dancing Classrooms program.

In Alpine, California, a program called EduDance (see www.edudance.net/newsroom.htm) similarly connects professional ballroom dancers to classrooms in order to help students meet physical education requirements. Many teachers learn of such programs from conducting Internet searches or by reading testimonials from other teachers on blogs and forums. The Internet allows teachers to stumble across innovative ideas and programs that they may not have been exposed to otherwise.

But teachers' use of technology now far surpasses surfing the Internet for information-gathering purposes. Depending on the commitment and training of the teacher, the following technology elements can be incorporated into the middle and high school levels of dance:

1. Web-based interactive activities like *A Dancer's Journal*, http://artsedge.kennedy-center.org/marthagraham, provide one-of-a-kind resources that engage students in active learning as they explore an arts-related topic.

2. Sophisticated computerized weight equipment can help develop and maintain a dancer's muscle structure.

3. Laptops can be used to take notes quickly as a dance is being choreographed. These notes are of particular value to those learning-disabled students who have difficulty writing or those who have sequencing problems.

4. Hour-long satellite programs on various dance-related subjects can be viewed in real time so that artists appearing on the program can answer students' questions live. The Kennedy Center's Performing Arts Series, for example, offers arts-based educational programming free to teachers and students via satellite and web.

5. Teachers can use laptops to take notes during their reviews of students' work, and then quickly send these notes to students via email. Or, if the notes are projected for a class or production team, students can scrutinize and discuss the notes as a team.

6. Software programs, such as DanceForms 1.0 (see www.charactermo-

tion.com), allows teachers to bring their choreography ideas to three-dimensional life by posing dance figures. Another software program, Dance 5.0, www.download.com.ph/DANCE.htm, allows users to design their own dance patterns and print them. The program also contains:

- A database from which users can download basic patterns for a variety of ballroom dances.
- Performances, which can be enhanced by projecting a slideshow of images or a video onto a backdrop behind the dancers.
- Computer-generated lighting systems, which allow users to program lighting patterns that correspond to sound.

Programs like MiniPads and KidiPads Interactive Performance System, www.tsof.edu.au/resources/dance/drama/, are relatively low-cost and user friendly—simple enough to be used in elementary school. The many uses of technology in dance are ever-changing and ever-growing as new programs spring up every day.

Drama and technology in the classroom

A master can tell you what he expects of you. A teacher, though, awakens your own expectations.

Patricia Neal

Just as it is up to the teacher to awaken students' expectations, it is up to the teacher's integration of technology into instruction to enhance these expectations. Teachers are now able to access an unparalleled amount of material through the Internet to help them provide drama education opportunities for students in the classroom. From the availability of reference materials that aid students in writing plays to the wealth of tips, interviews, and guides related to producing plays in schools, the Internet has provided ample opportunities to expand knowledge and skills. With additional opportunities and resources comes an increased expectation for what students produce and perform.

Since a drama teacher is a rare commodity on a school's faculty, it is often up to the classroom teacher or English teacher to incorporate drama techniques in the curriculum or during extracurricular activities. Those teachers who do bring drama into their classrooms are rewarded with students who:

- have a higher self-confidence
- can speak articulately in public
- are more personally involved in learning
- tap hidden resources and skills that may not have been accessed in other subject areas
- can be assessed through varied means

Technology is useful for the teacher who balances drama activities with duties related to teaching the core curriculum. The Internet alone has vastly improved drama education, simply by providing access to resources useful to classroom teachers and drama teachers alike. Teachers can find step-by-step instructions on various production processes, such as making a shadow puppet theater. For example, see the Old Sturbridge Village Kids Club at www.osv.org/kids/crafts2.htm. Through sites like ARTSEDGE's Shadow Puppets: An Introduction to Shadow Puppetry, http://artsedge.kennedy-center.org/shadowpuppets/, teachers can explore the art of shadow puppetry with students in an in-depth way through animated instructional resources. Students can explore the site on their own or work with their teacher to learn the ins and outs of shadow puppetry, then create their own shadow puppet play on a virtual stage.

In the comfort of their classroom, students can access countless reference materials that can enhance their understanding of plays, playwrights, and production. Students can access articles and interviews with actors and playwrights or find information about the clothing, music, scenery, and general lifestyle that would be historically accurate in a period piece. They can view digital images of original scripts that may contain handwritten notes that give insight into a writer's process or a director's take on a play. Students can also find information that would help them portray a character, particularly when the character's way of life and experiences is foreign to the student portraying that character. In history classes, students can research information about former presidents then recite a famous presidential speech.

The Internet is also helping teachers to work with students with disabilities who are enrolled in mainstream classes. Through web sites like The Council for Exceptional Children's Information Center on Disabilities and Gifted Education, ericec.org, teachers can link to invaluable resources, teaching strategies, adaptations, and ideas to ensure that no child is *truly* left behind. On a web page at the above site titled "Arts Activities for Children with Disabilities," ericec.org/faq/arts.html, the Council for Exceptional Children lists ways arts activities can be structured for students with disabilities, including employing role-play in public speaking activities.

Utilizing the Internet is just the tip of the iceberg when it comes to incorporating technology in drama education. In the realm of playwriting and dramatic performances, technology allows students to:

- Record oral histories with hand-held devices, then use quotes from interviewees in monologues and oral storytelling projects.
- Create blogs about current events then role-play as newscasters to report their findings to the class.
- Use PowerPoint in oral presentations on any given topic related to playwriting or specific plays and writers.

- Digitally record a character's lines then download the file to an iPod to help memorize lines and improve delivery.
- Write dialog then film and edit them to produce short films. English language learners can review such films to improve their pronunciation skills and their ability to convey subtleties of meaning through appropriate inflections and tone.
- View video clips of musicals, plays, and monologues that might be available on the web or in DVD form.

On the technical and administrative side of play production, technological advances have made many jobs easier—from sound design to publicity. Students and teachers have been using technology to produce dramatic events in the following ways:

- Directors and assistant directors take notes during rehearsals on laptops then print them and share them immediately with the cast.
- Rehearsals can be filmed and critiqued by the production team and cast.
- Directors and producers can find scripts on sites such as Pioneer Drama, www.pioneerdrama.com.
- Desktop publishing software is used to produce tickets, posters, programs, etc.
- Business programs like Microsoft Excel are used to keep track of the financial aspects of production costs.
- School performances can be filmed and edited for a video archive of school productions or to be sold in fundraising drives.
- Sound effects and music to accompany performances can be created in software programs such as Garage Band.
- Plays and skits can be shared with other classes in the school through closed-circuit television.

For those schools lucky enough to have a theater dedicated to performances, the possibilities for incorporating technology are endless. However, with endless possibilities comes a lot of work. Keeping up with all the new technologies being created for theater productions can be overwhelming. Sound and lighting boards, walkie-talkies and headsets used to communicate cues, scrims, projectors and screens to project images for backdrops, and smoke machines can all be quite costly. Moreover, they are continually being replaced with newer, more advanced technologies. In order to have a good sense of which technical tools are necessary, teachers can refer to online resources such as the Internet Public Library's "Dance & Performance" guide, www.ipl.org/div/subject/browse/hum20.40.00/, for links to pertinent information. Unfortunately, most schools must battle budget constraints and do not have the luxury of deciding between a new lighting board versus a new scrim. Luckily, the most important tool in theater is imagination. With so many resources available on the Internet, teachers can bring the joy of drama to their students for free.

Media production and technology in the classroom

Film provides an opportunity to marry the power of ideas with the power of images.

Steven Bochco

Video editing technologies, computer graphics, web authoring software, animation programs, blogs and podcasts; these tools are being used more and more to strengthen and enhance lessons and to make concepts more meaningful for students. Whether surfing the Internet, watching television, playing video games, or walking in high-density urban areas like Times Square, visual media surrounds students. By incorporating media production in their lessons, teachers are tapping into a genre that fascinates—or at least entertains—many students. Fortunately, prices continue to drop for many video cameras, graphics software, and other media technologies. It is easier to purchase such tools for use in the classroom or apply for grants that provide funding for such tools (see www.edweek.org/grants/). Students with access to these resources are learning skills that are vital in today's media-saturated society. They are also telling their stories, documenting them, and presenting them to an audience—and learning a variety of subjects along the way.

Many students are fascinated by the ways still and moving images can be produced and manipulated with technology; however, most elementary and middle schools and many high schools do not offer courses in media arts. Faced with the challenge of addressing students' growing interests, classroom teachers and visual art teachers often take the gauntlet and march ahead. In Bowie, Maryland, Jim Lipiano is one example of a teacher who has taken the gauntlet. Currently the Computer Graphics Teacher and Coordinator at Bowie High School, Lipiano was formerly a visual arts teacher. Interested in combining his love of art with his love of technology, Lipiano created an award-winning computer graphics program. Students in Lipiano's Computer Graphics class can expect to learn a little bit of everything. Not only are they learning several graphics programs, but they are also engaged with reading and creative writing activities, traditional and online research, math, art history, and design principles. "Most students come in with limited experience in art and computer technology and soon begin creating sophisticated projects," Lipiano wrote in a recent email. Many graduates of his class have continued to work in the field: one currently works as a graphic designer for Disney, one illustrated a children's book, and another founded a graphic design business in New York.

At Thomas Pullen Creative and Performing Arts Magnet School in Landover, Maryland, literacy, computers, and media production come together with students' imaginations. In a unit created by several teachers to enhance language arts skills, students were asked to write original stories then use a word processing program to type, edit, rewrite, and refine their stories. The class picked one story to convert into a film. Students assumed roles of actors, production assistants, camera operators, editors, and set designers, and worked together to create a film from beginning to end. In some instances, students added animation to the final product.

Many teachers across the country now have access to video cameras, and this resource has not gone unnoticed. Video cameras and video editing programs like iMovie are being used more and more to enrich learning experiences. Even pen pals have taken on a new meaning. Replacing the pen with video cameras, many schools are creating videos to send to their sister schools in other parts of the United States or the world. With these videos, students are given the opportunity to observe a school in another region first-hand and can compare and contrast their environments.

Morning announcements are also being transformed. Once a task for administrators to broadcast over the loudspeaker, morning announcements have become morning television shows that are produced in a studio and aired in each classroom. Programming for such shows might include interviews of faculty and guests, footage of events taking place both in and out of the school, and commercials about upcoming school events.

Socially conscious students are taking film to the next level by creating documentaries on everything from cafeteria food to school clean-up projects. In 2003, students from Moanalua High School in Honolulu Hawaii won the Hawaii Student Film Festival for their documentary on child labor, www.edutopia.org/php/article.php?id=Art_1047&key=137.

Not all media projects have to be so complicated. Going on a field trip? Students can document their observations with Polaroid or digital cameras and record pertinent audio samples using tape recorders or digital recorders. Teachers are finding that recording devices help students notice small details they might not have observed otherwise. A trip to Washington, DC is always a learning experience. But with hand-held recording devices that force students to observe their environment closely, students are more likely to notice—and then remember—architectural elements of historical buildings, information on plaques at monuments, and details about exhibits they viewed. The audiovisual materials students record can be incorporated into a report about the field trip. This project gives each individual a chance to share his/her view and listen to the views of others. As a result, the trip becomes more personal and relevant for the students. As for the teachers, they can use students' final projects to assess what has been learned.

There are many more ways media projects can be used to enhance learning. Additional examples include the following:

- Students can create podcasts on topics relevant to assigned research projects.
- Teachers can play podcasts that contain relevant material for class discussions.
- Students can learn how to design web sites that showcase school activities or feature individual projects.
- Images can be manipulated and enhanced using Adobe Photoshop Elements to create unique works of art. (Students can be rewarded for such effort through contests like Portraits of Learning (see www.adobe.com/education/digkids/contest/), an annual photography competition sponsored by *Technology & Learning* and Adobe Systems).

Teachers are finding that media projects offer a perfect vehicle through which students can share ideas and opinions in a creative and exciting format. Given that myriad forms of media technology have surrounded students since they could barely type their names, it is only fitting that schools embrace projects that speak to students in a familiar language. Media production not only engages students in active learning, but also teaches them important skills for the twenty-first century workplace. The challenge for teachers will be staying on top of the media tools in existence so that they can at least point students in the right direction. Most likely the student will know more than the teacher about how to move forward in any given direction. It is not realistic to train teachers in all aspects of media production—even at a rudimentary level. Rather, educators should be well versed in media literacy so that they can teach students how to view and interpret visual images and how to think critically about the ways information is presented to an audience to fulfill various goals. With media technologies saturating all aspects of society, students should be able to discern which tactics are being used to sell a product as well as which artistic choices can enhance the quality of a work. One of the Polaroid Education Program's (www.polaroid.com/education) workshops for educators introduced visual imaging into the classroom explaining that the camera is just a tool and we use it in six different ways: exploring, recording, expressing, communicating, motivating, and imagining. The way we handle or present this information requires another set of six skills that will need to be taught. They are the ability to:

- Organize images for effective display.
- Establish visual criteria and arrange images in a visual database.
- Substitute images for words and establish a visual language.
- Combine images with text to communicate more effectively.

- Integrate images with live presentations to communicate more powerfully.
- Manipulate or transform existing images to envision something new.

If students understand the above and can decode visual information in photos, they will understand how an individual or company's viewpoint is being expressed through various media formats and what aspects of the viewpoint are controlled by outside forces.

While we agree with Steven Bochco when he says "Film provides an opportunity to marry the power of ideas with the power of images," we would like to take the quote one step further, i.e., *technology* provides an opportunity to marry the power of ideas with the power of the imagination. Behind every great idea lies an imaginative mind, and vice versa. When it comes to media production, technology allows students to produce works that result from sound ideas and logical decisions as well as creative and reflective thinking.

Conclusion

I like a teacher who gives you something to take home to think about besides homework.

Lily Tomlin as Edith Ann in *Laugh-In*

For students who share Edith Ann's sentiments, projects that incorporate technology go beyond "homework" because learning is made fun, exciting, and interesting. In addition, by training students to use technology at an early age, teachers are giving students the tools for success in the workplace. It in no way takes the place of the content and pedagogy, i.e., the teacher, we have and use in the classroom, it is an innovative set of tools for tying content to pedagogy and connecting with people around the world. Students in the classroom can communicate with peers through email, instant messaging programs, teleconferencing, and blogs. Teachers can share lessons and ideas with colleagues and take students on virtual field trips to museums and performances anywhere in the world. Teachers and students foster lifelong learning by listening to podcasts or video interviews with experts of virtually any subject.

Technology never takes the place of subject matter content in the arts. Rather, technology:

- Makes content knowledge more meaningful.
- Creates excitement about learning.
- Addresses different learning styles as described by Howard Gardner in his Multiple Intelligences theory.
- Assists in the research process through databases and the Internet.
- Exposes students to diverse styles of music, dance, theater, and visual arts from around the world no matter where we live.

- Brings the global community into our homes and classrooms.
- Develops creative thinkers.
- Allows us to see ourselves create and perform—as well as critique our performances—through video documentation.
- Allows students with disabilities the chance to participate in the production of the arts.

The benefits of technology integration in the arts classroom are numerous. Both in-service teachers and education majors need to be made aware of the importance of technology in enhancing arts learning and need to be trained in the appropriate use of technology in the development of lessons and units. They must also learn how the arts can be used to meet standards and reach goals in core curriculum subjects. Whether admiring a mural on the side of a building or listening to music on your iPod at the gym, the arts surround every aspect of our life.

In the wake of the No Child Left Behind Act, many school systems are cutting what they consider the extras—the arts—and focusing on subjects assessed in standardized tests—reading and math. At a recent Association for Supervision and Curriculum Development (ASCD) conference in Maryland, the Assistant Superintendent of Maryland Schools, Dr. Skip Sanders, pointed out that nowhere in the No Child Left Behind Act are educators told how to teach, so the arts need not be absent from the curriculum. Rather, the arts can offer a strong foundation to one's teaching methods. According to Dr. Sanders, the arts are the magic in education. Indeed, the arts work wonders in enhancing student learning and in addressing all multiple intelligences identified by Howard Gardner. The many benefits of arts education warrant its inclusion in the educational process.

Integrating the arts across all subject areas ensures that students are receiving the benefits of arts education. To be clear, we are not advocating for the elimination of art-specific courses in favor of integrating arts in other subject areas. Regardless of how many art teachers are on a school's faculty, we believe classroom teachers should still integrate the arts in their lessons to reach kinesthetic as well as visual and auditory learners, to make learning more meaningful and enjoyable, and to allow students' creative voices to be heard. Whenever possible, classroom teachers across all subject areas should collaborate with the arts teacher to make learning more meaningful and active.

In the June 2006 issue of *The American School Board Journal*, author Ruth E. Sternberg described in an article titled "Arts at the core" how six different school systems around the country are integrating the arts. Each school is integrating the arts with the aid of technology. One science class uses smart labs to project images of cell structures, which students then use to draw scientific illustrations. In another class, students created a movie about a fellow student who claims to be telepathic. All of the projects are varied and fascinating—and ambitious.

For those teachers just starting out who are interested in finding ways to integrate the arts into their curriculum, they can access step-by-step lesson plans on ARTSEDGE, www.artsedge.kennedy-center.org, the premier website for arts integration. ARTSEDGE provides standards-based, arts-integrated lessons and activities, dynamic interactive activities for students, videos and audio clips of performances and artist interviews, and a wealth of articles, guides, and reference materials on the topics of arts education and arts integration. With so many resources available to educators for free, there is no reason why the arts should remain in the background in education.

In the State of Maryland, teaching majors are now required to take a course in arts integration. Many other states are following suit. To give teachers the tools to integrate arts in the classroom, it is imperative that teaching majors are taught how best to use technology to enhance the arts components of their lessons. Teachers must stay a step or two ahead of the students. To learn how to most effectively use technology in the classroom, education majors should—at the very least—be trained on how to search the Internet for the most age- and skill-appropriate tools available in the rapidly evolving arena of technology and learning. At best, professors should model TPCK best practices to help integrate the arts across all subjects, and teacher preparation programs should require their credential candidates to complete multiple projects that use technology to integrate the arts in the core curriculum.

With arts programs being scaled back across the board, it is necessary to keep teachers trained in educational uses of technology so that teachers continue to share the joy of art-making and art appreciation with their students. TPCK in the arts will enable teachers to combine their knowledge of the arts with technological and pedagogical skills to provide the best education for their students making optimal use of the available technological resources. "The TPCK framework offers insight … into how the myriad complexities and tensions of teaching and learning can be brought together to mutually develop teachers' and students' knowledge" (Koehler & Mishra, Chapter 1).

References

Agrelo, M. (Producer/Director). (2005). *Mad Hot Ballroom* [Motion Picture]. USA: Paramount Classics.

Brown, A., Cocking, R., & Bransford, J. (eds) (2000). *How people learn: Brain, mind, experience, and school.* Washington, DC: National Academy of Sciences.

Csikszentmihalyi, M. (2002). *Flow: The classic work on how to achieve happiness.* London: Rider.

Feuerstein, R., Hoffman, M., & Miller, R. (1980). *Instrumental enrichment.* Baltimore: University Park Press.

Gardner, H. (2006). *Multiple intelligences: New horizons.* New York: Perseus Books Group.

Goleman, D. (2006). *Social intelligence: The new science of human relationships.* New York: Bantam Dell Books.

Jensen, E. (2000). *Brain-based learning: The new science of teaching and training* (rev. edn). San Diego: The Brain Store.

Reese, S. (2002). *Strategies for teaching: Technology.* Lanham, MD: Rowman & Littlefield Education.

Rittel, H., & Webber, M. (1973). Dilemmas in a general theory of planning. *Policy Sciences, 4*(2), 155–169.

Sternberg, R. (2006). Arts at the core. *The American School Board Journal, 193*(6), 44–47.

Sylwester, R. (2003). *A biological brain in a cultural classroom* (2nd edn). Thousand Oaks, CA: Sage Publications.

Thornburg, D. (2002). *The new basics: Education and the future of work in the telematic age.* Baltimore: Association for Supervision & Curriculum Development.

Vygotsky, L. (1978). *Mind and society: The development of higher psychological processes.* Cambridge, MA: Harvard University Press.

9
Science, technology, and teaching
The topic-specific challenges of TPCK in science

RAVEN McCRORY

Introduction

Science and technology are natural, long-standing partners in school and out. Scientists develop technologies for use in their work and they develop technologies for commercial purposes. The science classroom is a natural place for technology use since so much of science today depends on technology. It is fair to say that one cannot be a scientist without being knowledgeable about computers and other advanced technologies.

This chapter explores the question of what knowledge teachers need in order to integrate technology into their science teaching in ways that might help students learn science and prepare them for future work in scientific fields. It starts from the assumptions that technology should be used to do things that would otherwise be difficult or impossible to do, not to replicate the same things ordinarily done; and that technology has a place in science classrooms when it is integral to the science being taught or when it solves a particular pedagogical problem.

The sections that follow consider first, the general idea of pedagogical content knowledge in science and how it has been defined and used; then the uses of technology in science education; and finally, teachers' knowledge for teaching science with technology, TPCK in science.

Pedagogical content knowledge in science

Pedagogical content knowledge is a teacher's understanding of how to help students understand specific subject matter. It includes knowledge of how particular subject matter topics, problems, and issues can be organized, represented, and adapted to the diverse interests and abilities of learners, and then presented for instruction.

(Magnusson, Krajcik, & Borko, 1999, p. 96)

The term pedagogical content knowledge—PCK—has been used to mean many different things. Since Shulman's (1986) seminal work on PCK, researchers have pushed and pulled on the concept to understand how to define and use it in specific domains and to make more crisp the distinction between this kind of knowledge and other knowledge teachers use in practice. The most commonly used definition comes from Grossman (1989, 1990) who delineates four elements of PCK: (a) conceptions of purposes for teaching subject matter, (b) knowledge of students' understanding, (c) knowledge of instructional strategies, and (d) curricular knowledge. Magnusson, Krajcik, and Borko (1999) provide a more comprehensive definition, delineating five components of PCK as knowledge and beliefs about (a) orientations toward science teaching, (b) curriculum, (c) students' understandings, (d) assessment, and (e) instructional strategies. Van Driel, Verloop, and Vos (1998) review versions and adaptations of the concept of PCK in research on science teaching and suggest that most include at least two of the elements proposed by Grossman: (a) knowledge of students' understandings (and misconceptions) of particular topics, and (b) instructional strategies and representations for teaching particular topics.

In science education, researchers have used the concept of PCK as a way to understand what teachers know and how they teach particular topics. Some research has investigated how teachers develop PCK. For example, van Driel and colleagues (1998) studied preservice teachers' knowledge of chemical equilibrium, focusing on their use of representations. They found that for the topic of chemical equilibrium, textbooks at both high school and post-secondary levels do not address the elements of PCK that they found important in challenging students' naïve conceptions of chemical reactions. They suggest that representations of the reversibility of chemical reactions are not adequately addressed in textbooks, although they appear to be an important aspect of teachers' PCK. In another study de Jong, van Driel, and Verloop (2005) investigated preservice teachers' knowledge and use of particle models in teaching chemistry. In this study, they found they could teach PCK for this topic by connecting the prospective teachers' experiences in the classes they taught with their learning in the classes they were taking, emphasizing and supporting learning from their own teaching. Along with other research on PCK in science (Daehler & Shinohara, 2001; Loughran, Milroy, Berry, Gunstone, & Mulhall, 2001; Zohar & Schwartzer, 2005), these studies make clear that PCK is a topic-specific and context-specific kind of knowledge, and that teachers seem to develop PCK in response to their experience as teachers.

Unfortunately, the lack of clarity about the construct makes it difficult to draw conclusions across studies, for the range of definitions of PCK is very broad: some researchers include nearly all teacher *reasoning* as part of PCK; others use nearly all content and pedagogical knowledge; and others restrict PCK to the two categories mentioned above, briefly, student errors and misconceptions, and representations. In all cases, PCK includes at least specific knowledge of student thinking about science topics and knowledge of representations and instructional strategies for teaching particular topics, but beyond that, the definition becomes unclear. In the next section, we use the narrower definition of PCK—knowledge of students' understanding and mis-conceptions, and knowledge of instructional strategies and representations for particular topics—and consider how to extend it to include technology in a way that makes visible the knowledge needed to teach science with technology.

Elements of technological PCK in science

Teachers' knowledge of technology, science, and pedagogy comes together in knowing *where* (in the curriculum) to use technology, *what* technology to use, and *how* to teach with it. These three aspects of TPCK are discussed below.

Where to use technology

In deciding to use technology in science teaching, it is fundamental to decide where technology can help students learn or help the teacher teach. Technology is good for some purposes, but not for others, especially in K-12 class-rooms where uses of technology are determined in part by the characteristics of the technology that is available. In science, two considerations guide decisions about technology use:

1. Identifying parts of the curriculum that are hard to teach where technology might help overcome pedagogical or cognitive difficulties.
2. Identifying topics in the curriculum for which technology is an essential element of the science being taught.

These considerations are important and not trivial, and they define two kinds of technology use: pedagogical and scientific. We next consider what constitutes pedagogical and scientific uses of technology.

Pedagogical uses

There are many ways that technology could be pedagogically useful in science teaching:

- Speeding up time via simulations of natural events.
- Saving time through data collection devices.
- Seeing things that could not otherwise be seen:
  - through multiple linked representations
  - through dynamic representations
  - through models and simulations
- Recording data that would otherwise be hard to gather.
- Organizing data that would otherwise be hard to organize.
- Sharing information in new ways across time and/or space.
- Communicating with experts or others remotely located.
- Having access to real-time data and current information.

The teacher needs to know, with respect to her subject and her students, where technology could solve a pedagogical problem that she faces. For example, if she is teaching biology, she may face the common problem that students do not learn much from dissecting real animals. Some students are repulsed by dissection and do not engage in it, and those who do often make a mess of it and fail to learn the intended lessons about animal biology. A technological solution could be to supplement or replace real dissection with virtual dissection.

Another example of a pedagogical problem is teaching the importance of accurate and organized data collection. Because time is short in school science, it often happens that students are unable to collect enough data to experience for themselves the need for precision and organization of data. Technology could be used in several ways to change this. For example, technology can speed up experiments through simulation or by pooling and sharing data from multiple experiments. Or, technological devices can be used to collect and simultaneously record data in the lab or in the field. In each of these uses, the increased volume of data collected could be used to teach students about the importance of methods for collecting and organizing data in science.

A third example is helping students understand a complex cycle, such as the oxygen cycle in a pond. A computer-based modeling program can help students visualize the processes involved and they can manipulate variables in ways that would be impossible if studying a particular body of water or reading and solving problems from a textbook. Such a model involves speeding up time to see results in minutes that might usually take days or years. Modeling is surely one of the major changes in science teaching made possible through technology.

Scientific uses

There are times when technology is integral to the topic being taught, when science is embedded in technology. For example Niess (2005) describes a preservice teacher's use of a computer-based laboratory (CBL) pH probe. This teacher expressed her reluctance to have the students explore how the probe worked or how its function differed scientifically from litmus paper or cabbage juice tests. Niess argues that in this case, the probe technology is part of the science itself, not merely a tool for data collection, suggesting that students could learn science both by *using* the tool and by *learning about* the tool. In fact, in the world of science outside of schools, many technologies are part of science, not simply tools to do science. It is important for teachers to consider when technology is such an integral part of science that it is essential to doing science or even becomes the object of study.

Another example of a technology that is integral to science, already embedded in our expectations for science teaching, is the microscope. Using a microscope is fundamental to the study of biology to the point that it would seem inadequate to teach *about* using a microscope, or to teach *about* what might be seen with a microscope, without actually having students use a microscope (or more recently, using a remote or simulated microscope on a computer). At more advanced levels of scientific practice, critical technologies are pervasive. Some of them have become available in schools via the Internet, offering a wider range of options for teaching with or about technologies integral to doing science. Even in high school or earlier, technology has changed what is possible in science, not only what is possible to do as a scientist (e.g., using a telescope at a remote location) but also what is possible to teach and learn. There is evidence, for example, that through technology, students can learn physics before (and without) calculus. Or, they can create and learn from intuitive models of advanced processes much earlier than they could acquire the technical (mathematical) skills to model those processes quantitatively.

In summary, we see many reasons for using technology in science teaching that relate directly to a pedagogical opportunity to offer students something that would be hard to do without technology. There are also opportunities to teach with and about technologies that are integral to doing science in the twenty-first century. Next, we look at technologies in schools and consider what is available.

What technology to use

The second piece of teachers' TPCK is knowing what technology is available and deciding what technology to use. The range of technologies that might be found in science classrooms is enormous. Hardware possibilities include handheld devices, laptop computers, calculators, and probes, as well as remote devices available via the Internet. Local devices may be connected wirelessly or through wired hubs. Devices may be loaded with software designed for classrooms (such as SimCalc for graphing calculators)[1] or they may be available as platforms to which software can be added.

We can classify technology for science teaching in three categories:

1. Technology that is unrelated to science but is used in the service of science. Word processing, spreadsheets, or graphic software fall into this category.
2. Technology designed for teaching and learning science. Programs like Model-It™, Virtual Frog, Cooties™, BIOKids, and WISE have been developed specifically for teaching K-12 science.[2]
3. Technology designed and used to do science. This includes instruments such as microscopes, remote (web-based) telescopes, CBL probes, and scientific calculators.

Science teachers at all grade levels have reasons to use each of these categories of technology, yet the focus of teaching may be quite different in each case. In addition, because every school is different, a large element of each teacher's knowledge is knowing his own school's resources. Having a lab full of desktop computers has different implications for teaching than having a portable set of wireless laptops or individual handheld devices. The conditions of use, the possibilities for teaching and learning, and the timely availability of resources all change from school to school, or even classroom to classroom. In some schools, science teachers have been leaders in obtaining technology for teaching, and when that happens, they can be much more proactive in choosing technology that is appropriate for their classes.

How to teach with technology

The final piece of TPCK is knowing how to integrate technology into teaching and learning. As with using any new resource in teaching, this is a risky business. No matter how ineffective previous teaching has seemed (e.g., the messy frog dissection from which some students learned very little), it has been successful in some degree, if only in getting through the content without delay. Using something new means risking failure. Anticipating how to use technology is hard and calls on teachers' knowledge in many different ways. Technology failure often occurs at the first attempt, and for many teachers the first attempt is the last one.

It is at this stage that teachers need to mine their own internal resources—their knowledge of science, of students, and of pedagogy—to anticipate and prepare for what will likely happen when the technology is used.

For example, to use graphing calculators to simulate time and distance problems with SimCalc, what might a teacher consider before his first use? This teacher has identified a problem: students have a hard time understanding the relationships among time, rate, and distance especially as shown on graphs. He has identified a technology that is available: his school has calculators with SimCalc software and he has a classroom computer, a wireless hub, and a projector that can be used to collect data from individuals or groups of students and display it to the class. Some things he will want to consider before launching the project include:

- Teaching students about the calculators before starting the project.
- Giving them time to "play" with the system before starting with the desired subject matter teaching.
- Identifying possible or likely failure points for the software or hardware and developing alternate plans in case of a breakdown.
- Organizing the classroom for the activity, individual or small group work; timed or open-ended activities; all working on the same problem or doing a variety of problems; one–one ratio of calculators to students or some other arrangement, etc.

- Planning the specific activity students will engage in with attention to how it engages them with the desired subject matter and how it will help them learn the intended content.
- Considering what kind of activity, noise level, and student talk to expect or accept during the activity.
- Planning for assessment of what students learned as well as evaluation of the activity itself.

The more specific the scenario he can build about likely events when he uses the technology, the more likely he is to experience success. This is not unlike planning for any new activity in the classroom using any new resource. One main difference is the near certainty that something will go wrong with the technology and the consequent need for detailed backup planning. Another difference is that teachers have ample experience with other kinds of activities such as individual or group seatwork, presentations by individuals or groups, going over homework, managing a standard lab activity, etc. With technology, especially using hardware or software for the first time, even an experienced teacher becomes a novice. The classroom experience of teaching and learning with technology can be unlike any prior experience, depending on exactly how new and how different the technology is for teacher and students.

In the process of building a scenario for teaching with technology, and then reflecting on what happened when the class is over, a teacher develops knowledge that he can use the next time he uses the technology. It is very context- and content-specific knowledge, depending on the technology available, the students, and the subject matter. It is TPCK.

This chapter has proposed three elements of TPCK for science teaching, (1) *Where* technology can help, (2) *What* technology is available, and (3) *How* to teach with technology. The next section discusses the implications of these three elements for teacher knowledge.

Teacher knowledge

What is the knowledge that enables teachers adequately to answer the questions of where, what, and how to teach with technology? It is a combination of things including knowledge of subject matter, of students, of pedagogy, and of technology. Each of these is discussed below.

Knowledge of science

The first demand on teacher knowledge is knowing the science they are teaching. Although the precise content knowledge teachers need has not been well specified (by theory or empirical research), it is certainly true that they need at least to know the science they expect their students to learn. Beyond this, they probably need to know much more science. For example, it may be helpful and important to know what comes after the content they are teaching, e.g., what a student might learn next; to know what science precedes or is a prerequisite for the topic being studied; to know how what they teach relates to applications in the world and to the work scientists actually do; and to know the big open questions in the field related to the topic at hand.

In a review of literature on pedagogical content knowledge in science teaching, van Driel and colleagues (1998) conclude that "teaching experience [is] the major source of PCK, whereas adequate subject-matter knowledge appears to be a prerequisite" (p. 673). In their study, the prospective teachers needed to have their own deep understanding of chemical equilibrium before they could develop the pedagogical content knowledge needed to help their students develop a similar understanding. In this case, PCK consisted of knowledge of representations and examples that addressed students' naïve ideas about chemical reactions. One of the conclusions of their study is that, while previous research on PCK has focused in a general way on the nature of this knowledge and whether it is a different kind of knowledge, the knowledge itself is topic specific and not at all general in content. They suggest that more research is needed to identify specific PCK for topics in science education, while understanding that the foundation for PCK is the basic subject matter knowledge for the topic in question.

Knowledge of students

One aspect of teacher knowledge that is critical is knowing for the particular students being taught, what they find hard to learn and where they hold misconceptions or stubborn misinformation. Teachers learn this in at least two ways: from their formal education in teacher preparation, and from their own experience as teachers. Experienced teachers have a long list of specifics in their subject where students stumble. They may know, for example, that students hang on to the idea that an eclipse is caused by the shadow of the earth or that seasons are caused by distance from the sun. Students misinterpret graphs of velocity as graphs of location. They confuse temperature and heat. And so on. Science teachers use detailed knowledge of students' knowledge as they decide what to emphasize and what tools and techniques to use. Their knowledge of students helps them define a landscape of teaching and learning that is appropriate to both the subject matter and the characteristics of their particular students.

Knowledge of students is an especially important aspect of teachers' knowledge that is related to TPCK, because there have been many programs or technologies developed specifically to address student misconceptions in science. For example, the WISE project has units addressing misconceptions about light, heat and temperature, and energy, among others. Other web sites feature widgets that address specific problems students have in understanding astronomy, Newtonian physics, and other topics from high school science.[3]

Knowledge of pedagogy

Teachers need to know how to teach. They need knowledge of pedagogy both general to all teaching and specific to their subject matter. At a general level, they need to know how to manage the classroom effectively to avoid unnecessary disruptions and delays. In the subject-specific domain, teachers need a repertoire of tools and techniques to address the particular content they are teaching. They may have supplementary materials like films, posters, or extra readings; they may have lesson plans incorporating a range of activities such as simulations or modeling; they may have outside experts they call on for particular pieces of the curriculum.

At a more detailed level, a teacher's knowledge of pedagogy extends to how she presents and explains material, how she organizes a lab activity to enhance learning, and how she designs group and individual assignments. These are all closely connected to subject matter, probably falling into what Shulman called pedagogical content knowledge.

Knowledge of technology

The fourth domain of knowledge science teachers need is knowledge of technology. Some would argue that knowledge of technology is practically synonymous with knowledge of science, or that science is a form of technology. Derry (1999) describes the difference between science and technology this way:

> Science is a way of understanding the world … Technology, on the other hand, is a way of controlling the world, a set of tools that we can use to make things happen as we wish. So science and technology can sometimes be separate and unrelated … More typically, science and technology are highly intertwined.
>
> (pp. 133–134)

Technology defined broadly includes any tools or techniques used for practical purposes. In this broad definition, technology includes not only computers and machines, but also methods, skills, and processes. Using the expansive definition, knowledge of technology might include knowledge of curriculum and pedagogy, since the latter are themselves technologies. In this case, TPCK and PCK tend to merge, since pedagogy itself is a form of technology. Certainly, conventional tools for teaching science are also technologies: microscopes, Bunsen burners, wind tunnels, and other lab equipment have been used in science teaching for decades. Teachers' knowledge of these technologies is essentially taken for granted, even though the issues for TPCK with respect to these technologies are the same as for computers and other newer technologies.

To avoid this collapsing of categories, we consider here the technologies that are new and currently problematic in schools: digital technologies like computers, hand-held devices, digital cameras, networks including the Internet, and software to make all of these devices function. As to these, teachers need knowledge of what they are, what is available, and how to use them, as outlined earlier in this chapter. Unlike more conventional lab equipment, there is no standard, expected configuration of digital technologies for science teaching. The set of possibilities is large, for not only do many technologies appear on this list, but they also change rapidly and regularly. What is "high-tech" today is outdated tomorrow, and consequently, what is available today becomes unusable tomorrow.

What does this rapid turnover of devices and software mean for teacher knowledge? It is unreasonable to expect science teachers to be "techies" who keep up with every current trend in technology. What, then, is reasonable?

A proposal for reasonable and manageable technology knowledge for a science teacher might have these characteristics: he or she should be a regular computer user who knows how to use and manage her own computer; she should be able to troubleshoot problems she encounters on her own computer; she should be able to approach a new technology with confidence and should know where to get help; she should be willing to try new technologies, even if not first in line to do so.

This list is vague and does not include specifics. Should a science teacher know how to set up a wireless network? To make DVDs or edit video? To create web pages? These are specifics that depend on the teacher's circumstance and what is available in the school. Although there are lists of skills and dispositions that define adequate technology knowledge for teachers (e.g., International Society for Technology in Education, 2000), what is suggested here is that no list of skills is appropriate for all teachers because technology availability and use is highly dependent on context. It is much easier to make a list of what a high school science teacher needs to know about biology or physics than about technology.

Technological pedagogical content knowledge

Four elements are critical to science teachers' development of technological pedagogical content knowledge: knowledge of science, students, pedagogy, and technology. All four come together when a teacher uses technology in his teaching. Ideally, this happens for one of two reasons: (a) He knows a topic or place in the curriculum that is problematic for teaching and/or learning and, because of characteristics of technology as related to the subject, he believes that technology could be used to solve the problem; or, (b) he is teaching a topic in science which is embedded in a technology or for which a technology is essential. These reflect the pedagogical and scientific uses of technology described above.

What is special about this knowledge? Two characteristics are fundamental: (1) it is local and specific, and (2) it is usually developed in practice in response to specific students and contexts.

LOCAL AND SPECIFIC

TPCK is about a specific topic within a domain using a specific technology. There is no general version. For example, TPCK for teaching the weather cycle could include a wide range of technologies and models, but for a specific teacher with a specific class, it means knowing many things in detail: e.g., that her 9th grade students studied weather in the 6th grade; that the American Meteorological Society web site[4] has a set of tools that make generating simple weather maps possible; that her classroom has an Internet connection; that she can get the set of laptops the days she need them, etc. It also means knowing how to design a lesson that uses the AMS maps as a representation of some aspects of weather.

For another teacher, at a different grade level in another school, all of this would be different. If the teacher did not have Internet access, he might use television weather broadcasts recorded on a DVD or videotape; or he might printout the day's weather maps at the start of the day from an Internet connection in the library. There would be tradeoffs: is it the same to have students "watch" the weather change over several days by using Internet resources as it is to watch a television broadcast or work from printed maps? There may be differences in what students are able to learn in each of these modes that relate in part to motivation, and in part to substantive differences in content and affordances. For example, students may be more interested in using the Internet than watching a video, especially if the Internet is not routinely used in their classes or homes. Substantively, on the Internet, the weather maps can be modified in real time to focus on particular areas of the world or on particular aspects of the weather, whereas the content of a video is static.

DEVELOPED IN RESPONSE TO SPECIFIC STUDENTS AND CONTEXTS

Knowledge of technologies for teaching a particular topic, such as that described for weather, could be taught in teacher education programs or professional development, but two problems with trying to teach such specific content are (a) it may prove to be useless to some or all of the students when they become teachers and find that they do not have access to the technologies required or that the class they are teaching does not include the topic they learned about; and (b) it is impossible to "cover" the terrain of science to teach either TPCK or PCK across the domain. Even with a PCK class to accompany every science class a prospective teacher takes in college (an impractical if not absurd idea) it would not be possible to anticipate the contexts in which students would teach.

What can be done then to help teachers develop TPCK? In teacher education programs, the content courses must themselves include uses of technology integral to the subject matter. That way, teachers develop first-hand knowledge of learning science with technology and at the same time are exposed to technological tools that they may be able to use in their own teaching. At the same time, methods courses could include explicit attention to the features and affordances of technology for science teaching, concentrating on in-depth use of a few powerful examples of technologies that are widely available. The aim overall is to have new teachers graduate from their teacher preparation programs with a repertoire of tools, albeit small, and a deep understanding of the role of technology in science and science teaching and learning.

On the one hand, these teachers will have specific knowledge, constituting a repertoire of tools and techniques, rather than a list of items. On the other hand, they will have an overarching perspective about technology in science. It is important to keep in mind, though, that what works for one teacher in one school for one class may be impossible for another, even someone in apparently similar circumstances. Part of a teacher's TPCK is knowing what will not work, what is outside of one's repertoire of technologies for teaching. This is the kind of knowledge that develops in practice when a teacher is aware of possibilities and reflective about his or her own teaching.

This knowledge allows teachers to pinpoint spots in the curriculum where a different approach to teaching might help. Knowing what to do in these hard spots is part of what Shulman called pedagogical content knowledge. Adding technology to the mix, we identify this as TPCK—knowing the places in the subject matter where technology can be used to improve pedagogy.

Discussion

Describing or discussing TPCK in science parallels the problem of describing science knowledge itself. Even if we know exactly what it is when we see it, there is so much of it, and it is so varied across the domains of science, that discussing TPCK in general, or science knowledge in general, is not especially helpful. TPCK is made up of very specific knowledge that happens to live in the boundary between subject matter and teaching. Technology adds a layer of complexity to the demands on teacher knowledge because of the unpredictability of what will be available, and how it will change over time.

What can we say in general about TPCK? Although it would clearly be useful for teachers to have knowledge that lets them use technology effectively in science teaching, they face the same problem with technology as with other tools, techniques, and even subject matters for teaching. Because there is not enough time to learn everything that would be useful to know—or even to learn everything that others could teach them in their undergraduate education or professional development experiences—the best teachers can do is equip themselves to learn from their practice and from ongoing education. Teachers must choose what technologies to use, a choice based on availability and their own knowledge along with factors outlined above related to science itself. Here we see something of a vicious circle—teachers choose technology based on knowledge, yet sometimes the only way they can gain knowledge is through experience. TPCK in science depends on teachers learning about technology in their undergraduate education, in professional development, or on their own initiative.

What should be taught in preservice and in-service education for teachers? Time is not elastic and it is limited, so choices must be made. Teacher educators can now assume that their students—both prospective and practicing teachers—have basic technology skills such as using email, searching the web, and using a word processor. More advanced skills like creating a web page or setting up a wireless network are less common. That still leaves a lot of territory to consider, and since time is limited, if we add a technology to the semester or session, something else will get less attention.

The answer to the problem of TPCK must be that we teach teachers as we wish them to teach. When teacher educators routinely use technology to teach science and make explicit how and why they use technology in particular ways, prospective teachers learn from this experience as they will later learn from their own teaching. As with other issues for teacher education, detailed answers to these questions are surely local. There is one general proposition, however, that may hold up to scrutiny: in formal in-service and preservice education, teachers can learn to learn about teaching with technology. No matter what technologies are used or what topics are taught, the goal can be to equip teachers with the knowledge, skills, and dispositions to try new technologies and to learn from their own experience; to anticipate problems that may arise and to persist in using technology in ways that support their students' learning.

Notes

1. SimCalc information is available at http://www.simcalc.umassd.edu.
2. Information about these technologies can be found at the following web sites:
   Model-It™: http://goknow.com/Products/Model-It
   Virtual Frog: http://froggy.lbl.gov/virtual
   Cooties™: http://goknow.com/Products/Cooties
   BIOKids: ttp://www.biokids.umich.edu
   WISE: http://wise.berkeley.edu.
3. cf., WISE Project: wise.berkeley.edu;
   A Private Universe project, www.learner.org/teacherslab/pup;
   Misconception widgets, www.physics.montana.edu/physed/misconceptions;
   Interactive Physics, www.design-simulation.com/IP.
4. American Meteorological Society education web site: www.ametsoc.org/amsedu.

References

Daehler, K. R., & Shinohara, M. (2001). A complete circuit is a complete circle: Exploring the potential of case materials and methods to develop teachers' content knowledge and pedagogical content knowledge of science. *Research in Science Education, 31*(2), 267–288.

de Jong, O., van Driel, J. H., & Verloop, N. (2005). Preservice teachers' pedagogical content knowledge of using particle models in teaching chemistry. *Journal of Research in Science Teaching, 42*(8), 947–964.

Derry, G. N. (1999). *What science is and how it works.* Princeton, NJ: Princeton University Press.

Grossman, P. L. (1989). A study in contrast: Sources of pedagogical content knowledge for secondary English. *Journal of Teacher Education, 40*(5), 24–31.

Grossman, P. L. (1990). *The making of a teacher: Teacher knowledge and teacher education.* New York: Teachers College Press.

International Society for Technology in Education. (2000). *National educational technology standards for teachers.* Eugene, OR: International Society for Technology in Education (ISTE) NETS Project.

Loughran, J., Milroy, P., Berry, A., Gunstone, R., & Mulhall, P. (2001). Documenting science teachers' pedagogical content knowledge through PaP-eRs. *Research in Science Education, 31*(2), 290–307.

Magnusson, S., Krajcik, J., & Borko, H. (1999). Nature, sources, and development of pedagogical content knowledge for science teaching. In J. Gess-Newsome & N. Lederman (eds), *Examining pedagogical content knowledge: The construct and its implications for science education* (pp. 95–132). The Netherlands: Kluwer Academic Publishers.

Niess, M. L. (2005). Preparing teachers to teach science and mathematics with technology: Developing a technology pedagogical content knowledge. *Teaching and Teacher Education, 21*, 509–523.

Shulman, L. S. (1986). Those who understand: Knowledge growth in teaching. *Educational Researcher, 15*, 4–14.

van Driel, J. H., Verloop, N., & Vos, W. D. (1998). Developing science teachers' pedagogical content knowledge. *Journal of Research in Science Teaching, 35*(6), 673–695.

Zohar, A., & Schwartzer, N. (2005). Assessing teachers' pedagogical knowledge in the context of teaching higher-order thinking. *International Journal of Science Education, 27*(13), 1595–1620.

10

The role of TPCK in physical education

LUKE E. KELLY

The goal of this chapter is to explore how the concept technological pedagogical content knowledge (TPCK) applies to physical education. Like most of the other academic disciplines in education, much has been written about physical education content knowledge and pedagogical content knowledge. An analysis of this literature reveals that while there are many similarities in the basic components of the undergraduate preparation programs used to prepare physical educators and other teachers in areas like math and science, there are also some fundamental differences (Siedentop, 2002). The TPCK model presented by Koehler and Mishra in the beginning of this book will be used to highlight these similarities and differences. Before the interactions between content, pedagogical, and technology knowledge can be examined it is important to briefly review a few unique aspects of physical education in these foundation knowledge areas.

Content knowledge in physical education

Like many other fields, there has been much discussion within the profession as to what should constitute the content knowledge or academic discipline of physical education (Henry, 1964; Siedentop, 2002; Tinning, 2002; Wright, 2000). Today, physical educators are typically trained in Kinesiology or Exercise Science departments which may or may not be housed in schools of education. The core of these degree programs is heavily weighted toward science course work and application of these foundation principles to human movement and development in more applied courses such as biomechanics, motor development, motor learning, motor control, sport psychology, sport history and philosophy, and exercise physiology. These courses serve as the core of the undergraduate kinesiology degree. After the core is obtained students then specialize in a major that applies this content to a specific area of kinesiology (e.g., athletic training, exercise/fitness specialists, physical educators) or use it as the basis for pursuing graduate work in related areas such as sports medicine, physical therapy, or occupational therapy to name a few. The subsequent course work and experiences used to apply the kinesiology content knowledge to a specific area define the pedagogical content knowledge.

Pedagogical content knowledge (PCK) in physical education

Pedagogical content knowledge then is defined by the specific kinesiology speciality or major pursued. For this chapter we will focus on the PCK kinesiology majors need to become physical education teachers. Much has also been written within the profession about what PCK is and its applications to different curriculum models used in physical education (Lynn, 2002; Morh & Townsend, 2002; Metzler, 2000; O'Sullivan, 1996). Like the other academic disciplines discussed in this book, pedagogy in physical education must address the four dimensions of PCK (Grossman, 1990; Shulman, 1986) related to physical education:

- Knowledge and conceptions about the purposes for teaching physical education.
- Knowledge about students' understanding, conceptions, and misconceptions about the content.
- Knowledge of instructional strategies.
- Curricular knowledge.

The fundamental difference here is that physical educators must focus on teaching physical and motor skills with the goal that the learners must not only understand what the skill is and how it can be used in games and sports, but they must also be able to perform it to a certain level of proficiency.

Using an example from a developmental curricular approach to physical education (Kelly & Melograno, 2004), a teacher would need to be able to apply their content knowledge so that they could assess and then teach the basic components of motor skills. For example, the components of the underhand roll, which would be considered a relatively simple motor skill, are presented below:

1. Stand with body square to target, weight evenly distributed on both feet, feet shoulder width apart, eyes on target, ball held in palm of dominant hand at waist level in front of body.
2. Arm swings back, elbow extended, until dominant hand is behind the thigh, with trunk rotation back.
3. Arm swings forward below the shoulder until dominant hand is in front of the thigh, with trunk rotation forward.
4. Weight shift to the foot on the arm-swing side of the body during the arm swing back, and stride forward with weight shift to the foot on the opposite side of the body during the arm swing forward.
5. Ball released close to ground, bending hips and knees with trunk near vertical, palm facing forward toward target.
6. Arm follows through well beyond ball release toward the target.
7. Smooth integration (not mechanical or jerky) of the previous components.

To teach this skill, physical educators must know a variety of things from their content knowledge such as:

- how to perform this skill,
- when students are typically developmentally ready to learn this skill and what prerequisite skills and abilities (e.g., strength, range of motor, motor control) the student must possess,
- the learning needs and attributes of the students,
- the biomechanical analysis of the skill.

For students to learn this skill, the teachers must know pedagogically how to communicate such things as:

- what the skill is and why it should be learned,
- what the skill looks like when done correctly,
- what the key components are and what they look like when performed correctly,
- how to accurately assess these components,
- which specific components each student needs to work on,
- what specifically students need to do to change their performance on the components,
- how the students can practice this skill for many practice trials with corrective feedback so that they know when they are doing the components correctly,
- how to accommodate and address the diverse ability levels and learning styles of the students,
- how to design and present a progression of learning tasks that are both challenging and achievable,
- provide a safe and secure learning environment where students are comfortable taking learning risks.

The point to be stressed here is that the teacher must know when and how to teach the skill and the student must know specifically what to work on and then practice it numerous times with feedback. This highlights one of the uniqueness's of the content in physical education. Students must not only know the content, they must be able to perform it to a level of proficiency.

The curriculum in physical education is cumulative requiring students to develop competency in many fundamental motor skills during the early elementary years. These fundamental motor skills then become the building blocks and are combined to form more complex skills which are taught in the subsequent grades. These complex skills constitute the skill sets needed to participate in our societal games and sports. For example, for students to eventually play a pick-up game of basketball with their friends, they would need basic skill proficiency in the following fundamental skills (running, changing directions, dribbling, catching, passing, and shooting) and in combining these skills as well as knowing the rules, and basic offense and defense strategies of the game.

Physical education also presents some unique pedagogical demands. First, skill acquisition takes time and practice. Learning motor skills involves more than simply knowing what to do. The learners must also be able to make their bodies do the movements and be willing to take the risk of trying to do it. Using an adult example to illustrate this point, can you do a front flip off a diving board? All you need to do is jump up and out from the board, bring your chin to your chest as you raise your knees to your chest, this will rotate your body forward, when you have rotated approximately 270 degrees, begin to lift your chin and extend your legs so that you enter the water vertically. Now that you know what to do, how confident are you that you can do a flip? Most motor skills involve learning to quickly move multiple body parts in new ways that must be carefully coordinated and timed in order for the skill to be performed successfully. A second pedagogical challenge for physical education is that learning motor skills is done in a public setting. When students perform they typically receive immediate feedback and this feedback is also visible to all the other students in the class. Unfortunately, the type of feedback most readily available to students is not the type that is most conducive to early learning. What students typically receive is knowledge of results or the end result of their performance. If the students were trying to catch, was the ball caught. If the students were shooting a basketball, did the shot go in the basket. Of course, if the students were not successful in terms of the results and these results were seen by the other students, this can reduce the students' motivation to try again. What students actually need during skill acquisition is feedback on how they performed the skill or what is called knowledge of performance. This type of feedback involves providing the student with information about what component of the skill was performed incorrectly and how to correct it and is dependent on the teacher either providing it directly or designing the activity so that it provides the student with relevant performance feedback. Returning to the front flip example used above, landing on your back after attempting to perform a flip is knowledge of results. Being told that you did not keep your chin on your chest during the flip is knowledge of performance.

Many people who have tried to teach themselves a new skill like how to play golf can relate to the challenges of learning a motor skill where there is abundant knowledge of results and an absence of knowledge of performance feedback. Even though beginning golfers have access to countless sources of video information and expert advice on what they should do (e.g., keep their head down, wrist stiff, etc.), few succeed with just this information. What is needed is assessment-based instruction providing knowledge of performance and then thousands of practice trials with corrective performance-based feedback to train the brain to initiate the right neural messages to trigger the correct muscles to contract with appropriate timing and force to hit the ball just right. And then, even this performance can fail on the first tee when being watched by several other golfers waiting to tee off!

Technology knowledge in physical education

With a basic understanding of the unique content knowledge and pedagogical knowledge of physical education, we can now explore the role of technology knowledge and how it can be used to enhance acquisition of content knowledge and pedagogical knowledge and whether there is a unique TPCK for physical educators teaching K-12 physical education. If an argument can be made that technology plays a significant role in teachers acquiring their content and pedagogical knowledge and that teachers need to use technology in order to maximize their teaching effectiveness, than it can be deduced that there is justification for both technology knowledge base and specific TPCK for physical educators.

The first question then is whether technology plays a significant role in the acquisition of physical education content knowledge. If technology is defined broadly as tools and devices, the answer to this question is clearly yes. Given the scientific nature of much of the content in kinesiology, technology has been an integral part of instruction for years. This technology ranges from using video clips in motor development to illustrate different developmental stages, to using three-dimensional models to illustrate the anatomy of a joint like the knee, to sophisticated computer-generated applications that allow students to peel back layers of skin and muscle to explore biomechanics such as the mechanics of the shoulder joint. Most content areas in kinesiology are also heavily dependent upon computer-controlled devices for the collection, analysis, and graphic summary of large amounts of data that are invaluable for allowing students to interact and learn this respective content.

In terms of using technology to facilitate the acquisition of content knowledge in kinesiology, the greatest challenges are in developing these applications and equitably distributing their use. In some cases, applications developed for medical applications can be adopted and used in kinesiology at a reasonable cost (e.g., anatomy and biomechanics examples used above). In other cases, technology developed and used primarily for research can also be used for instruction. However, this technology is largely limited to research universities and would be cost prohibitive for many non-research colleges and universities to purchase purely for instructional purposes. Finally, higher education faculty have to be trained in how to use this technology to enhance student learning and not just how it can be used in research.

The second question is what is the role of technology in teaching pedagogical content to physical educators? As with content knowledge, technology plays a significant role in developing pedagogical skills in physical educators. Physical education can benefit from all the common technologies used in teacher education to enhance the development of teaching skills such as computer-based teacher observation systems, video analysis of teaching, and computerized case studies. In addition, technology can play a major role in developing assessment skills in physical educators (Walkley & Kelly, 1990). As discussed earlier, assessment is critical for children to receive knowledge of performance when learning motor skills. To provide this type of feedback, the teacher must know the key components of the motor skills being taught, how to accurately observe these components, determine where errors are being made, and then know how to provide appropriate instruction so that the students can change their motor behavior on these components. While many of the sub-skills of assessing are cognitive and can be learned independently, learning how to accurately observe the components is a skill that can only be acquired through guided practice with corrective feedback. This can be challenging because many skills have multiple components and are performed very quickly. For example, performing an overhand throw involves seven key components that are performed in less than a second. Many beginning teachers require numerous practice trials just to see the components before they can start making judgments regarding their quality. This is further complicated by the fact that there are natural variations in children's performance of motor skills and the skills must be evaluated efficiently within two or three trials before fatigue and motivation begin to become factors. This means a preservice teacher must observe a student performing the target skill and make judgments regarding which components are being performed incorrectly and then immediately receive feedback regarding the accuracy of their judgments. Traditionally, this would mean that this skill would have to be practiced with an expert, someone who could accurately evaluate the accuracy of the preservice student's judgments. When errors are made, an explanation would be provided by the expert on why the teacher's observation was wrong and how the error could be corrected. In the past, this was a difficult issue to address in teacher education programs due to the amount of content physical educators needed to be competent in assessing, the ratio of experts (i.e., higher education faculty) to students (preservice teachers), and the fact that an expert was needed to evaluate the judgments and provide constructive feedback.

This turns out to be an excellent example where technology can enhance both instruction and student learning. A self-paced computer-assisted instructional program (Kelly, Walkley, & Tarrant, 1988) can be used to teach the key components of the motor skills as well as common errors associated with each component. The program can then provide the preservice teachers guided practice using a library of video clips of the motor skills, which have already been evaluated by experts. During the guided practice the students can watch the clips an unlimited number of times and at different speeds (frame-by-frame, slow motion, and real-time) until the key components are learned and can be accurately observed. Then the program can evaluate their performance, using a dedicated pool of clips, under simulated field conditions where the preservice teacher must accurately evaluate the performance of students after seeing only three trials in real speed. This approach to teaching assessing has all the advantages associated with computer-assisted instruction (Kelly, 1987): individualized, self-paced, can be accessed when it is convenient to the learner, and is competency based.

While it is clear that technology can and at many institutions of higher education does play a significant role in the teacher training of physical educators, it is not without challenges. As mentioned earlier there are many different philosophical approaches to physical education which complicates the development of technology tools and applications. As with many other education areas, physical education is a small specialized market that is not attractive to commercial software developers. As a result, many of the applications that are created are developed as part of research projects. The challenge is then developing these specialized applications to scale so that they can be used by the profession for instruction across universities.

Physical education TPCK

From the above examples, it is safe to conclude that since technology plays a significant role in physical educators' acquisition of content and pedagogical knowledge, they must have a foundation in TK. The critical question now is whether there is a unique TPCK that physical educators must possess to effectively teach physical education to K-12 students. The answer to this question is yes, but its role is limited due to many of the constraints imposed on K-12 physical education and the nature of learning physical and motor skills.

The goal of physical education is to develop students' physical and motor skills so that they can live healthy and active lives during and after their school years. To achieve this goal students must know how to learn motor skills, in most cases they must practice them thousands of times with corrective feedback, and they must be motivated to learn these skills. So how can physical educators use technology to maximize their effectiveness and enhance communication of what is to be learned, provide students feedback during learning, and motivate students to learn and practice physical and motor skills? Three examples will be presented to explore these issues. The first two examples illustrate how physical educators can use technology to enhance instruction. The third example highlights how physical educators can use technology for evaluating their effectiveness and for student and program evaluation.

While most people would agree that one of the goals of physical education should be the development of physical fitness, this is a challenge to accomplish in most school settings. There are several components of physical fitness: cardiorespiratory endurance, flexibility, balance, body composition, coordination, power, speed, agility, muscular strength, and muscular endurance. For the purpose of this example we will focus on just one of these components, cardiorespiratory endurance (CRE). The principles of developing CRE are relatively straightforward. To achieve a CRE training effect, students must participate in activities that raise their heart rates to 70 percent of their maximum heart rate and then maintain this heart rate in this training zone for 20–30 minutes a day at least three to five times a week. One of the challenges of working on CRE in physical education is monitoring the effort and compliance of the students. In other words, how do the students and the teacher know when the students are in their target training range or how long they stay in this range? Here is a case where technology in the form of heart rate monitors can be a valuable teaching adjunct. Small watch-size heart rate monitors can be worn by students and easily programmed to provide corrective feedback in the form of audio alarms when students go over or fall below their assigned training rates. The data collected by these monitors can also be downloaded so that they can be used both by the teacher to guide future instructional planning and students to learn how their hearts respond to CRE training in terms of their resting and recovery heart rates over time.

One of the major challenges when working on fitness objectives like CRE is maintaining student motivation. This is another area where technology can play a significant role. Today there is a wide range of CRE training equipment (e.g., exercise bikes, treadmill, stair climbers) that can be used by students to work on their CRE. The advantages of these devices is that they have a variety of motivating training programs built into them and they also provide the students with constant feedback on their performance. The training programs can be programmed around the specific needs and capabilities of the students. Some of the newer systems provide video of actual courses so the students see what they would see if they were riding the real course. Other systems allow users to share the same program and train with other students on the same course, which for some students may make exercising for 30 minutes more enjoyable.

Now let's examine an example of using technology to teach motor skills. The key to learning motor skills in physical education is students actually physically performing them. Physical educators can use technology to develop instruction materials such as posters and student task cards, which remind students of the key components of the skill being learned and/or focus their attention on how to correct specific performance errors. Technology can also be used to provide students with feedback during practice so that they can self-evaluate. This technology can range from very simple forms such as performing in front of a mirror to more sophisticated forms such as video recording student performance so it can be reviewed and analyzed in slow motion to detect performance errors. The important point here is that the technology should be used so that it maximizes the number of correct performance trials and does not take away from the students' limited practice time. In most cases, the key to learning motor skills is repeated practice. To the degree technology can be used to motivate students to perform more trials and give corrective feedback to ensure that the practice done is correct, it can be a valuable tool for physical educators.

One area where technology can play a major role in K-12 physical education is in evaluation. Physical educators are faced with a daunting amount of data to manage. For example, a typical physical educator would have a case-load of 300–500 students and would be responsible for achieving a minimum of ten objectives each year. Each of these objectives would have several components that would need to be assessed at a bare minimum at the beginning and end (i.e., pre/post or entry/exit) of instruction. Using just these rough minimal estimates that would be 12,000 data points (300 students × ten objectives × five components × two measures) that would need to be managed. To handle this large amount of data, physical educators need to use technology at all phases of the data management process (Kelly & Melograno, 2004). The first and probably the most critical phase is the collection of the actual student entry and exit performance data on the components of each skill being taught. These data need to be collected via PDAs or tablet PCs so that the data are directly entered into a database. Once the data are in a data-base they can be analyzed to guide daily instructional planning and periodi-cally to provided summative progress reports to students and parents. Figure 10.1 shows a sample computer-generated physical education student progress report. To generate this report, information on the students and objectives (e.g., objective name, number of components for each objective, and mastery criteria) in the curriculum must be entered once when the database is initially defined. Then the teacher must enter three scores for each student on each

---

ABC School District Physical Education Student Evaluation Report

Student name: Brian McElroy   **Number of students in class:** 24   **Teacher:** Luke Kelly
Grade level: 8   **Report date:** 06/10/03

Objectives	Entry level	Target exit	Actual exit	Net change	Target met	Mastery criteria	% mastered	Class average	Teacher comments
Abdominal strength	25	35	37	12	Yes	40	92.50	31.25	Good progress—maintain program
Leg strength	8.20	7.80	7.70	0.50	Yes	7.80	100.00	8.52	Excellent
Cardiorespiratory endurance	629.00	607.00	548.00	81	Yes	600.00	100.00	713.45	Excellent
Forehand stroke	8	13	16	8	Yes	15	100.00	14.66	Excellent
Backhand stroke	6	12	12	6	Yes	15	80.00	14.41	Focus on racket preparation
Tennis serve	4	10	9	5	No	15	60.00	13.12	Focus on ball toss and slow-ing down
Knowledge of rules test	61.00	85.00	100	39.00	Yes	85.00	100.00	87.04	Excellent
Cooperative behavior	12	16	16	4	Yes	20	80.00	16.53	Good improvement
Tennis etiquette	8	18	20	12	Yes	20	100.00	17.65	Excellent

Figure 10.1 Sample computer-generated student physical education progress report.

Reprinted, by permission, from L. E. Kelly and V. J. Melograno, 2004, *Developing the physical education curriculum: An achievement-based approach.* (Champaign, IL: Human Kinetics), 246.

objective during the year. The entry and exit scores reflect the student's performance on the objective at the beginning and end of instruction. The target score is the teacher's individualized goal of how much progress each student is expected to make during this unit. This report is typically accompanied by two additional forms that define the objectives (see Figure 10.2) that

ABC School District Physical Education Student Evaluation Report
Description of Physical Education Objectives

The ABC School District physical education curriculum identifies 12 objectives to be mastered during the eighth grade. This report focuses on student progress on 9 of these objectives. For more information on these objectives or other objectives in the curriculum, please contact Mr. Kelly.

1. Abdominal strength (i.e., strength of the abdominal muscles) is a physical fitness objective measured by the number of curl-ups a student can perform in 30 seconds. The desired performance level of achievement (i.e., mastery) for all students is 40 curl-ups.

2. Leg strength is a physical fitness objective measured by the speed (in seconds) a student can run 50 yards. The desired level of achievement (i.e., mastery) is for all students to be able to run 50 yards in 7.8 seconds or less.

3. Cardiorespiratory endurance is a physical fitness objective designed to measure the efficiency of the heart, lungs, and circulatory system. Cardiorespiratory endurance is measured by the amount of time (in seconds) it takes a student to run a distance of one mile. The desired level of achievement (i.e., mastery) is for all students to be able to run one mile in 600 seconds (10 minutes) or less.

4. Forehand stroke is a tennis objective that is measured by whether the student demonstrates the 15 qualitative performance standards that are used to define the mature forehand tennis swing. The specific performance standards are defined in the physical education curriculum. The desired achievement level (i.e., mastery) is for all students to be able to perform all 15 standards.

5. Backhand stroke is a tennis objective that is measured by whether the student demonstrates the 15 qualitative performance standards that are used to define the mature backhand tennis swing. The specific performance standards are defined in the physical education curriculum. The desired achievement level (i.e., mastery) is for all students to be able to perform all 15 standards.

6. Overhead tennis serve is a tennis objective that is measured by whether the student demonstrates the 15 qualitative performance standards that are used to define the mature forehand tennis stroke. The specific performance standards are defined in the physical education curriculum. The desired achievement level (i.e., mastery) is for all students to be able to perform all 15 standards.

7. Knowledge of rules test is a cognitive objective designed to measure students' knowledge of the rules and strategies of the game of tennis. The test is composed of 50 multiple choice questions. Students' scores are the percentage of answers they get correct on a scale from 0 to 100. The desired level of achievement (i.e., mastery) is for all students to achieve a score of at least 85%.

8. Cooperative behavior is an affective objective designed to measure the degree to which students can work cooperatively with other students. This objective is rated on a scale with a range from 0 to 25. The desired level of achievement (i.e., mastery) is for all students to achieve a score of at least 20.

9. Tennis etiquette is a performance objective designed to measure whether students demonstrate correct tennis etiquette when they play tennis. This objective is rated on a scale with a range from 0 to 25. The desired level of achievement (i.e., mastery) is for all students to achieve a score of at least 20.

Figure 10.2 Sample objective definitions for student progress report.

Reprinted, by permission, from L. E. Kelly and V. J. Melograno, 2004, *Developing the physical education curriculum: An achievement-based approach.* (Champaign, IL: Human Kinetics), 247.

Instructions for Interpreting a Student Evaluation Report

Column heading	Explanation
1. Objectives	The first column of the report contains names or phrases used to label the objectives that were taught during this reporting period. For more detailed descriptions of the objectives, see the attached objective descriptions or consult the ABC School District Physical Education Curriculum.
2. Entry level	This column contains the student's entry performance level on each objective. Entry level indicated the performance level of the student prior to instruction. The entry level score is the basis for measuring improvement.
3. Target exit	This column contains the performance scores the teacher expects the student to achieve on each objective during this reporting period. Target achievement scores are set individually for each student.
4. Actual exit	This column contains the student's actual performance level on each objective at the end of the reporting period.
5. Net change	This column contains the difference between the student's entry and exit performance levels for each objective. This value is indicative of the amount of progress the student made on each objective during this reporting period.
6. Target met	This column contains either a yes or no depending on whether the student's actual exit performance on each objective was equal to or surpassed the target achievement score set by the teacher at the beginning of the unit for each objective.
7. Mastery criteria	This column contains the mastery criterion for each objective that has been established in the physical education curriculum that all students are expected to achieve.
8. % mastered	This column indicates what percentage of the mastery criterion the student has achieved to date on each objective. This value is calculated by dividing the student's actual exit performance score by the mastery criterion for each objective. Values over 100% are possible, but are reported as 100%.
9. Class average	This column contains the class average exit performance score for each objective. This value is provided to assist the reader in evaluating a student's performance in relation to the other students in the class. The class average exit value for each objective is the sum of the students' actual exit scores divided by the total number of students for each objective.
10. Teacher comments	This column may contain brief comments or codes provided by the teacher regarding the student's performance on the various objectives.

Figure 10.3 Sample student progress report interpretation instructions.

Reprinted, by permission, from L. E. Kelly and V. J. Melograno, 2004, *Developing the physical education curriculum: An achievement-based approach.* (Champaign, IL: Human Kinetics), 248.

are listed down the left side of the report and the column headings (see Figure 10.3) across the top of the report. These two additional reports are typically reduced and printed on the back of the student report. The point here is that after the database is defined and minimal student performance data entered, physical educators can produce relatively sophisticated and professional reports using technology that otherwise are too time consuming to produce. The same entry, exit, and target performance data can also be analyzed to provide ongoing feedback on teacher effectiveness and to guide teacher instructional planning. Over time, these same data can also be used to evaluate the degree to which the physical education curriculum is being achieved by the students at the completion of each phase of the program (e.g., unit, grade, program level).

The use of technology in physical education is not without some significant challenges. The single greatest obstacle is probably cost. Even when relatively simple devices like heart rate monitors (cost = $100) are used, the cost for initial purchase and ongoing replacement/maintenance (i.e., 300–500 students using 30–50 watches) can be significant (e.g., $5,000–8,000 a year for 50 watches). This is in addition to the lost instructional time related to checking the equipment in and out each class and individually setting the parameters on the watch at the start of each class. It is important to note that the costs in this example are all related to working on just one physical education objective—CRE. Given the cost of technology devices and applications for physical education and the limited budgets most physical education programs have, the first priority for acquiring and using technology in physical education should be devoted to managing student performance data. Once student performance data can be collected and managed, a data-based case can be made to justify the benefits of purchasing and using other forms of technology in physical education. In the future there is tremendous potential for more extensive use of technology in physical education. Sophisticated video analysis systems have the potential of assessing student performance and giving them immediate feedback on a large number of motor skills. These systems are currently designed for adults and for only a few select motor skills in the areas of golf and tennis. These future systems could also be integrated with high-end video simulators that could allow students to practice the skill in highly motivating conditions (e.g., throwing a pass to a famous NFL receiver or kicking a soccer ball to a soccer superstar). The advantages of these systems would be that they would:

- assess and provide students with immediate knowledge of performance feedback,
- reduce the audience effects,
- allow learner to try different techniques and immediately see the results,
- allow independent practice and be highly motivating, which would enhance practice and performing the number of practice trials needed to learn a motor skill.

In addition to cost, the other challenge for TPCK technology in physical education is the development/availability of sophisticated applications that can be used to assist physical educators in providing feedback to students. Some of these applications will be commercially developed for select motor skills related to popular sports (e.g., batting for baseball, kicking for soccer, golf swing) and can be adopted/adapted for use in physical education. Unfortunately, there will be the need for these applications to be developed to address many other foundation motor skills that will not be commercially viable.

So what unique TPCK do physical educators need? In review, teaching motor skills is conceptually relatively straightforward. The teachers need to know and present to the students the key components of the skill being taught. The teachers must be able to assess the students, determine which components they need to work on, and then communicate how to correct the errors they are making. Then the teachers need to create fun and highly motivating instructional activities that allow the students to perform many practice trials with corrective feedback on the components they need to work on. The TPCK physical educators need is similar to other instructional areas in that they need to know how to use technology to develop appropriate instructional materials for their content. They therefore need basic web skills to tap the wealth of information available from sites like PESOFTWARE.com, PECENTRAL.org and PELINKS4U.org. To provide feedback, they need TPCK related to using low-cost and relatively easy to use technology such as activity and heart rate monitors. In the future, they will need TPCK related to using more sophisticated analysis and feedback applications as they become commercially viable for use in physical education. In terms of current teacher training of physical educators, the greatest TPCK needs are in the areas of using technology to collect, manage, analyze, and report student performance data. In particular, they need specific skills in using data entry tools (e.g., PDAs and tablet PCs) to collect student performance data and knowledge of how to analyze their student performance data to evaluate their instructional effectiveness and guide their instructional planning (Kelly & Melograno, 2004). Just like their students, teachers need knowledge of performance feedback to change their teaching behavior. In other words, physical educators need specific feedback on their effectiveness of teaching specific skills and skill components. In the absence of data-based feedback, it is hard for physical educators to accurately evaluate their effectiveness. Effectively managed student performance data can also be used to guide in-service planning and peer mentoring programs. In the short term, teachers need to know how to harness and use the technology resources they have available in their schools to begin to manage their student performance data. They also need to know how to communicate their data management needs to the central administration so that they are incorporated into the school's overall student data management system.

In summary, technology plays a significant role in physical educators learning their physical education content knowledge and pedagogical content knowledge. Physical educators also require specific technological pedagogical content knowledge to deliver effective physical education instruction to K-12 students. Physical educators greatest TPCK needs are in the areas of data collection, management, analysis, and reporting. The type and amount of TPCK related to direct instruction in physical education is limited in scope and sophistication at this time due to instructional time, cost, and access constraints within the K-12 schools.

References

Grossman, P. (1990). *The making of a teacher: Teacher knowledge and teacher education.* New York: Teachers College Press.

Henry, F. (1964). Physical education: An academic discipline. *Journal of Health, Physical Education and Recreation, 37,* 32–33.

Kelly, L. E. (1987). Computer management of student performance. *Journal of Physical Education, Recreation and Dance, 58,* 12–13, 82–85.

Kelly, L. E., & Melograno, V. J. (2004). *Developing the physical education curriculum: An achievement-based approach.* Champaign, IL: Human Kinetics.

Kelly, L. E., Walkley, J., & Tarrant, M. (1988). Developing a computer managed videodisc application. *Journal of Physical Education, Recreation, and Dance, 59,* 22–26.

Lynn, L. (2002). Pedagogical content knowledge for teachers. *Teaching Elementary Physical Education, 13*(4), 6.

Metzler, M. W. (2000). *Instructional models for physical education.* Needham Heights, MA: Allyn and Bacon.

Morh, D. J., & Townsend, J. S. (2002). Using comprehensive teaching models to enhance pedagogical content knowledge. *Teaching Elementary Physical Education, 13*(4), 32–36.

O'Sullivan, M. (1996). What do we know about the professional preparation of teachers? In S. Silverman & C. Ennis (eds), *Student learning in physical education: Applying research to enhance instruction* (pp. 315–337). Champaign, IL: Human Kinetics.

Shulman, L. S. (1986). Those who understand: Knowledge growth in teaching. *Educational Researcher, 15,* 4–14.

Siedentop, D. (2002). Content knowledge for physical education. *Journal of Teaching in Physical Education, 21*(4), 368–377.

Tinning, R. (2002). Engaging Siedentopian perspectives on content knowledge for physical education. *Journal of Teaching in Physical Education, 21*(4), 378–391.

Walkley, J., & Kelly, L. E. (1990). The effectiveness of an interactive videodisc qualitative assessment training program. *Research Quarterly for Exercise and Sport, 60,* 280–285.

Wright, L. J. M. (2000). Practical knowledge, performance, and physical education. *Quest, 53*(3), 273–283.

III
Integrating TPCK into teacher education and professional development

11
Guiding preservice teachers in developing TPCK

MARGARET L. NIESS

If we teach today as we taught yesterday, then we rob our children of tomorrow.

John Dewey

Two hundred years ago, the predominant belief about preparing teachers for teaching was that knowing the content at a particular level was adequate preparation for teaching that content at that level. Teachers needed to know and understand the content determined by the grade they planned to teach. An elementary reading teacher needed to be able to read, write, and compute at the elementary level. At the secondary level, a geography teacher needed a secondary level geography understanding and a mathematics teacher needed a secondary level mathematical understanding. Teachers taught what they were taught, as they were taught. That was *yesterday.*

Today beliefs about what preparation teachers need for teaching have significantly changed. Yes, teachers need to know the content they are to teach, but they must also have knowledge about teaching and learning that content—the pedagogy of teaching. Shulman (1986) challenged this framework for preparing teachers indicating that effective teachers rely on a specialized knowledge that is more than simply knowing the subject matter and the pedagogy of teaching. He contended that effective teachers need an integrated knowledge base—one that relies on an integration of multiple domains of knowledge (knowledge about subject matter, learners, pedagogy, curriculum, and schools) in order to translate the content in ways that students are able to grasp. Shulman described this vastly different teacher knowledge as pedagogical content knowledge or PCK.

Yet, if teacher preparation methods courses continue *as they have been*, focused on the teaching strategies and classroom management, planning for instruction, and assessment of learning developed from the directions of the twentieth century, they will most certainly *rob the children of tomorrow*. With the addition of an integration of new and emerging twenty-first century technologies as tools for learning, the preparation of teachers must evolve toward

223

preparing preservice teachers to teach in ways that help them to guide their students in learning with appropriate technologies. Today, the twenty-first century, teacher preparation methodology courses must assume the task of guiding preservice teachers toward the abilities, strategies, and ways of thinking for teaching *today and tomorrow*.

Technological pedagogical content knowledge (TPCK) defines that body of knowledge that teachers now need for teaching with and about technology in their assigned subject areas and grade levels. TPCK is described as the interconnection and intersection of content, pedagogy (teaching and student learning), and technology (Margerum-Leys & Marx, 2002; Mishra & Koehler, 2006; Niess, 2005a; Pierson, 2001; Zhao, 2003). However, TPCK is more than a set of multiple domains of knowledge and skills that teachers need for teaching their students particular subjects at specific grade levels. TPCK is a way of thinking within these multiple domains of knowledge. uit Beijerse (2000) offers a useful description of knowledge as

> the amount of information necessary to function and achieve goals; the capacity to make information from data and to transform it into useful and meaningful information; the capacity with which one thinks creatively, interprets and acts; and an attitude that makes people want to think, interpret and act.

Shavelson, Ruiz-Primo, Li, and Ayala (2003) bring clarity to thinking about the thinking involved in TPCK: *declarative* (knowing that, including definitions, terms, facts, and descriptions), *procedural* (knowing how that refers to sequences of steps to complete a task or subtask), *schematic* (knowing why by drawing on both declarative and procedural knowledge, such as principles and mental models), and *strategic* (knowing when and where to use domain-specific knowledge and strategies, such as planning and problem solving together with monitoring progress towards a goal). Accumulating these notions suggests that TPCK is a way of thinking strategically while involved in *planning, organizing, critiquing,* and *abstracting* for specific content, specific student needs, and specific classroom situations while concurrently considering the multitude of twenty-first century technologies with the potential for supporting students' learning.

Incorporating TPCK as a way of thinking strategically into the curriculum of the preservice methods courses exposes the "wickedness" (Koehler & Mishra, Chapter 1; Rittel & Webber, 1973) of the preservice teacher preparation problem because preservice teachers have not traditionally experienced learning their subjects with these new and emerging technologies. They have not learned how to learn their content with these technologies as tools for learning. As Putnam and Borko (2000) indicate, "How a person learns a particular set of knowledge and skills, and the situation in which a person learns, become a fundamental part of what is learned." The challenge then becomes one of overcoming and enhancing preservice teachers' experiences in learning the content that they learned without such technologies. How can preservice teachers gain the experiences that require a change in their mindsets and beliefs about how students need to learn the subject matter content? In other words, how can a teacher preparation program challenge future teachers to develop new ways of learning their subject with appropriate new and emerging technologies so they are prepared to teach the children of tomorrow?

The wickedness of this issue is elevated with the recognition of and concern for what these teachers will be expected to teach. As described in the Partnership for 21st Century Skills (2004), new teachers must be prepared to redesign and create a curriculum and instruction to prepare their students with the skills of a twenty-first century literate citizen—an expanded form of literacy that includes new communication and information skills, the ability to think critically and creatively in problem-solving and decision-making situations in response to and recognition of the interconnections among systems, a respect for diverse perspectives, and basically the knowledge and skills to "successfully face rigorous higher education coursework career challenges and a globally competitive workforce." Through their Information and Communication Technology Literacy Maps, they describe significantly different student outcomes in mathematics, science, English, and geography than those that preservice teachers learned *yesterday*. The recognition of this changing curriculum in the content these teachers will be expected to teach raises even more challenges for programs designed to prepare them for teaching. How can programs prepare future teachers for teaching in ways that incorporate unlearning and relearning their content with appropriate new and emerging technologies so they are adequately prepared to teach the children of tomorrow?

Tomorrow's teachers must be prepared to rethink, unlearn and relearn, change, revise, and adapt. Their teacher preparation programs must confront and challenge these future teachers with the myriad of issues and concerns in teaching as they learn to plan and organize lessons that effectively engage students in learning new subject matter goals and in meeting outcomes reflected in the enhanced vision of literacy highlighted by the Partnership for 21st Century Skills. Integrating technology with the content and pedagogical issues and concerns for this new era elevates the wickedness of the problem. Elementary preservice teachers must deal with issues of engaging children in digital storytelling—experiences that they themselves have not had (Schmidt & Gurbo, Chapter 3). Mathematics preservice teachers are faced with questions about when and how students should use calculators or how dynamic spreadsheets can showcase the power of algebra in exploring and making decisions about real-world problems (Grandgenett, Chapter 7). Social studies preservice teachers are challenged with developing strategies that guide students in wading through the breadth of Internet resources in ways that involve a critical analysis of the data rather than acceptance without question (Lee, Chapter 6). Science preservice teachers must determine whether students learn better with direct experiences (such as in a frog dissection or investigation using a microscope) or whether a technological model or simulation provides the best classroom experience (McCrory, Chapter 9). And, all preservice teachers are faced with learning to incorporate goals and outcomes beyond their own content areas—guiding student learning *about* the new and emerging information and communication technologies while students are also learning the content *with* these technologies.

This book provides a multitude of ideas about what preservice teachers need to learn in gaining TPCK. The question remains: How must preservice preparation programs be arranged to assure that the preservice teachers gain the declarative, procedural, schematic, and strategic ways of knowing and thinking involved in TPCK? Researchers have explored various models for integrating technology into teacher preparation programs and have concluded the importance of inclusion in all courses and experiences in the programs (Brush *et al.*, 2003; Niess, 2005a; Strudler & Grove, 2002). Thus, a more salient question is: What experiences and how should the experiences be arranged so that the preservice teachers develop their TPCK given that they bring to the program a lack of experiences in learning the content with new and emerging technologies, along with the recognition of a shifting set of content outcomes and expectations for guiding student learning about the technologies as they learn with the technologies?

Teacher preparation methods courses are typically directed toward helping future teachers gain effective teaching methods and strategies while carefully considering the students' background knowledge and experiences, the school environment, and the learning goals in the curriculum—i.e., a way of thinking that results in guiding a diversity of students in the classroom toward learning the content that is taught. These courses provide a foundation upon which preservice teachers build their developing knowledge about teaching and learning. The foundation is used and expanded in the other program courses as well as in their practicum and field experiences including student teaching. With conscious attention to the development of TPCK as a way of thinking, methods courses potentially establish environments for engaging preservice teachers in integrating their developing understandings of content, teaching, and learning along with a conscious consideration of the integration of technology in the learning environment. Integrating technology in teaching and learning also exposes broader issues and concerns that preservice teachers must consider when designing lessons. Therefore, enhancing methods courses to consider developing TPCK's ways of thinking requires that the preservice teachers are more likely engaged in changing their mindsets and behaviors established from their own personal learning experiences when learning to plan, organize, critique, and abstract for their specific content, specific student needs, and specific classroom situations. Such methods courses provide experiences that enhance the course goals in emphasizing the preparation of preservice teachers in:

- understanding the diversity of students and their learning needs in a technology-mediated classroom,
- planning and designing learning environments and experiences that meet the diversity of student learning needs in a technology-mediated classroom,
- developing effective instructional strategies to adequately attend to the diversity of student learning needs in a technology-mediated classroom,
- identifying effective classroom management strategies to support the diversity of students in learning in a technology-mediated classroom, and
- assessing the diversity of student learning in a technology-mediated classroom.

While these pieces may seem to present individual topics, the topics are intertwined in the development of the strategic thinking that preservice teachers need as they develop TPCK. Planning lessons relies on knowledge of effective instructional strategies that meet specific student learning needs and considers how to integrate technology that effectively guides students in learning. Structuring the curriculum and instruction of methods courses to prepare preservice teachers to teach with technology in their lesson designs requires attention to the pedagogical reasoning that integrates their knowledge about the students, of the content, of the instructional strategies, managing the classroom, and assessing student learning along with a careful consideration of how technology impacts on how students interact with the subject matter. Equally important, these various topics need to be integrated with appropriate field experiences where the preservice teachers are provided with opportunities to test their developing ways of thinking for teaching with technology.

Understanding students

To teach is to learn.

Chinese Proverb

Methods courses potentially provide an important context for guiding preservice teachers in understanding the diversity of the students and how that diversity affects their learning. Including experiences in learning with technology requires more than "more of the same" kinds of experiences because preservice teachers so often rely on their own personal learning experiences to guide their thinking about students. If they rely only on personal experiences, they are not typically sensitive to multicultural issues that impact learning, either with or without an integration of technology. Through *teaching* preservice teachers gain opportunities to *learn* TPCK ways of thinking. But, before they are ready to *teach*, they need to *learn* methods for teaching. To deal with this issue, methods courses can coordinate practical experiences with actual students working with technologies along with opportunities to interact with teachers teaching with technologies. At least two types of experiences have potential for supporting the development of TPCK's strategic thinking in the methods courses: (1) communicating with multiculturally diverse students in technology-mediated environments, and (2) exploring students' thinking and understandings when learning with technology. Each of these experiences is supported and enhanced through the content in the methods courses.

Enhancing multicultural sensitivity

Teachers often are required to support students' written communications, guiding them in developing their writing in ways that clearly present their ideas. How does this support change in a technology-mediated environment? McClanahan (2006) appreciates the importance of preservice teachers gaining personal experiences as they learn to communicate in a technology-mediated context and recognizes the importance of guiding preservice teachers toward increasing their sensitivity to multicultural issues. This responsibility that all teachers (not just language arts teachers) have in the development of twenty-first century general literacy skills is an important recognition that must be considered in the preparation of future teachers.

From this perspective, McClanahan designed a research project to engage her preservice methods course students with an authentic audience for teaching literacy skills with the intent of increasing their sensitivity to multicultural issues amid a technology-mediated context. A partnership with a school located in the village of Mekoryuk on Nunivak Island in Alaska provided the context where she paired her preservice teachers with secondary students in the Alaskan village. The school housed approximately 40 students ranging from pre-K through grade 12 from a population of 97 percent Alaskan natives. The technology for their communication was electronic mail while the technology for the development writings was word processing, admittedly not considered new and emerging technologies, but nevertheless, technologies available for connecting the preservice teachers with their Alaskan partners.

After the initial introductions, the Alaskan students supplied their preservice partners with pieces of writings in progress, persuasive essays on a topic of personal concern. One student titled her paper as "Preserving our culture" where she focused on describing the culture and its importance. The preservice teachers provided their student-partners with feedback directed at improving the communication of the writers' thinking and experiences. Through their writings, the Alaskan students shared information about themselves, their surroundings, and their families inviting the preservice teachers into a different culture. Both partners benefited from interacting with people who had "very different lifestyles and cultures."

The preservice teachers *learned* about students through *teaching* in this electronically mediated environment. The preservice teachers benefited from the "authentic" student texts where they practiced giving written feedback to students. More importantly, the preservice teachers gained an understanding of the cultural implications of the students' writings. Their student-partners benefited from the writing assistance of someone other than their teachers, by interacting with someone who was "still in school" who valued education and going to college, worked for a living, and who was functioning in a modern society. One preservice teacher noted that this technology-mediated experience provided an opportunity to see that literacy "is going on all around us, and to deem one type (formal essays) more valid than 'naturally occurring literacies' (note writing, participating in electronic chat rooms, blogs, etc.) may be doing those of us who teach literacy a disservice." Ultimately, the preservice teachers experienced a technology-mediated instructional environment that helped them enhance their personal understandings about how diverse students used technology as a tool for communication that shared their knowledge and thinking. In the *teaching* process, they gained important *learning* experiences for developing "fluency and cognitive flexibility [of technology, pedagogy and content] ... in the manner in which these inter-relate with each other in order to attempt solutions that are sensitive to the contexts within which they occur" (Koehler & Mishra, Chapter 1).

Exploring student understandings in a technology-enhanced learning experience

Students funnel their individual understandings through personal experiences as shown when the preservice teachers communicated with the Alaskan natives. But, are students with similar cultural experiences as the preservice teachers considered? Can preservice teachers assume they "understand" how these students are thinking and interacting? Prensky (2001) describes students of the twenty-first century as "digital natives"—students with significantly different experiences with information technologies than their teachers. Methods courses structured to develop TPCK must not only attend to the typical diversity of students that the preservice teachers will encounter; they must attend to the preservice teachers' understandings of what this digital diversity adds to the mix of students they will encounter. How these children learn and understand ideas in a technology-enhanced context is likely quite different from how the preservice teachers learned and understood similar ideas as they were learning—without the use of technology. In other words, preparing preservice teachers to develop TPCK strategic thinking strategies requires attention to more than the physical, cognitive, cultural, personal, and social developmental levels of the students they will be teaching. Preservice teachers need opportunities that unveil how students think and learn in technology-enhanced learning environments. Recognition of this broader perception of diversity impacts their planning, teaching, and reflection on instruction.

Having preservice teachers conduct observational case studies is a useful strategy that helps them examine and learn about both students and teachers (Good & Brophy, 2003). While finding out what students know about technologies is perhaps a good beginning, a more valuable understanding comes from interactions with students while they are learning about specific concepts, ideas, and procedures with access to the technologies. How does student writing develop when they are engaged in a collaborative writing process in a blog environment? How does students' description of their understandings of accepted views of the past shift after analyzing original U.S. Census Bureau data rather than reading about the views in a textbook? How do students communicate their understanding of slope after investigations of gathering and analyzing digital pictures of various real-world expressions of slope? The more varied the cases that preservice teachers are able to examine the better.

The preservice teachers need to be organized in research groups to conduct focused observations and interviews in multiple classrooms where students use a variety of technologies as learning tools. Initially, the group members might interview the teachers prior to observing in the classrooms, using questions like: What are the goals and objectives for the lesson? Why did they plan to engage students in this lesson with the particular technology? What experiences have the students had with the technology prior to the lesson? What about the diversity of student experiences with the technology? Which students do you recommend that I observe and why? After gathering the teacher's ideas about the lesson, the group members should observe the students as they work with technology and specifically focus on a diversity of students—a diversity that represents physical, cognitive, cultural, personal, social, and technological developmental differences and similarities. After the observations, the various group members should interview some of the identified students with challenges and questions such as: Describe what you were learning in the lesson today. Did the technology you used today interfere with your learning or help you understand the ideas in the lesson? What is your background with this technology prior to this lesson? Are you comfortable using this technology in learning?

Afterwards, the research group members need to gather and analyze the information for their observations and interviews. Were the teachers' goals and objectives met? Did the technology divert or enable understanding and, if so, how? What were the students' backgrounds with the technology prior to this activity? Had the teacher provided previous instruction with the technology? Did student diversity affect the impact of the lesson? If so, how? As they frame their analyses, they need to consider the students' physical, cognitive, cultural, personal, social, and technological developmental levels, specifically noting the impact of technology on what the students learned in the activities.

Subsequently, the research groups need to share the results with the intent of identifying similarities and differences in student learning and thinking with technologies as tools for learning. Have them share what they learned about students at various grade levels. Summarize student development with respect to physical, cognitive, personal, cultural, social, and technological levels by educational levels (elementary, middle, and high school). A cumulative summary and analysis might be organized to compare the various grade level descriptions with a similar description that the preservice teachers had developed prior to their observations. What impact does this comparison have on their thinking about students' attitudes and capabilities for learning with technologies across the various grade levels? What are the implications for planning lessons that incorporate learning with various technologies and at the same time consider student learning diversities that they have identified? What accommodations are needed for the various diversities of the students—physical, cognitive, personal, cultural, social, and technological?

Planning and designing instruction

Plans are nothing; planning is everything.

Dwight D. Eisenhower

Learning to design lessons, sequences of lessons, and units of study encompasses an important content area in methods courses that must be followed by field-based experiences where preservice teachers can test and reflect on their developing ideas and understandings. Integrating technology in these plans requires that they develop a *pedagogical reasoning* that integrates what they know about the subject, teaching, student learning, and the technologies. The goal is for them to design lessons in ways that transform the content into a form accessible to the learners (Wilson, Shulman, & Richert, 1987). This reasoning process is essential in the development of TPCK strategic knowledge—the knowledge of when, where, and how to integrate knowledge of content, teaching, student learning, and technology (Ruiz-Primo, Shavelson, Li, & Schultz, 2001). The end result of *planning* is the enhancement of the reasoning process. The learning in the *planning* process is essential; the *plan* may be inconsequential.

Dynamic thinking tool for developing TPCK

Teacher educators can lecture about the knowledge that preservice teachers need for developing TPCK, but lectures do not adequately provide experiences upon which preservice teachers can rely in the development of their TPCK. One strategy for guiding them in the development of TPCK in the methods course begins by organizing them in collaborative study groups with similar student grade levels and content interests (Niess, Lee, & Kajder, 2008). Study groups might be organized by different school levels—elementary, middle, and high school levels or by different content areas—such as language arts, social studies, mathematics, science, and foreign languages. Each study group is charged with identifying a specific topic that they want to plan to teach for a specific group of students (e.g., heterogeneous groups of students or even homogeneous groups of students in a targeted content area). The study groups collaboratively identify a specific content topic for the unit of instruction they plan to design. These initial decisions provide the context for exploring important ideas for designing lessons/units, understanding student needs, considering various instructional strategies, managing classroom activities, and assessing student learning.

In their early thinking for developing a unit, the study groups need to consider a role for technology in their decision-making processes. The matrix in Table 11.1 initiates their pedagogical reasoning in the processes of clarifying their units as they are engaged in thinking about the content, teaching, student learning, and the possibility of integrating technology in the instruction. The important feature of this matrix is that it is a dynamic tool where the study group members enter their thoughts and make changes as their thinking evolves as a result of the instruction in the methods class. They might have their matrices prepared in a word processor and attach the documents as they communicate via electronic mail. Or, they might use a wiki (as in Figure 11.1) to dynamically allow each member of the group to work interactively on the document as the class progresses. With the wiki, when individuals select specific cells in the matrix, they are entering a space where they are able to insert their ideas as well as review the ideas of others.

Table 11.1 Matrix organization of the thinking for designing a unit of instruction

Knowledge dimension	Content	Teaching and student learning	Technology
Declarative			
Procedural			
Schematic			
Strategic			

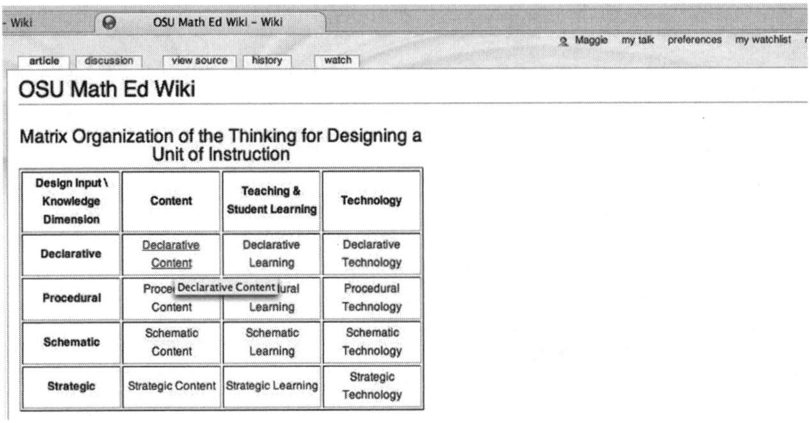

Design Input \ Knowledge Dimension	Content	Teaching & Student Learning	Technology
Declarative	Declarative Content	Declarative Learning	Declarative Technology
Procedural	Proce[Declarative Content]ural Content	Procedural Learning	Procedural Technology
Schematic	Schematic Content	Schematic Learning	Schematic Technology
Strategic	Strategic Content	Strategic Learning	Strategic Technology

Figure 11.1 A wiki presentation of the matrix of the thinking in designing a unit of instruction.

Using a backward design approach (Wiggins & McTighe, 2006), the study groups begin with the ends they have in mind—what they plan for students to do at the conclusion of the unit. What problems will these students solve at the end of the unit? What skills will they demonstrate? How will they demonstrate their knowledge of the content? Such questions help the study group members in clarifying their ideas about the content while carefully considering different knowledge levels (declarative, procedural, schematic, strategic) that distinguish the thinking required in the end-of-the-unit problems or expectations. Table 11.2 provides an example of how one study group began their thinking about the content in a unit focused on 4th grade students learning about making change for amounts tendered in particular transactions. In working with the matrix, the preservice teachers might begin with a problem at the declarative level that depends on students being able to identify the values of specific coins; then, they may shift to the strategic level at the upper boundary of the students' learning in the unit where the students make decisions about the number and types of coins that might be needed in preparation for running a lemonade stand operation. Alternatively, they might begin by thinking about procedural level skills (how to make change for the amount received for a specific purchase), move to what students as managers of a lemonade stand might do at the strategic level, and then return to the procedural level to adjust their ideas at that level. The intent is that this matrix simply provides a dynamic space for presenting ideas while in the process of framing, organizing, and clarifying their thinking about the content they plan to include in the unit. The process is not necessarily linear, rather it allows for the evolutions in their thinking about the unit.

From the initial considerations of the content, the study groups then must think about teaching and student learning as well as integrating technology in

Table 11.2 Content students are expected to demonstrate at the conclusion of the unit

Knowledge dimension	Content	Teaching and student learning	Technology
Declarative	• Recognizes that change is the amount to be returned after providing money in excess of the cost of specific items • Identifies the values for coins such as pennies, nickels, dimes, quarters, and dollars		
Procedural	• Knows how to use "count on" as a means of making change • Knows how to use subtraction to find the amount of change		
Schematic	• Explains why a set of coins is the least number of coins needed for returning the excess of the cost of the items		
Strategic	• Makes change in a lemonade stand simulation. Determine money transactions and the appropriate coins needed for returning change for different purchases		

the unit. Web searches and investigations of other curriculum materials are useful for identifying potential activities, technologies, and instructional strategies. Table 11.3 presents a draft of the progress of one group's thinking where the group has identified multiple technologies that might be useful in the unit and where they identify some strategies for teaching and student learning. The online flashcards that display sets of coins provide a way for students to gain practice in recognizing and comparing the values of coins while the online money change game engages the students in the procedural aspects of making change.

Goals and objectives of instruction

As the preservice teachers' thinking evolves, the methods course needs to direct their attention toward specific goals and objectives for the instruction. Typically, preservice teachers focus on subject matter goals and objectives, but with the addition of the challenge of developing TPCK, methods courses have the potential to expand the students' thinking beyond the subject matter

Table 11.3 One group's initial thinking about all dimensions of the matrix

Knowledge dimension	Content	Teaching and student learning	Technology
Declarative	• Recognizes that change is the amount to be returned after providing money in excess of the cost of specific items • Identifies the values for coins such as pennies, nickels, dimes, quarters, and dollars	• Students practice recognizing and comparing the values of coins, e.g., two dollars, three quarters, two dimes and a penny is more than $2.80 • Students engage in multiple experiences in counting amounts composed of a variety of coin amounts	Online flashcards that display sets of coins where students need to count the value of the coins http://www.aplusmath.com/Flashcards/index.html
Procedural	• Knows how to use "count on" as a means of making change • Knows how to use subtraction to find the amount of change	• Students practice giving change for specific costs • Whole class teacher demonstration for making change using "counting on" to determine the excess • Worksheets focused on using subtraction to find the change	• Online money changing game http://www.funbrain.com/cashreg/index.html • Provide exercises with calculators where students enter the total and find the amount to be returned using subtractions
Schematic	• Explains why a set of coins is the least number of coins needed for returning the excess of the cost of the items	• Small group confirmation to determine multiple ways to return the change • Whole class exploration to form conjectures for the number of ways that change could be made for the cost of the items	Teacher-created spreadsheet that identifies cost of the items, amount tendered and allows the user to determine the change in multiple ways using various types and numbers of coins
Strategic	• Makes change in a lemonade stand simulation. Determine money transactions and the appropriate coins needed for returning change for different purchases	• Students have opportunities to make decisions about making change: organize groups where each group has a lemonade stand in a different location in the town. Each business is a student collaboration for investigating the types of transactions that might occur and the change returned	Create a movie showing the progress of different businesses in running a lemonade stand to sell different sizes of lemonade, collecting money, and demonstrating different ways to determine the change for specific sales

content. Certainly, methods courses do consider various pedagogies that might be used. But with the inclusion of technology, methods courses need to direct preservice teachers' thinking about the content goals and objectives with regard to pedagogical/instructional rationales along with those for including technology in the instruction. How does the inclusion of technology affect the content that is to be taught and thus the goals and objectives of the instruction? Are the students prepared to learn with the technology? What strategies can be used to maximize the learning experience for the students? These considerations focus their thinking about the content, pedagogy, and technology concurrently, where they are expected to identify reasons for their decisions based on the impact on student learning.

The pedagogical/instructional rationale highlights the thinking in the development of the strategies to be used in the unit. In the strategic dimension of Table 11.4 the preservice teachers must describe a pedagogical goal for organizing the class in managing various lemonade stands where the students must return change for specific purchases given an amount tendered. How does this activity support student learning? Perhaps they site the importance of authentic activities for helping students see when, where, and how they might be engaged in making accurate change. They might site a constructivist perspective, indicating the importance of personal experiences in learning.

For identifying the technological goals/objectives, the preservice teachers might rely on the framework provided by the National Educational Technology Standards for Students (NETS·S), with six areas promoting the use of technology as an "integral component or tool for learning and communications within the context of academic subject areas" (International Society for Technology in Education (ISTE), 2000, p. 17). These standards are useful for focusing their thinking about the technology goals/objectives: basic operations and concepts; social, ethical, and human issues; technology productivity tools, technology communication tools, technology research tools; technology problem-solving and decision-making tools. In the "making change" example, the technology goal for using the online flash cards might include a consideration of developing basic operations with the Internet, along with using the technology as a productivity tool since the online versions allow for more dynamic versions than pre-made flash cards. The pedagogical goal for either of these formats might be to provide students sufficient practice in making change for automating their abilities in making change. Table 11.4 shows how a study group might explain their thinking around a content goal and objective. Initially, they might consider only the handmade flash cards, but as they discuss the opportunities provided by the online flash cards, they might shift their thinking to the importance of providing varied activities for keeping the students engaged in the practice.

Table 11.4 Reasons generated for pedagogy and technology options in meeting content goals/objectives

Type	Goal	Objective	Rationale
Content	Students become fluent in making change	Students make change for amounts less than $5	• NCTM Number and Operations standard: Students understand numbers, ways of representing numbers, and relationships among numbers
Pedagogy	Multiple stations for practice: • Work with handmade flash cards in dyads • Work with online flashcards in dyads		• Students learn to work together and have practice recognizing correctness of change to return for purchase, less than $5 • Varied activities for making change more motivational for practice
Technology	• Students work in pairs with online flash cards that identify charge and amounts tendered • NETS-Student standard for basic operations of applications on the Internet plus technology as a productivity tool		• Students have opportunities to work collaboratively with online technologies and to practice making change for purchases less than $5 • NETS-Student Standards: Basic operations (I) of applications on the Internet plus technology as a productivity tool (III)

Scaffolding instruction

As preservice teachers clarify the goals and objectives for their units along with the rationale for their pedagogical and technological decisions, they must consider how the unit might be organized and what the students need to know before becoming engaged in this unit. Are the students familiar with the multiple coins and paper money values? Do they need opportunities for working online in preparation for activities in future lessons? If the students will be making a movie during the unit, have they had adequate opportunities to learn to make the movie? Can learning about how to create a movie be integrated with the unit?

Preservice teachers need to learn to *scaffold* students' learning of the content where they also become familiar with the various technologies as tools for learning (Niess, 2005b). As they consider the possibilities of integrating technology in the unit, they must face the issue of scaffolding students' learning about the technology—considering prerequisite lessons that develop students' learning about the technology. Skipping this step often results in a unit of instruction that misses its intent—a unit that is focused on learning about the technology, rather than maintaining the focus on learning the subject matter content using the technology as a learning tool. The challenge for preservice teachers is to identify the skills students need with the technology in order to be prepared to work on the content in the unit. They need to identify places in the curriculum where they can help students add to their knowledge and skills about the technology while also learning the subject matter. Careful planning results in students becoming more comfortable with the technology as a tool for learning because they are learning about learning with the technology tool.

Developing effective instructional strategies

Hope is not a strategy.

Thomas McInerney

As preservice teachers design lessons that integrate various technologies, they have the opportunity to plan for student learning. However, simply *hoping* that the lesson will "go well" is definitely not a *strategy* for insuring effective learning. Methods courses must engage preservice teachers in the identification and exploration of instructional strategies for supporting the learning needs of a diversity of students. Incorporating the proposals from the dynamic matrices used in developing their units provides study groups with experiences in meta-cognitive reflections on the effects of particular strategies for integrating technology in the lessons—what the strategies afford them to do with technology and how the strategies constrain the integration of technology for effective student learning.

Affordances and constraints

Affordances and *constraints* are two key terms for guiding their thinking about potential instructional strategies. Gibson (1979) declares *affordances* as opportunities for action for the observer provided by an environment, and proposes that observers perceive these affordances rather than abstract physical properties of objects and environments. They further suggest that *constraints* "limit possible actions" (p. 78). While much of the literature on affordances and constraints has been embedded in technology design, the ideas offer interesting adaptations for investigating the notions in the methods course (Niess, Lee, & Kajder, 2008). Calculators afford students with opportunities to easily compute, while they are constrained to problems that require a fixed number of decimal places. Word processing tools afford opportunities to easily edit documents while the work is constrained by keyboarding skills.

Preservice teachers' understandings of various instructional strategies can be enlightened through a consideration of the affordances and constraints of the strategies. Direct instruction affords students opportunities to master content through a carefully designed presentation of the ideas followed by student practice. However, direct instruction is constrained in its ability for presenting complex material that requires analysis, synthesis, and evaluation. Cooperative learning affords students opportunities to engage in higher level thinking, yet the level of thinking can be constrained by the diversity of the students in the group.

Borrowing from Brown, Stillman, and Herbert's (2004) discussions on affordances and constraints, preservice teachers might be guided in understanding the affordances and constraints of their instructional plans to include actions that support and allow for the affordances. The existence of an affordance does not necessarily imply that the activity will occur. Thus, as the preservice teachers explore the affordances of various strategies and methods, they must think about the actions that support or detract from the affordances—they need to consider ways to organize lessons so that the affordances are likely to occur. For example, student work with the Internet affords them the opportunities to access a wide range of resources. However, they need to learn how to use the Internet safely, accurately, and efficiently; this development requires careful attention to scaffolding this learning amid the instruction with the subject matter.

In introducing the various instructional strategies, such as direct and indirect strategies, preservice teachers can be focused on a consideration of the affordances and the constraints offered by each strategy as a way of helping them make decisions about which strategy will be most effective for particular cases. They need to concurrently consider the integration of technology along with these strategies. What strategies support students in learning about the technology as they are learning with the technology? This effort provides a way to engage preservice teachers in an evaluation of the values offered by each strategy and to consider when and how to use those strategies when technology is a part of the learning.

Consider an example for using a teacher demonstration of the spreadsheet suggested in Table 11.3. The study group proposes to engage students in determining the change to be returned for the cost of the items and the amount tendered. A teacher demonstration affords the opportunity to direct the whole class toward the procedures for working with the spreadsheet, illustrating the ideas in the spreadsheet and challenging the students with the overall question they plan to explore when they work with the spreadsheet. A constraint for such a demonstration is that students do not have the opportunity to explore the spreadsheet while the teacher is demonstrating the ideas. From these ideas, the challenge for the preservice teachers is to determine how to provide the students with the hands-on work and opportunities for asking the individual questions that arise as students begin to explore with the technology. Perhaps the preservice teachers might plan for the demonstration to include having students propose ideas for consideration by the whole class. Perhaps the teacher even invites the students to come to the demonstration table to actually enter the information. Maybe the demonstration is conducted in the computer lab where the students are able to follow the instructions at their computer stations after the initial demonstration; this type of demonstration allows for students to do what "students will do with technology"—explore the capabilities, test the functions, and see what they can do with the technology.

Gaining effective classroom management strategies

If the only tool you have is a hammer, you tend to see every problem as a nail.

Abraham Maslow

Integrating technology in instruction calls for a teacher's careful attention to classroom management strategies that have potential for guiding students toward a successful learning experience. With technology integrated in learning activities, effective classroom managers must consider (1) motivation and problem prevention as well as (2) coping with problems effectively (Good & Brophy, 2003). Research findings suggest that teachers who approach classroom management as a process of establishing and maintaining effective learning environments tend to be more successful than teachers who place more emphasis on their roles as authority figures or disciplinarians (Cotton, 1999; Emmer & Strough, 2001; Evertson & Harris, 1992; Gettinger, 1988; Jones, 1996).

A toolkit of strategies

The question then is how to prepare preservice teachers for the multitude of variables that impact the potential effectiveness of classroom activities when technology is integrated as a learning tool. Learning to manage a classroom is definitely not an algorithm that says, "If this happens, do this ... then do this ... then do this." The variables in a classroom are simply too dynamic to be reduced to a finite set of algorithms for managing the classroom. More appropriately, effective classroom management is a heuristic process of problem solving that requires experience. But, this too is a wicked problem. Simply placing preservice teachers in the classroom and *hoping* they gain the needed experiences is not the best way for them or the students. They need an educational preparation that guides them in seeing the issues involved in establishing a classroom climate conducive to learning and in developing a *toolbox* of potential strategies for establishing such a climate. Without this preparation, they will indeed see the issue as a *nail* for which they only need to use a *hammer.*

Incorporating work with classroom cases during a methods course provides initial preparation for their student teaching experiences where they put their understandings in action. Cases can be used to help preservice teachers think about and react to key management issues involved when integrating technology in the classroom activities. Box 11.1 provides just two examples of technology-related cases for engaging preservice teachers in dealing with the key issues.

When developing the cases that specifically attend to the development of their TPCK with respect to managing classroom management, you need to create cases that are less generic and more integrated with content, pedagogy, and the technology to help them recognize and develop an appreciation for the intersection and interactions of these domains in working toward effective classroom interactions. The cases in Box 11.1 were created using information from two sources to assure attention to these three domains:

1. Two of the common types of classrooms described by Good and Brophy (2003, p. 111): (1) chaos and uproar, (2) noisy but positive.
2. Descriptions of technology activities in the NETS Student Standards (ISTE, 2000) as an example of relying on recommendations from the myriad of technology integration resources (either in print or on the Internet).

One idea for using these cases is to divide the class into small groups of preservice teachers as case study investigators where each group has responsibility for investigating and responding to one of the cases, identifying actions that may prevent the case from erupting (prevention) as well as actions to take with the case during the class (coping). For example, in Case number 1,

Box 11.1 Technology-related classroom management cases

Case number	Observed classroom actions
1.	A middle school mathematics class is investigating the question of designing their own bedrooms. The students are required to select the floor covering, paint for the walls and ceiling, and air-conditioning and heating unit appropriate for the room's volume. To get started with this lesson, the students needed to determine the areas and volumes of their rooms at their home. To accomplish this activity, they needed to bring the measurements for walls, ceilings, and floors of their homes. The goal of this lesson is for the students to enter the data into a spreadsheet, calculate the area of the walls, floors, and ceilings along with the volumes for each of the rooms (ISTE, 2000, p. 3).
	The class began in the computer lab where the students were assigned to work individually at their computer workstations. The teacher reminded them that they were to enter the data and find the appropriate measurements and then told them to get busy. Almost immediately, hands were raised and the students started talking. The teacher tried to answer as many questions as quickly as possible but the noise level continued to increase. Some students did not have data to enter, some students were confused on what package to use, some students were confused about how to set up the spreadsheet, some were confused about what formulas would be appropriate for the dimensions required, some were confused about entering formulas and copying the formulas, and a few finished the activity with time to spare. When the class ended, less than half of the students had completed the work and some students had begun playing with graphics packages, games, and the Internet to fill the time.
	How could the teacher have prevented and coped with the chaos and uproar that resulted in this lesson?
2.	A fourth grade science teacher organized the classroom so that the students were to analyze, compare, contrast, and classify characteristics of their fingerprint styles with their peers. For this lesson they worked in teams of four to fingerprint each other and then to scan, enlarge, and print digital images of the fingerprints (ISTE, 2000, p. 144). The materials for the activity were placed at each of the workstations along with a set of instructions of what they were to do. The class had four digital cameras and one scanner.
	The teacher introduced the activities, instructing the students to work in their groups. The students enthusiastically began following the instructions for making their fingerprints with the graphite pencil to create a swatch of "ink" on a piece of paper. As the students worked in their groups, they talked and laughed at how the fingerprints looked. Some students began making their fingerprints on the faces of others. As soon as a group was ready for a digital camera, some, one, or all of the group members went to the front of the room to check out a camera. Along the way they were showing other groups their fingerprints and asking to see what they had created. The teacher was busy guiding the students in getting the images from the digital camera to the scanner and in working with the scanner. Many groups seemed to need the equipment at the same time so while they waited they were going from group to group to compare their fingerprints and were talking about how they might classify their fingerprint styles. With the need for the teacher to be with the equipment, the room became noisier and noisier.
	How could the teacher have reorganized this lesson to prevent and/or better manage this noisy but positive classroom lesson?

the students appeared to be at a loss for working with the spreadsheet. The teacher might have planned a prior lesson to demonstrate the specifics of setting up a spreadsheet to find areas and volumes from classroom measurements. Such a demonstration provides an opportunity for students to focus on what they will be asked to do and to ask clarifying questions while also allowing the teacher to guide them as a whole group. Since demonstrations do not allow all students to have hands-on work, the teacher might also plan for extra time for students to practice. The preservice teachers might discuss a variety of ways to provide this additional practice, particularly if access to the technology is limited. Of course, when the students are actively working on the computers in the classroom, issues arise and students have questions. In this case, teachers need to have prepared their students with strategies for getting answers to their questions. Students might check with the persons on their right to see if they can answer the question. They check with the persons on their left if the question remains unanswered; if the question is still not answered, they raise their hand for the teacher to help. This action allows students to problem solve and try to answer their own questions while at the same time allows the teacher extra time to get to those students who are in the most need.

As the case study groups lead the class in investigating these cases, the other groups in the class need to record the variety of strategies for preventing and for coping with classroom management issues. Upon completion of the investigations, the discussion shifts to guiding the preservice teachers in making connections of teaching their content with technology with two key pedagogical principles that have emerged from the research:

1. Good management is preventive rather than reactive.
2. Teachers help create well-managed classrooms by identifying and teaching desirable behaviors to their students (Emmer & Stough, 2001).

Simultaneously, the preservice teachers have an opportunity to develop their own toolkits of classroom management strategies that specifically consider important issues when integrating technology in teaching their content. In the process they begin to see the variety of problems and issues that arise and realize that the problems are not all *nails* to be pounded with a *hammer*.

Effective plans for teaching with technology

With the importance of prevention for establishing a well-managed classroom, methods classes must provide intensive guidance in helping preservice teachers in thinking through the lessons they plan to teach with technology. Preservice teachers typically struggle to consider and verbalize the detail needed when planning to teach with technology and for this reason need experiences in planning these technology-enhanced lessons. They must be

Table 11.5 Sample prompts for thinking and preparing for effective classroom management of technology-enhanced lessons

General area	Question prompt samples
Preparation for teaching	• What preparation must be done prior to the lesson with respect to the technology and other classroom materials? If lab stations are to be set up, what must be available at each station? When does this happen? • Are the materials needed for the lesson clearly identified? • What knowledge/skills do students need in advance of the lesson?
General lesson expectations	• Does the flow of the lesson prepare, motivate, and encourage the students to engage in the experiences? • What questions are proposed for engaging the students in the ideas and assessing student understanding? • Are the time estimates reasonable for each of the activities in the lesson? • Do the directions and transitions assure student understanding and maintain student attention? • Is there closure to the lesson?
Integration of technology	• Why is the technology included in this lesson? • How is the technology maximized to support the learning of the subject matter ideas? • What preparation will the students need for successfully using the technology as a tool for learning the subject? • What instructions with the technology should students have prior to their work? How is student understanding of the instructions assessed? • Is the problem for the incorporation of technology clear? How do the students know what they are trying to determine? • What worksheets/handouts might support students with information and instruction for working with the technology?
Instructional strategies with the technology	• Are the affordances and constraints of the strategies considered in the plan? • Should the technology be demonstrated in order for students to use it as a learning tool? • If the lesson incorporates hands-on use of technology by students, have the students been prepared to work individually or in the small groups with the technology? • Are all students involved and held accountable for learning in the lab/hands-on experiences? Are tasks assigned in advance to assure accountability? • What does the teacher do while students are working in lab groups? • How does the teacher assure that students are making progress and that the technology is working? Is the teacher responsible for answering all questions or are there specific procedures for asking neighbors first when questions arise? • What if the students finish early? What if time runs out and some groups are not finished? • What are the clean-up procedures? What about the materials? Are they to be cleaned for future labs? Are they to be placed in a specific location? The teacher should not be responsible for cleaning up the materials and lab because of a lack of time. • Is there closure to the lesson that integrates considerations of what they learned with the technology?

challenged to consider effective classroom management techniques when integrating technology in the instruction and to incorporate these ideas in their plans. With the active, hands-on nature of many technology lessons, preservice teachers need to think about and develop lesson plans for guiding students with hands-on uses of technologies in ways that continue to value the importance of the focus on the subject matter content. As they think through such a lesson, they are forced to consider important factors for establishing effective classroom management.

Again study groups provide an effective strategy for engaging them with an in-depth discussion of their plans. First, the preservice teachers must prepare lesson plans where they propose strategies for introducing students to a particular technology used in learning. These plans provide the framework for a discussion about strategies and methods for integrating technologies in specific subject area lessons. Then study groups of two or three students analyze each of their plans, using the question prompts similar to those in Table 11.5. Ultimately, they consider the question: Does the lesson plan provide sufficient detail to assure effective classroom management?

Assessing student learning with technology

> However beautiful the strategy, you should occasionally look at the results.
>
> **Winston Churchill**

Assessment of student learning is as important in the methods course as planning lessons for student learning. However *beautiful* the strategies in the plans, preservice teachers must determine the extent to which the students met the objectives of the lessons and units—*the results*. With the addition of learning both *with* and *about* the technology, preservice teachers need to learn how to assess students' knowledge of the subject matter content in an environment where technology is integrated as a tool to think and learn with the technology—as a productivity tool, a communication tool, a research tool, and a problem-solving and decision-making tool. If the students learn with the technology and are assessed without the use of the technology, was the assessment about a different objective of instruction?

When technology is added to the educational environment, teachers must consider (1) how technology can be applied to enhance learning, (2) how use of technology changes what is learned, and (3) how technology can be used to enrich the evidence of student learning. New methods, new tools, and new approaches that apply technology to learning must be accounted for when applying technology to the assessment of what is learned and how that learning is known and displayed. Considering the affordances and constraints for multiple assessment strategies when thinking about what students learned with technology is an important experience in learning about different assessment techniques. Classroom tests have been a traditional assessment of learning. Yet, does a paper–pencil assessment accurately assess how and what students have learned with technology? Performance-based and portfolio assessments have risen in the consideration as they recognize the impact of the technology on the students' learning of the subject matter content. Thus, as preservice teachers learn about the various assessments, they must be engaged in a careful consideration of the validity and reliability of the assessment instruments in reflecting what students learn as they learn with technology as a tool for learning. If students are allowed to use calculators for solving problems in their mathematics classes and are tested in solving problems without access to calculators, the results are likely not a valid assessment of what the students have learned.

Practice field experiences

Learning is not a spectator sport.

Anonymous

A variety of additional approaches for preparing teachers to teach with technology have been proposed to move toward the other end of the continuum in a teacher preparation program where (1) technology considerations are included in all courses in the program in order to be more supportive of the development of TPCK with particular attention to content-specific applications, and (2) preservice teachers are required to teach with technology in their student teaching experiences (Duhaney, 2001; Niess, 2005a; Wetzel & Zambo, 1996; Young *et al.*, 2000). No mater how marvelous the coursework is in providing them with knowledge about teaching with technology, they must have opportunities to apply this knowledge. For them to *learn* to teach with technology, preservice teachers must be more than *spectators* in the classroom. Microteaching provides opportunities for them to test their developing ideas for establishing classrooms conducive to learning with technology. But, this type of experience is not with the appropriate student levels—the students they would be teaching when they are teachers. During their student teaching experiences, they connect *words from the professors* with *actions in the classroom*. Reflections on their teaching experiences often result in comments such as these from student teachers I prepared in the teacher preparation program at Oregon State University:

- When using technology, I have to spend time on what directions are absolutely necessary ... then think about how to make the directions succinct.
- Overall I was pleasantly surprised by the technology lesson. I think my paranoia of chaos breaking out forced me to plan and prepare enough so the lessons flowed in a logical, orderly manner.

- The lab activity required that I give a very accurate description of the steps that students were to follow before they began … it was important to constantly be checking their understanding during the activity. I felt that this was difficult to do adequately … nothing really went wrong, but it was a big headache. I think that by going over all the chemistry concepts covered in the activity again in class salvaged the lesson, but it was an additional chunk of time going over the same things.
- … it … gave me the opportunity to learn some new things and help my students learn some new things. Once the steps have been taken to use the technology, I think the students definitely benefited.
- I feel that how I introduced the equipment and helped them learn how to use it was also very important in their success. I first modeled the use, then gave them guided practice, and then worked with individuals while others got started on the lab.
- It took some extra planning and some extra time to set up, but I think the payoff of enhanced student interest and learning made it worthwhile … I think teaching with technology is definitely a little different than standard teaching. It forced me to do more planning and more setup than I had previously.

Field experiences help preservice teachers understand the importance of planning and preparation. Field experiences help them realize the value of specific instructional strategies. And, ultimately field experiences help them comprehend and appreciate the complexities involved in teaching with technologies, thus developing and extending their TPCK. Preservice teachers need to be more than *players* in teaching with technology. Critical reflection is an important aspect of both their teaching and learning. It is the reflection, not the experience alone, that provides the instruction. As Clarke (1995) indicates, reflection is not about a single event in time, but occurs over time as teachers begin to construct meaning for themselves. This reflective behavior is an essential ingredient in developing TPCK's strategic thinking—for knowing when and where to use domain-specific knowledge and strategies.

In conclusion

On being asked how he had "discovered" the law of gravitation, Newton replied "by thinking on it continually."

Isaac Newton

An essential goal for methods courses is typically directed toward the development of pedagogical content knowledge (PCK)—that knowledge that distinguishes teachers' knowledge, skills, and dispositions from those who are simply content experts. With the rapid integration of technology in the fabric of the twenty-first century society, integrating instruction for teaching *with* and *about* new and emerging technologies has been recognized because future citizens need to work and continue learning with technology. Thus, as important as the development of PCK is for methods courses, TPCK and its way of thinking have emerged as needing to be included throughout the preparation of teachers, including in the methods courses. And, guiding preservice teachers in *discovering* their own TPCK requires experiences that engage and even require them to *think of it continually.*

Extending Grossman's (1989, 1990) four components of PCK, TPCK is revealed as the knowledge, skills, and dispositions that teachers have for teaching with technology—or knowledge that includes:

- an overarching conception of what it means to teach the content with technology,
- knowledge of instructional strategies and representation for teaching the content with technology,
- knowledge of students' understanding, thinking, and learning the content with technology, and
- knowledge of curriculum and curriculum materials that integrate technology in their subject (Niess, 2005a).

In essence, preservice teachers need to develop the strategic thinking involved in TPCK—the thinking that involves *planning, organizing, critiquing,* and *abstracting* for specific content, specific student needs, and specific classroom situations. Methods courses provide a natural environment for building on the knowledge, skills, and dispositions identified in TPCK—for helping them *discover* the TPCK that supports them in teaching with technology. Methods courses focus on guiding preservice teachers in planning lessons, units, and sequences of instruction. Their learning experiences with the content they plan to teach has been primarily without access to technology as a learning tool. Moreover, their content has emerged and shifted with the impact of the new and emerging technologies. Their overarching conception of what it means to teach their content with technology is certainly a naïve conception that requires attention. Their knowledge of instructional strategies and representations relies on their personal experiences, experiences primarily with little if any access to technology. Their knowledge of students' understanding, thinking, and learning with technology needs to provide them experiences where they interact with and explore student thinking in technology-rich experiences. Their knowledge of curriculum and curriculum materials is similarly deficient.

Methods courses focus the development of TPCK by providing conscious attention to the question of whether technology might enhance the learning experiences. This integration needs to be directed toward the development of the strategic thinking of TPCK so that preservice teachers are prepared to actively consider when, where, and how technology might enhance student learning. Throughout all of the experiences identified for methods courses, an essential experience in guiding preservice teachers' development of TPCK through planning and problem solving around designing instruction is to have them monitor their progress in their development of the knowledge, skills, and dispositions of TPCK. A reflective expectation with each experience is essential for their development of TPCK. The reflection is a challenge to improve the lesson, the strategies, and the assessments. In sum, reflection is an important experience in the making of a teacher for the twenty-first century—a teacher with the knowledge, skills, and dispositions for teaching with newer and emerging technologies, a teacher with knowledge and understanding of the intersection and integration of content, pedagogy, and technology in ways that ultimately affect student learning.

References

Brown, J., Stillman, G., & Herbert, S. (2004). Can the notion of affordances be of use in the design of a technology enriched mathematics curriculum? In I. Putt, R. Faragher, & M. McLean (eds), *Proceedings of the 27th Annual Conference of the Mathematics Education Research Group of Australasia, Townsville, Vol. 1* (pp. 119–126). Sydney: MERGA.

Brush, T., Glazewski, K., Rutowski, K., Berg, K., Stromfors, C., & Hernandez Van-Nest, M. (2003). Integrating technology into a pre-service teacher training program: The PT3@ASU project. *Educational Technology Research and Development, 51*(1), 57–72.

Clarke, A. (1995). Professional development in practicum settings: Reflective practice under scrutiny. *Teaching and Teacher Education, 11*(3): 243–261.

Cotton, K. (1999). *Research you can use to improve results.* Alexandria, VA: Association for Supervision and Curriculum Development.

Duhaney, D. C. (2001). Teacher education: Preparing teachers to integrate technology. *International Journal of Instructional Media, 28*(1), 23–30.

Emmer, E., & Stough, L. (2001). Classroom management: A critical part of educational psychology, with implications for teacher education. *Educational Psychologist, 36*, 103–112.

Evertson, C., & Harris, A. (1992). What we know about managing classrooms. *Educational Leadership, 29*, 74–78.

Gettinger, M. (1988). Methods of proactive classroom management. *School Psychology Review, 17*, 227–242.

Gibson, J. J. (1979). *The ecological approach to visual perception.* Boston: Houghton Mifflin.

Good, T. L., & Brophy, J. E. (2003). *Looking in classrooms.* Boston: Allyn and Bacon.

Grossman, P. L. (1989). A study in contrast: Sources of pedagogical content knowledge for secondary English. *Journal of Teacher Education, 40*(5), 24–31.

Grossman, P. L. (1990). *The making of a teacher: Teacher knowledge and teacher education.* New York: Teachers College Press.

International Society for Technology in Education. (2000). *National educational technology standards for teachers.* Eugene, OR: ISTE NETS Project.

Jones, V. (1996). Classroom management. In J. Sikula, T. Buttery, & E. Guyton (eds), *Handbook of research on teacher education* (Vol. 2). New York: Macmillan.

Margerum-Leys, J., & Marx, R. W. (2002). Teacher knowledge of educational technology: A study of student teacher/mentor teacher pairs. *Journal of Educational Computing Research, 26*(4), 427–462.

McClanahan, L. G. (2006, April). Using technology to foster literacy instructions: The benefits for pre-service teachers. Paper presented at the *Annual Meeting of the American Educational Research Association*, San Francisco, CA.

Mishra, P., & Koehler, M. J. (2006). Technological pedagogical content knowledge: A framework for integrating technology in teacher knowledge. *Teachers College Record, 108*(6), 1017–1054.

Niess, M. L. (2005a). Preparing teachers to teach science and mathematics with technology: Developing a technology pedagogical content knowledge. *Teaching and Teacher Education, 21*, 509–523.

Niess, M. L. (2005b). Scaffolding math learning with spreadsheets. *Learning and Leading with Technology, 32*(5), 24–25, 48.

Niess, M. L., Lee, J. K., & Kajder, S. B. (2008). *Guiding learning with technology.* Hoboken, NJ: Wiley & Sons.

Partnership for 21st Century Skills. (2004). *Framework for 21st Century Learning.* Retrieved September 30, 2006 from: http://www.21stcenturyskills.org.

Pierson, M. E. (2001). Technology integration practices as function of pedagogical expertise. *Journal of Research on Computing in Education, 33*(4), 413–429.

Prensky, M. (2001). Digital natives, digital immigrants. *On the Horizon, 9*(5).

Putnam, R. T., & Borko, H. (2000). What do new views of knowledge and thinking have to say about research on teacher learning? *Educational Researcher, 29*(1), 4–15.

Rittel, H., & Webber, M. (1973). Dilemmas in a general theory of planning. *Policy Sciences, 4*(2), 155–169.

Ruiz-Primo, A., Shavelson, R., Li, M., & Schultz, S. (2001). On the validity of cognitive interpretations of scores from alternative concept-mapping techniques. *Educational Assessment, 7*(2), 99–11.

Shavelson, R., Ruiz-Primo, A., Li, M., & Ayala, C. (2003, August). Evaluating new approaches to assessing learning (CSE Report 604). Los Angeles, CA: University of California, National Center for Research on Evaluation.

Shulman, L. (1986). Those who understand: Knowledge growth in teaching. *Educational Researcher, 2*, 4–14.

Strudler, N., & Grove, K. (2002). Integrating technology into teacher candidates' field experiences: A two-pronged approach. *Journal of Computing in Teacher Education, 19*(2), 33–39.

uit Beijerse, R. P. (2000). Questions in knowledge management: Defining and conceptualizing a phenomenon. *Journal of Knowledge Management, 3*(2), 94–109.

Wetzel, K., & Zambo, R. (1996). Innovations in integrating technology into student teaching experiences. *Journal of Research on Computing in Education, 29*(2), 196–215.

Wiggins, G., & McTighe, J. (2006). *Understanding by design.* Upper Saddle River, NJ: Pearson Education, Inc.

Wilson, S. M., Shulman, L. S., & Richert, A. E. (1987). "150 different ways" of knowing: Representations of knowledge in teaching. In J. Calderhead (ed.), *Exploring Teachers' Thinking* (pp. 104–124). London: Cassell.

Young, S., Cantrel, P., Bryant, C., Archer, L., Roberts, C., & Paradis, E. (2000). The state of technology in university teacher preparation and public schools in Wyoming. *Teaching and Change, 8*(1), 134–144.

Zhao, Y. (2003). *What teachers should know about technology: Perspectives and practices.* Greenwich, CT: Information Age Publishing.

12
TPCK in in-service education
Assisting experienced teachers' "planned improvisations"

JUDITH B. HARRIS

Jazz today, as always in the past, is a matter of thoughtful creation, not mere unaided instinct.

Duke Ellington

To an experienced educator, teaching is much like jazz performance: a well-practiced fusion of careful, creative planning and spontaneous improvisation. Like jazz music, much of good teaching is context-dependent, serendipitous improvisation, yet it still follows predetermined, somewhat predictable structures sequenced in virtually infinite permutations.[1] Functional and effective learning activity designs and implementation strategies for teachers' use must build upon such educational improvisation, so that students' needs, preferences, and reactions can be accommodated. Yet they must also be carefully planned, so that curriculum standards are addressed in appropriate ways within the time constraints of the school day and year. For even the experienced teacher, assisting students' learning "is a matter of thoughtful creation, not mere unaided instinct," as Mr. Ellington reminds us.

What happens when experienced teachers seek to integrate educational technologies into curriculum-based learning and teaching, and how can teacher educators assist this professional development process? This chapter will suggest answers to this question in both conceptual and practical forms, framed within the notion of technological pedagogical content knowledge development (Mishra & Koehler, 2006; Koehler & Mishra, Chapter 1).

Technology integration: a "vamp"

"Swing" is an adjective or a verb, not a noun. All jazz musicians should swing. There is no such thing as a "swing band" in music.

Artie Shaw

A "vamp" in jazz music is a brief, repeated chord progression, usually used to introduce a performance, like the piano chords that serve as a musical preamble to Frank Sinatra's famous "That's Life!" song. Technology integration is a vamp of sorts, in that it appears often in today's educational literature, but its definitional parameters, as expressed and implied currently—like Artie Shaw's notion of a "swing band" cited above—can be shallow (Pierson, 2001) and technocentric (Papert, 1987). Yet educational technologies, like Shaw's use of "swing" as an adjective or verb, may be applied appropriately in many types of teaching and learning. In doing so, they should assist with—not overshadow—teachers helping students to meet curriculum-based standards.

Recent conceptions of technology integration (e.g., Gunter & Baumbach, 2004) focus upon curriculum-based, educational *uses* for digital tools and resources, rather than the affordances of the technologies themselves. As Earle (2002) asserts,

> Integrating technology is not about technology—it is primarily about content and effective instructional practices. Technology involves the tools with which we deliver content and implement practices in better ways. Its focus must be on curriculum and learning. Integration is defined not by the amount or type of technology used, but by how and why it is used.
>
> (p. 8)

For the purposes addressed in this chapter, I suggest a basic definition for technology integration: the pervasive and productive use of educational technologies for purposes of curriculum-based learning and teaching. Note that this definition does not specify or imply a particular educational approach, philosophy, or goal. More on this below.

Studies of K-12 teachers' instructional applications of educational technologies to date show many of the uses to be pedagogically unsophisticated; limited in breadth, variety, and depth; and not well integrated into curriculum-based teaching and learning (e.g., Cuban, 2001; Earle, 2002; McCrory-Wallace, 2004; Zhao, Pugh, Sheldon, & Byers, 2002). In a 20-year retrospective on U.S. educational technology policy, Culp, Honey, and Mandinach (2003) describe a mismatch between educational technology leaders' visions for technology integration, and how most practitioners use digital tools, by saying:

> Technological innovations favored by the research community intended to support inquiry, collaboration, or re-configured relationships among students and teachers continue to be used by only a tiny percentage of America's teachers.... Instead, teachers are turning to tools like presentation software, resources like student-friendly information sources on the Internet, and management tools like school-wide data systems to support and improve upon their existing practices ...
>
> (p. 22)

McCormick and Scrimshaw (2001) label these currently predominant uses for information and communication technologies as "efficiency aids" and "extension devices," differentiating them from "transformative devices" (p. 31), which "transform the nature of a subject at the most fundamental level" (p. 47). These authors suggest that such curricular transformation happens only in those few content areas (e.g., music, literacy, and art) that are "largely defined by the media they use" (p. 47). (More on educational technologies as transformative devices in literacy and the arts can be found in Chapters 3 and 8, respectively.)

Given this discrepancy between leaders' visions and practitioners' actions, perhaps teacher educators' choices among efficiency, extension, and transformative applications of educational technologies in professional development for experienced teachers should be strategic and context-dependent, rather than automatic and unilateral. In each unique professional development situation, a customized and collaborative decision about the nature of the approach could be made along with school stakeholders. In situations in which pervasive educational use of digital technologies is more important than transformative use, professional development can be designed to incorporate more efficiency- and extension-focused integration. In situations in which curricular transformation is sought, professional development can encourage transformative educational technology use.

Yet to date—and perhaps due to the largely transformative agendas of most organized technology integration efforts—persistent and pervasive technology integration in classroom practice has been notoriously difficult to sustain, and almost as challenging to catalyze. Two notable exceptions to this pattern, however, are instructive. In less than a decade, more than 90 percent of secondary mathematics classes in the U.S. have adopted use of graphing calculators (as described in Chapter 7)—so pervasively that they are now required of students taking Advanced Placement exams (Bull & Garofalo, 2004). During an even shorter time period, WebQuests (Dodge, 1995) have pervaded elementary-level classrooms and Internet-related professional development for teachers in North America (March, 2003/2004; Molebash, n.d.). The keys to the rapid adoption rates for these particular curriculum-based uses for educational technologies are also key to successful, self-sustaining professional development for experienced teachers: recognizable *content, structure,* and *advantage.* Each of these factors will be addressed below.

TPCK content: jazz "riffs"

I'll play it first and tell you what it is later.

Miles Davis

Jazz riffs are short, recognizable melodic phrases that are repeated within and across different songs. Some blues riffs, for example—like the melodic phrases that we associate with B. B. King playing his guitar "Lucille"—are so recognizable that even beginning musicians can use them to "jam." Other riffs are unique to particular performers and jazz traditions. Riffs can therefore be used to help more sophisticated listeners recognize and focus upon jazz musical characteristics, style, development, and innovations. In a sense, riffs express the "content" of jazz music in ways that help listeners to recognize and appreciate it.

Clearly, teachers need curriculum-related content knowledge to do their jobs effectively. Windschitl (2004) defines this as "understanding of a domain's concepts, theories, laws, principles, history, classic problems, and explanatory frameworks that organize and connect its major ideas" (A framework for thinking about teacher knowledge section, para. 4). As Shulman (1986, 1987) proposed more than two decades ago, however, content knowledge alone is not sufficient. Teacher knowledge must also encompass disciplinary, general pedagogical, and pedagogical content knowledge. All of these together and in dynamic relationship with each other comprise the "content" of teacher expertise. Shulman's unique contribution to the educational literature on teacher knowledge at the time was his crystallization of the notion of pedagogical content knowledge, or a

> special amalgam of content and pedagogy that is uniquely the province of teachers, their own form of professional understanding ... it represents the blending of content and pedagogy into an understanding of how particular topics, problems, or issues are organized, represented and adapted to the diverse interests and abilities of learners, and presented for instruction.
>
> (1987, p. 8)

Windschitl explains that pedagogical content knowledge is focused upon how *students* understand subject matter, including the developmental appropriateness of and prerequisite understandings necessary to learn particular discipline-related ideas, concepts, and other subject matter. As it complements that developmentally focused understanding, teachers' pedagogical content knowledge (PCK) also encompasses "how to select representations, analogies, and activities" (p. 5) that assist learners' content-related conceptualizations. Hughes (2005, p. 279) explains the use of PCK pragmatically, saying,

> Pedagogical content knowledge is specific for each content area; teachers within a discipline make pedagogical decisions about instruction and learning based on what they believe to be the purpose(s) for teaching the content, what knowledge they believe students should be devel-

oping (noting what has been taught in previous and subsequent grade levels), what discipline-based teaching materials are available, and what representations or activities have been successfully used in their past teaching.

Koehler & Mishra (Chapter 1) are among a growing number of scholars (e.g., Pierson, 2001; Hughes, 2003; Franklin, 2004; Gunter & Baumbach, 2004; McCrory Wallace, 2004; Irving, n.d.) who have recognized that a particular type of pedagogical content knowledge—that is, *technological* PCK, to use Pierson's term—is what teachers must develop to be able to effectively integrate use of educational technologies into curriculum-based instruction. Though the terms differ somewhat—Gunter and Baumbach, for example, consider this type of PCK to be a form of literacy that they call "integration literacy" (p. 193)—the concepts and constructs across theorists are similar.

It is important to note that technological pedagogical content knowledge (TPCK) is interdependent with content, pedagogical, and technological knowledge; and also pedagogical content, technological content, and technological pedagogical content knowledge, as Koehler and Mishra's diagram and explanations in Chapter 1 show. Moreover, each and all of these are influenced by contextual factors, such as culture, socioeconomic status, and organizational structures. Thus, TPCK as it is applied in practice must draw from each of these interwoven aspects, making it a complex and highly situated educational construct—a "wicked problem," as was asserted in Chapter 1. Given the nature of this type of problem,

> *There is no single technological solution that applies for every teacher, every course, or every view of teaching.* Quality teaching requires developing a nuanced understanding of the complex relationships [among] technology, content, and pedagogy, and using this understanding to develop appropriate, context-specific strategies and representations.
> (Mishra & Koehler, 2006, p. 1029)

The ways in which teacher educators help teachers to develop TPCK and concomitantly integrate educational technology use into their practice should therefore reflect the interdependence of technology, pedagogy, and content, so that knowledge of each aspect is developed concurrently (Cochran, DeRuiter, & King, 1993), and is as philosophically, pedagogically, and contextually flexible as Mishra and Koehler recommend.

Experienced teachers' knowledge is situated, event-structured, and episodic. It is "developed in context, stored together with characteristic features of … classrooms and activities, organized around … tasks that teachers accomplish in classroom settings, and accessed for use in similar situations" (Putnam & Borko, 2000, p. 13). Attempts to assist experienced teachers' development of TPCK should accommodate these characteristics if more pervasive technology integration is a goal of a particular professional development effort.

There is also some evidence that well-developed TPCK may be positively correlated with general teaching expertise. Though TPCK can be demonstrated at a beginner's level in an experienced teacher with little technology integration expertise, it probably develops more quickly for a seasoned educator than for a teaching intern (Pierson, 2001). Logically, this suggests that TPCK-focused professional development for experienced teachers should be qualitatively different from similar professional learning opportunities for most novices. Koehler and Mishra (2005) demonstrated that TPCK can be developed measurably using a design-based approach in authentic instructional planning contexts. Considering all of these ideas, along with the complex and very situated nature of TPCK, plus the time-strained realities of teachers' schedules, suggests the provision of *flexible design scaffolds* to assist experienced teachers with development and practice of curriculum-based TPCK. These will be described in the next section.

TPCK structures: "lead sheets"

You don't know what you like, you like what you know.
In order to know what you like, you have to know everything.

Branford Marsalis

A "lead sheet" is what jazz musicians use to guide performances of a particular song. It's a shorthand musical score, usually containing only the song's melody (also called the "head") and its harmonic progression. Lead sheets are analogous to what practicing teachers use to plan learning activities for their students. Fully itemized lesson plan documents are used more often to help people learn to plan instruction than to support day-to-day instructional interactions in classrooms. Most practicing teachers use shorthand versions of lesson plan documents, which specify essential elements only: the curriculum topics or standards addressed, instructional activities scheduled, special resources and materials needed, and formal or informal evaluation strategies to be used.

One approach to helping teachers learn to plan technology-integrated learning activities—or "performances of understanding" in the Teaching for Understanding framework's terminology (Wiske, 1998)—focuses upon creating awareness of the range of possible learning activity types, and helping teachers to know how to select and combine these to help students meet content and process standards in ways that are congruent with their differentiated learning needs and preferences. Based upon a metaphorical understanding of Branford Marsalis' statement above, it is only after teachers are familiar with the full range of learning activity types that they can appropriately choose among and effectively implement them in each learning situation. Since content, pedagogy, and technology knowledge are so interrelated and interdependent (Koehler & Mishra, Chapter 1), and given the socially situated, event-structured, episodic, and pragmatic nature of experienced teachers' knowledge (Moallem, 1998; Putnam & Borko, 2000), it serves to reason that there are identifiable TPCK-related activity types, within and across curriculum-based disciplines.

There is some evidence that learning activity types—called "activity structures" in social semiotic and science and mathematics education literature—are cognitive structures that experienced teachers use regularly (albeit subconsciously at times) to plan and carry out instruction. Windschitl (2004), for example, when examining recommended pedagogical practice for science labs, identifies several lab-related activity structures, defining the term as follows.

> The term "activity structure" is borrowed from the sociocultural theorists, meaning a set of classroom activities and interactions that have characteristic roles for participants, rules, patterns of behavior, and recognizable material and discursive practices associated with them. "Taking attendance," "having a discussion," and "doing an experiment" could all be considered activity structures. While the term "activities" refers to specific phenomena occurring in classrooms, the structures underlying these are more general and applicable across multiple contexts.
>
> (p. 25)

Polman (1998) sees activity structures operating on both classroom (e.g., whole-group question-and-answer session) and school levels (e.g., academic credit units). He also asserts that, from a sociocultural standpoint, dominant activity structures are cultural tools that perpetuate and standardize interaction patterns—and therefore interaction norms and expectations—primarily according to teachers' memories of dominant discourse patterns from their own school-related childhood experiences. When a paradigmatically new teaching approach is attempted, Polman argues, since there isn't an "obvious set of well-established cultural tools to structure their interaction" (p. 4), the resulting confusion and resistance can undermine reform efforts. It would seem, then, that some activity structures could also represent a mismatch between teachers' and students' differing socioculturally based expectations for teacher–student and student–student interaction (e.g., preferences for competitive or collaborative work on school assignments), and therefore should be selected from as culturally competent a stance as possible. (More on TPCK and cultural competence can be found in Chapter 2.)

The notion of activity structure is rooted in the study of classroom-based discourse, with Mehan's (1979) I–R–E (teacher initiation, student reply, teacher evaluation) sequence being the first commonly cited discursive structure in educational literature. Lemke (1987) applied the notion of recurring discourse structure to the social semiotics of science education more broadly, noting that "every meaningful action in the classroom makes sense as part of some recurring semiotic pattern" (p. 219) and that every action has both interactional and thematic meaning. That meaning unfolds, according to Lemke, within two independent discourse structures: activity structures and thematic structures. Activity structures are "recurring functional sequences of actions" (p. 219) and thematic structures are familiar ways of speaking about a topic, such as the curriculum-based focus of a unit or lesson (Windschitl, 2004). Lemke's underlying assertion is that meaning cannot be separated from action; the structure of curriculum content cannot be separated from the structure of content-related learning activities. Given similar underlying assumptions of TPCK's interdependence, it is probable that tool and resource use—both digital and nondigital—can similarly not be separated from content/theme and activity structure. Therefore, TPCK-related activity structures for teachers' use should be conceptualized and presented thematically, in terms of particular disciplinary discourses.

Several educational researchers have begun to examine the intentional cultivation and use of activity structures in professional development for teachers. Kolodner and Gray (2002), for example, proposed a system of "ritualized" learning activity structures to assist learning and teaching in project-based science work. (More on science learning and TPCK can be found in Chapter 9.) These authors recommend ritualizing activity structures at both strategic and tactical levels—that is, in terms of sequencing both the steps for participating in a particular type of activity and the ordered succession of activities in a project or unit. Kolodner and Gray's activity structures are specific to the skills that each helps students to develop. For example, there are three different types of presentations included: for experimental results, for ideas, and for experiences with multiple problem solutions. These researchers discovered that, contrary to common expectations that too many different activity structures would overwhelm students and teachers, such fine-grained differentiation actually assists both learners and instructors in knowing what to expect, how to participate in, and how each activity type is connected to the development of content-specific processes. The structures "articulate[ed] and normalize[ed] a sequence of activities and setting expectations about how and when to carry them out." ("Ritualized" Activity Structures section, para. 3.)

Polman's (1998) two-year classroom-based research study sought to document a project-based alternative to the traditional I–R–E activity structure. He discovered a B–N–I–E structure being used in a middle school science class, in which students "bid" by suggesting topics that they would like to research, then "negotiated" the details of the projects based upon those possible topics, then "instantiated" their understanding with work on the project according to their understanding of the instructor's guidelines, then received and considered formative "evaluation" from the teacher on their work. The evaluation results then formed the basis for a new recursion of the B–N–I–E sequence.

Polman's research continued as he then tested the B–N–I–E activity structure in a different discipline: history. He found that the structure could be modified to accommodate an alternate curriculum area, but that the adaptation must involve choices "along the dimensions of act (what) and agency (how)" (p. 22) because the nature of inquiry and expression in different disciplines differ in essential ways—for example, between a lab report and an historical narrative. Polman's work with the same activity structure in two disparate disciplines raises the question of the extent to which activity structures or types are discipline-specific or transdisciplinary. I will address this issue below.

During an in-depth study of science education practices in Japan, Linn, Lewis, Tsuchida, & Songer (2000) compared the presence and use of science activity structures in multiple classrooms, finding them to be consistently present and similarly described by both students and teachers, framed in terms of what students do during each science-related learning experience. The researchers also explored how these activity structures are connected to larger system structures, including teacher professional development. They hypothesized that the highly collaborative nature of Japanese teacher interactions may be a factor determining the consistency of both the structures and discussion of them by teachers and students. Contrary to popular U.S. perceptions, "Japanese teachers ultimately choose the instructional approaches they will use in the classroom," but "shared research lessons may offer opportunities for teachers to collectively build and refine not just instructional techniques, but also norms about what is good instruction" (p. 11). This points to an essential feature of successful use of activity structures as instructional planning/design tools: as Linn, Lewis, Tsuchida, & Songer recommend, they are best used flexibly and in the context of active teacher discourse communities to "enable deep, coherent instruction" (p. 4).

Dodge's (2001) recommendations to teachers of "five rules for writing a great WebQuest" illustrate what can happen when an activity structure is used without the active professional discourse that Linn *et al.* suggest. In Dodge's own words,

> A quick search of the Web for the word *WebQuest* will turn up thousands of examples. As with any human enterprise, the quality ranges widely.... Some of the lessons that label themselves WebQuests do not represent the model well at all and are merely worksheets with URLs.
>
> (p. 7)

Table 12.1 Telecollaborative and telecooperative activity structures

Genre	Telecollaborative/ telecooperative activity structure	Description
Interpersonal exchange	Keypals	Students communicate with others outside their classrooms via email about curriculum-related topics chosen by teachers and/or students. Communications are usually one-to-one.
	Global classrooms	Groups of students and teachers in different locations study a curriculum-related topic together during the same time period. Projects are frequently interdisciplinary and thematically organized.
	Electronic appearances	Students have opportunities to communicate with subject matter experts and/or famous people via email, videoconferencing, or chatrooms. These activities are typically short-term (often one-time) and correspond to curricular objectives.
	Telementoring	Students communicate with subject matter experts over extended periods of time to explore specific topics in depth and in an inquiry-based format.
	Question and answer	Students communicate with subject matter experts on a short-term basis as questions arise during their study of a specific topic. This is used only when all other information resources have been exhausted.
	Impersonations	Impersonation projects are those in which some or all participants communicate in character, rather than as themselves. Impersonations of historical figures and literary protagonists are most common.
Information collection and analysis	Information exchanges	Students and teachers in different locations collect, share, compare, and discuss information related to specific topics or themes that are experienced or expressed differently at each participating site.
	Database creation	Students and teachers organize information they have collected or created into databases which others can use and to which others can add or respond.
	Electronic publishing	Students create electronic documents, such as Web pages or word-processed newsletters, collaboratively with others. Remotely located students learn from and respond to these publishing projects.
	Telefieldtrips	Telefieldtrips allow students to virtually experience places or participate in activities

Table 12.1 continued

Genre	Telecollaborative/ telecooperative activity structure	Description
		that would otherwise be impossible for them, due to monetary or geographic constraints.
	Pooled data analysis	Students in different places collect data of a particular type on a specific topic and then combine the data across locations for analysis.
Problem solving	Information searches	Students are asked to answer specific, fact-based questions related to curricular topics. Answers (and often searching strategies) are posted in electronic format for other students to see, but reference sources used to generate the answers are both online and offline.
	Peer feedback activities	Students are encouraged to provide constructive responses to the ideas and forms of work done by students in other locations, often reviewing multiple drafts of documents over time. These activities can also take the form of electronic debates or forums.
	Parallel problem solving	Students in different locations work to solve similar problems separately and then compare, contrast, and discuss their multiple problem-solving strategies online.
	Sequential creations	Students in different locations sequentially create a common story, poem, song, picture, or other product online. Each participating group adds a segment to the common product.
	Telepresent problem solving	Students simultaneously engage in communications-based realtime activities from different locations. Developing brainstormed solutions to real-world problems via teleconferencing is a popular application of this structure.
	Simulations	Students participate in authentic, but simulated, problem-based situations online, often while collaborating with other students in different locations.
	Social action projects	Students are encouraged to consider real and timely problems, then take action toward resolution with other students elsewhere. Although the problems explored are often global in scope, the action taken to address the problem is usually local.

Source: Dawson & Harris, 1999, p. 2.

Table 12.2 Teleresearch activity purposes

Genre	Teleresearch activity purpose	Process description
Teleresearch	Hone information skills	Practicing information-seeking and information-evaluating skills
	Explore a topic or answer a question	Exploring a topic of inquiry or finding answers to a particular question
	Reviewing multiple perspectives	Discovering and investigating multiple beliefs, experiences, etc., upon a topic
	Generate data	Collecting data remotely
	Problem-solving	Using online information to assist authentic problem-solving
	Teleplant/telepublish	Publishing information syntheses or critiques for others to use

Source: Harris, 1998.

Dodge and March (Dodge, 1995) specifically intended for the WebQuest to be an inquiry-based activity that emphasizes students' use of information located online at analysis, synthesis, and evaluation levels primarily. With posted evaluation standards now available and encouraged for teachers' use (Dodge, Bellofatto, Bohl, Casey, & Krill, 2001), Dodge hopes that a greater proportion of newly created WebQuests will reflect the purposes for and types of learning originally conceptualized.

My own work with TPCK-based activity structures began as explorations of curriculum-based telecomputing applications for K-12 students (e.g., Harris, 1993, 1995–1996, 1998) that were assumed to be cross-disciplinary, like WebQuests. This taxonomy of 24 activity structures, organized into "telecollaborative"—later: "telecollaborative" and "telecooperative" (Harris, 2005)—and "teleresearch" genres, were embraced by many teachers and teacher educators as a viable way to think about and design curriculum-based learning that integrated appropriate use of online tools and resources. The structures are still in active use today, as a Google search demonstrates (Tables 12.1 and 12.2).

TPCK structure combinations: "fake books"

Imitate, assimilate, and innovate.

Clark Terry

In using this first activity taxonomy to design curriculum-based learning experiences for and with students, I encouraged teachers to combine activity types, digital and nondigital tools used, and curriculum standards. Yet as the years passed and access to hardware, software, and technology-related professional development improved in many schools, my work with teachers began to suggest that learning activity structures should no longer be classified, even in part, by technology type. To do so, I realized, was technocentric and therefore unnecessarily limiting.

In a reconceptualization of activity structures as "activity types" (Harris & Hofer, in press)—a term that seems to be preferred by many teachers—it is possible to combine the advantages of using design-based conceptual tools for planning, this time differentiated by curriculum area, while considering the full range of educational technologies available. Using this particular approach to professional development in technology integration, teachers learn to recognize, differentiate, discuss, select among, combine, and apply TPCK-oriented activity types in curriculum standards-based instructional design. In this way, teachers can function as designers in time-efficient ways that accommodate the nature of their daily schedules, which unfortunately don't allow sufficient opportunities for as much in-depth design-based planning as teachers may wish to do, or as teacher educators may recommend.

Social studies is the first curriculum area for which my colleague and I have developed a taxonomy of TPCK-related activity types that can be supported by a full range of digital and nondigital tools and resources. (For information on TPCK and social studies beyond learning activity design, please see Chapter 6.) Twelve examples of these 40 activity types are described below. The group is divided into 13 knowledge-building and 27 knowledge expression social studies-based activity types. Knowledge expression activity types are further divided into activities that emphasize either convergent or divergent thinking processes.

Knowledge-building activities are those in which students build content-related understanding through information-based processes. Five knowledge-building activity types follow. In the *view images* activity type, digital and/or nondigital images can be used to reinforce readings or points made in class presentations, provide a different and complementary means to present content, and/or generate reactions and discussion. In an *artifact-based inquiry* activity, online archives of artifact reproductions—such as primary source documents—provide students with a focused set of resources around a particular historical topic of interest, such as the Boston Massacre, the Holocaust, or *Brown* v. *The Topeka Board of Education*. These resources can then be used in a number of ways, encouraging students to ask questions of interest, while providing resources rich enough for them to begin to find answers. In developing an *historical chain*, students explore and then sequence documents (text, images, maps, etc.) in chronological order, using clues found within the documents. This challenges the students to carefully examine the documents, apply their knowledge of their historical contexts, and make inferences about how the documents may be justifiably combined. By contrast, in an *historical weaving*, students explore multiple historical documents or other resources concerning a person, place, or event, and piece them together into an integrated narrative. This activity goes beyond an historical chain in that it is not necessarily just a linearly structured story. An historical weaving may contain multiple chains of events happening simultaneously, challenging students not only to sequence events, but also make connections among these parallel stories. The challenge of this activity type requires students to understand, sequence, and synthesize events to tell the story of what may have happened. By contrast, in an *historical prism* activity, students compare and contrast multiple historical sources representing different perspectives upon a particular person, place, or event. This type of work often involves students stepping outside their comfort zones and reconciling divergent—if not contradictory—viewpoints.

Knowledge expression activity types help students to deepen their understanding of content-related concepts through various types of communication. *Convergent* knowledge expression activities, such as *completing charts or tables* based upon a classroom lecture or discussion, content-based reading, or as a synthesis activity after careful review of multiple sources, help students to take information and summarize it in another form. Charts, tables, and other graphic organizers can be projected for whole-group discussion/analysis using anything from printed overhead transparencies to editable digital documents that can be updated extemporaneously. Blank charts and tables created by the teacher also can be provided to students to complete in paper-based or electronic forms. Alternatively, to help students to express their understanding of historical cause and effect, creating cognitive contexts for complex events or topics, they can *create a timeline*. Whether in history, government, economics, or even sociology, when students sequence information, people, and events on a timeline, they can see connections and chronology much more clearly than when relying exclusively upon paragraphed text. While timelines can be and are created with paper and pencil, students can also use Web authoring or multimedia presentation software to create interactive timelines in which the dates or entries are linked to additional pages or slides that provide more detailed information about each.

Divergent knowledge expression activities in social studies help students to extend their content-related understanding via alternative forms of communication. For example, as an alternative to writing a report, *developing a presentation* enables students to share their understanding of a topic or concept using their own voice and a variety of visual or audio aids. The presentation may be given in either a formal or more casual way; either individually or with a small group; either face-to-face or "packaged" in some way to allow viewers to explore the presentation on their own. Another activity type that helps students to make abstract social studies concepts more accessible is *building a knowledge web* of the interconnected components of an idea, issue, occurrence, or concept being studied. Developed as a class, in small groups, or individually, the creation and use of webbed graphic representations of complex topics and concepts can help students to develop questions and understanding beyond what is presented more didactically in textbooks and similarly structured instructional materials.

Other *divergent knowledge expression activity types* help students and teachers to use educational technologies in ways that go beyond digitally enhancing traditional knowledge expression methods. Three of these activity types are described here. For example, films—rich and engaging stories leveraging visuals, sound, and music—are significant and ubiquitous artifacts of modern culture. Proponents of positioning students as filmmakers assert that students approach storytelling and writing in very different ways when multimedia options for expression are available. When students *create their own films* related to course content, their unique voices can be heard in diverse and rich ways that simply are not possible in written or oral forms of expression. Another divergent knowledge expression activity type—the *historical impersonation*—takes the historical diary assignment to another level. Using this approach, students are challenged not only to understand the past through the eyes of a particular person; they actually "become" the person and either make an oral presentation in first-person or interact with others—face-to-face or online—using the voice of an actual or historically possible figure from the past. Impersonating an historical figure challenges students to develop a rich understanding of a person's temporal context, experience, and viewpoints. Finally, when tied to coursework, *engaging in civic action* is active and purposeful, and can be transformative for students and their understanding of what it means to be a citizen, both locally and globally. Use of global, multimodal information networks helps students to not only learn about distant communities, but also to connect with people from around the world, making new and numerous civic action opportunities easily accessible. Through email exchanges, discussion forum conversations, and desktop video conferencing, students can share local information and perspectives, connecting with and learning from people around the world, thus expanding their notions of both citizenship and community.

Note that each of these example activity types, as they have been described here, do not typically privilege one particular type or class of educational technology. The same is true for the nascent research in developing and applying curriculum-based activity types done by other researchers and mentioned earlier in this chapter. Rather, in identifying and sharing activity types, the intention is to help teachers to become aware of the full range of possible curriculum-based learning activity options, and the different ways that digital and nondigital tools support each, so that they can select among, customize, and combine activity types that are well matched to both students' differentiated learning needs and preferences, and contextual realities, such as computer access and class time available for learning activity work. Using this design approach, as teachers plan classroom-based learning experiences, they keep students' needs, preferences, and relevant past experience in front-and-center focus, with curriculum standards and possible activity type selections in close visual peripheries, so that all are considered concurrently, albeit with differing emphases at different times and under different conditions.

Yet experienced teachers' planning for students' learning is not an activity-by-activity endeavor. Curriculum-based units, projects, and sequences are much more than the sums of their respective parts. Analogously, jazz "fake books" are collections of "lead sheets" that jazz musicians use to improvise a night's performance. In this sense, "faking" is jazz improvisation, with minimal but essential pre-performance notation recorded for the musicians to use as a guide—like most experienced teachers' lesson plans. Following through with this metaphor, if lead sheets are realistic lesson or learning activity plans based upon riffs as learning activity structures/types, then when lead sheets are combined into fake books, metaphorically they form the basic plans for longer-term educational projects and units of study. Part of what a curriculum-based activity types approach to the development of TPCK addresses is how to combine individual activity types into engaging, appropriate, and authentic project or unit plans.

For many experienced teachers, selecting, adapting, and designing learning activities, projects, and units is review work, but the awareness of how different digital and nondigital tools can be used in service of students' learning within each of the activity structures/types encompasses new information and/or new ways of thinking about the planning/instructional design process. Like jazz, much of experienced teachers' work is context-dependent, serendipitous improvisation, but it still follows a predetermined, somewhat predictable structure. Some jazz improvisationalists compose music of their own—as some teachers prefer to design and implement original projects and lessons—and others base their work completely upon their own interpretations of others' songs. It is important that professional development for experienced teachers that emphasizes TPCK be flexible enough to accommodate the full range of teaching philosophies, styles, and approaches. One way to ensure that flexibility is to share the full range of curriculum-based activity types within each discipline area, encouraging experienced educators to select among them based upon perceived appropriateness and advantage—and to engage in this selection/combination process each time a new lesson, project, or unit is planned.

TPCK and relative advantage

It's taken me all my life to learn what not to play.

Dizzie Gillespie

Knowles and his colleagues (e.g., Knowles, Holton, & Swanson, 1998) remind us that to be effective, adult education must operate according to a completely different set of principles than instruction of children and adolescents. Knowles stresses the importance of andragogical, rather than pedagogical approaches. Andragogical principles are especially important to keep in mind when planning and providing professional development for experienced teachers.

Andragogical assumptions suggest that adults need to know why they should learn something, and how, if at all, it will benefit them directly. Adults "resent and resist situations in which they feel others are imposing their wills on them" (Knowles, Holton, & Swanson, 1998, p. 65), and respond better to learning if their past experience and expertise can be acknowledged and used in the present learning act. Adults prefer authentic learning, in which direct ties to particular tasks, problems, or similarly real-life situations are made. Adults are motivated more internally, rather than externally, to learn, and become ready to do so when "they experience a need to learn … in order to cope more satisfyingly with real-life tasks or problems" (Knowles, Holton, & Swanson, 1998, p. 44). Yet in spite of a preference for autonomy, many adult learners—experienced teachers included—are accustomed to more dependent forms of learning.

For all of these reasons, TPCK-related professional development for experienced teachers should promote both autonomous and collaborative instructional decision-making while simultaneously encouraging open-minded consideration of new instructional methods, tools, and resources. Activity types that are keyed directly to required curriculum standards can provide both flexible scaffolding and authenticity of purpose for experienced teachers' TPCK-related learning—a balance of helpful, non-constraining structure/scaffolding for new implementation ideas while acknowledging experienced teachers' agency and expertise in the classroom.

Ultimately, each teacher will decide the relative advantage (Rogers, 2003)—and therefore the probability of use—of each unfamiliar TPCK-related instructional design idea. As Zhao and Cziko (2001) remind us, teachers are "goal-oriented, purposeful organisms" (p. 6) who will choose actively *not* to integrate use of educational technologies if they do not recognize the need to do so—even if access and support for technology integration are readily available. In practical terms, each new instructional possibility is assessed by each teacher using an implicit equation: utility = value/effort (Fischer, 2002). Approaching experienced teachers andragogically, rather than pedagogically, acknowledges the reality of this dynamic. TPCK-related professional development for experienced teachers is, after all, more a process of persuasion than prescription.

Given these recommendations, a final underlying issue should be addressed. In her literature review about issues of scale in school reform efforts, Coburn (2003) states:

Because teachers draw on their prior knowledge, beliefs, and experiences to interpret and enact reforms, they are likely to "gravitate" toward approaches that are congruent with their prior practices ..., focus on surface manifestations rather than deeper pedagogical principles ..., and graft new approaches on top of existing practices without altering classroom norms or routines.

(p. 4)

As described in this chapter and as recommended by Mishra and Koehler (2006), an activity structures/types approach to TPCK-focused professional development for experienced teachers does not preference any particular teaching philosophy or approach. In not doing so, it is probable that teachers learning to use TPCK-based design scaffolds will more often assimilate—as Coburn suggests—comparatively familiar activity types and combinations, rather than accommodate existing teaching ideas and approaches to use more unfamiliar activity types in ways that demonstrate and exemplify deep philosophical change.

Does this present a challenge to be addressed? Perhaps—but only if the goal of a particular professional development effort is qualitative philosophical change in teachers' beliefs and practices. To accomplish a goal of better or more extensive *technology integration* does not necessarily require a philosophically transformative agenda for professional development. Instead, the primary goal of such professional learning and reflection could be to develop and act upon TPCK in and to whichever forms and extents experienced teacher practitioners choose. Though it is necessarily a topic for a different chapter, it bears mention here that the automatic coupling of methodological and philosophical reform in current-day educational technology professional development efforts—such as was demonstrated in the much-publicized ACOT research (Sandholtz, Ringstaff, & Dwyer, 1997)—may be ill-advised if technology integration/TPCK development is the primary goal of a particular professional development program.

After all—as in jazz music, there are many different styles and traditions of teaching in which experienced teachers situate themselves via their practice. There are different styles of jazz (e.g., Dixieland, swing, big band) and jazz combines with other musical genres (e.g., blues, classical, hip-hop) just as there are different styles of teaching, which often borrow from and fuse with work in multiple disciplines. In the end, if students' differentiated curriculum-based learning needs and preferences are being accommodated well, it is both a practical and an ethical imperative to support and respect—in addition to helping to inform—experienced teachers' pedagogical choices. To assume that a particular instructional approach is privileged by educational use of digital technologies is as silly as assuming that a guitar should only be used to play the blues, or a pianist should only attempt ragtime. The development of pedagogical approaches, like the development of jazz traditions, is an additive, recursive, and expansive process, rather than a linear series of replacements of "old" with "new." Experienced teachers learning to develop and apply technological pedagogical content knowledge is an essential aspect of that expansion.

One of the things I like about jazz, kid,
is I don't know what's going to happen next. Do you?

Bix Beiderbecke

Note

1. Sincere thanks are offered here to my colleague, Mark Hofer, for suggesting this metaphor and collaborating with me to construct its components.

References

Bull, G., & Garofalo, J. (2004). Internet access: The last mile. *Learning & Leading with Technology, 32*(1), 16–18, 21.

Coburn, C. E. (2003). Rethinking scale: Moving beyond numbers to deep and lasting change. *Educational Researcher, 32*(6), 3–12.

Cochran, K. F., DeRuiter, J. A., & King, R. A. (1993). Pedagogical content knowing: An integrative model for teacher preparation. *Journal of Teacher Education, 44*, 263–272.

Cuban, L. (2001). *Oversold and underused: Computers in classrooms.* Cambridge, MA: Harvard University Press.

Culp, K. M., Honey, M., & Mandinach, E. (2003). A retrospective on twenty years of education technology policy. Washington, DC: U.S. Department of Education, Office of Educational Technology. Retrieved May 15, 2006, from www.nationaledtechplan.org/participate/20years.pdf.

Dawson, K., & Harris, J. (1999). Reaching out: Telecollaboration and social studies. *Social Studies and the Young Learner, 12*(1), P1–P4.

Dodge, B. J. (1995) *Some thoughts about WebQuests.* Retrieved June 4, 2006, from http://webquest.sdsu.edu/about_webquests.html.

Dodge, B. (2001). FOCUS: Five rules for writing a great webquest. *Learning & Leading with Technology, 28*(8), 6–12.

Dodge, B., Bellofatto, L., Bohl, N., Casey, M., & Krill, M. (2001). *A rubric for evaluating WebQuests.* Retrieved June 4, 2006, from http://webquest.sdsu.edu/webquestrubric.html.

Earle, R. S. (2002). The integration of instructional technology into public education: Promises and challenges. *ET Magazine, 42*(1), 5–13.

Fischer, G. (2002). Beyond couch potatoes: From consumers to designers and active contributors. *First Monday, 7*(12). Retrieved June 4, 2006, from http://firstmonday.org/issues/issue7_12/fischer.

Franklin, C. (2004). Teacher preparation as a critical factor in elementary teachers: Use of computers. *Society for Information Technology and Teacher Education International Conference 2004*(1), 4994–4999. Retrieved May 30, 2006, from http://dl.aace.org/15272.

Gunter, G., & Baumbach, D. (2004). Curriculum integration. In Kovalchick, A. & Dawson, K. (eds), *Education and technology: An encyclopedia.* Santa Barbara, CA: ABC-CLIO, Inc.

Harris, J. (1993). Using Internet know-how to plan how students will know. *The Computing Teacher, 20*(8), 35–40.

Harris, J. (1995–1996). Telehunting, telegathering and teleharvesting: Information-seeking and information-synthesis on the Internet. *Learning and Leading With Technology, 23*(4), 36–39.

Harris, J. (1998). *Virtual architecture: Designing and directing curriculum-based telecomputing.* Eugene, OR: International Society for Technology in Education, University of Oregon.

Harris, J. (2005). Curriculum-based telecomputing: What was old could be new again. In G. Kearsley (ed.), *Online learning: Personal reflections on the transformation of education* (pp. 128–143). Englewood Cliffs, NJ: Educational Technology Publications.

Harris, J., & Hofer, M. (in press). *Technology integration in social studies: Teachers as chefs, not cooks.* Thousand Oaks, CA: Corwin Press.

Hughes, J. (2005). The role of teacher knowledge and learning experiences in forming technology-integrated pedagogy. *Journal of Technology and Teacher Education, 13*(2), 277–302.

Hughes, J. E. (2003). Toward a model of teachers' technology-learning. *Action in Teacher Education, 24*(4), 10–17.

Irving, K. E. (n.d.). *Effective and appropriate uses of educational technology in science classrooms.* Retrieved May 31, 2006, from http://www.ohiorc.org/cor/student_learning/Effective_and_Appropiate_Uses.pdf.

Knowles, M. S., Holton, E. F., & Swanson, R. A. (1998). *The adult learner: The definitive classic in adult education and human resource development* (5th edn). Woburn, MA: Butterworth-Heinemann.

Koehler, M. J., & Mishra, P. (2005). What happens when teachers design educational technology? The development of technological pedagogical content knowledge. *Journal of Educational Computing Research, 32*(2), 131–152.

Kolodner, J. L., & Gray, J. (2002). Understanding the affordances of ritualized activity structures for project-based classrooms. *International Conference of the Learning Sciences,* April. Retrieved May 15, 2006, from http://www-static.cc.gatech.edu/projects/lbd/pdfs/activity-structures.pdf.

Lemke, J. L. (1987). Social semiotics and science education. *The American Journal of Semiotics, 5*(2), 217–232.

Linn, M., Lewis, C., Tsuchida, I., & Songer, N. (2000). Beyond fourth-grade science: Why do U.S. and Japanese students diverge? *Educational Researcher, 29*(3), 4–14.

March, T. (2003/2004). The learning power of WebQuests. *Educational Leadership, 61*(4), 42–47.

McCormick, R., & Scrimshaw, P. (2001). Information and communications technology, knowledge, and pedagogy. *Education, Communication and Information, 1*(1), 37–57.

McCrory Wallace, R. (2004). A framework for understanding teaching with the Internet. *American Educational Research Journal, 41*(2), 447–488.

Mehan, H. (1979). *Learning lessons.* Cambridge: Harvard University Press.

Mishra, P., & Koehler, M. J. (2006). Technological pedagogical content knowledge: A framework for integrating technology in teacher knowledge. *Teachers College Record, 108*(6), 1017–1054.

Moallem, M. (1998). An expert teacher's thinking and teaching in instructional design models and principles: An ethnographic study. *Educational Technology Research and Development, 46,* 37–64.

Molebash, P. E. (n.d.) *Scaffolding inquiry using WebQuests and Web inquiry projects.* Retrieved June 2, 2006, from http://edweb.sdsu.edu/courses/edtec470/sections/resources/Inquiry_ article.pdf.

Papert, S. (1987). A critique of technocentrism in thinking about the school of the future. Retrieved May 15, 2006, from http://www.papert.org/articles/ACritiqueofTechnocentrism.html.

Pierson, M. E. (2001). Technology integration practice as a function of pedagogical expertise. *Journal of Research on Computing in Education, 33*(4), 413–429.

Polman, J. L. (1998, April). Activity structures for project-based teaching and learning: Design and adaptation of cultural tools. Paper presented at the *Annual Conference of the American Educational Research Association,* San Diego, CA. Retrieved May 15, 2006, from http://www.cet.edu/research/papers/CPpolman98.html.

Putnam, R. T., & Borko, H. (2000). What do new views of knowledge and thinking have to say about research on teacher learning? *Educational Researcher, 29*(1), 4–15.

Rogers, E. M. (2003). *Diffusion of innovations* (5th edn). New York: The Free Press.

Sandholtz, J., Ringstaff, C., & Dwyer, D. (1997). *Teaching with technology: Creating student-centered classrooms.* New York: Teachers College Press.

Shulman, L. (1986). Those who understand: Knowledge growth in teaching. *Educational Researcher, 15*(2), 4–14.

Shulman, L. S. (1987). Knowledge and teaching: Foundations of the new reform. *Harvard Educational Review, 57*(1), 1–22.

Windschitl, M. (2004). *What types of knowledge do teachers use to engage learners in "doing science?"* Paper commissioned by the National Academy of Sciences. Washington, DC: Board of Science Education. Retrieved May 15, 2006, from http://www7.nationalacademies.org/bose/MWindschitl_comissioned_paper_6_03_04_HSLabs_Mtg.pdf.

Wiske, M. R. (1998). *Teaching for understanding: Linking research with practice.* San Francisco: Jossey-Bass.

Zhao, Y., & Cziko, G. A. (2001). Teacher adoption of technology: A perceptual control theory perspective. *Journal of Technology and Teacher Education, 9*(1), 5–30.

Zhao, Y., Pugh, K., Sheldon, S., & Byers, J. L. (2002). Conditions for classroom technology innovations. *Teachers College Record, 104*(3), 482–515.

Advancing TPCK through collaborations across educational associations

GLEN BULL, LYNN BELL, AND TOM HAMMOND

In 1986 Lee Shulman described a blind spot in the teaching research of his day:

> The missing paradigm refers to a blind spot with respect to content that now characterizes most research on teaching and, as a consequence, most of our state-level programs of teacher evaluation and teacher certification.... What we miss are questions about the *content* of the lessons taught, the questions asked, and the explanations offered.
>
> (Shulman, 1986, pp. 7–8)

Shulman argued that crucial aspects of pedagogical practice are uniquely connected to specific content areas and coined the term "pedagogical content knowledge" (PCK).

Extension of the concept to "technological pedagogical content knowledge" (TPCK) brings much-needed recognition of the central role of content and pedagogy in uses of educational technology—a role typically missing in discussions until recently. Even though some technologies may indeed facilitate student learning, content and pedagogy are crucial ingredients in this success. And if the pedagogical content knowledge required for each discipline differs, it follows that the ways in which technology might best be used for each discipline may also differ.

Coincident with the early articulations of TPCK (see Koehler & Mishra, 2005), several teacher educator content associations and educational technology associations began working together to examine uses of technology in teacher preparation. The participating representatives possessed a common intuition that technology should be introduced in the context of content instruction and that teachers should take advantage of the unique features of technology to teach content in ways they otherwise could not. It can be said that this consortium, which eventually became today's National Technology Leadership Coalition (NTLC), was grounded in the framework that later became known as TPCK.

This collaboration among associations over the years has involved dialog about the intersection of technology, pedagogy, and content. This dialog has been invaluable, but has also revealed that cultures, perspective, and values in these diverse disciplines can be very different—and understanding these differences can lead to new insights about TPCK.

The other chapters in this monograph provide in-depth perspectives regarding technology use in individual content areas. The first half of this chapter provides a perspective across disciplines and content areas gained from our work within the context of the NTLC. In the second half of the chapter we describe in more detail the evolution of the collaboration across educational associations that led to this dialog. Because this consortium of associations from different disciplines is grounded in the framework of TPCK, future advances in this area seem likely to emerge from the collective work of the NTLC.

Differing perspectives across content areas

A cursory reading through the previous chapters in this monograph demonstrates that every content area has different learning goals and requires a different set of strategies and technology tools to meet those goals—or at least a different way of using those tools. These differences frequently are not apparent to those outside the content area. They are obvious to those within the discipline, however, and vital to the success of efforts to enhance student learning. The following examples illustrate this point.

Spreadsheets

Spreadsheets, for example, are often used in both mathematics and science classes, and on the surface the uses would appear identical. In both classes, students are using spreadsheets to organize and calculate. However, once the *purpose* of the activity is investigated, it becomes evident that a common technology (a spreadsheet) is being used for opposite goals (see Figure 13.1).

In a sequence activity, a mathematics teacher leads students through generating, manipulating, and displaying data. As the students modify the coefficients, the function plot changes. The mathematics teacher's objective here is to allow the students to control the numbers and refine their algebraic thinking (Dugdale, 1998).

A science teacher, on the other hand, asks students to use spreadsheets to record, analyze, and summarize data. Rather than intentionally produce a pattern, students examine the data summary to seek a pattern. (In fact, manipulating data would be anathema to the nature of scientific inquiry!)

Digital narratives

In the humanities, student creation of digital narratives provides another example of an application being used in seemingly similar ways but for very different purposes (see Figure 13.2). Digital storytelling has emerged as an instructional technique in language arts classes, often in a unit on autobio-

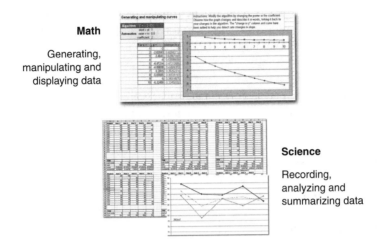

Math

Generating, manipulating and displaying data

Science

Recording, analyzing and summarizing data

Figure 13.1 Sample spreadsheet activities from a mathematics class and a science class.

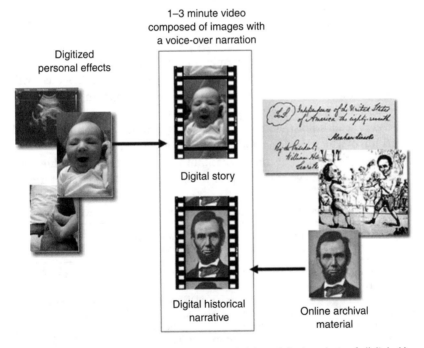

Digitized personal effects

1–3 minute video composed of images with a voice-over narration

Digital story

Digital historical narrative

Online archival material

Figure 13.2 Schematic diagram illustrating raw materials and final products of digital video creation in a language arts class and a history class.

graphical writing. After reflecting on personal experience, students identify a dramatic question and then compose and refine a script with an eye toward economy and pacing (Lambert, 2003). The final product features a voice-over narration against a visual track of thought-provoking images that students create and/or select.

In history classes, on the other hand, teachers are beginning to experiment with digital historical narratives, brief films that explore some topics of historical interest. Digital historical narratives commonly use primary source images as the visual track; the audio track, as in a digital story, is a voice-over narration composed and recorded by the student. The two products look (and sound!) deceptively similar, but are entirely different.

When we look at the criteria for evaluating digital stories and contrast them with the criteria for evaluating digital historical narratives, the two products' contrasting pedagogical purposes become more visible (see Table 13.1). In assessing a digital story, the language arts teacher places primary value on the student's ability to craft and refine a story of the self. The tools at the student's disposal are his or her life experiences, writing skills, speaking skills, and selection of digital images.

In a digital historical narrative, the teacher asks that the student critically address the story of an *other*, be it another person, an artifact, an institution, a society, or even a concept. The premium here is placed on getting the facts right and thoughtfully integrating specific primary source images used with the larger ideas of history. Manipulating the facts or images in the service of more powerful storytelling would violate a cardinal rule of the discipline. These distinctions illustrate how TCPK comes into play in both design and evaluation of educational technologies in specific content areas.

Building TPCK, then, is no easy task. In instructional uses of technology, things are not always what they appear to be. These two very different uses of

Table 13.1 Differences in criteria for student-created digital video in two content areas

Language arts: criteria for a digital story	Social studies: criteria for a digital documentary
• Display of an authorial voice • Construction of an engaging narrative • Inclusion of appropriate narrative information, exclusion of irrelevant information • Creative conceptualization, composition, and display of information • Use of engaging film-making techniques • Display of correct grammar and usage	• Accuracy of substantive knowledge (historical content, facts) • Display of procedural knowledge (historical thinking skills, discipline-specific ways of knowing) • Inclusion of appropriate historical information, exclusion of irrelevant information • Using appropriate film-making techniques to convey historical information and avoid misinterpretation

similar tools emerged from completely different specializations and communities. These communities normally remain separate, unless conscious action is taken to encourage dialog between disciplinarily dissimilar practitioners. Collaborations across educational associations are invaluable in facilitating such interactions.

Differing perspectives across teacher educators: pedagogical content versus educational technology

In 2004, Debra Sprague, editor of the *Journal of Technology and Teacher Education*, published an editorial titled "Technology and teacher education: Are we talking to ourselves?" This editorial highlighted a growing concern about a divide between the field of educational technology and pedagogical content specialists. This chasm has developed as a result of the natural order of academic enterprises. Within the field of education, subject matter specialists, teacher educators, and educational technologists have traditionally been housed in different departments, have attended different professional conferences, and have approached integration of technology from different cultural perspectives. These differing perspectives and values become more apparent when educational technology specialists and pedagogical content specialists evaluate the same innovation, as was the case for a recent technology leadership award nomination.

The Society for Information Technology and Teacher Education (SITE) sponsors two journals: *Journal of Technology and Teacher Education* (print) and *Contemporary Issues in Technology and Teacher Education* (electronic). SITE's journals co-sponsor annual Technology Leadership Awards, with selection panels composed of teacher educators both from content areas and from the field of instructional technology.

One nomination for an award in the category Exemplary Use of Technology to Teach Content in a Methods Course described the preparation of K-8 preservice teachers to teach science using computer modeling and simulation software. The preservice teachers used the software to learn science content themselves and also evaluated simulations and wrote lesson plans for potential use in their future teaching. The instructor used the modeling software to help preservice teachers learn not just scientific facts but the processes and nature of science as they dealt with the open-endedness of the models. In assessing the preservice teachers' beliefs about the technology, according to the nomination, the instructor learned that they valued software that was "fun, easy to use, aesthetically pleasing, and provided a source for scientific information.... They remained highly skeptical of the value of research-based modeling tools—particularly the ones that did not impart direct scientific information." From this point of dissonance, the instructor launched epistemological discussions about the characteristics of science and the nature of science pedagogy.

The science teacher educators on the panel gave this nomination the highest possible rating. They recognized the value of the teacher educator's use of the software as not just a teacher-tool for classroom practice but as an opportunity for teacher formation regarding beliefs about the discipline. In contrast, panel members from the discipline of instructional technology gave this nomination the lowest rating in the group. (One comment noted that the course was "not all that innovative.") This difference of opinion is illustrative of a recurring pattern we have observed, in which pedagogical content experts and educational technology specialists view the same innovation from markedly different perspectives, even when the evaluators are using identical rubrics. The rubrics are interpreted through the lens of expertise and experience, yielding different results.

Debra Sprague summarized the current state of affairs, observing that

> Some teacher educators do not understand the type of teaching and learning technology supports. They have developed a culture that does not include technology and are uncomfortable when that culture is challenged. On the other hand, some educational technology faculty members are familiar with, at best, one pedagogical content area and are unaware of some of the issues teacher education needs to address.
>
> (Sprague, 2004)

Her perspective as a journal editor is that few instructional technologists have sufficient depth in pedagogical content knowledge beyond a single discipline, and few methods professors are fluent in all possible technology integration strategies. Since it is not feasible to master all the domains involved, a collaborative approach can bring together these complementary skill sets. A venue that engages pedagogical content experts and educational technology specialists in constructive, cross-disciplinary dialogs is invaluable.

Toward TPCK: establishing a teacher education coalition

In 2004, a five-year collaborative relationship among professional associations was formalized as the National Technology Leadership Coalition (NTLC). The initial members of the NTLC included two educational technology associations (SITE and the International Society for Technology in Education [ISTE]) and four teacher educator associations representing the core content areas (ASTE, AMTE, CEE, and CUFA; see Table 13.2).

Some goals of the coalition include the following:

- An increased focus on PCK within the educational technology associations.
- A corresponding focus on TK (technological knowledge) within the teacher educator content associations.
- Identification of a research agenda to further effective use of TPCK.

Table 13.2 The initial educational associations that became the founding members of the NTLC

Content area	Teacher educator content associations	Educational technology associations
Science	Association for Science Teacher Education (ASTE)	Society for Information Technology and Teacher Education (SITE)
Mathematics	Association of Mathematics Teacher Educators (AMTE)	
English	NCTE Conference on English Education (CEE)	ISTE Teacher Education Special Interest Group (SIG-TE)
History	NCSS College and University Faculty Assembly (CUFA)	

- Facilitation of research and professional development advancing this agenda.

To accomplish these goals, each of the four participating teacher educator content associations

- established a standing educational technology committee,
- established an ongoing technology strand at its annual conference, and
- established an annual award for an exemplary paper related to technology integration in the respective content area (the "National Technology Leadership Awards")

At the same time, SITE established a teacher education council with special interest groups (SIGs) in each of the pedagogical content areas. A strand for each content area was also established at the SITE annual conference.

These parallel advances within the respective participating organizations provided an important foundation for collaboration across associations.

Interdisciplinary structures

It was recognized at an early stage in the joint collaboration that some mechanism for communication across associations would be required. The NTLC representatives from the teacher educator content associations serve both on the technology committee of their home association and on the corresponding special interest group at SITE (Figure 13.3).

These liaisons provide an important channel of communication, creating a mechanism through which continuity can be established for cross-association activities.

Over time, the NTLC has expanded. The National Association of Early Childhood Teacher Educators (NAECTE) joined the coalition in 2003, providing connections with elementary education. In 2005 the American Association of Colleges for Teacher Education (AACTE) and the Association of Teacher Educators (ATE) both joined the NTLC.

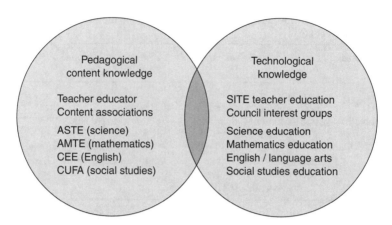

Figure 13.3 Interdisciplinary structures for TPCK. Establishing mechanisms for collaboration between pedagogical content associations and educational technology associations, with TPCK at the intersection.

Although there is not currently a formal relationship between NTLC and the American Educational Research Association, the founders of the AERA Technology as an Agent of Change in Teaching and Learning special interest group (SIG-TACTL) were also instrumental in establishment of NTLC. Consequently, it has been possible to coordinate NTLC initiatives with SIG-TACTL activities.

NTLC leadership summit

NTLC representatives convene at a retreat held in September of each year. These retreats have raised issues about technology in education that cut across the disciplines and have catalyzed the content associations to think more concretely about appropriate uses of technology. They have also become a place where teacher educators with an interest in educational technology broaden their perspectives and solidify their roles as leaders in the area of content-specific technology.

One of the initial tasks assumed by NTLC representatives entailed development of appropriate guidelines for integration of technology into teacher preparation. The resulting guidelines for each pedagogical content area were published in the premier issue of a peer-reviewed journal established through the NTLC, *Contemporary Issues in Technology and Teacher Education* (CITE Journal):

- Promoting appropriate uses of technology in mathematics teacher preparation (Garofalo, Drier, Harper, Timmerman, & Shockey, 2000).
- Preparing tomorrow's science teachers to use technology: Guidelines for science educators (Flick & Bell, 2000).

- Preparing tomorrow's English language arts teachers today: Principles and practices for infusing technology (Pope & Golub, 2000).
- Guidelines for using technology to prepare social studies teachers (Mason *et al.*, 2000).

The guidelines identified in these papers reflect differences in the ways teachers in different content areas are prepared to use technology in their instruction.

Subsequent retreats considered topics such as ubiquitous computing in schools, uses of open source software, digital images across the curriculum, uses of projectors to bridge the "last mile" from computers to learners, and open educational content.

In the past couple of years, NTLC representatives have been working to facilitate high quality research on technology in education. Their work includes identifying key research issues in the core content areas, clarifying acceptable evidence in research on educational technology, and presenting models of research that helps answer significant questions in the field. A subgroup of participants interested in legislative advocacy for technology in education also meets at each summit to plan strategies for the coming year.

The National Technology Leadership Summit (NTLS), as it is now called, is held at the beginning of the academic year, allowing representatives of NTLC associations to plan ongoing collaborations that will span educational conferences and content areas (see Table 13.2). The process culminates the following summer at ISTE's National Educational Computing Conference (NECC), the largest U.S. educational technology conference.

A topic considered at NTLS is typically discussed in panels and presentations at other associations throughout the following academic year (see Table 13.3). This mechanism is important for cross-disciplinary dialog. A summary of coalition outcomes for the year is published in the May issue of *Learning*

Table 13.3 Calendar for teacher education conferences with sessions that build upon dialog emerging from the NTLC leadership summit

Date	Association
September	NTLC (Annual Technology Leadership Summit)
November	NCTE/CEE (English Education)
November	NCSS/CUFA (Social Studies Education)
January	ASTE (Science Education)
January	AMTE (Mathematics
February	ATE (Teacher Education)
February	AACTE (Teacher Education)
March	SITE (Technology and Teacher Education)
May	AERA SIG-TACTL (Educational Research)
June	NAECTE (Early Childhood)
June	ISTE (Educational Technology)

and Leading with Technology. This issue is distributed to participants at NECC, who include not just teacher educators and education researchers, but practitioners and school administrators as well.

NTLS is typically held in Washington, DC, to provide an opportunity for participation of policy makers as well as educational foundations (see Figure 13.4). To ensure that the innovations discussed at the leadership retreats are feasible from a business perspective, each year selected corporate representatives are invited to participate and provide important insights. The Software Information Industry Association (SIIA) has also become an important NTLC member and contributor at the leadership summits.

Establishing a journal for TPCK in teacher education

One of the first tangible outcomes of the NTLC was establishment of an academic journal jointly sponsored by the participating associations. *Contemporary Issues in Technology and Teacher Education* (CITE Journal) is unique in one regard: each partner association assumed editorial responsibility for the section of the journal related to its discipline. These sections include:

- Contemporary Issues in Technology and Social Studies Teacher Education (NCSS/CUFA)
- Contemporary Issues in Technology and Mathematics Teacher Education (AMTE)
- Contemporary Issues in Technology and Science Teacher Education (ASTE)

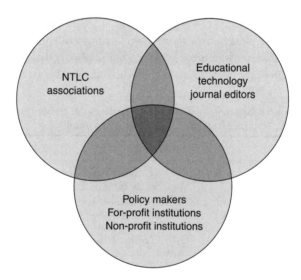

Figure 13.4 National Technology Leadership Summit (NTLS). A leadership summit at the beginning of the academic year allows leaders from NTLC associations to consult editors of educational technology journals and educational policy makers in an annual retreat.

- Contemporary Issues in Technology and English/Language Arts Teacher Education (NCTE/CEE)

A "General" section and a "Current Practice" section of the journal are devoted to more generic discussions of technology in teacher education and are sponsored by SITE.

Establishing sections with editorial control maintained by organizations representing specific subject areas entailed conscious acknowledgment of the domain-influenced nature of TPCK. Consequently, the *CITE Journal* provides a venue in which teacher educators can locate information relevant to integration of technology in their own subject areas and also identify corresponding perspectives in other content specializations. In order to make this information readily available to students enrolled in teacher educator programs, the peer-reviewed content of the *CITE Journal* is available electronically without charge (www.CITEjournal.org).

The journal itself has created a cross-disciplinary organization, as it brings together the editors from each section for annual meetings concurrent with the SITE conference. Not only do the editors enjoy vigorous discussions among themselves about the similarities and differences of technology uses in their content areas, but they disseminate their work and experiences by presenting to the wider SITE audience.

As noted previously, the *CITE Journal* co-sponsors with the *Journal of Technology and Teacher Education* annual awards for an "Exemplary Use of Technology to Teach Content in a Methods Course" and an "Exemplary Use of Technology to Teach Content in an Introductory Technology Course." Each year journal editors review nominations and select innovative technology uses that prepare teachers to improve student learning of discipline-based content (e.g., mathematics, science, social studies, and English).

The *CITE Journal* editors provide another important channel of communication between pedagogical content associations and educational technology associations. Because they participate in both the annual meeting of their teacher educator content association and the SITE conference, they are conversant with perspectives in both domains. These ongoing interactions provide opportunities to advance TCPK across disciplines and associations.

Interpreting TPCK across content areas: an NTLC initiative

To refine and articulate TPCK, collaborative work across the disciplines must be conducted with full awareness of the differing goals, inquiry processes, and habits of mind of each content area. One example of such a collaborative effort is the initiative to explore the affordances and constraints of digital images for the core content areas. The process began with an NTLC retreat and culminated with the publication of the book, *Teaching with Digital Images* (ISTE, 2005). At an NTLC retreat, content specialists, methods

Table 13.4 Primary affordances of digital images in the core content areas as delineated in the cross-associational publication, *Teaching with Digital Images*

	Science	Math	Language arts	Social studies
Observation	✓			
Contextualization		✓		
Expression			✓	
Object of study				✓

instructors, instructional technologists, and technology industry representatives discussed the unique possibilities that digital images afforded the core content areas and how they might be used to overcome conceptual challenges for students. These conversations were followed by the preparation of a book intended for teachers and teacher educators. The volume addresses issues native to the medium (e.g., copyright, editing tools, and techniques) and thoroughly explores its application to each content area. The process illustrated a pattern: in each core content area, digital images have a common use but satisfy different instructional needs (Table 13.4).

The common use across the content areas is visualization. Through digital images and digital video, students can record, view, explore, and manipulate visual representations of curricular concepts. In science instruction, for example, digital images can help students overcome problems of scale: small objects (e.g., a bee's wing) can become large; large objects (e.g., floodplains) can become small; slow processes (e.g., the growth of crystals) can be sped up, and fast processes (e.g., a solar eclipse) can be slowed down. This alteration of the physical or temporal scale allows students to grasp concepts that otherwise might be inaccessible or confusing. The use of visualization in science class, then, helps overcome a problem of *observation*: without the support of the digital imaging technology, students will not be able to observe clearly the objects or processes being studied.

In mathematics classes, on the other hand, the primary task of digital images is one of providing real-world *contexts* to abstractions. The concept of slope, for example, can be applied to rooflines; area and approximation can be explored using tree leaves. Through digital images, mathematics teachers can help students situate mathematics concepts in their daily observations and actions and not just in textbook diagrams.

In language arts, digital images can be used to address the problem of *expression*. Students who struggle with text can use images or video as a bridge to textual comprehension or as a bridge to writing. Finally, social studies teachers' use of digital images might address any of these problems of observation, contextualization, or expression. Additionally, in history classes, the images may themselves be part of the content being studied (see Table 13.4).

Future cross-disciplinary collaborations will help map the affordances and constraints of different technologies for the specific pedagogical challenges faced by content area instructors. Unified, thorough explorations such as *Teaching with Digital Images* will help articulate TPCK, especially as it varies across the content areas.

NTLC editors: working within the incentive structure

The NTLC editors, representing six of the leading educational technology journals and periodicals, are an important component of the cross-disciplinary strategy of the NTLC. Journals and periodicals represented by editors who participate in NTLC activities currently include:

- *Journal of Research on Technology in Education (JRTE)*
- *Journal of Computing in Teacher Education (JCTE)*
- *Learning and Leading with Technology*
- *Computers in the Schools*
- *Journal of Technology and Teacher Education (JTATE)*
- *Contemporary Issues in Technology and Teacher Education (CITE Journal)*

The interaction and collaboration of NTLC editors with leaders from pedagogical content associations plays an important role in advancing the goals of the coalition. Editors of educational technology journals most often come into contact with those who have chosen educational technology for their career—educational technology coordinators at the K-12 level, and instructional technology faculty members (for example) at the post-secondary level. Consequently, the opportunity for in-depth discussions that have pedagogical content knowledge as a focus provides a way of gaining greater insight into this perspective and places the editors in a position to better facilitate needed work.

There are equal benefits to participants from content associations. The existing incentive structure is a strong potential barrier to cross-associational collaboration, since faculty members typically advance through publication and presentation within their own professional disciplines. Consequently, participation in cross-disciplinary collaborations requires addition of one or more professional meetings beyond those within their home associations, with the associated extra time and expense. Collaboration and interaction with a coalition of journal editors from leading educational technology periodicals provides an opportunity to gain insight in needed research and publications, at least from the perspectives of these editors. This opportunity may be particularly valuable for those who have chosen technology as an emphasis or focus of their careers.

Establishing bridges between educational technology editors and the editors of the content association journals is critical. The focus of other activities during the formative years of the cross-associational collaborations described has limited these interactions to date—although in one instance, an article was simultaneously co-published in an educational technology journal and a science and mathematics education journal in order to reach the constituents of both associations. However, there are many additional opportunities that could potentially accrue from this type of dialog in the future.

The most important outcome is collective identification and dissemination of activities judged to be crucial for advancing the field of educational technology as it pertains to teacher preparation and learning outcomes in schools. Many of these collaborative outcomes have been communicated in a series of editorials jointly authored by the NTLC editors (Bull, Knezek, Robyler, Schrum, & Thompson, 2005; Schrum *et al.*, 2005; Thompson, Bell, & Bull, 2005). These editorials have appeared in the *Journal of Research on Technology in Education* (JRTE), the *Journal of Computing in Teacher Education* (JCTE), the *Journal of Technology and Teacher Education* (JTATE), and *Contemporary Issues in Technology and Teacher Education* (CITE Journal). This coverage provides a means of reaching many of those who have an interest in educational technology and teacher preparation. A natural next step would be to extend the dialog to the journals of the teacher educator content associations.

Summary

In the absence of dialog across disciplines, there is little opportunity to develop a unified direction of research or implement findings regarding TPCK-related best practice in teacher preparation programs. Efforts to establish cross-disciplinary organizational structures represent a deliberate attempt to ensure that preservice and in-service teachers develop TPCK and that the potential of technology to facilitate learning in specific content areas will be realized through successful curriculum-based technology integration in classrooms.

The founding of the NTLC, the establishment of standing technology committees within the pedagogical content area associations, the establishment of awards for exemplary papers on use of technology, the founding of a cross-disciplinary journal, and collaborative work related to facilitating research in the core content areas all represent activities designed to ensure that our field's understanding of TCPK continues to expand.

References

Bull, G., Knezek, G., Robyler, M., Schrum, L., & Thompson, A. (2005). A proactive approach to a research agenda for educational technology. *Journal of Research on Technology in Education, 37*(3), 217–220.

Dugdale, S. (1998). A spreadsheet investigation of sequences and series for middle grades through precalculus. *Journal of Computers in Mathematics and Science Teaching, 17*(2/3), 203–222.

Flick, L., & Bell, R. (2000). Preparing tomorrow's science teachers to use technology: Guidelines for science educators. *Contemporary Issues in Technology and Teacher Education* [Online serial], *1* (1). Retrieved August 2, 2006, from http://www.citejournal.org/vol1/iss1/currentissues/science/article1.htm.

Garofalo, J., Drier, H., Harper, S., Timmerman, M. A., & Shockey, T. (2000). Promoting appropriate uses of technology in mathematics teacher preparation. *Contemporary Issues in Technology and Teacher Education* [Online serial], *1* (1). Retrieved August 2, 2006, from http://www.citejournal.org/vol1/iss1/currentissues/mathematics/article1.htm.

Koehler, M. J., & Mishra, P. (2005). What happens when teachers design educational technology? The development of technological pedagogical content knowledge. *Journal of Educational Computing Research, 32*(2), 131–152.

Lambert, J. (2003). *Digital storytelling cookbook and traveling companion.* Berkeley, CA: Digital Diner Press.

Mason, C., Berson, M., Diem, R., Hicks, D., Lee, J., & Dralle, T. (2000). Guidelines for using technology to prepare social studies teachers. *Contemporary Issues in Technology and Teacher Education* [Online serial], *1*(1). Retrieved August 2, 2006, from http://www.citejournal.org/vol1/iss1/currentissues/socialstudies/article1.htm.

Pope, C., & Golub, J. (2000). Preparing tomorrow's English language arts teachers today: Principles and practices for infusing technology. *Contemporary Issues in Technology and Teacher Education* [Online serial], *1*(1). Retrieved August 2, 2006, from http://www.citejournal.org/vol1/iss1/currentissues/english/article1.htm.

Schrum, L., Thompson, A., Sprague, D., Maddux, C., McAnear, A., Bell, L., & Bull, G. (2005). Advancing the field: Considering acceptable evidence in educational technology research. *Contemporary Issues in Technology and Teacher Education, 5*(3/4), 202–220.

Shulman, L. S. (1986). Those who understand: Knowledge growth in teaching. *Educational Researcher, 15*(2), 4–14.

Sprague, D. (2004). Technology and teacher education: Are we talking to ourselves? *Contemporary Issues in Technology and Teacher Education, 3*(4), 353–361.

Thompson, A., Bull, G., & Bell, L. (2005). A proactive approach to a research agenda: A call to action. *Journal of Research on Technology in Education, 21*(3), 74–76.

Afterword: TPCK action for teacher education
It's about time!

THE AACTE COMMITTEE ON INNOVATION AND

TECHNOLOGY (ANN D. THOMPSON, KIM BOYD,

KEVIN CLARK, JOEL A. COLBERT, SHARON GUAN,

JUDITH B. HARRIS, AND MARIO ANTONIO KELLY)

The contents of this book suggest that technological pedagogical content knowledge is the key to successful curriculum-based technology integration. Each chapter author has carefully explained TPCK within his/her chapter's context. Given this detailed analysis of TPCK, with reference to curriculum content, teaching experiences, and digital equity, it is now time to reconsider, reconceptualize, and revise goals, processes, and policies for technology in teacher education to accommodate and express this new understanding of teachers' professional knowledge. As the title suggests, the final chapter of this book focuses on using the material from each of the previous chapters as a basis for action toward significant change in teacher education programs, courses, structures, and procedures. We begin with a description of a new direction for teacher education programs suggested by the contents of this book and then summarize several unifying themes that inform this call to action. The chapter concludes with specific recommendations for teacher educators working to assist both preservice and in-service teachers as they build TPCK.

New direction for technology in teacher education

Taken together, the chapters of this book point clearly toward a new direction for educating teachers about the effective use of educational technologies in their classrooms. Although a quarter century has passed since Richard Clark suggested that, "Media are mere vehicles that deliver instruction but do not influence student achievement any more than the truck that delivers our groceries causes changes in nutrition" (Clark, 1983, p. 445), teacher educators have continued to focus upon technology as a discrete subject, and teacher education in educational technology use has consisted primarily of learning about various tools and resources. Clark's insights have been applied to some extent to research on technology use in education, but applying this insight to teacher education has proven to be a wicked problem. Although numerous researchers have suggested that knowledge of technology is not enough for meaningful integration into learning and teaching, in both in-service and pre-service teacher education technocentric approaches to educating teachers have continued to dominate practice. "It's not about the technology" is a familiar statement to teacher educators who are keen to integrate technology in their practice and to inspire their students to do the same, but changing professional development to enact this idea has been problematic. We believe that the frame presented in this book provides a useful way to reconceptualize the interdependent technological, pedagogical, and content knowledge needed to understand and develop specific technologically facilitated practices that address the curriculum-based learning needs of an increasingly diverse student population.

One of the major premises underlying most of the chapters in this book is that individual teachers must work as *designers* to create the most appropriate technologically inclusive learning plans in their subject areas with their students. Throughout the book, chapter authors suggest that teacher education programs must work to help both preservice and in-service teachers to develop such adapted design skills. The "wickedness" of the problem (Rittel & Weber, 1973) specific to TPCK and teacher education rests in the demand that teachers develop the skills to design technologically integrated instruction in time-efficient ways, with the acknowledgment that teacher education programs therefore cannot provide "recipes" or scripts on how to teach with educational technologies.

Beginning in Chapter 1, the T in TPCK is defined broadly and includes all types of educational technologies. Koehler and Mishra suggest that newer, digital technologies may require a greater level of thought and work on the part of teachers seeking to integrate them into their teaching. Teacher educators, however, need to be sensitive to the fact that all technologies—digital and nondigital—have pedagogical affordances and constraints, and in that sense the TPCK framework can be applied to any technology. Thus, teacher education programs may seek to develop TPCK in a gradual and spiral-like manner, beginning possibly with more standard and familiar technologies (with which teachers may already have developed TPCK), and moving on to more advanced or non-familiar technological tools and resources.

This book provides both a theoretical frame for TPCK and specific applications as well as interpretations of this frame in each of the primary content areas taught in K-12 schools. The design-based, curriculum-keyed contents of the book imply a call to action for teacher education programs to restructure technology experiences for both preservice and in-service teachers. The authors agree that TPCK can provide the conceptual frame for moving teachers toward effective and meaningful applications of technology that are directed at improving both learning and teaching. Each content-area chapter also includes specific ideas and approaches for fostering teachers' TPCK.

Unifying themes

Although the majority of the chapters in this book focus on explicating TPCK within particular content areas, there are several themes that appear across chapters that can inform the directions in which the authors of this book believe that teacher education as a whole should move. These themes include:

- The acknowledgment that developing and using TPCK is a wicked and significant problem for both teachers and teacher educators.
- The need to use TPCK throughout the teacher education curriculum as a conceptual frame to help preservice and in-service teachers fully integrate the use of all types of educational technologies in their teaching.
- The importance of context in helping teachers to develop TPCK and the insistence upon and celebration of the potential of the individual teacher to make powerful, effective design decisions about tool and resource use in his/her classroom.
- The potential for teachers to use TPCK to effectively address students' diverse learning needs.
- The importance of teachers understanding the changing lives of children with respect to technology, including how children interact with technologies in ways that are qualitatively different than teachers' technological encounters and histories.

Using examples from individual chapters, we now develop each of these themes individually in preparation for providing specific suggestions for teacher education practitioners and programs.

The acknowledgment that developing and using meaningful technology integration is a wicked and significant problem for both teachers and teacher educators

Beginning with Koehler and Mishra's definition of a wicked problem in Chapter 1, each content area chapter author has acknowledged the complexity and ill-structured nature of achieving meaningful technology integration within each content area. Each author uses the TPCK model to clearly define each component of the problem, and each also acknowledges the interactions and interdependence of each of the parts of the model. Thus, all authors use the TPCK model as a conceptual frame to help identify the interrelated components involved in successful technology integration and some of the dynamic relationships among technology, content, and pedagogy. For example, in the mathematics chapter, Grandgenett, explains how technology has altered the content in mathematics and how this relationship illustrates the interdependence of technology and content in the model. He suggests that knowledge of topics such as fractals, statistics, graphing, coordinate geometry, matrices, probability, combinatorics, and many others are in an ongoing state of change and evolution and that much of this change can be related to new technologies.

Similarly, in the chapter on TPCK for English education, Hughes and Scharber illustrate how the advent and increased use of technology lead to the call for the redefinition and reconceptualization of literacy. The portrayal of developing and using TPCK as a wicked and significant problem for both teachers and teacher educators is also prevalent in the chapter on K-6 literacy. Schmidt and Gurbo suggest that technology has not only changed the definition of literacy, it has changed the way we read. Students who access information on the Internet use different decoding and reading strategies as they follow hyperlink after hyperlink that lead to information about a specific topic. As researchers grapple with defining literacy in the context of TPCK, Schmidt and Gurbo describe the process as a "moving target" that continually changes according to what society expects from a literate person. Literacy will constantly be redefined as new technologies emerge and as expectations change for what it means to be literate. In all three examples, the complex and dynamic relationship of technology and content is emphasized.

Though technology-related teacher education has been over-simplified historically by focusing upon primarily operational knowledge of particular educational technologies, each of our authors acknowledges the complexity of effective technology integration, using TPCK as a tool to define and address this issue. Through carefully defining the nature of content and pedagogy in each curriculum area, each author describes a similar, but disciplinarily differentiated notion of TPCK in action. Acknowledging, understanding, and accepting these differences mark a significant step forward for teacher educators. Within TPCK's frame, technology integration is no longer a broadly generalizable set of skills and concepts. Instead, it emerges differently within each curriculum specialization, pedagogical approach, and learning context. In this book, TPCK becomes a tool for providing multiple, differentiated solutions to one cross-disciplinary, wicked problem.

Implicit in the acknowledgment of the wickedness of the technology integration problem is the suggestion that teacher education programs have tended to over-simplify how technology integration is addressed, as was stated above. The classic example of this over-simplification was the separation of educational technology as a field of study for preservice and in-service teachers. Examples of these phenomena include single courses on technology applications for preservice teachers and workshops on how to use particular tools for in-service teachers. Understanding TPCK and acknowledging the reality of comparatively well-equipped classrooms in which educational technologies are used either infrequently, ineffectively, or both makes it clear that these approaches focused upon the "T" and tended to ignore content, pedagogy, and the reciprocal "essential tension" among these components.

The need to use TPCK throughout the teacher education curriculum as a conceptual frame to help preservice and in-service teachers fully integrate the use of all types of educational technologies in their teaching

Material presented in this book suggests that reframing the development of teacher knowledge in both in-service and preservice teacher education programs to accommodate TPCK is a logical step in the reform of teacher education programs. Focusing on developing curriculum and pedagogy within content areas that are rooted in TCPK will allow teachers to build the knowledge and skill necessary for them to develop meaningful learning experiences for their students that integrate technology use effectively.

To affect this conceptual shift in teacher education practice, content-based and educational technology professional organizations must collaborate across disciplinary, epistemological, and pragmatic boundaries to explore and disseminate the technological content and technological pedagogical knowledge necessary for the effective TPCK development that Koehler and Mishra describe in Chapter 1. In a sense, collaborations among these heretofore pedagogically independent professional organizations must reflect the interdependence of the TPCK model itself. Bull, Bell, and Hammond describe, in Chapter 13, such interorganizational efforts that are already underway and that show much promise.

Using TPCK can shift the emphasis away from focusing upon technology itself and toward appropriate applications of technologies of all types within curriculum areas, based upon operational knowledge of the unique affordances and constraints of particular tools and resources used for learning in particular content areas. As Koehler and Mishra describe in Chapter 1, technologies are not neutral additions to classrooms. By virtue of their affordances and constraints, they concomitantly facilitate and restrict different types of learning and teaching within each content area. Therefore, teacher educators must assist both preservice and in-service teachers in understanding and utilizing these affordances and constraints in both planning and teaching. In the chapter on TPCK for English Education, Hughes and Scharber illustrate, through literature review and case studies, various ways for preservice and in-service teachers to acquire skills in TPCK development. They emphasize that content-focused technology learning experiences can yield content-based technology integration in the classroom. Although defining K-6 TPCK literacy is complex, Schmidt and Gurbo provide numerous rich resources and examples for teachers and teacher educators who are willing to take ownership of their responsibilities for developing TPCK in K-6 literacy. Examples include the use of electronic or talking books to serve as motivational tools for struggling readers; the use of digital still and digital video cameras to enhance visual literacy; the use of educational software such as GoKnow to provide opportunities for children to write and draw; and the use of learning tools such as Inspiration and Kidspiration to create graphic representations for many literacy learning tasks. Additionally, the authors present three case studies describing teachers integrating technology throughout entire lessons, providing models for teachers who perhaps are struggling with what it looks like to authentically implement TPCK in K-6 literacy lessons.

Similarly, Luke Kelly details specific curriculum-based ideas for developing TPCK in the physical education curriculum in his chapter. He suggests that teachers need to develop skills to use technology as individual assessment tools for students, and points out that new video technologies provide rich possibilities for collecting data on student progress in physical education competencies.

Several chapter authors suggest that teachers should be taught to use technologies to carry out activities that would otherwise be impossible to accomplish and that this type of focus moves the attention from the technology to the content and pedagogy. van Olphen, author of the chapter on world languages, indicates that world language students often cannot afford to study abroad and are not being exposed to the artistic works housed in museums such as the Louvre, the Prado, or even national art galleries. In this case, a virtual tour of a museum or another culturally relevant place can provide students with a better understanding of their target language. Both van Olphen and Grandgenett reinforce the point that teacher educators must help future teachers think imaginatively about new ways in which technology can support learning and teaching in their content areas.

Content-rich technology learning experiences gained through professional development programs and/or collaboration with colleagues can assist practicing teachers with existing content and pedagogical knowledge to develop TPCK. This can help them to make instructional decisions that put the technologies into students' hands for learning content-based concepts. Focusing upon developing TPCK will help teacher educators move away from approaches that treat technology as a separate subject area that is uniformly applicable across all curriculum areas.

The importance of context in helping teachers to develop TPCK, and the insistence upon and celebration of the potential of the individual teacher to make powerful, effective design decisions about tool and resource use in his/her classroom

The need to view teachers as designers and to provide them with the skills necessary for effective design of instructional activities is a recurring theme in this book. Our authors agree that the nature of the wicked problem—effective technology integration—requires that individual teachers design and implement customized uses of technology in their teaching. Since there are no generalizable solutions to the problem of technology integration in different content areas and for students' differing learning needs, it is the job of the individual teacher to combine his/her knowledge of content, pedagogy, and technology to offer effective teaching and ensure meaningful learning in his/her particular context. As teachers develop TPCK during their preservice and in-service experiences, they are forming the knowledge necessary to design effective, contextually sensitive learning environments for their students.

Throughout this book, teachers are viewed as creative designers who work to meet the individual needs of learners. Both Chapters 10 and 11 emphasize the notion of teachers as designers. In the chapter on TPCK in preservice education, for example, Niess emphasizes the need to educate preservice teachers as designers and provide specific opportunities for them to practice this skill. In the chapter on TPCK for English education, Hughes and Scharber present cases on teachers' ability to adjust their teaching strategies and uses of technological tools based upon instructional goals, technical resource availability, and their own comfort levels with different technologies. In the chapter on TPCK for in-service teachers, Harris offers a particular professional development approach that is differentiated for experienced, rather than novice teachers: the overt identification of content-based, technologically inclusive learning activity types to use as tools for instructional design. In the science chapter, McCrory contextualizes the need to educate teachers to become designers when she asserts that

> No matter what technologies are used or what topics are taught, the goal can be to equip teachers with the knowledge, skills, and dispositions to try new technologies and to learn from their own experience; to anticipate problems that may arise and to persist in using technology in ways that support their students' learning.

The design-based ideas included in the chapters of this book suggest that teachers can select among and combine curriculum-keyed activity types and approaches, each of which is supported by a defined range of technological tools and resources, using them as design aids instead of seeking out and following previously created recipes for curriculum-based learning experiences for students.

The potential for teachers to use TPCK to effectively address students' diverse learning needs

As preservice and in-service teachers develop TPCK and experience designing context-specific technology applications for their classrooms, they will also expand their abilities to meet the diverse needs of their students. The emphasis on teacher as designer throughout this book recognizes the need for teachers to adapt technology applications to the specific and sometimes individual needs of their students. In the chapter on bridging digital and cultural divides, Mario Antonio Kelly focuses on designing technology applications for a context that is typical of many American classrooms—students diverse in their ethnicity, socio-economic status, home language, and culture. He argues that these context elements must be incorporated into teachers' TPCK applications if they are to be effective with all children, and provides specific suggestions and examples to encourage teachers to use technology to foster equitable learning contexts.

Kelly discusses the concept of attribute-treatment-interaction in his chapter and suggests that it is the responsibility of the teacher to deduce which instructional strategies will be the most compatible with individual student's learning styles to result in the highest achievement. The individualized instruction suggested by the concept of attribute-treatment-interaction can be facilitated by appropriately differentiated technology use. Similarly, TPCK can assist teachers in designing classroom instruction that includes the basics of good teaching and avoids a "pedagogy of poverty."

In the social studies chapter, Lee provides specific examples for how teachers can effectively address the diverse needs of their students through the use of TPCK. Lee argues that social studies is the study of subject matter directed at civic preparation and that technology use provides opportunities for teachers to better address the individual needs of students in the learning of social studies. He notes the following TPCK-related prerequisites for representing and adapting the use of social studies-related resources:

- Teachers locating and adapting digital resources.
- Teachers facilitating their students' work in non-linear environments.
- Teachers developing critical media literacy skills.
- Teachers providing students with opportunities to utilize the presentational capabilities of the Web.
- Teachers using the Internet to extend collaboration and communication among students.
- Teachers extending and promoting active and authentic forms of human interaction using networked technologies.

Lee provides specific strategies for how each of these activities can be accomplished so that social studies teachers who are committed to the use of TPCK will have both a feasible plan and appropriate resources to help them prepare students for participation in our democratic civic culture. Similarly, Grandgenett suggests that TPCK can help mathematics teachers develop strategies that will better meet the individual needs of students and better address the different ways in which students learn mathematics. Ultimately, TPCK can help all teachers to provide more appropriately differentiated experiences so that more children learn curriculum-based content and process in meaningful, culturally competent ways.

The importance of teachers understanding the changing lives of children
with respect to technology, including how children interact with
technologies in ways that are qualitatively different than teachers'
technological encounters and histories

Several of the authors of this book's chapters have described the emerging divide between children's and teachers' experiences with and attitudes toward technology, and the resulting need to better connect the technological worlds of children and teachers. In recent years, both researchers and educators have acknowledged the divide between generations with respect to digital capabilities. Mark Prensky (2001) described the situation quite vividly when he pointed out that young people tend to be natives to the digital world, while older people come to digital technologies as immigrants. He suggests that "if Digital Immigrant educators really want to reach Digital Natives—i.e. all their students—they will have to change" (p. 6).

Specific strategies for addressing this challenge are described in this book. In the chapter on preservice teacher education, Niess suggests using case studies to help preservice teachers examine technology use in a variety of classrooms. She suggests engaging preservice teachers in research groups to conduct focused, field-based observations in multiple classrooms in which students are using technological tools for learning. The groups then develop a unit, including technological possibilities, actively in the decision-making process. Niess's suggestion to provide authentic opportunities to connect preservice teachers with the realities of technology use in schools provides a feasible way to educate preservice teachers about children's relationships with technology.

In the TPCK in the arts chapter, DePlatchett argues that the lives of children today are infused with media and that teachers need to use this reality in their teaching. She suggests teachers are finding media projects to offer appropriate vehicles through which students can communicate and share ideas and opinions in creative and exciting formats. DePlatchett suggests that the challenge is for teachers to stay current with available media tools and to integrate those tools into instruction so that students engage in learning projects that are standards-based, creative, and collaborative. Her example of Maryland teacher Jim Lipiano, who created a high school computer graphics program that integrates media skill development with reading and creative writing, traditional and online research, mathematics, art history, and design principles, provides a realistic view of the possibilities of engaging learners through curriculum-based, arts-related technology use.

Recommendations for teacher educators

The contents of this book suggest several rather radical changes for teacher education programs' approaches to technology integration. Although most address educational technologies, most also tend to treat technology as a separate topic or in a separate course. In many cases, educational technology faculty work in their own department, which may or may not be part of the teacher education program. The frame of TPCK suggests that these separations between technology and content areas do not provide teacher education students with the TPCK they need for successful technology-integrated teaching. The contents of this book clearly suggest that technology is not separate from content nor pedagogy and that teacher education programs need to create structures and experiences that support and reflect the integration and interdependence of technology, pedagogy, and content.

This realization may suggest that teacher education programs do not need more faculty members with expertise solely in educational technology, but rather that they need content area specialists who know how to model and encourage the development of TPCK. Separate technology departments, sections, and courses do not seem to be appropriate structures for developing TPCK. Should decision-makers opt to act in accordance with this supposition, it is probable that instituting this type of structural change will be challenging for educational technologists and content area faculty alike. Educational technology faculty will need to develop content expertise relative to TPCK, while content area faculty members will need to develop TPCK expertise relative to their disciplinary specializations.

Beyond this rather radical notion of restructuring the basis of teacher educators' professional knowledge and work, the contents of this book suggest several very specific recommendations for teacher educators and teacher education programs that can be used as stepping stones to the restructuring recommendation presented above. We believe that teacher education programs need to:

- Move away from offering technology experiences and courses in isolation and toward providing these experiences within content area courses.
- Work with teacher education faculty members to define and implement TPCK within each of the content area methods courses.
- Emphasize the concept of teacher as designer in both preservice and in-service teacher education experiences.
- Hire new content area teacher education and arts and sciences faculty who have rich design experiences with educational technologies.
- Help teacher educators and both preservice and in-service teachers understand the affordances and constraints of the complete range of educational technologies in each of the content areas.

- Help teacher educators and both preservice and in-service teachers understand the nature of the wicked TPCK problem, along with context-dependence of their multiple solutions to the problem.
- Foster research and development work on the development of TPCK and the effectiveness of teachers who have and demonstrate TPCK.

Clearly, there is much substantive change recommended here. To best effect these changes within and across existing educational organizations requires levels of interdisciplinary and interorganizational collaboration typically not experienced to date in either pre-K-12 or higher education contexts, much less between or among them. Yet given the interdependent nature of the TPCK framework itself, these collaborations are not just recommended; they are *required*. By their very nature, these types of teacher knowledge can only be developed in highly collaborative, cogenerative professional working contexts and relationships.

Conceptualizing, developing, researching, and teaching technology integration as TPCK *requires* close collaboration among university, school, and community partners in multiple disciplines. Without equal, adaptable contributions from content specialists, practicing educators, assessment specialists, and technologists, TPCK-based research, development, and practice cannot hope to yield useful results.

Summary and conclusion

Although the idea of technology integration is not new to most teacher educators, the notion of technological pedagogical content knowledge is epistemologically distinct and probably foreign. The work in this book marks a major step forward in the application of TPCK to both preservice and in-service teacher education programs. Through defining and providing examples of TPCK within each subject area, this book moves the concept of TPCK beyond theory and toward practice. The chapters on equity of access and preservice and in-service teacher education operationalize this practical explication of the concept to provide effective, equitable TPCK-based professional development to assist this transition. The chapter on collaboration across professional organizations relative to TPCK provides a similarly effective national-level approach to leadership and development for TPCK in teacher education.

This book demonstrates specifically how TPCK can be incorporated throughout preservice and in-service teacher education programs and what it might look like in practice. Taken together, the chapters in this book are a call to action for teacher educators to reconceptualize the role of technology in teacher education.

References

Clark, R. E. (1983). Reconsidering research on learning from media. *Review of Educational Research, 43*(4), 445–459.

Prensky, M. (2001). Digital natives, digital immigrants. *On the Horizon, 9*(5), 1–6.

Rittel. H., & Webber, M. (1973). Dilemmas in a general theory of planning. *Policy Sciences, 4*(2), 155–169.

About the AACTE Committee on Innovation and Technology

The American Association of Colleges for Teacher Education (AACTE) Committee on Innovation and Technology is charged to develop the Association's classroom reform and technology agendas as it relates to K-12 and postsecondary education. The Committee should promote the use of innovative strategies and technological interventions in schools and professional education preparation contexts through gathering information about resources and uses; providing leadership related to professional preparation; and facilitating communication and interaction about innovations in learning and technology among faculty in schools, colleges, and departments of education (SCDEs) through the dissemination of proven methods and processes in professional education. The Committee's work includes but is not limited to the activities listed below:

- To assist AACTE in developing informed public policy regarding the application of technology in professional education programs;
- To assist AACTE in exploring broader questions raised by innovation and reform for teaching, learning, and the preparation of teachers; and
- To monitor and disseminate the information about best practices in educational practice.

About the contributors

Lynn Bell works with the Center for Technology and Teacher Education at the University of Virginia. She is co-editor of the online journal *Contemporary Issues in Technology and Teacher Education* with Glen L. Bull. She also co-edited the book *Teaching With Digital Images: Acquire, Analyze, Create, Communicate* (Bull & Bell, 2005), and is currently working with the National Technology Leadership Coalition on a book entitled *Framing Research on Technology and Student Learning in the Content Areas: Implications for Teacher Educators.*

Kim Boyd (AACTE Innovation and Technology Committee Member) has served as Associate Dean of the School of Education since 1998. Previous to her current position she served for over nine years as an instructor/professor in the School of Education and over eight years as a classroom teacher in the Sapulpa Public Schools. Dr. Boyd received her doctorate degree in Curriculum and Instruction from Oklahoma State University. Her Masters degree is in Reading from Northeastern State University and her Bachelors Degree is from Oral Roberts University. She has been a professional educator serving as a teacher and professor in elementary and postsecondary education since 1979.

M. Christopher Brown II is Professor and Dean of the College of Education at the University of Nevada, Las Vegas. He previously served as Vice President for Programs and Administration at the American Association of Colleges for Teacher Education, Director of Social Justice and Professional Development for the American Educational Research Association (AERA), as well as Executive Director and Chief Research Scientist of the Frederick D. Patterson Research Institute of the United Negro College Fund. Dr. Brown earned a national reputation for his research and scholarly writing on education policy and administration. He is especially well known for his studies of historically black colleges, educational equity, and institutional culture. Dr. Brown is the author/editor of 12 books and more than 100 other journal articles, book chapters, monographs, and publications related to education and society. He earned the B.S. in Elementary Education from South Carolina State University, the M.S.Ed. in Educational Policy and Evaluation from the University of Kentucky, and the Ph.D. in Higher Education from The Pennsylvania State University with a cognate in public administration and political science.

Glen Bull is a Professor of instructional technology in the Curry School of Education at the University of Virginia. In the 1970s he taught the first educational computing courses offered in the Curry School. In the 1980s he participated in a reorganization of the Curry School in which educational technology was designated as one of three strands integrated throughout the teacher education program. The Curry School subsequently became the recipient of the first American Association of Colleges for Teacher Education (AACTE) *Innovative Use of Technology Award.*

He is a founding member and past president of the Virginia Society for Technology in Education (VSTE) and a recipient of VSTE's *Honors of the Association.* He also is a founding member and past president of the Society for Information Technology and Teacher Education (SITE). He was the first recipient of the Willis Award for *Outstanding Lifetime Achievement in Technology and Teacher Education.* He currently serves as editor of the journal, *Contemporary Issues in Technology and Teacher Education,* and is co-director of the Curry Center for Technology and Teacher Education.

Bobby L. Cato, Jr., received his B.S. in Elementary Education from North Carolina A & T State University and M.S.A. in Educational Administration and Policy from Trinity College. A former classroom teacher, K-12 Technology Administrator and Director of Technology Programming and Initiatives for AACTE, he has trained hundreds of teachers in school systems across the country on how to integrate digital technologies into the classroom. Mr. Cato has a passion for developing initiatives that will provide equity and access to technology for disadvantaged youth. He ardently works to establish after-school programs focusing on helping disadvantaged students obtain computer skills and serves as a consultant in a variety of education and technological communication arenas.

Kevin Clark (AACTE Innovation and Technology Committee Member) is an Associate Professor of Education in the College of Education and Human Development at George Mason University. Dr. Clark has been involved in the design and development of innovative educational software and online learning environments for more than 12 years. Dr. Clark is currently the Program Coordinator of the Instructional Technology program, and has authored several publications and made numerous presentations regarding digital equity, online learning environments, and the role of gaming in education.

Dr. Clark's scholarly activities include conducting a needs analysis of community technology centers, bridging the digital divide using self-directed learning communities, examining online study groups, and identifying best practices in technology integration in schools. Dr. Clark's current research project examines the use of gaming to improve the motivation and achievement of students with science and mathematics content.

Dr. Clark and his work have been honored by the Education Techno-logy Think Tank and the Congressional Black Caucus Education Brain-trust for his outstanding technology leadership in the community, and has been selected as a Fulbright Senior Specialist Roster Candidate. For more information, please go to http://mason.gmu.edu/~kclark6

Joel A. Colbert (AACTE Innovation and Technology Committee Member), Professor and Director of the Ph.D. program in Education at Chapman University, is a lifelong educator. He earned his Ed.D. in Curriculum and Instruction, with a specialization in science education, from the University of Kansas.

He began his teaching career as a classroom teacher in south central Los Angeles. Prior to coming to Chapman University, he was a Professor of Clinical Education and Director of the Undergraduate and Teacher Educa-tion Program at the University of Southern California. Prior to that he was on the faculty and an administrator at California State University, Dominguez Hills.

His research interests include using case studies in teacher education, science education, and technological pedagogical content knowledge. He is very active in professional organizations, serving as Vice President of the California Council on Teacher Education (CCTE) and Chair of the Ameri-can Association of Colleges of Teacher Education (AACTE) Committee on Innovation and Technology.

He teaches and advises students in the Ph.D. program.

Nancy DePlatchett is currently the Curriculum Advisor for ARTSEDGE, The Nations Arts and Education Website at The John F. Kennedy Center for the Performing Arts in Washington, DC. She is also an adjunct professor at Montgomery College in Rockville, Maryland in the Department of Educa-tion. Nancy taught visual arts to elementary school students in Puerto Rico and to middle and high school students in Prince George's County Public Schools in Maryland. She helped open the Thomas Pullen K-8 Creative and Performing Arts School in Prince George's County where she served as Arts Coordinator for 13 years. During this time she was honored as one of the County's Outstanding Teachers and also received the Outstanding Educator Award from the Prince George's County Chamber of Commerce. She also received two National Endowment for the Humanities summer grants, was named one of the *Outstanding Women In The Arts* by the Women's Commission of Maryland, and one of the *Women of Achieve-ment* in Prince George's County History. Nancy has presented at numer-ous conferences, at workshops for various school systems, and at the Kennedy Center's Professional Development Opportunities For Teachers Workshops. She has acted as a consultant to various school systems including the American School in São Paulo, Brazil, the Alexandria Public

Schools in Virginia, and the Montgomery County Public Schools in Maryland. Recently she spoke to the arts community in Montevideo, Uruguay as the guest of the American Embassy. Her graduate and undergraduate work was done at Edinboro University of Pennsylvania. As a visual artist Nancy's interests are many and she currently creates jewelry and fabric arts.

Neal F. Grandgenett is the Peter Kiewit Distinguished Professor of Education at the University of Nebraska at Omaha. His research interests include the examination of technology-based learning environments for mathematics and science and he has authored nearly 100 articles and research papers related to those topics. He has directed numerous externally funded technology-based learning projects for NASA, NSF, the U.S. Department of Education, and various private foundations. Many of these funded projects have focused on the use of the Internet in instruction, collaboration, and online coursework. He has worked particularly closely with NASA Education on several educational technology-related curriculum development efforts including the Jet Propulsion Laboratory's DataSlate project, the NASA Learners Project, and NASA's Earth System Science Education Alliance. He is a former middle school mathematics teacher and he is currently a co-principal investigator on two NSF-funded educational robotics projects that focus on the teaching of mathematics and science concepts at the middle school level using robotics as motivating context for student learning. Dr. Grandgenett is a frequent program evaluator for federal projects related to mathematics and science education and he has designed and led program evaluations for more than 20 federally funded projects associated with various initiatives from NSF, NASA, and the Departments of Education, Labor, and Commerce. He is also a review editor for new software applications in the international *Mathematics and Computer Education Journal* and a frequent writer of educational software reviews for that journal.

Sharon Guan (AACTE Innovation and Technology Committee Member) is the Director of the department of Instructional Design and Development at DePaul University. In this role, she leads a team of instructional technology consultants to provide consultation services to faculty on the use of cognitive theories, instructional design method, and educational technology to enhance teaching and learning. She has been a member AACTE Technology for Teacher Education Committee and is the co-chair of the Portal Governance Board and the Teaching, Learning and Technology Committee at DePaul. She has published/presented research papers on learning science, online course design, game-based education, language education, ePortfolio, and faculty development. Dr. Guan received her undergraduate degree in International Journalism from Beijing Broadcasting Institute and her Masters and Ph.D. degree in Curriculum, Instruction and Educational Technology from Indiana State University.

Marina Gurbo is a senior expert for InVITe Consulting, Ltd, in Riga, Latvia. Her area of expertise is education policy research and analysis. She conducts research on Latvian teacher professional development and education quality evaluation systems, and consults with several projects financed by the European Social Fund on teacher professional development. These latter projects include those focusing on the integration of technology into science teaching in secondary schools, as well as use of technology to improve educational access among socially disadvantaged groups. She also works as an institutional and organizational capacity-building expert for the United Nations Development Program in Riga.

Tom Hammond is an Assistant Professor in the Teaching, Learning, and Technology program at Lehigh University, where he teaches courses in instructional technology and social studies education. He received his doctorate in instructional technology from the University of Virginia. Prior to entering academia, he taught secondary social studies for ten years at schools in the United States, Haiti, and Saudi Arabia.

Judith B. Harris (AACTE Innovation and Technology Committee Member) is a Professor and the Pavey Family Chair in Educational Technology in the School of Education at the College of William & Mary in Virginia, where she coordinates the Curriculum and Educational Technology doctoral program.

Dr. Harris' research and service focus upon K-12 curriculum-based technology integration and teacher professional development. During the past 24 years of her work in educational computing, she has authored *Way of the Ferret: Finding and Using Educational Resources on the Internet* (1994 & 1995, ISTE), one of the first books about K-12 educational use of the Internet; *Virtual Architecture: Designing and Directing Curriculum-Based Telecomputing* (1998 & forthcoming, ISTE); *Design Tools for the Internet-Supported Classroom* (1998, ASCD); and more than 180 research and pedagogical publications on curriculum-based applications of educational technologies. Her work is used by teachers, technology specialists, and teacher educators internationally; especially her "activity structures" method for designing curriculum-based learning activities that incorporate use of online tools and resources. She and colleague Mark Hofer have adapted this notion to introduce content-based "activity types" that help teachers integrate the full spectrum of digital and nondigital tools and resources into planning social studies learning experiences.

Prior to moving to William & Mary in 2002, Dr. Harris served on the faculty of the University of Texas at Austin for ten years, where she founded and directed WINGS Online ("Welcoming Interns and Novices with Guidance and Support Online"), a suite of online services that support new teachers in multiple ways. That work became the foundation of William & Mary's ENDAPT ("Electronic Networking to Develop Accomplished Professional Teachers;" http://endapt.wm.edu/), a second-generation suite of online services for new teachers. Her nonprofit Electronic Emissary (http://emissary.wm.edu/) telementoring service and research effort, begun in 1992, is the longest-running K-12 effort of its kind, and has served students and teachers worldwide.

Joan E. Hughes is an Associate Professor of Instructional Technology in the Curriculum and Instruction department at the University of Texas at Austin. Her research focuses on teachers' technology knowledge, technology integration in K-12 classrooms, technology professional development, and technology leadership. Her research on teacher learning and knowledge has been published in the *Journal of Technology and Teacher Education, Contemporary Issues in Technology and Teacher Education*, and *Action in Teacher Education*. She has published her recent research on technology inquiry groups as a form of professional development in the *Journal of Research on Technology in Education*, while also organizing and chairing an AERA symposium and co-editing a special issue for the *Journal of Educational Computing Research* (vol. 32, n. 4) on "situated professional development programs." At the University of Minnesota (2000–2007), she was a principal investigator of the School Technology Leadership Program, a project federally funded through the Fund for the Improvement of Post-Secondary Education (FIPSE) to develop the first academic program that comprehensively meets the National Educational Technology Standards for Administrators (NETS-A). Research and outcomes from this project have been presented at AERA, published in *Academic Exchange Quarterly, Technological Horizons in Education (T.H.E.)*, and are in preparation for publication. She collaborates with, mentors, and co-authors with numerous Ph.D. students within the Learning Technologies program and across the university (e.g., Rhetoric, Educational Policy and Administration, Educational Psychology). She teaches Ph.D. seminars and Masters-level courses on K-12 Technology Integration such as facilitating technology integration in schools, technology tools for educators, technology planning, and designing and planning technology-supported lessons and curriculum. She earned her Ph.D. in Educational Psychology from Michigan State University and her B.A. in English from Pomona College.

Luke E. Kelly is Professor of Kinesiology, holder of the Virgil S. Ward endowed professorship, director of the graduate programs in adapted physical education, and chief technology officer for the Curry School of

Education at the University of Virginia. He has 30 years of experience working with public schools in evaluating and revising their physical education curricula to meet the needs of students with disabilities. Dr. Kelly has written extensively about the achievement-based curriculum model, assessment, and the use of technology in physical education. Dr. Kelly has served as the president of the National Consortium for Physical Education and Recreation for Individuals with Disabilities (NCPERID) and directed the NCPERID adapted physical education national standards project from1992 to 1999. Dr. Kelly is a fellow in the American Academy of Kinesiology and Physical Education. He has also received the G. Lawrence Rarick Research Award and the William H. Hillman Distinguished Service Award from the NCPERID.

Mario Antonio Kelly (AACTE Innovation and Technology Committee Member) is Associate Professor of educational foundations at Hunter College, City University of New York. His research and teaching interests include minority youth development and achievement, the impact of culture and other issues of diversity on the teaching–learning process, and technology-mediated instruction. He is a co-author of the book, *Challenging the Potential: Programs for Talented Disadvantaged Youth* (Oden, Kelly, Ma, & Weikart, 1991), and frequently presents papers at national and international conferences.

Matthew J. Koehler is an Associate Professor with appointments in the Educational Psychology and Educational Technology program and in the Teacher Education program in the College of Education at Michigan State University. His background includes undergraduate degrees in Computer Science and Mathematics, a Masters degree in Computer Science, and a Ph.D. in Educational Psychology. His research and teaching focus on understanding the affordances and constraints of new technologies; the design of technology-rich, innovative learning environments; and the professional development of teachers. He has collaborated with Punya Mishra to develop theoretical, pedagogical, and methodological perspectives that characterize teachers who effectively integrate content, pedagogy, and technology. He has received over $6 million in grants for his research and development work. He has recently published in several research journals, including *Teachers College Record, Cognition and Instruction, Journal of Technology and Teacher Education, Journal of Computing in Teacher Education*, and the *Journal of Educational Computing Research.*

John K. Lee is an Associate Professor in middle grades social studies education at North Carolina State University. His research is embedded in recent scholarship on technological applications of teachers' pedagogical content knowledge in social studies, most specifically in the emerging field of digital history. Dr. Lee's research includes case studies of teacher practice, empirical investigations of student learning, local and national surveys of teachers' uses of historical resources, and theoretical considerations of the pedagogy of digital history. He has worked over the last several years to help describe and conceptualize general technological applications in social studies as well as in the specific field of digital history. Dr. Lee has authored or co-authored numerous descriptions of teachers' practice using a wide range of technological resources. He also has numerous published empirical research reports on students' learning with digital historical resources. Dr. Lee is the recent recipient of a $500,000 grant from the Fund for the Improvement of Post Secondary Education to investigate the uses of local digital historical resources in social studies teacher education. He is currently editor of the social studies section of the AACE online journal *Contemporary Issues in Technology and Teacher Education.* Dr. Lee also serves on the executive committee of the College and University Faculty Assembly of the National Council for the Social Studies. He has recently served on the advisory committee for the drafting of the 2006 U.S. History Test for the National Assessment for Educational Progress.

Raven McCrory is a graduate of Smith College with a major in mathematics. She completed a Masters degree in mathematics at the University of Massachusetts, and a Ph.D. in education at the University of Michigan. Dr. McCrory's research interests include teacher knowledge for teaching mathematics and science and for teaching with technology; teacher learning in preservice teacher education and professional development settings; and the impact of teacher community on practice. In her current research, she is studying the undergraduate mathematics education of prospective elementary teachers and investigating teacher knowledge for teaching algebra. She is a recipient of the NSF CAREER grant studying the mathematical education of elementary teachers. McCrory is co-PI on the NSF-funded Knowledge of Algebra for Teaching project and co-PI on a project studying National Board certified teachers as a resource for school improvement. McCrory's publications include a book chapter on teaching science with technology (McCrory, R. (2006). Technology and teaching: A new kind of knowledge. In E. Ashburn & R. Floden (eds), *Meaningful learning using technology: What educators need to know and do* (pp. 141–160). New York: Teachers College Press) and journal articles about science teachers' use of the Internet (McCrory Wallace, R. (2004). A framework for understanding teaching with the Internet. *American Educational Research Journal,* 41(2), 447–488; Wallace, R. M. (2002). The Internet as a site for changing practice: The case of Ms. Owens. *Research in Science Education,* 32(4), 465–487).

Punya Mishra is Associate Professor of Educational Technology at Michigan State University. He has an undergraduate degree in Electrical Engineering,

Masters degrees in Visual Communication and Mass Communications, and a Ph.D. in Educational Psychology.

His research has focused on the theoretical, cognitive, social, and aesthetic aspects related to the design and use of computer-based learning environments. His other interests include online learning, visual literacy, and creativity. He has worked extensively in the area of technology integration in teacher education and teacher professional development both in face-to-face and online settings. He is the developer (with Dr. Matthew J. Koehler) of the technological pedagogical content knowledge (TPCK) framework for understanding the process and nature of teacher knowledge for technology integration.

He has received over $4 million in grants from national and international agencies to support his research and development work. He has published his work in peer-reviewed research journals such as *Teachers College Record, Communications of the ACM, Journal of Technology and Teacher Education, Journal of Educational Computing Research, Computers & Education, Computers & Human Behavior,* and *Journal of Visual Literacy.*

Dr. Mishra teaches courses at both the masters and doctoral levels and has received many accolades for his teaching. These include a Lilly Faculty Fellowship, the MSU Teacher Scholar Award, and the College of Education's Teaching Excellence Award. He is also an accomplished visual artist and poet. His work has been featured in international design and puzzle magazines and websites. You can find out more about him and his work by going to http://punyamishra.com/

Margaret L. Niess is currently Professor Emeritus of Mathematics Education at Oregon State University (OSU). At OSU she was Department Chair of the Department of Science and Mathematics Education (1987–2001), Director of Science and Mathematics Teacher Preparation (2001–2003), and Faculty Senate President (1998). Since 2003, Dr. Niess has conducted research, worked on grants, actively engaged in national associations, and written a teacher preparation textbook, *Guiding Learning with Technology* (released in August, 2007). Her research efforts focus on the integration of technology in teaching science and mathematics with specific attention to the knowledge teachers need to teach with technology—a technological pedagogical content knowledge (TPCK). Her research is directed toward the identification of teachers' levels of TPCK as they learn more about teaching with technology as well as framing professional development and other educational experiences that support teachers in developing TPCK. Dr. Niess is the chair of the Technology Committee for the Association of Mathematics Teacher Educators (AMTE), the Vice President for the Mathematics Teacher Education Committee for the Society of Information Technology and Teacher Education (SITE), and co-chairing the Teacher

Education Council for SITE beginning in March 2007. Dr. Niess is PI for the Central Oregon Consortium (an Oregon ESEA Title IIB MSP), a three-year professional development in support of improving the mathematical content knowledge and pedagogical content knowledge for teaching mathematics in the middle grades (under the No Child Left Behind federal initiative); she is also a co-PI responsible for the Education and Outreach for the EUSES End User Software Engineering NSF grant focused on engaging and supporting teachers for teaching with spreadsheets. Previously, Dr. Niess was editor of the *Journal of School Science and Mathematics* (1996–2001), a board member of the SSMA (2002–2005), and Mathematics Section Editor for *Learning and Leading with Technology* (1995–present).

Cassandra M. Scharber is a doctoral student in the Department of Curriculum and Instruction at the University of Minnesota. Majoring in both Learning Technologies and Literacy, her research interests include K-12 technology integration, digital equity, digital literacies, and automated essay scoring. She has expertise in developing online curricula for both K-12 students and preservice teachers. Throughout her graduate school experience, Cassie has been involved with federally funded research projects including Educational Theory into Practice Software (ETIPS), www.etips.info and the Partnership for Accessible Reading Assessments (PARA), www.readingassessment.info. Her efforts on these projects as well as with many professors have enabled her to co-author journal articles that have been published in journals such as *The Journal of Educational Computing Research* and *Reading Psychology* as well as co-author several book chapters on technology integration. A former secondary English teacher, Cassie earned her M.A. in Curriculum and Instruction from the University of Minnesota and her B.A. in English education from the University of Wisconsin—Eau Claire.

Denise A. Schmidt is an Assistant Professor in the Department of Curriculum and Instruction in the College of Human Sciences at Iowa State University. In addition to teaching instructional technology and reading methodology courses, Denise coordinates the undergraduate educational computer minor program offered in the department. Denise directs a number of grants that link K-12 teachers, area education agencies, and university faculty and students in collaboratives that support the diffusion of technology-supported innovations in schools. Keenly interested in K-12 outreach, she has made significant research contributions in the area of computer applications to teaching and learning in K-12 classrooms. She also conducts research that examines technology use and integration in teacher education.

Ann D. Thompson (AACTE Innovation and Technology Committee Member) is a University Professor of Curriculum and Instruction and the

Founding Director/Senior Advisor for the Center for Technology in Learning and Teaching in the College of Education at Iowa State University. Dr. Thompson is Past President of the Society for Information Technology in Teacher Education and the editor of the International Society for Technology in Education journal, *The Journal of Computing in Teacher Education.* She has published more than 40 articles and four books in the area of technology in teacher education. Dr. Thompson has served as the principal investigator on contracts and grants totaling more than $5 million. Her grant projects have focused upon collaborative work between teacher education and K-12 schools in the area of technology use.

Marcela van Olphen received her M.A. in Spanish Linguistics and her Ph.D. in Foreign Language Education from Purdue University. Currently, she is an Assistant Professor of Foreign Language Education and ESOL at the University of South Florida (USF). She joined the Department of Secondary Education in August, 2004. Before coming to USF, Dr. van Olphen served as an Assistant Professor of Modern Language Education at the University of Wyoming. While in Wyoming, she taught foreign language methods and second language acquisition courses to student teachers as well as ESL classes at the Wind River Reservation. During the same period, she was responsible for supervising student foreign language teachers who were placed across Wyoming and in Colorado for their professional residencies.

Her research agenda focuses on foreign language teacher education and the integration of technology in the curriculum, heritage learners, and bilingual education. She has presented at several national and regional conferences and has been invited to conduct workshops for Argentinean foreign language teachers. In addition, she has done consulting work for Wyoming and Colorado school districts as well as at Purdue University.

Dr. van Olphen is the recipient of teaching awards from the University of Nebraska-Lincoln and Purdue University, where she taught courses in all levels of Spanish language, literature in translation, culture, and foreign language methods.

Dr. van Olphen has been very active in her profession and has served on several professional and university committees. She has also enjoyed the challenge of developing new curricula with the goal of meeting changing educational requirements.

Prior to coming to the United States, Dr. van Olphen earned her undergraduate degrees in elementary education, preschool and kindergarten education, and adult education in Argentina, her native country. She taught PK-12 in urban (private and public) and rural schools for almost seven years in Buenos Aires province and has additional experience as a Spanish teacher at the elementary school level in both Indiana and Nebraska.

Index